W9-BVJ-293

The Flowering

of

Modern Hebrew Literature

The Flowering of Modern Hebrew Literature

A Volume of Literary Evaluation

by

MENACHEM RIBALOW

Edited and Translated by Judah Nadich

TWAYNE PUBLISHERS
NEW YORK

Library of Congress Catalog Number 59-8385

MANUFACTURED IN THE UNITED STATES OF AMERICA
PRINTED BY RECORD PRESS, NEW YORK, N. Y.

Table of Contents

Translator's Preface

Great literature serves as a stimulus for the reawakening of a people's national consciousness. In turn it is one of the great creations of a people's renaissance. So has it been with the relationship between modern Hebrew literature and Jewish national revival, that has reached its political climax in the reborn State of Israel.

The essays, novels, short stories, and especially the poetry written by Hebrew authors during the past three generations, have aroused the folk consciousness of the Jewish people and stirred them to self-emancipatory action. At the same time this literature—and again the poetry in particular—has reflected the spirit and action of the people. Henry Wadsworth Longfellow aptly contrasted poetry with history when he wrote, "The history of a nation is the external symbol of its character; from it we reason back to the spirit of the age that fashioned its shadowy outline. But poetry is the spirit of the age itself—embodied in the forms of language, and speaking in a voice that is audible to the external as well as the internal sense."

Modern Hebrew poetry is the spirit of the Jewish age and he who would understand the contemporary Jewish renaissance and the building of the Third Jewish Commonwealth must have some familiarity with it and the poets who have penned its lines.

The essays in this volume are designed to acquaint the English reader with some of the writers who have been instrumental in laying the foundation for modern Hebrew literature and in fashioning its character. They deal with the great triumvirate of modern Hebrew poetry, Bialik, Tchernihovsky and Shneur, and with four other top-ranking poets, Fichman, Shimoni, Hameiri and Shalom. Other branches of literature are discussed as well: the novels and folk tales of Agnon, the legends written by Bialik, the novels of Hameiri, the short stories of Shoffman and the plays of Shoham.

These essays have been selected from the five Hebrew books on literary criticism written by the late Menachem Ribalow, leader of the Hebrew movement in America and for almost thirty-three years editor of the *Hadoar,* the American Hebrew weekly. A great soul, completely in love with the Hebrew language and its literature, he rejoiced in every new literary creation. Yet his standards as a literary critic and editor were high and if he did not look upon the critic in Shelley's words, as "a general of the armies of the mind," he did see him as a cultural agent in league with the serious author against the anarchic tides of tastelessness which are always ebbing and flowing like the sea-water. Therefore, he chose to write only about such authors whom he could evaluate in positive manner and with whom, at times, he could feel an emotional affinity. His distinction as a critic is marked by his attempt to see a novel or group of poems not only in the critic's terms but in terms of what the author was trying to do, by the existence of basal critical values carefully developed out of a remarkable working knowledge of the best in literature and by a final neat loop of appraisal that could be easily grasped by the inquiring reader. An inveterate optimist, he argued strongly but without stridency for idealism without self-deception, for awareness of living issues without meaningless immersion and for recognition of the power of hope.

He himself described the function of criticism as he saw it. "True criticism is not a means but an aim in itself. It instructs and refers to the works of writers as illustrations, but its purpose is creative, namely to reveal truth and beauty, to inject a glow in the heart of the reader and to help him appreciate the function of art in life."

To be faithful to the original language of his essays and yet accurately to convey his ideas in idiomatic English is not a simple task. Long ago, in 132 B. C. E., it was already said by the grandson of Ben Sira in the introduction to his Greek translation of his grandfather's book, "Things once expressed in Hebrew do not have the same force when put into another language." To this must be added the fact that Ribalow's essays are distinctive by their beauty of expression, richness of vocabulary and poetic quality—he began his own literary career as a poet.

Almost all of the essays were translated by the undersigned and several translations had the advantage of being seen and approved by the author. A few translations had been done by others years ago but have been completely revised so that I must bear the responsibility for the translation. Brief biographical sketches written by myself have been prefaced to the essays and selections of each author's work have been added by way of illustration.

I am grateful to my wife, Hadassah Ribalow Nadich, true daughter of her father, for her constant help in the preparation of this manuscript.

If this book will contribute to a greater appreciation of modern Hebrew literature among the English reading public and if it will spur a few to go to the original Hebrew works themselves, it will effectively serve as my tribute of love and admiration to a man to whom I owe so much—Menachem Ribalow.

JUDAH NADICH

Menachem Ribalow: An Appreciation

Menachem Ribalow, who enjoyed a lifelong love affair with the Hebrew language, was one of the most influential spokesmen of modern Hebrew literature. When he died in September, 1953, at the height of his career and still in his energetic fifties, his passing was as deeply mourned in Israel as it was in the United States. His loss was a grievous one to all Jews who recognize in the continuation of living Hebrew a vital element in the survival of the Jewish people.

For more than three decades, Menachem Ribalow was the heart and brain of the Hebrew movement in America. As editor of *Hadoar,* the only Hebrew weekly in the world outside of Palestine and, later, Israel; as the prime mover of the Histadruth Ivrith, the federation for the dissemination of Hebrew culture in the United States; as an eloquent public speaker and communal leader—and, of course, as a major literary critic—Ribalow, more than any other single individual, helped keep modern Hebrew alive in America.

There are those who have called impossible the task of maintaining Hebrew as a spoken and written language in this country. Ribalow was not among them. He believed in America's cultural pluralism and himself was a symbol of the happy blend of American and Hebrew culture. He had faith in American democracy and in the democratic ideals of this country. His admiration for America was deep: he was in love with its history, its physical beauty, its writers and its dynamism. He wrote a great deal about New England and was thrilled by the thought that the Hebrew Bible was so influential in coloring American character, from Puritan days up to the present. His faith in the values and abilities of the creators of Hebrew literature and in an audience for their work is evident in the essays included in this volume.

To Ribalow it was inconceivable that the Jewish people could exist, let alone survive, without Hebrew. Hebrew was more than a vehicle for daily expression, more than a prosaic everyday language, more, even, than a holy tongue. It was part of his religion as a man and as a Jew. He judged Jews on their knowledge of Hebrew, their attitude toward it, their support of it, their love for it. When you talked with Ribalow about Hebrew, or read his essays, or heard him exhort an audience from a public platform, you fell under his spell and you accepted the primacy of Hebrew in the collective life of the Jewish people.

Ribalow's command of the language was remarkable. His vocabulary was, of course, rich, full of Biblical and poetic allusions. When he spoke in public, he intuitively called forth precisely the right word, the exact lyric phrase, the glowing literary passage. He could utilize, with equal skill, the Ashkenazic or the Sephardic accent, a rare ability, as any Hebraist can testify.

He brought to his work as editor, as essayist, and speaker an unassailable faith in the value of Hebrew. It was an end in itself, not merely a language of expression. Franz Kafka once called writing an act of faith, a prayer. If, then, one writes in the Holy Tongue, in the language of the Bible, in Hebrew, how much greater is that act of faith! How much more eloquent a prayer!

As a literary critic, Ribalow, who wrote and edited scores of books, was happiest when he could call attention to good writers and writing. There was no envy in him. He did not write fiction himself, and he thought of himself primarily as an expounder, a guide, a cultivator of talent. That a Jew could write well and meaningfully in Hebrew was, he believed, a wonderful experience to be shared by all lovers of the language. It was his gift that he had the ability to transmit his excitement to his devoted readers, who recognized in him a devout servant of his cause.

Faced continually with overwhelming responsibilities as editor of *Hadoar,* Ribalow never ceased to search for new work. He was always eager to encourage writers to produce new poems, stories and books. He was a jealous but proud caretaker for the language. Each Hebrew Year Book he edited, every weekly issue of *Hadoar* to roll off the press, delighted him. He would take pains with the typography, with the quality of the paper, with the binding of a book. He would read the issue of *Hadoar* anew, as though he had never seen it before, as if he had not slaved over the galleys and the makeup and the layout and the original manuscripts. He never lost his enthusiasm for his work.

He was not a provincial unacquainted with other literatures and cultures. He was well-versed in American creativity and journalism and he knew that high quality English-language literary periodicals seldom survived without subsidy. His magazine, he said, was no exception and so there was no reason to be depressed. If the *Atlantic* had to struggle to remain alive, why should the fate of *Hadoar* be different? Culture was a product hard to sell in America, he said, regardless of language. He was prepared to give all he had for the cause that moved him. He was immovable in his belief in the glory of Hebrew.

When Israel was established, Ribalow mistakenly believed his dreams of economic security for *Hadoar* would somehow come to fruition. He thought American Jewry now would automatically realize the significance of Hebrew in the pattern of Jewish life and would come forward with practical aid. But he learned once again that literature must be nurtured by the few, not by the many. He discovered that his own passion could be transmitted not to the masses but to the already convinced core of Hebraists. There were more of them, but not enough. Israel's re-establishment was a miracle to him, as it was to thousands of others. Yet he slowly realized that the struggle he had undertaken was not to be appreciably eased.

He had visited the Holy Land twice and had been astonished by the attention and recognition he had received. A modest man with simple tastes, he could not restrain his pleasure that his name was known to the Jews of Israel; that his essays were included in Hebrew schoolbooks and that Israeli cultural and political spokesmen looked to him as the leading Hebraist in the Diaspora. He was so driven by his dream of Hebrew Reborn that he did not have the time to look back at the career he was building, the reputation he was earning.

Born in poverty in Russia, Ribalow was accustomed to hard work and he was consecrated to Hebrew. The language was his muse and he was faithful to her. As a youngster, he met the great Hebrew poet Hayyim Nahman Bialik, who recognized in the young boy a kindred spirit. In many ways they were similar. Both vividly remembered and loved their humble parents, and their work was permanently colored by the knowledge of poverty. Both were extraordinarily gifted, yet modest. They were plain-spoken, generous to talent and romantics in their writings and their approach to life. Bialik was Ribalow's literary idol and Ribalow never ceased reading, studying, analyzing his poetry and prose.

Once, on a visit to Chicago, Ribalow came upon some original manuscripts of Bialik's earliest verses. The experience was a high point of Ribalow's life and he never tired of describing how he had stumbled upon this literary treasure. Characteristically, he never thought of keeping what he had found. Instead, he contributed the rare manuscripts to the Bialik Museum in Israel, but, of course, he first wrote a series of essays on the find and considered the entire event of major importance to him and to Hebrew letters.

Both men loved to hear spoken Hebrew. Bialik would walk the streets of Tel Aviv and listen to youngsters jabber and, in spite of their slang and grammatical errors, would crow in triumph that he had lived to hear Hebrew used in everyday commerce. Ribalow experienced the same pleasure from his annual visits to Hebrew-speaking summer camps. He would walk across the camp grounds, strain to hear the American-born youngsters talk in Hebrew and when the Hebrew phrases would pour forth from their lips, he would return to the city to face his complex chores with new faith and ambition.

In 1921, Ribalow arrived in the United States. At first he earned his livelihood as a Hebrew teacher, but soon turned to journalism and became a staff member of *Hadoar,* which was a daily newspaper at the time. When it became obvious that American Jewry was not prepared to support a Hebrew-language daily, the editors of *Hadoar* were ready to give up the struggle. Ribalow suggested that the newspaper be converted into a weekly—and from that day until he died, Ribalow *was Hadoar.* He wrote the lead editorials every single week for more than thirty years. He wrote prodigiously, courageously and eloquently on the most ticklish issues in Jewish life. He attacked Communism when it was unfashionable to do so and, at the same time, refused to bow to the power or prestige of the leaders of those Jewish organizations who felt that they ought to be immune from criticism because they gave financial aid to *Hadoar.* The magazine Ribalow edited was like himself: fiercely independent, lively, and full of character and integrity. Around *Hadoar,* Ribalow created a Hebrew movement.

He was, however, unable to concentrate on editing alone. There were daily problems: bills could not be put aside forever; rabbis had to be appealed to for aid; wealthy Jews had to be persuaded to unloosen their purse-strings for a literary cause which could scarcely "promote" the giver. And, simultaneously, the Histadruth Ivrith had to be strengthened, if the Hebrew movement was to represent more than a weekly journal. It became the task of the editor of *Hadoar* to coordinate all these elements.

Gradually, and scarcely aware of the change that added responsibility had made in him, Ribalow was transformed from a writer into an organizer. He was now a leader of a movement. He accepted engagements to lecture all over the United States because he was invited to do so and because he thought he could help disseminate the message of Hebrew's importance. In time, he made fast friendships all over the country and in times of crisis he was able to call upon these friends to help him in his program.

His integrity earned him enormous respect, and his utter devotion to Hebrew infected other Jewish leaders. They cooperated with him when they would not even agree to meet with others. But this situation led him to delay his literary labors and this turn in his career upset him. He accepted it because he was a servant of his language. That he wrote as prolifically as he did proves only that he worked without halt. He was a compulsive writer and nothing could keep him from his desk and pen, not even rising demands on his time as a communal leader.

There were isolated moments in his life when Ribalow suspected he might be trying to plant seed in barren soil. But he was an optimist and never really wavered in his faith. Shortly before his death, he founded a new Hebrew quarterly, *Mabua;* accepted the co-Presidency of the World Hebrew Union together with Itzhak Ben-Zvi, President of Israel; and conceived new editorial ideas for both *Hadoar* and *Mabua*.

When he was stricken with a fatal heart attack at the age of fifty-eight, the outpouring of grief from all over the world gave impressive evidence of Menachem Ribalow's stature as one of the truly important Jews of the twentieth century.

That *Hadoar* continues to appear regularly and the Hebrew movement is still expanding is in large measure due to Menachem Ribalow's lifetime of labor. He believed in the *Word* above all, and the continuation and enrichment of Hebrew as a movement and a vehicle of expression for new generations of American Jews must please him now as he looks down upon us. All friends of Hebrew will be grateful that Ribalow pioneered in this difficult area of American Jewish life.

Every published essay, each book a writer leaves behind reflects and reveals the man behind the words. Ribalow's lifework is to be found not only in his books, in the bound issues of *Hadoar* and in the memory of those who knew him, but in the survival of *Hadoar* and the Histadruth Ivrith. He built solidly.

Because he was American as well as Jewish, he would like to have seen some examples of his finest work made available to the English-language reader. This volume, published some five years after his death, presents, for the first time to the American public, an important critic on a significant literature. If the essays in this book win friends for Hebrew and its writers, Menachem Ribalow will live again, this time in another tongue and for a new audience. It would be good if this comes to pass.

HAROLD U. RIBALOW

Introduction—Hebrew: Revival and Redemption

I

The love of the Jew for the Hebrew language, popularly called "the sacred tongue," is one of the most precious national possessions of the Jewish people. This love is woven, like a golden thread, throughout Jewish history, for the Jew knows that "the sacred tongue" is the eternal tongue of his people. One generation passeth away and another generation cometh; and the Hebrew language abideth forever. Exile may end and redemption come and the root-language of the land of Israel stands firm.

Although the Jewish people made use of many different languages, corresponding with the many lands into which it was driven by its fate of exile, it never—even for a day—betrayed or rejected its language. The Jew would use Hebrew in his prayers, his lamentations, his liturgical poetry; in its accents he would pour forth his heart to God in stirring and plaintive psalms. Week in and week out he would review the weekly Biblical portion according to the traditional practice, twice in the Hebrew original, once in the Aramaic translation, and the entire history of his people would pass before his mind's eye.

"The universe was created by means of the holy tongue"—thus spoke the Jewish sages because to them the universe was revealed in Hebrew. They felt, and many feel with them today, that through the Hebrew language the Jewish national and cultural character is most truly revealed. Actually, the reasoning is simple. There live in this language historic Jewish concepts and Hebrew expressions that are peculiar and unique and find their like in no other language. There are words, phrases and verses whose roots go so deep that they touch the limits of time and thus can have their comparison in no other tongue. Every word bears the scent of ancient eras and has the savor of old wines that stir up longings that transcend the boundaries of language.

Therefore, the man who speaks or writes such a language becomes a partner with the great of distant epochs and enters a mystical enclosure with those noblemen of spirit who lived most richly and he draws sustenance from their fountain. He feels that a great and majestic hand casts him—in the phrase of Hayyim Nahman Bialik—into "an unexplored height, an unknown remoteness."

For it was through the Hebrew language that the God of Israel revealed Himself to His people and it was in this language that the covenant was sealed between them. This is the language of the Jewish people's past—as it is the language of its future, in Israel.

The Hebrew language is the language of the Jewish beginnings, for it was in Hebrew that God revealed Himself in a vision to Abram, before he became the patriarch Abraham, when He commanded him to gaze heavenward and to count the stars, even before He had made His covenant with Him.

It was in Hebrew that God disclosed Himself to Moses, out of the bush that burned with flame, yet was not consumed.

It was in Hebrew that Moses and the people of Israel burst forth into song at the Red Sea, a song of national glory and rebirth, after their departure from Egypt.

It was in Hebrew, too, that Moses spoke from Sinai's peak and "God answered him by a voice"—and the Torah was given to Israel.

All the statutes and ordinances of the Torah, by which the Jewish people has lived for thousands of years, were written in Hebrew. Similarly, the Hebrew language has been warp and woof of the Jewish fabric from the conquest of Canaan, to the destruction of the first Temple and the Babylonian captivity; from the first King to the last Prophet; from the return from Babylonian exile to the destruction of the second Temple. Hebrew has been branch and root of the Jewish creations of the spirit from Ezra and the men of the Great Synagogue to the days of the writing of the Mishnah and the Gemara; from the Halakhic literature to the literature of mysticism; from the Gaonic literature and that of the Middle Ages through the Kabbalah and Hassidism and the Haskalah—up to our own time, to the restoration of the Jewish State.

The entire Jewish approach to life, in which are united the earthly and the heavenly, the material and the spiritual, finds full and exact expression in the Hebrew language. Abstract and lofty concepts are blended together with the concrete and simple. Symbolic images of the completely incorporeal divine dwell honorably side by side with very human descriptions, converting the spirit into matter and the godly into human. The anthropomorphic element is characteristic of the Bible and, therefore, of Hebrew.

The Jew is fond of concreteness, of the figure of bas-relief, the definiteness of the idol—the forbidden idol. He ascribes even to God human characteristics. God is not only *the God of hosts;* he is also *the man of hosts.* He can wax angry at His people. Light is His garment; His tent—the heavens. He rides upon the thick clouds and flies upon the wings of the wind. He speaks and remembers, loves and hates. He is jealous and avenging, merciful and compassionate.

These are human qualities and it is these human qualities which philosophers and theologians have labored so hard to explain, qualities which the Jewish people have illustrated so perceptively in the Bible. These qualities are safeguarded in the Hebrew language alone, for the other languages into which these qualities and expressions have been translated are not Hebrew—and these expressions have lost their essence and their sacred character has become secularized. But in Hebrew there are retained the naiveté of the folk in its childhood and something of the strength of primeval man whose flesh yearned for the living God.

Yes, generations come and generations go, languages and cultures enter the world and pass on, but the Hebrew tongue remains, it stands forever. Actually, the word "stands" is inaccurate, for Hebrew moves; it is alive, constantly developing and rejuvenating itself with new vitality.

This is an inner vitality, one of the soul, for Hebrew has lived within the Jewish people, in all periods and ages, in all lands and in all its exiles. In Babylonia and Persia, in Greece and Egypt, in Spain and Africa, in Germany and Poland, in Italy and France, in Lithuania and Rumania and now in North and South America, the Hebrew language, like a good and faithful angel, accompanied the people it loved.

In every age and in every land, there arose redeemers for Hebrew in the shape of poets and scholars and codifiers and grammarians. They played upon the harp of the language so that the chords of the people vibrated. Not all Jews knew or spoke Hebrew, for a people's fate in exile is a harsh one—exile is like a stepmother with an ill-tempered face—but the majority of the people, if not all of them, used Hebrew in prayers and hymns, in psalms and lamentations and, for that matter, in daily affairs. Legal documents and accounts, memoirs and family records of births and deaths, letters and wills—these were all written in Hebrew. For the people knew for a certainty that the tongues they used in the lands of exile were alien tongues and that these languages, acquired during the long exile, were not as important or as sacred as their first and national language—Hebrew.

The most Jewish of the alien tongues, one used a great deal for a long period of time, was Aramaic. Most of the Talmud was written in Aramaic, as was the sacred book the Zohar. The *Kaddish* and *Kol Nidrei* are recited in Aramaic and the wedding *ketubah* is written in that language. But Aramaic remains in the treasure-house of Jewry because of the precious books written in it, and not because of the language's own intrinsic value. It cannot be imagined that at some future time a movement will arise for the revival of Aramaic because it is the language of the Talmud and the Zohar. These vast works are studied in their original language by students and by scholars, but they are gradually being translated into Hebrew. Aramaic itself belongs to the past; it can have no future.

Arabic too has left Jewish life never to return, although Jews like Saadya Gaon, Judah Halevi, Solomon ibn Gabirol, Maimonides and others created in Arabic. Their greatest works, those that plumbed the profoundest depths, were written in Hebrew. These, and the works they wrote in Arabic which were translated into Hebrew, remain. The rest were not preserved. Maimonides made this point when he said to his son, "My son, I know the sin I have sinned against my people and I pray to God that I may be found worthy to return the stolen article to its rightful owners and to translate my books into the sacred tongue."

The philosopher Philo, who wrote in Greek, also recognized the truth when he wrote, "From Aramaic nothing has remained; from Arabic nothing has remained; and from Greek nothing has remained." He foresaw that he himself was to remain something of a concealed spirit.

The language that has stood the test of time, that has overcome the tempests of history and the waves of wrath that threatened to swallow it and its people, has been the Hebrew language.

When the Yiddish language encompassed millions of Jews some centuries back, what did the Hebrew language then do? It found for itself a dwelling place in the concealed depths of the Yiddish language. More than three thousand Hebrew words, expressions and concepts were assimilated into Yiddish. These filled the language with charm and with Jewish flavor. Religious and sacred concepts thus entered Yiddish in their original tongue. Expressions like: *Hakadosh barukh-hu; Ribbono shel olam; Yom Tov; Huppah, Mazal Tov, Torah, Tefilah,* these and hundreds and hundreds more were gathered together and absorbed by the Yiddish language. Similarly, the "salt and pepper" of Yiddish comes from Hebrew, including words like *efshar* and *afilu* and *ad'raba* and *halila* and *halvai* and *mayla.*

Thus Yiddish was filled with the scent of Hebrew expressions and the flavor of Hebrew verses. The sayings of the sages would hover on every lip and out of both casual and serious conversation there would flow a stream of the wisdom of the ages. The splendor of the Hebrew language shone through the life of the Jewish people.

II

There is something beautiful about a person's love for an ancient language. Every spiritual love has in it something of a revelation of the divine, for through it man lays bare his transcendental "I," bringing him closer to God. It is a true love, for it depends on no material thing. A charming woman, a beautiful tree, a lovely field excite man's imagination and sensuality and his body trembles with longing. Not so is a spiritual love—love of God or of Torah or of language. For here a man rids himself of the material and frees himself from the yoke of the physical. He climbs higher and becomes the more refined, the cleaner, the purer. He ascends into the sphere of the pure spirit.

Love for a language is one of the highest rungs in the ladder of human culture. Usually it is the possession of the few—poets, authors, philologists. For them it is not only the precious gem preserved from the days of Creation but also the instrument by which they can peer into the future and by their own ability fashion that which they most desire. For them it is a magic harp. Every word, every expression are precious images by which they achieve self-fulfillment.

The poet calms the tempest of his spirit with the sound of a word that blends exactly with the next word, joining it in a melody that answers his heart's yearning. So too with the author of prose who creates living personalities in his story or constructs a world of ideas by the use of words, words which others may use for idle or evil purpose or not at all. By the use of the delicate and mysterious mechanism of language, the scholar or philosopher, the essayist or the critic brings distant subjects near and makes the complex understood, permitting him to enter the inner sanctum of thought and creation. For the philologist too every word is a definite spiritual entity, whose roots lie in the life of a people, in the history of culture and religion. Every word has a long development and many faces. It lives a life both public and secret. The philologist, like the poet, is sensitive to its existence, feels its vibration, understands its spirit, observes its peculiarities and transmigrations and rejoices at its every new meaning and nuance.

The sages of the Mishnah and the masters of the Kabbalah knew the secret life of the letters of the alphabet. They plumbed its depths and revealed new forms and new meanings.

But it is not only the poet, the author, the philosopher or the philologist who finds in the Hebrew language a matter of life and of creativity. The ordinary Hebraist too, the earnest reader, the lover of Hebrew sees in it a precious gift given him by the God of the Hebrews to be the object of his love. He derives joy from every new creation in Hebrew not only for its own intrinsic worth, but also because of its linguistic value. Hebraists are grammarians and linguistic stylists *par excellence*. And for them "the joy of language" is akin to "the joy of the Sabbath" to the traditional Jew.

III

It is because of the Jew's great and enduring love for the Hebrew language that there has come to pass the great marvel of the renaissance of the Hebrew language in our generation. And through this revival has come, in part, the rebirth of the Jewish State, for it was the Hebrew language that was a powerful force in the revival and redemption both of the people and of the land.

It was the Hebrew language that, through all the vagaries of time, was the fortress of strength in which the Jew, cleaving to the rock whence he was hewn, entrenched himself. Through the language of the prayers and hymns, the lamentations and penitential psalms, his heart would cleave not only to his Father in heaven but also to his desolate land for which he yearned and to whose redemption he looked forward. This land would live in his heart through the poetic descriptions of the Bible that were included in the prayer book and that became the daily bread of the Jew. The distant Palestinian landscapes would overshadow the landscape of the country in which he dwelt. When he recalled the wonders of God, the Creator of the Universe, he would remember the Exodus from Egypt and *his* wandering in the desert and *his* war with the kings of old until *he* finally entered the land given by God as "an inheritance to Israel His servant." The early rains and the later rains, the grain, the wine and the oil of far-off days in a geographically-distant land became real entities and influential factors in his life in the diaspora. On Passover the Jew would pray for dew and on Sukkot for rain.

Even the incense of spice of the Temple and the various sacrifices brought upon its altar accompanied him upon the path he trod. As he sang the Hallelujah psalms, he would recall the servants of the Lord "who stand in the house of the Lord, in the courts of the house of our God." And how did his prayers conclude? With the entreaty that "May the Temple be rebuilt speedily and in our days" and with the hope that "May our eyes behold Thy return to Zion in mercy" and with "A redeemer shall come to Zion."

All of these desires and yearnings formed such an integral part of the Hebrew language that it became impossible to distinguish between the two. It is possible to say without exaggeration that the essence of the chant of the prayers in their gentle and soulful language would quiet the sighing of the heart and calm the storm of longing. Thus the uttering of the Hebrew words of the prayers was not only a means to an end but an end in itself in no small measure. In itself it became a great individual and national achievement. Because of it, Zionist sentiment lived in the heart of every Jew through all the years of the Exile.

Is it any wonder then, that with the Haskalah period, the period of enlightenment, and after it, the age of the renaissance, the Hebrew language became so precious and powerful an instrument for revival and redemption? All of modern Hebrew literature was born and grew with this concept of the redemption of the people and the land. From Abraham Mapu's *The Love of Zion* up to the latest story of the new Israel, and from the Zionist and Biblical poems of Micah Joseph Lebensohn to the Biblical and pastoral poems of the contemporary young Hebrew poets, there can be felt the yearning for the motherland that helped create the Zionist movement and cleared the way for the State of Israel.

Now that Israel has been established, great days lie in store for the Hebrew language, days of creativity and development, the like of which has not been experienced in many generations.

Thus a generation goeth and a generation cometh, a language goeth and a language cometh, exile goeth and redemption cometh—and the Hebrew language endureth forever.

Hayyim Nahman Bialik, Poet Laureate of the Jewish People

Hayyim Nahman Bialik is without question the greatest name in modern Hebrew poetry, one of the greatest in the entire history of Jewish literature. One must go back to the prophets for a parallel to Bialik in the use of the Hebrew idiom. Since the close of the Biblical canon, no writer has ever used the Hebrew language with such perfection.

Bialik was born in the year 1873 in Radi, in the province of Volynia, Russia. When he was six years old, his family moved to the city of Zhitomir. A year later his father died and Bialik was taken to his grandfather's home. It was in his grandfather's library that Bialik at the early age of eleven read such philosophic works as Judah Halevi's *Kuzari* and Maimonides' *Guide for the Perplexed,* as well as books on Kabbalah and Hassidism. Most of his days were spent in the *Bet Hamidrash* studying the Talmud and its commentaries, and evenings and late into the night he would read the works of modern *Haskalah* literature. After much argument, his grandfather finally consented to Bialik's leaving home to attend the famous Yeshivah of Volozhin.

Bialik gives us a picture of the life he led in his Volozhin days in his famous poem, *Hamatmid* (*The Talmud Student*). He studied the Talmud voraciously but he also found time to work on modern Hebrew literature, the Russian language and other secular subjects. It was at this period that he came under the influence of the writings of Ahad Ha'am (*nom de plume* of Asher Ginzberg) who was emerging as the great Jewish intellectual leader of the time. Bialik's respect for Ahad Ha'am was as life-long as was Ahad Ha'am's love and admiration for him. Moved by the philosophy of Ahad Ha'am, Bialik could remain in Volozhin no longer. Without informing his grandfather, he left for Odessa, the home of the philosopher. There in 1892 appeared his first published poem, *To A Bird.*

The next year he married. He unsuccessfully tried his hand at various kinds of business and then settled for a time in Sosnowice earning his livelihood as a tutor. All the while he continued with his own literary efforts, one magnificent poem following another.

In the year 1900, Bialik's friends rescued him from want and isolation and brought him back to Odessa, then a center of great literary activity. Before long he, Ahad Ha'am, and Mendele Mokher Sefarim, the novelist, became the presiding triumvirate over the Odessa school of Hebrew literature.

Together with I. H. Ravnitzky and Ben-Zion, he established the publishing house known as *Moriah*. Bialik also became co-editor with Ahad Ha'am of the monthly *Hashiloah,* taking over the department of fiction and poetry. He lived in Odessa until the advent of Bolshevism, when his publishing house was disbanded.

For a short time thereafter he resided in Berlin, and in 1924 he settled in Palestine. Bialik was regarded as the first citizen of the new Palestine and the favorite son of the all-Jewish city of Tel Aviv, which honored him by calling a street by his name. On this street Bialik built a beautiful home which became the mecca not only for the intellectuals of Tel Aviv, but for visitors the world over. Today the home is a national museum.

In 1926, accompanied by Dr. Shmaryah Levin, Bialik visited the United States on behalf of the Palestine Foundation Fund and was accorded a royal welcome. Thousands of enthusiastic admirers turned out to hear his message. His visit awakened great interest on the part of the Jewish masses in the rebuilding of Palestine.

Bialik undertook a tour of Poland in the interest of Hebrew culture in 1927 and upon his return founded the *Oneg Shabbat* in Tel Aviv. This cultural observance found a quick response in the hearts of the citizens of Tel Aviv and has been the model for similar undertakings in other parts of the world.

Bialik's sixtieth birthday in 1933 was an event celebrated by Jewry the world over. A year later his physician advised an operation. Bialik left for Vienna after having delivered a touching farewell address to a large *Oneg Shabbat* assembly. It was in Vienna that death overtook him on the 21st day of Tammuz, July 4, 1934, one day after the thirtieth anniversary of Dr. Theodor Herzl's death in the same city. Bialik's body was brought to Tel Aviv and the day of his funeral was a day of mourning in Palestine and throughout the diaspora.

Literature on Bialik has been continuously mounting. It may be said without fear of contradiction that hardly a week passes without a study in some Hebrew publication of phases of Bialik's poetry. A Bialik cult has arisen in modern Hebrew literature similar to the cults of Shakespeare and Goethe in world literature. His collected works and selections of his poetry have appeared in numerous editions and have been translated into nearly all the European languages. In English translation there are volumes of poetry by L. V. Snowman, by Maurice Samuel, and the most recent one, edited by Israel Efros, in 1948. *Far Over the Sea* is a collection of poems and jingles for children. Short stories and legends have been published in *Aftergrowth and Other Stories,* translated by I. M. Lask, and *And It Came To Pass,* translated by Herbert Danby.

In addition to his poetry, Bialik wrote excellent prose—Biblical legends, short stories, tales for children (as well as songs and poems for children) and essays. Several volumes of his letters and addresses have also appeared.

Together with Ravnitzky he published *The Book of Legends.* He composed a lucid commentary on the first order of the Mishnah and issued carefully edited volumes of the medieval poetry of Solomon Ibn Gabirol and Moses Ibn Ezra.

He translated into Hebrew Cervantes' *Don Quixote,* Schiller's *William Tell,* and Anski's *The Dybbuk.*

I

Hayyim Nahman Bialik was one of those creative personalities who are unique and everlasting in the annals of literary history. When such personalities appear, they set their sign and seal upon the life and spiritual creativeness of their generation. A great poet is more than the product of his age or the child of his environment. Great poets stand above their times. They cannot be fitted into a Procrustean bed of neatly formulated concepts that tend to delimit and diminish their world. On the contrary, in their case there is a distinct and palpable influence by the individual upon the group. It is the poet that affects his environment. He imparts new energy and new values to old concepts and accepted norms. He opens new vistas in the life of his people. As the old Hebrew saying has it, he renews the work of Creation.

Bialik was such a force. Through his poetic creations he brought about the Hebrew literary renascence of his period and the rejuvenation of the Hebrew language. And with his cry of revolt and protest he quickened the pulse of his people and moved them to historic action.

In addition to his poetic genius, Bialik was endowed with the divine spark of prophecy. He was a man of inspiration. More than that, he was a child of the *Shekhinah*—the Divine Spirit. As he once wrote in a letter to Professor Joseph Klausner, "At times it seems to me that I am the only begotten son of the Holy One, blessed be His name, the favorite child of His divine spirit." Inspiration is the heritage of any poet who sings of himself and to himself. But the divine spirit, the *Shekhinah,* is the soul of a people, revealed only to chosen ones and to prophets of God.

The ordinary poet sings about his own life, nature, man's tribulations or the mystery of existence. But the prophetic poet not only sings; he preaches and chastises, he lashes out against the people and its God. The artist-poet, singing his individual song, reflects upon the world and upon man who inhabits it, and he sings his song with poetic imagery. But the prophet-poet, even when he is alone, never concentrates only upon himself. His is a threefold visual front: himself, his people and his God. This threefold conflict takes place within his inner soul: between himself and his people, between both and their God.

Bialik was able to lift himself above his environment, above his time, to penetrate the great beyond once trodden by the divine prophets. He took the linguistic symbolism and prophetic allegories of Amos, Isaiah, Jeremiah and Ezekiel, sparked them with new fire and hurled them into our lives, kindling our souls thereby. He was the only one of our contemporaries who had the kind of moral strength with which he opened his Yiddish poem, *The Last Word* (which he called prophetic), with the daring lines, "I was sent to you by God," and to complete his first stanza with these words, "And God remembered you and brought me to you." The end of the poem is reminiscent of Jeremiah:

> "And God said unto me:
> 'And now go down to the potter's house
> And buy a pot,
> And hurl it down and say in a loud voice
> So that everyone may hear:
> Thus will you be shattered!
> Then speak no more,
> Cry not, scream not.
> Bow your head in silence.
> The day will dawn—it comes, it comes!' "

With the boldness and candor of a prophet does Bialik address himself to the heavens and to the God who dwells in them.

> "Heavenly spheres, beg mercy for me!
> If truly God dwells in your orbit and round,
> And in your space is His pathway that I have not found,—
> Then you pray for me!"

He does not beguile himself with hollow hopes, and does not salve his and our wounds with false prophecies of consolation.

Here you have the primitive simplicity of Biblical style, the deep moral conviction that leads a Job to his unsilenceable revolt.

All of his national and social poetry bears this seal of high courage and supreme unrest. It gains added power from the fact that, barring a few exceptions, they are purely individualistic. In these poems there is no trace of the rhetoric that marks so-called patriotic poetry. In most of the poems one looks in vain for such collective terms as people, nation—for such abstract generalizations as ideal, faith, etc. His national poetry assumes the expression of a personal tragedy, stemming from the national self and flowing toward universal significance.

"Heavenly spheres, beg mercy for *me*!"
"I know *I* shall fade like a star on some dark night,
No star shall know *my* grave."

All intensely personal and therefore so convincing, so immediate, and so intelligible. Even *The City of Slaughter,* as is true with all the other poems of pain and wrath, is permeated to the core with the deep personal sense.

"Of steel and iron, cold and hard and numb,
Now forge thyself a heart, O man! and come
And walk the town of slaughter. Thou shalt
With thine own eyes see, and touch with thine own hands,
On fences, posts, and doors . . . "

And at the end of the poem—the same personal note:

"Now flee, O son of man, for ever flee,
And hide *thee* in the desert—and go mad!
There rend *thy* soul into a thousand pieces,
And fling *thy* heart to all wild dogs for food!
The burning stones shall hiss beneath *thy* tears,
And stormy winds shall swallow up *thy* cry!"

Thus, the national tragedy, having saturated every fibre of the poet's soul, becomes a deep personal experience for him—his own pain, the bane of his own existence, seeking redress, straining for redemption. The collective "I" of the people is identified with the individual "I" of the poet. He seeks and finds all the shortcomings of his people within himself. For the people's faults are his faults; their sins, his sins.

And this individual-communal emotion makes the prophet-poet a symbol of his people, a man who bears its burden, the magnitude of its destiny. And his soul's agonized cry is that of a man who is "roasted alive upon his own coals."

Deep in his heart the poet carries the proud painful sense of that higher solitude and the supreme loneliness of the chosen one. Between him, the seer, and us, the public, there yawns the gulf of obtuseness, deafness and unresponsiveness. We are immersed in the petty concerns of the day, caught in the meshes of the infinitely trivial, while he is being consumed by the inner fire not only to sing, but to shout. He is devoured by a "word," *the* word of the Lord, as the prophets understood it—aye, perhaps the *last* word.

> "And speak the curse that God puts in thy mouth,
> Let not thy lips know fear;
> Though thy word be bitter as death,
> Yea, death itself,
> We shall know and hear."

Death here means the death of our national life. We have strayed from its source, from its true self, and, therefore, have become impoverished, petty, reduced. We have become impatient and not only we, but even our Almighty God has lost his omnipotence.

> "For [says God] when you stand tomorrow at My threshold,
> When you remind Me, when you ask for payment,
> I shall but answer you: 'Come, see, I've nothing,
> It cries to heaven, I bear it, but I've nothing.
> For I am poor myself, I'm beggared also.' "

And again,

> "I have no further words for you,
> The word of God is dead to you;
> The hand of God is thrust aside,
> And ridiculed the Sacred Name!"

For good reason are such appellations as "national poet" and "prophet" applied to Bialik. The group sense is the very mainspring of his soul; he is the one who mirrors the many. His prophetic outbursts are not so much intended for the ears of others as the confessions of one aware of his own malaise, which happens to be that of his own people as well as of humanity as a whole. This accounts for the seeming ruthlessness of his poems written in the prophetic vein. This is the way of all great ethical personalities who feel in their own bones the decline of a world grounded in falsehood and cruelty.

The unique force of his exhortative poems lies in the fact that he does not reprimand others only, but himself as well. Not only is society as a whole sinful and wicked, but also the individual who is an infinitesimal part of it—not excepting the poet himself.

Some poets place themselves above the masses and look down upon them with scorn. They operate with two scales, one for all others, the other for the poet. Obviously the scale occupied by him, the chosen and anointed one, outweighs the other in wisdom and righteousness, in sweetness and light. This favorable balance soothes the poet's pride and flatters his *amour propre*. He has outweighed them all; he can now bask in a justifiable complacency.

But Bialik is never complacent, for Bialik's strictures are of a different nature. They are addressed to none but his own people—himself. The pain he inflicts upon his people is felt by the poet himself; hence the poignant and personal sorrow that broods over these prophetic poems. His pessimism is not of a general nature, but a directly personal one. When he seems to struggle most bitterly against the people, it is with himself that he wrestles. In his poems, *The Last Word, God's Chastisement* and *Summon the Serpents* his pessimism mounts in its bitterness, in its vitriolic rage. "Villains," he hurls at his people, in *The Last Word*:

"Pluck, O prophet, the fire brand from your altar,
And cast it to the villains—
Let it serve them for roasting, to set their kettles on,
And to warm their palms.
Fling the ember from your heart
And let it light their pipes,
Let it illumine the stealthy smirk on their lips
And the evil cunning in their eyes.
Lo, they come, these villains,

Mouthing the prayers you've taught them,
Feeling your pain and sharing your hope,
Their souls straining toward your ruined shrine,
So as to pounce upon the wreckage,
Burrow in its rubble heap,
And cart away its scattered stones
To pave their floors and fence their gardens,
To mount as tombstones over graves."

And again, in *God's Chastisement,*

"When thus you shall have spurned your best ones from you,
One after another, you shall sit bereaved,
Your tent despoiled, all beauty fled your dwelling,
A dread and desolation to be seen,
God's blessing nevermore shall cross the threshold,
Salvation's joy stand tapping at the window.
And when you turn to pray, the words shall fail you,
To weep—the tears, because your heart shall dry
And fade and shrink. . . .
The hearthfire, when you crave it, shall have died,
The cat mew loudly in the chilly ashes. . . ."

Has everything come to an end?

"And say no more nor utter cry nor shed a tear,
But bend thy head and bury it in silence . . ."

No. In the last dark lightning lies hidden the very power that must indeed compel a new rebuilding, a re-creation. The will to create breaks a path through the dark mazes of individual and national pessimism. From deep hidden sources a fresh, sparkling stream forces its way through the entangled forest—it is nothing other than the fountain-head of Bialik's creativity.

II

The embodiment of will power, a dynamic creative energy, an irresistible vitality that must burst forth into full blossom—such is the artistic profile of Bialik. Expressive and forceful, concise and quick—such is the song of Bialik. His language is rich and lucid, his sentiments earthy and wholesome. His preference for the particular and the individual comes from his desire to lay bare, to sense and perceive all the isolated moments which in the aggregate make up life.

The *tsafririm* (the morning breezes which, according to the kabbalists, herald the glad tidings of the rising sun) wake him at dawn; they peck like pigeons on his window pane, calling him. The *tsafririm* are calling their playmate. Let him come out and join them; and full of bubbling joy, they will waft over the broad open spaces. They will scatter rays of light everywhere—upon hairy spears of corn, the ocean's waves, the smile of a slumbering child, the heart of a tender mother, the drops of morning dew, the cheeks of a lovely lass, the wing of a butterfly, a glass bead, a soap bubble.

In this colorful mosaic is heard the unifying harmony of man and nature; the miscellany throbs with the pulse of the world. In this blending together of isolated particulars there is the wholesome oneness of all that lives and sprouts and blossoms.

Bialik possesses an uncanny sense of balance and proportion. Whether it be realism or a closeness to the earthy, he is able to draw together two worlds, the shadowy and the real. He brings everything closer, towards the earth, towards reality. Perhaps this is because there is so strong a *drang,* so much of tradition pulling him higher, heavenward. Hence his burning will to counter that pull and to draw the heavens down to earth and to implant its sunlight in our hearts. The morning breezes, whispering host of kabbalistic *tsafririm,* he converts into so many mischievous, frolicsome beings. They beckon unto him, they call him, and he, drunk with light and with the zest of living, refuses to be persuaded. And the light and nimble *tsafririm* are invited into his home.

> "O, come to me, pure ones, pure Spirits of morning,
> Come under my cover, my sparkling white sheet,
> And there let us play till the day gives us warning,
> Let me feel your bright warmth from my head to my feet."

This concentration and transmutation of the general into the individual and the specific, the all into the one, is characteristic of

Bialik's poetry in general and his nature poetry in particular. In his two poems, *Splendor* and *The Pool,* in which he reaches the heights of his poetic expression and religious communion with nature's secrets, there is crystallized this deification of the human "I" as the very center of the universe.

It is a native gift. He has hewn it out of his own sub-conscious quarries. He owes it to no one but himself.

> "I have not won the light from freedom's courses,
> Nor from my father's part
> Came it to me; 'tis hewn from crags of mine,
> I carved it from my heart.
> One spark is hid in the fortress of my heart,
> So small, but mine alone;
> I asked it of no man, I stole it not,
> 'Tis in me, and my own."

With this child-like integrity, which in its remote windings derives from some primitive sources, he walked the Jewish world with distinction, a scion of those who blazed new paths, divine heralds and seers. He looked deep into the eye of the world. There his "playmates" revealed themselves to him. He absorbed their secrets and sealed their echoes deep in his being.

In *Splendor* and *The Pool,* that are essentially one poem of light and radiance, a whole world is astir—a mirrored, refined and distilled world. The myth of childhood has come to life again. It is an undefiled and sacred precinct whither no speck of sinfulness or baseness finds its way. It is the Garden of Eden whence the man of today has been banished. Now this world appears to us as congealed, where ancient forms and images have become hardened into cold crystal, a world upside down in which the tree stands with its branches downward, a heroic world lying like Samson bound in the coils of a Delilah. We no longer feel the great strength of that world, its reality has receded in our memory and has taken on a dreamlike insubstantiality. But to Bialik it is the most real world, the most beautiful. He lavishes all the passion of his soul upon that crystal-clear life which he has conjured up from his union with the mystic sources of creation.

III

Bialik is classic. The ephemeral and the temporary separate themselves from the essential and the eternal. The dark shadows of his early poems are banished by the bright sunshine of the later ones. His first poems, which are of a social character, he valued less highly than those which came after. The poems, *On the Threshold of the House of Prayer, If Thou Wouldst Know* and others of a similar character, singing the praises of the old house of study, hailing it as a fountain source from which our people in their long exile drew strength and comfort—even these poems, so gratefully acknowledged by many, are not fully expressive of Bialik. However, in this group of poems, and particularly in *The Talmud Student, Before a Bookcase* and *On the Threshold of the House of Prayer,* the poet does reveal one important aspect of his being.

The Talmud Student is the great poem about Israel's love of Torah which preserved the Jewish people throughout all the periods of the diaspora. The figure of the student in the poem symbolizes Bialik himself and all the other Jewish Talmud students. There is both protest and compassion in the poem. He bemoans the fate of the Jewish child who devotes his days and nights to the study of Torah and who denies himself every joy of life. There is deep admiration and wonder at the young spiritual hero who checks every natural instinct and who isolates himself from the delights of life for the sake of the great ideal of studying Torah for its own sake.

The House of Study appears as the strong fortress of the spirit of the Jewish people. It was

> ". . . A mystic fount from whence
> Thy brethren going to their slaughter drew
> In evil days the strength and fortitude
> To meet grim death with joy, and bare the neck
> To every sharpened blade and lifted axe,
> Or pyres ascending, leap into the flame
> And saintlike die with *Ehad* on their lips."

Thus Bialik placed a wreath of glory and heroism even around the brow of the diaspora because of the great light which arose from the students of the Torah.

His songs that speak of the House of Study are the last shadows of the night and the first harbingers of dawn. At the time they were written, the first poetic steps of Bialik were still uncertain. Like the Talmud student he walks in the early dawn towards his corner in the House of Study. Gentle breezes whisper to him, caress him, intoxicate him. They would have his soul. Often he succumbs to them. He becomes the singer of twilight, of the comrades of his youth, of his own penurious childhood.

But Bialik quickly overcomes all that. With true poetic impetus he brings to light another kind of childhood, another type of world. Bialik's real world is a strong, firm world. Nothing in it is weak, soft, unreal. Here all is sculptured. The shadowy takes on form. The mists disappear in an ocean of brilliant sunshine. And each ray, as it falls, is caught and reflected by the frost on the window.

"See! A forest! On the glass pane
Fresh it grows in winter glory;
Overnight, like Aaron's rod,
Into blossom bursts my window."

For now winter has come upon the earth, a winter which gathers all the wandering rays and imprisons them in its own rigidity, converting them into frost and snow. They shimmer and sing without speech in the light of the brilliant sun.

"Radiance fresh and cold and lucid
Filled my chamber and renewed it;
Seems, an angel, feeling festive
Whitewashed all the walls with wonder!

And my heart, too, fresh irradiated
Cold and calm and new reposes;
Seems, an angel, snow-winged, clear eyed,
Moved into my heart and shrived it."

In the white, clear snowy world, old powers are forged into newness, the human will becomes firmer, stronger. Man becomes the pivotal center of all existent force. He is ready to contend with the superhuman powers of Nature itself.

"Now my arm again is iron:
Give me mountains—I'll uproot them!
Give me lions—I shall rend them!
Og or Goliath—I shall crush him!"

Long suppressed youthful energies assert themselves; desire celebrates its triumph.

"Grasp me, clasp me, O thou frost!
Burn me and blight and scald and stab!
Pour thy steel into my heart,
Make me sword-like, sharp and swift!

Line my breast with ironmail,
Lest it burst with excess might.

Glow and frolic, O thou frost!
Burn and blight and scald and stab!"

Did this really happen to the frail Yeshivah lad? Did the Talmud student of yesteryear, the intellectual of today, really experience this?

"True, I am a Yeshivah lad. My face is white as chalk. But, like the winter, I have stored great power under my glazed shield."

"Freedom, freedom! All is free!
Whip up, sledmen! Flit! Fly!
Cast me into the storm's swirl,
Hurl me to the whirling winds!"

Great energies are undammed; they burst forth, seeking deliverance in light and might.

"From my ice exudes a fragrance
Of an unknown, glorious spring,
A new spring, rich, resplendent,
Ne'er yet seen by child of man."

IV

Bialik who grew up in Czarist Russia, which taught the world a lesson in unprincipled barbarism, said of himself, "My father is bitter exile, my mother—black poverty." This was the Jew who saw his people sink to the lowest depths, living "a life without hope and without light, the life of a chained and hungry dog. . . ." He was the greatest revolutionary in the diaspora and called for total war against the insufferable conditions of life in exile.

He chastised his people for living such a life, he thundered against them with all the fire of his indignation; shook them with all the strength of his anger. His heart was filled with deep Jewish pride and dignity, which intensified his disgust with the ways of his people. He could not endure their submissiveness, their slavishness, the bending of the necks beneath the yoke of their taskmasters, and their acceptance of their agony with resignation. He sought to put an end to their shame, to stir again the ancient pride and dignity of the ones who were being led like sheep to torture and massacre and who did not rise in revolt.

The City of Slaughter, written after the Kishenev pogroms in 1904, shook the Jewish world to its foundations. Bialik was sent to the city of slaughter by the Jews of Odessa who wanted a first-hand report of what had happened there. Instead of a routine report to the committee, he let loose a thunderbolt of prophetic denunciation.

After the holocaust of Hitler, the incident of Kishenev appears pale in comparison. But in the eyes of the prophet-poet, that small-scale pogrom was a hint of what was to come. Indeed, *The City of Slaughter* was the beginning of those tragic circumstances in the life of the Jewish people in the European diaspora which reached their climax in the Hitler atrocities.

Bialik walked among the ruins of Kishenev and beheld the maniacal fury of anti-Semitism and the bitter shame of Israel's exile. The heart of the delegate from Odessa bursts with his suppressed shame and agony. He controls his tears, for he knows that "the time to bellow is when the ox is bound for the slaughter," not after. But his heart not only writhes in pain at the sight of the ruins and the atrocities visited upon his people; it constricts at the sight of the terrible degeneration of this chosen people. From the cemetery where the martyrs were buried, he comes to the synagogue on a fast day proclaimed as a day of mourning. There he is horrified at the weeping and the wailing of the survivors. He writes, "Thus groans a people who is lost. . . . They beat upon their hearts and confess their sins saying: 'We have sinned, we have dealt treacherously.'" The self-accusations of a people who are butchered alive shake him to the roots of his being. And he, as one of the people, as its spokesman, feels his own unworthiness, his own shame.

The poet, feeling the inadequacy of poetry when the dignity of man has been trampled, when the sanctity of life has been desecrated, lifts himself up above poetry and is clothed with the spirit of prophecy. He demands retribution for all the generations put to shame from time immemorial. He grasps the pillars—not only of our national structure—but of the universe, as if prepared to pull them down. He flagellates himself and his people, and flings defiance against the All-Highest.

It is in this mood that he writes his poems *Upon the Slaughter* and *I Knew In a Dark Night.* In these poems he grasps at the Throne of God in order to shake it and demand the justice due him. More than the prophets and more than Job, he challenges the Creator and his creations.

"If Right there be—why, let it shine forth now!
For if when I have perished from the earth
The Right shine forth,
Then let its Throne be shattered and laid low!
Then let the heavens, wrong-racked, be no more!
While you, O murderers, on your murder thrive,
Live on your blood, regurgitate that gore!
Who cries *Revenge! Revenge!*—accursed be he!
Fit vengeance for the spilt blood of a child
The devil has not yet compiled. . . .
No, let that blood pierce world's profundity,
Through the great deep pursue its mordications,
There eat its way in darkness, there undo
Undo the rotted earth's foundations!"

With this outburst Bialik's national poetic genius reached cosmic proportions. His revolt against himself, against his people and against his God, brought him nearer to the folk. The more he goaded them, the more he captured their hearts.

It seemed as if the tortured body and the sick soul of his people thirsted for the healing hand of the one who whipped them into action. They needed to be whipped, cursed, chastised, purified, awakened from their lethargy and roused to revolt. His gift to national self-consciousness was of tremendous importance. Because of the world-shaking challenge in *The City of Slaughter,* a Jewish army of self-defense was organized among the Russian youth. Later when other Russian cities were attacked, the "sons of the Maccabees" did not flee for shelter in cellars or in attics. They organized into armed squads for self-defense and sallied forth to meet the enemy and return blow for blow. These partisans later developed into the Haganah, which is now the Army of Israel. The partisan bands of the ghettos of Poland and Lithuania in the days of Hitler were the sons of the original members of the self-defense squads inspired by Bialik's poem. The burning message of the prophet-poet was transformed into a life-giving force of a people yearning for redemption.

The idea of revolution in the diaspora found a powerful, epic expression in Bialik's great poem, *The Dead of the Wilderness.* He based this poem on a Talmudic injunction: "Come and I will show you the dead of the wilderness." On that one sentence he constructed a far-reaching poetic edifice.

Through the eyes of his imagination he beheld the desert generation of those who made their exodus from Egypt; those who died in the desert and who were not privileged to enter the land of Israel. These dead are sleeping giants who still wear their armor. In their life-time they were mighty warriors, determined to go from slavery unto freedom. They were the original explorers and undaunted pioneers. But with all their strength and determination, they could only go out of Egypt and wander in the desert. They were not destined to enter the Promised Land. They fell into an everlasting sleep in the midst of the desert.

As described by Bialik, this desert with its fearful stretches of wasteland, its misleading lights, its brooding silence and violent storms, its untold secrets, is the uncharted desert of the diaspora in which Israel wanders, lost and in a daze for generations. But even though the diaspora is a curse, in the eyes of the poet it has a magnificence and grandeur of its own. It is characteristic of Bialik that he looked at things, even unpleasant ones, not in their insignificance, but in their cosmic aspects, in their historical sweep and in their imaginary greatness.

The sleeping dead of the wilderness are not poor slaves who compromised with their destiny. They are:

> "Crouched like dragons primeval,
> Things from the dawn of creation."

They did not attain their goal because the wilderness closed them in. But they died or fell asleep like proud heroes, in the peace and glory of bygone aeons. And behold, after thousands of years, the great hour of redemption came, the hour of awakening for the giants.

> "And in that instant–
> Wakes the terrible power that slumbered in chains,
> Suddenly stirs and arises the old generation of heroes,
> Mighty in battle: their eyes are like lightning, and
> flame-like their faces.
> Then flies the hand to the sword.
> Sixty myriads of voices–a thunder of heroes–
> awaken,
> Crash through the tempest and tear asunder the rage of
> the desert.
> Round them is wildness and blindness. And they cry:
> 'We are the mighty!
> The last generation of slaves and the first generation
> of freemen!' "

The last sentence has become a classic quotation in Hebrew literature and in the life of the Jewish people. It seemed as if the thought waited for generations for Bialik to come and give it expression. It hovered in the air of the diaspora for hundreds of years waiting to be born. And when the hour arrived, it became the battle cry for our reborn generation.

The dramatization of the exile and the redemption is the basis of Bialik's renowned creation, *The Scroll of Fire,* the poem that aroused much controversy and difference of opinion because of its multiple motifs and ideas.

It deals with the destruction of the First Temple and the story of the abduction of its holy altar flame. According to legend the flame was spirited away to a secret hiding place on a desolate island. One of the exiled sons of Judah went out in search of the flame. The symbolism of the island and the flame is quite clear. Just like the desert in *The Dead of the Wilderness,* so the island in *The Scroll of Fire* is the diaspora. The flame is the spirit of the people—the soul of its culture. And he who goes in search of it is the man of vision who thirsts for redemption, who wishes to find the holy flame which would kindle the heart of the people anew.

Bialik drew upon other ancient Jewish legends as source material for this poem. One of them is the meaningful allegory about the two hundred youths and the two hundred maidens whom the enemy exiled from Jerusalem and brought to the desolate island. These young exiles were the remnants of the destruction, the youths who bore the seed of the future within themselves. Bialik invested them with all the depth of his yearning for redemption and with all his soul's desire for love.

In contrast to the epic spirit of *The Dead of the Wilderness,* a deep, lyric spirit pervades *The Scroll of Fire.* In the first poem everything is solid, stony; in the second, the words flow from a soul full of poignant melancholy. Instead of a unified expression, there is dualism. There are two camps: one for lads and one for maidens. There are two extraordinary youths, one delicate, with bright eyes, who looks up to the heavens as if seeking the star of his life; and the other, a man of awesome aspect with stormy eyes who looks down to the earth as if seeking something precious which he has lost. They symbolize the tragic conflicts in life which pull in different directions making it impossible to reach a set goal. There is an autobiographic flavor in the poem; the pain of unrequited love; the earthly and divine aspects of love; the divine and satanic sides of life; the loneliness of man, especially of the Jew in exile; the thirst for beauty, perfection and loftiness; the deep yearning to rise out of the bounds of reality into the spheres of dreams. All these elements combine to form a beautiful tapestry of poetic symbolism.

The two youths who walk along the island are two aspects of man, one has faith in his heart, the other, despair. One sings a song of hope and redemption, the other, a song of revenge and immolation.

Even the four hundred exiles are divided by the enemy into two camps that cannot come together. Their souls yearn to join each other, but they find it impossible. Disunity is the decree of exile, which devours the body and the soul with the fangs of assimilation. All the promising youths are sacrificed to the Moloch of strange civilizations.

One of the unforgettable scenes in *The Scroll of Fire* is the procession of both camps, the one facing the other. The maidens walk with eyes closed. They do not see the deep waters at their feet; neither do they hear the warning cries of the young men. They walk blindly until they fall into the waters. After them the young men descend with a desire to save them, only to drown together with the maidens in the waters of oblivion.

Only the delicate youth with the bright eyes remains on the island, the one who sacrificed his personal happiness on the altar of the holy flame and who was sent on a long mission to be a prophet and a man of vision unto his people and to find the flame that was hidden for a future day. The figure of the youth is all gentleness and deep yearning, resembling Bialik and his poetry. It is but a reflection of himself.

V

In *The Scroll of Fire* one of the important themes is that of unsatisfied love. For not all the maidens fall into the waters. The last and youngest of the girls does not leap. She stays there on the mountain cliff wreathed in the moonlight.

The one remaining youth, the blue-eyed lad who had sung of hope and redemption, speaks to the maiden. His speech, a confession, an outpouring of the spirit, is the climax of the poem. It is the cry of suppressed love and inhibited desires. He tells the maiden of his sorrowful past, of his abashed youth, his expectations unfulfilled. Here, as in other of Bialik's poems, the maiden-figure is exalted to symbolic heights. Earthly woman is enveloped in a mystic supernal light. The poet's love is a blending of prayer and yearning. His beloved is a reflection of the divine *Shekhinah*. Like twin sisters, love and religion are fused.

In *Where Art Thou?* the poet sings:

"Where art thou?
Long ere I had known who and what thou art,
Thy name trembled upon my lips,
And like a fire-coal at night upon my couch
Thou hast burned in my heart;
And I wept in night unrest, and bit my pillow,
And my flesh pined with thought of thee:
And all day long among the letters of the *Gemara*
In a ray of light, in a cloud's bright form,
In the purest of my dreams and harshest of my pangs,
My soul sought naught but thy revelation unto me,
Naught but thee, thee, thee. . . ."

Of her he had dreamt while sitting over his *Gemara,* that same ancient Talmud tome in which his soul had been captive from childhood on. For her he yearned in his holiest prayer and his purest joy. Purity—that is woman's greatest attribute. Holiness—that is the word for her.

"Too pure art thou to be my friend,
Too holy to sit by my side,
Be thou to me God and Angel,
Thee would I serve,
To thee would I pray!"

This purity and holiness are but facets reflecting all of life's yearnings. Woman is the incarnation of the light, the glow and the ardor which fill the universe. Therefore, should one have to leave her, all is not lost. For so is it in life. In order to unite with that which is most pure, one must sever one's self from the physical, from the corporeal form and be made one with spirit and holiness.

"No, my pure one, I have loved thee,
And to thee I still am loyal.
Even when I deserted thee,
It was all for love's own sake."

Better that her image remain to him forever undefiled—thus may the holiness of the universe shine out to him through her.

> "Be to me a holy memory,
> Shine to me from out the starlight,
> Call to me from out my heart's beat,
> Tremble to me from out of my tear-drop. . . ."

If, at time, he should stumble and yield to the intoxication of her hungry eyes, her thirsty lips, and drink at the fountain of carnal delight, he soon regrets it. For one moment of pleasure and a sip of delight, he has given up an entire world. He exclaims, "How great is the price I have paid for thy body!"

It is better to say, "Thou goest forth from me—go in peace." He does not remain alone. So much is yet left to him—green spring-tides, golden summer-ends, winter's whiteness—and over all shall hover her image, like God's loving kindness hallowing the Sabbath candles.

He beseeches her as she goes from him, to be calm, to behold the tranquillity of those on high, of the stars and the skies which will outlive generations of our kind . . . and to drink in something of their peacefulness and eternity.

VI

Bialik was blessed with the love of his people. For he is profoundly Jewish in his *weltanschaung*. He is firmly rooted in the Jewish spirit. He has the deep tribal feeling of the ancient Hebrew, the graces of the folk life of yesterday and today, and the might of the national awakening of today and tomorrow. Thus he unites within himself the oldest ancestral traditions, the lore of the immediate past, the tasks of the present, the hopes for the future.

That it why we feel germinal power and full-flavored ripeness in all of Bialik's words. He is the poet of strength and of forceful utterance. His word is a deed, a *davar* in prophetic parlance. He likens his word to an axe or a hammer. ("My word shall fall like a heavy axe"—"My hammer has found no anvil beneath"—"My axe has struck rotten wood.") It is an elementary metaphor, of the type the Prophets used, to compel sinners not merely to *hear* their Word but to *feel* it as though driven into their flesh. It is not only in isolated images that Bialik makes use of this metaphor. He wants us to see him completely in the character of a woodcutter. On the morning after the celebration of his fiftieth birthday Bialik wrote:

> "And wherefore have ye gathered about my dwelling?
> Wherein have I sinned? What power have I?
> I am no poet, no prophet—
> A mere woodcutter am I,
> A woodcutter, an axeman
> Doing my work by rote,
> And when the day passes, my hand grows weak,
> And dull rests my axe."

With great courage, with the enthusiasm and faith of a pioneer, without precedent to guide him and without assistance, through his own native talents, he carved a new language and hewed a new poetry, to be enshrined forever in the people's consciousness.

Bialik shunned the facile and superficial; he sought the difficult and the profound. He wrestled with himself and with his environment. He chastised and flagellated his people because their weakness insulted him. His feelings were outraged by his people's cowardly meekness, their patient callousness towards their own suffering. He poured forth a new prophetic castigation upon Israel. In this he obeyed not only the promptings of nationalist emotion; there was much in it of great personal drive, urging him to fight, to struggle, to rebel. Having the axe in his hand, he sought an object on which to wield it. His superabundant strength needed the stimulating presence of an obstacle, an opposition over which it might triumph.

His words reverberated like thunder in the clouded skies of the Jewish people. In him they were conscious of a new matchless power and they learned to love even his wrath and reprimand, his gall and sarcasm, his sorrow and tribulation. Though he lashed their flesh with burning rods, they came to cherish his violence for it was indicative of the driving force of the poet. They knew always that Bialik smote not out of hate but of love. So the people presented him with the greatest honor stored in their national treasury—the name *Prophet*.

But Bialik dug more deeply not only into the recesses of the people's soul, but into his own. For there can be no influence exerted on others unless it flow from an inner personal strength. Valuable though prophetic poetry be, it needs an object to receive its hammer-like blows. But the purely poetic, the lyrical impulse needs no such object, no sinner to chastise and seeks only to find itself, to become aware of its own light, to sense the flavor and truth of its own life.

It is then that Bialik goes into the Holy of Holies of his own ego. He goes forth to *The Pool* where he beholds a new world reflected in the clear, calm waters. There among the eternal trees which no axe has ever touched, the domain of wolf and huntsman, he wanders for many silent hours in lone communion with his heart and his God.

In *The Pool* and *Splendor* and other nature poems, Bialik reveals himself in his true greatness. The poet who has heard echoes of a hidden God looks into the pool's reflected landscape and perceives that

"There is a silent, divine language, a secret tongue,
No voice has it nor syllable, but hues of hues,
And magic has it and glorious pictures and a host of shows—
In this tongue God reveals himself to the chosen of His heart,
And in it the Master of the World thinks His thought
And the Master Artist bodies forth His heart's medication,
And in it finds interpretation for an unuttered dream—
Behold, it is the language of sight—"

In this silent, wordless language of many wondrous scenes and images, God also reveals himself to this chosen one as He had once taught him the beauty of the Word.

It would require a great artist to translate even with remote adequacy these poems in which Bialik's word mastery is displayed in all its charm. As earlier he had applied the language of the Prophets to his poems of power, so now he molds the richness and loveliness of the Hebrew tongue to suit the delicate nuances of the reflected lake-world. Strength and might are the fibre of his prophetic utterances. But here his words uplift the reader with their plastic beauty, their lyric clarity and purity. Indeed, they affect us like a prayer.

With Bialik, as with all great poets, language is not merely a means to an end. It is an end in its own right because through it the content and rhythm of a poem are formed. By its separate tiny parts, by the words which are wedded together, by the sounds engendered by their union and by their every slight stir, the desired result is attained, the image formed and the poet's goal reached. Content and form are completely and indissolubly united throughout the poetic writing of Bialik.

But what he did for the Hebrew language was more than a linguistic accomplishment, though that be sufficient when the language is a sacred tongue, the national tongue of Israel. Bialik probed the ultimate sources, the deepest origins of Jewish expression. And to him were revealed with a blinding light the hidden treasures of the language in which the Jewish spirit was first fashioned, in which the Law was given to mankind, in whose sharp and concise terms the Ten Commandments were hewn and a new morality created for man, whose flaming words spoken by divinely inspired prophets set afire the hearts of men and nations, teaching them justice and mercy, brotherhood and equality.

It was this very Hebrew language which first revealed a whole new world to the poet Bialik and then became the instrumentality for the awakening of his own powers and for the development of his rich talents for the greater glory of mankind.

THE TALMUD-STUDENT

(Excerpts)

There are abandoned corners of our Exile,
Remote, forgotten cities of Dispersion,
Where still in secret burns our ancient light,
Where God has saved a remnant from disaster.
There, brands that glimmer in a ruin of ashes,
Pent and unhappy souls maintain the vigil—
Spirits grown old beyond the count of time,
Grown old beyond the reckoning of days.
And when thou goest forth alone, at nightfall,
Wandering in one of these, the sacred cities,
When heaven above is quick with breaking stars,
And earth beneath with whispering spirit-winds—
Thine ear will catch the murmur of a voice,
Thine eye will catch the twinkle of a light
Set in a window, and a human form—
A shadow trembling, swaying back and forth,
A voice, an agony, that lifts and falls,
And comes toward thee upon the waves of silence.
Mark well the swaying shadow and the voice:
It is a *Matmid* in his prison-house,
A prisoner, self-guarded, self-condemned,
Self-sacrificed to study of the Law.

Within these walls, within this prison-house,
Six years have passed above his swaying form:
Within these walls the child became the youth,
The youth became the man, fore-ripened swift;
And swift as these went, swifter yet were gone
The cheek's bloom and the lustre of his eyes.
Six years have passed since first he set his face
To the dark corner of the inner walls;
Six years since he has seen, for joyous sunlight,
Gray limestone, lizards and the webs of spiders;
Six years of hunger, years of sleeplessness,

Six years of wasting flesh and falling cheeks—
He knows that Jews have studied thus of old,
He knows the fame and glory they have won . . .

In the *Yeshivah* is a holy silence
Which he, the Talmud-lad, is first to break;
For there, in the dark corner, wait for him—
Faithful companions since the day he came—
Three friends: his stand, his candle and his Talmud.
As if the moments could not move too swiftly
That lie between him and his trusted friends,
He hastens to his place and takes his stand,
And like a pillar stays from morn till night.
Still standing he will eat his mid-day crust,
Still standing he will half out-watch the night.
Granite is yielding clay compared with him—
A Jewish boy unto the Torah vowed . . .

MORNING SPIRITS

Was it my mother's kiss, was it the swallow
With its "twit-twitter," broke off my sweet dream?
Lo, I awoke and seemed crowned with a halo,
Legions of rays smote my eyes with their gleam.
Still on my eyelids the dream-web was clinging,
Still lingered its cherubs and would not retreat.
Already the glory of morning was swinging
In a galloping cart o'er the cobble-stone street.

The nest o'er my lintel awoke with a flutter,
Aroused itself quickly with shout and with song,
The Spirits of Morning poured in through the shutter
And frolicked and beckoned—a radiant throng.
They sparkled in dances so joyously soaring,
They beat on my pane as white doves in their glee,
They glided and vanished in light outpouring
And flowing abundantly down upon me.

They winked and they beckoned, their faces bright beaming:
"Come forth, roguish one, shine with us in our flight!
With childhood's exulting we'll send our rays streaming,
On all that we find we will sprinkle our light:
On the soft tufts of sheaves, on curls and on tresses,
On the smooth of the waters that sleep between crests,
In the smile of a child whose lips slumber caresses,
In the heart of a mother where soft pity rests,
In the dew of the morn, in the cheek of fair maiden,
In the pure tears of children, on the wing of a bird,
In fragments of glass, in a bubble air-laden,
On a door-knob of brass, in the poet's rhymed word.
Come forth, roguish one, let us send our rays streaming."
They wink and they beckon, their eyes brightly shine.
Their faces so tiny give light with their beaming,
Their pure brilliant bodies aflutter seek mine.
Great waves of warm light come and surge on my face,
My heart faints within me and melts at the sight!
I open my eyes and I close them apace—
O God, I am swept, I am flooded with light!

O, come to me, pure ones, pure Spirits of Morning,
Come under my cover, my sparkling white sheet,
And there let us play till the day gives us warning,
Let me feel your bright warmth from my head to my feet,
On my locks, on my lips, on my eyelids come beaming,
On the dimple of cheek; then through lens of my sight,
Oh, enter and flood me with radiance gleaming,
Cleanse my heart and my soul and suffuse them with light.
The charm overpowers me languid, sweet-flowing,
And each of my veins feels the flow warm and bright
'Til the banks of my heart, 'neath the surge ever growing,
Are flooded completely with radiance of light.
Like a fountain forth bursting, its brilliance outpouring.
How sweet! How my eyelids respond at the sight!
I open and close them, the radiance adoring—
O God, I am swept, I am flooded with light!

UPON THE SLAUGHTER

Heavenly spheres, beg mercy for me!
If truly God dwells in your orbit and round,
And in your space is His pathway that I have not found,—
Then you pray for me!
For my own heart is dead; no prayer on my tongue;
And strength has failed, and hope has passed:
O until when? For how much more? How long?

Ho, headsman, bare the neck—come, cleave it through!
Nape me this cur's nape! Yours is the axe unbaffled!
The whole wide world—my scaffold!
And rest you easy: we are weak and few.
My blood is outlaw. Strike, then; the skull dissever!
Let blood of babe and graybeard stain your garb—
Stain to endure forever!

If Right there be,—why, let it shine forth now!
For if when I have perished from the earth
The Right shine forth,
Then let its Throne be shattered, and laid low!
Then let the heavens, wrong-racked, be no more!
—While you, O murderers, on your murder thrive,
Live on your blood, regurgitate this gore!

Who cries Revenge! Revenge! —accursed be he!
Fit vengeance for the spilt blood of a child
The devil has not yet compiled . . .
No, let that blood pierce world's profundity,
Through the great deep pursue its mordications,
There eat its way in darkness, there undo,
Undo the rotted earth's foundations!

SURELY THIS TOO

Surely this too is a judgment of God and a great reckoning:
You deny your own hearts;
You broadcast your holy tears into every puddle
And string them on every beam of false light,
And pour out your spirit over outlandish marble
And sink your soul into the bosom of an alien stone.
While yet your flesh drips blood 'twixt the teeth of your devourers
You stuff also your soul down their throats.
When you build Pithom and Raamses for your deriders
You use your own children for bricks;
And when from the wood and the stone their souls entreat you,
Their cry dies out in the porch of your ears.
When one of your own sons proves an eagle and grows wings,
From his nest you cast him forever;
Even when he soars, sun-thirsty and mighty in space,
Not to you does he bring down the luminaries;
As he shatters the clouds with his wings and cleaves a path to the radiance,
Not on you does the splendor fall;
Far from you on a mountain peak when he shouts exultant,
Not even the echo to you descends.
Thus you lose one by one all your precious children
And are left deserted.
And lustre shall pass from your dwellings and your tents be destitute,
A terror and a desolation,
On whose threshold the mercy of God shall not tread
Nor the joy of deliverance rap on its windows.
When you come to the ruins to pray—you cannot.
When you coax a tear of consolation—there is none.
Your heart is dried out as a bunch of pressed grapes in the winepress,
Rubbish cast in a corner

Whence not a drop can be squeezed to revive the spirit,
To refresh the spent soul.
You shall finger the ruined hearth and find its stones cold,
And in its chilly ashes the cat whining.
There shall you sit mourning and moping, the world without
dreary
And dust and ashes in the heart.
You shall stare at the dead flies on the windows
And at the spiders in the desolate corners.
And want shall howl down to you through the chimney
And the ruined walls shall shiver with cold.

OUT OF THE DEPTH

I know that in the darkness of some night
Like a spent star my soul shall flicker out,
And not a star shall know its resting place.
But yet my wrath shall smolder like a crater
Whose flames have fallen; yea, my wrath shall live
While yet the thunder rumbles in the sky,
While ocean heavenward flings his troubled waves.
O God, would that my people's ageless woe
Were stored deep in the bosom of the world
To water the wide plains of sky and earth,
To nourish stars and plants, to live their life,
To pulse in all their throbbing, sense their growth,
With them to dwindle, rise and sprout afresh!
Outsoaring generations, let that woe
Witness to wrong eternal. Voiceless, dumb,
Oh, let that cry ring through the deep of hell
And pierce the heavens, everlastingly
Withholding the redemption of the world.
And when, at end of days, the sun of guile
And counterfeited righteousness shall rise
Upon your slain, when crimsoned with your blood
The banner of deceit shall flaunt the heavens
Unfurled above your slayers, when their flag

Emblazoned with the spurious seal of God
Shall pierce the sun's bright eye,
When haughty dance and noisy revelry
Of lying feasts shall waken from their graves
Your hallowed bones: the firmament shall shudder
And grow dark at your agony, the sun
Shall redden to an orb of pure blood
To brand the mark of Cain upon the front
Of all the universe, to testify
The broken arm of God. Yea, star to star
Shall flash its trembling message and cry "Behold
A world's deceit, a nation's agony!"
Until the Lord of Vengeance, stung to wrath
Shall rise and roar and with His sword unsheathed
Go forth to strike.

GO FLEE, O PROPHET!

Go flee! No! Such a man as I shall not retreat.
My flock taught me to step with gentle pace;
Nor has my tongue learned fear or base deceit,
My word shall fall as falls a heavy mace.

And if my strength is spent, 'tis not my wrong.
The sin is yours. Bear the iniquity!
My hammer found no anvil firm and strong,
My axe struck but the soft rot of a tree.

It matters not! I'll make peace with my fate
And to my girdle bind my tools, the same
As unpaid laborer when day grows late;
And then I'll leave as softly as I came.

Return to my own vales and habitat,
Make with the forest sycamores my stay,
But you, decaying moldiness and rot,
Tomorrow's storm shall fling you far away.

I DID NOT FIND THE LIGHT

I did not find the light drifting free,
My father bequeathed it me not.
I have hewn it of my own rock;
Of the heart's hiddenmost spot.

One spark's in the rock of my heart,
Tiny, but wholly my own,
Borrowed from none nor yet stolen,
But of me and in me alone.

'Neath the hammer of all I have suffered
When my heart bursts, the rock of my prime,
This spark dashes into my eyes
And from thence—to my rhyme.

From my rhyme it slips into your heart
And into your fire that I raise,
While with my own flesh and blood
I pay for the blaze.

Bialik, Teller of Legends

I

The legend plays a special role in the drama of Bialik's life and work. From his earliest days he was drawn, as though by magic bonds, after the inner charm that lies hidden in the legend.

In one of his first poems, *To The Legend,* upon which the freshness of youth rests like the morning dew upon garden blossoms, the Yeshivah student confesses to the pages of his Talmud tome:

"In you, my worn, moth-eaten Talmud-leaves,
Dwell ancient legends, captivating tales;
In you, my soul finds soothing from its woes,
To you I come whenever grief assails."

In the secret shelter of these pages of the Talmud that preserve in their columns those charming and bewitching legends "the sorrow-laden soul" of the young poet "finds its repose from the tyrant's wrath." When he walks in darkness in the vale of gloom there rise up to confront him these faded pages from which sparkle those legends like precious stones, opening wide "the gates of heaven" and

". . . into his anguished soul
A new supernal light streams ceaselessly."

Since Bialik was the kind of man who kept faith with all the sights and events, with all the precious images and early experiences of his distant childhood and since he was a poet with excellent memory and with his roots in the past, all his life he spun this web whose first strands he discovered in the springtime of his being. He kept faith with the legend and fulfilled the promise he had made to it. During the very years of his torrential poetic creativity, he was working diligently on the great undertaking of *Safer Ha-agadah (The Book of the Legend),* destined to become a most popular work, a glorious memorial to the poet and to his loyal co-worker, Ravnitzky.

Together with this collaborator, who could throw himself into uninterrupted research because of his devotion to the subject, the poet entered the inner sanctum of the legend and there in its secret gardens he plucked its choicest blossoms and became intoxicated with their fragrance, a fragrance with which he scented all of modern Hebrew literature and Hebrew education.

Thus the great poet of the Hebrew literary renaissance became the great exegete of the ancient legend. The relics of our distant forefathers' creative imagination, scattered over the expanse of the wide "sea of the Talmud" and concealed like pearls in its depths were gathered together and strung on one rope, arranged chronologically and presented in a most palatable Hebrew.

In this work of bringing to life again the ancient legend and finding a place for it within the framework of the Hebrew literature of our times, Bialik found final fulfillment for his creative talent and, at the same time, a specific for the sick soul of his generation that searched for the new while yet yearning for the old. He was most eager to discover the happy blend of past and present. He grasped the artistic preciseness and the ethical meaning, the Jewish *apercu* and the human wisdom of the legend and with poetic grace presented his readers with a rediscovered treasure. To the flavor of the Biblical Hebrew which Jews savored from the days of childhood and the time of the literature of the Haskalah, a new flavor was added.

The question may be raised, if Bialik's admiration and love for the legend be so great, what is the explanation for his excellent essay, *Halakha V'agadah (Law and Legend),* in which he so strongly argues that proper due be given the place of law in literature and life? Is there not in this defense of law, a diminution of the importance of legend and its subordination to the royal sceptre of *halakha?*

The answer is that even in this essay, marvellous in the beauty of its construction, in the richness of its language and in the depth of its emotion, Bialik reveals himself principally as a great master of the legend.

True, he does appear in this essay as the devoted and industrious defense attorney for one side, that of the *Halakha;* hence it would logically seem that he should be too the prosecuting attorney vis-à-vis the opponent, the *Agadah.* But his method in the "prosecution" is the method of the poet, the master of the legend, whose words are like a "consuming flame." He is zealous for the wholeness and the well-being of Hebrew creativity. He does not wish to see it weakened or dissipated; nor is he anxious to see Hebrew literature limited to the poem and the story alone. He is eager for its historic greatness, its Jewish originality and its universal sweep so that it may become a light unto our path as well as the path itself in life.

Such is the deep yearning of the ideal master of the legend who seeks to place a firm foundation to literature's structure so that it neither totter nor fall, who desires to strengthen poetry too so that it have not only feminine energy but masculine might, who wishes to pour into the roots of *Agadah* the blood of *Halakha* to give it firmness and vigor and long life, so as to make it a powerful light for those who walk in its paths. Thus this essay, whose purpose is to affirm in deliberative prose what the writer always sensed within the recesses of the soul of Hebrew poetry, is but an additional gift, luxurious and beautiful, to Bialik's rich treasure-trove of poetry or, as one may say, of legend.

II

Bialik was accepted as the people's poet with the speed of lightning, the kind of immediate acceptance won by few. However, in this blessing, to which so few attain, there lies also something perilous.

The peril lies in "the first impression." It is the strongest one and remains unchanging, preventing the readers, even the most faithful of them, from budging one whit from their first reaction to the poet so as to see him in a different light, in a new revelation. When the first edition of Bialik's collected poetry appeared in 1923 in honor of his fiftieth birthday (including also the rest of his works, short stories, essays and translations, all in four volumes), his stature had already been fixed in the imagination of the reader of Hebrew. But as a result, Bialik's own *terminus ad quem* was, as it were, also fixed. What he had created until that time was popularly known and accepted; while what he was to create henceforward would not be as widespread nor as greatly appreciated as it deserved. It was as though both reader and critic had agreed: What the poet has given us until now is more than enough—for what can be added to the unique and overwhelming gift he has given us? What more can be told that has not been told already? What more can be set to poetry that already has not been in the *Hamatmid (The Talmud-Student), B'ir Haharegah (The City of Slaughter),* in his nature poems and his poems of indignation, in *Megilat Ha'esh (The Scroll of Fire)* and *Metey Midbar (The Dead of the Desert)?*

However, now it is indeed known that more could have been added and, in truth, more was added, of basic and lasting value, to Bialik's poetry—even something new to his autobiographical poems (such as the poems of his "orphaned years"): *Avi (My Father), Shivah (The Seven Days of Mourning), Almenut (Widowhood), Pridah (Separation),* as well as other poems, and the writing of the legends collected in his book, *Vayehi Hayom (And It Came To Pass).*

The new elements in this book of legends are the lucidity and the penetration, the breadth of knowledge and the very joy of telling a story, of describing a scene, the good humor and the keen observation and, most important of all, the author's emergence upon the broad square of popular imaginative writing while climbing the heights of universalism, especially in *Agadat Sheloshah Ve'arba'ah (The Legend of the Three and the Four).*

It would seem that in these legends Bialik freed himself from the spiritual tension that had gripped him all through his years, years heavy with creative toil and weighty with the great national burden. In the legends he entered a world translucent and pure, a world for which his soul had ever yearned.

It would seem too that with these legends the poet finally went beyond the limits of the *Bet Hamidrash* and the village, the confines of the desert and the exile, and attained the peace of the Promised Land amidst the clime of the enchanting legend, which breathes the air of the free imagination and reflects the wisdom of the ages. Here, in this climate of light and freedom which characterizes the ancient folk legend, whose heroes are kings and singers—a David or a Solomon—here it is possible for the poet of exile and poverty, of anguish and indignation, for the prophet of the end and the beginning (the end of exile and the beginning of redemption), to rise to royalty himself—the royalty of the freedom of the spirit, of the glory of song, of the majesty of the past.

Into this arena Bialik stepped armed with all the necessary weapons, a great literary style, a mastery of Biblical Hebrew and a spiritual and aesthetic maturity. When one reads his book, *And It*

Came To Pass and, especially *The Legend of the Three and the Four, The Stalled Ox and the Dish of Herbs* and even the rhymed humorous story of *Duke Onion and Duke Garlic,* one marvels at the rare linguistic ability and the artistic and imaginative power of this contemporary poet who could so successfully penetrate to the very core of the Biblical idiom, to the manner of speech of ancient man and the way of thinking of the sage of the remote past.

Other authors who preceded him in the use of Biblical style, from Abraham Mapu to David Frischman, moved along a simple and straight path. Having grasped the general spirit of the Biblical story, they poured the hot metal of their own literary expression into the molds of phrases and sentences exactly as found in the Bible. The authors of the *Haskalah* period were enslaved to the complete literary structure of Biblical style. It was as though they were caught in self-imposed chains so that they could make no progress. When we read Mapu's *The Love of Zion,* for example, particularly the conversations between its characters, we know for a certainty that its setting is a world far removed from our own, a world with no relationship to ours. The complete consistency of the Biblical setting, as reflected in the Hebrew dialogue of the book, gives one the feeling that with all the skilled workmanship of the novel, it is basically an imitation, although a marvellously beautiful imitation.

The legends, *In the Wilderness* by Frischman, in turn, point to the fact that the author too belongs to the period of the Renaissance in modern Hebrew literature. He is a man emancipated from the Biblical verses that had enchained Mapu. He breathes freely; all his writing is in the Biblical *spirit* only. Yet in spite of all this, he is himself still in the wilderness, breathing the atmosphere of the ancient days he creates, without attempting to extend his stakes so as to include within his narrative allusions and shadows of the scenes and the emotions of contemporary man. The result is that he too is imprisoned and there is no breadth of scope to his work. Therefore, too, his language is limited by the boundaries of the concepts found in the Bible. But because Frischman possessed a facile style, easy running and pleasant, these legends of his flow freely along their course and make for delightful reading.

But Bialik, original creator that he was, was concerned about the essence and substance of things. Therefore, he could not be satisfied with a literary imitation, even though it be an imitation of great beauty. Nor was it enough for him merely to tell a story charmingly, for the sole purpose of creating delightful reading.

In the legend he sought an additional means, a new medium, for giving expression to his creative talents that had reached their climax in his long-perfected poetry and now looked for a new outlet along other paths and in new directions.

Perhaps it is this that explains the riddle that in its time puzzled all those who admired Bialik's poetry. There was that difficult unexplainable period when he was silent, a period that lasted a number of years and evoked a deep anxiety in the hearts of his readers together with many explanations by literary critics. Ears that had become accustomed to the clear tones of Bialik's poems could not bear his silence. His devotees, thirsting for his word, beat upon his doors, pleading, "O poet, give us your poetry!"

But the poet was then going through a severe spiritual crisis. He wished to be alone in his tent and to pray in solitude for his spirit that he might know the path to follow in his creativity. It was as though he stopped still for a moment to peer deep down into the pool of his poetic genius to see what yet lay hidden within it, what concealed message had not yet been revealed to him. He inquired, as it were, of his secret *Urim* and *Tumim* as to the way he should go henceforth, having already created his early poetry that had satisfied others but that had left him all the more hungry. He sensed that there was an unfinished account, a veiled and inner account, between himself and the wide world in which he lived, both the Jewish world and the world generally, and the account must be completed while yet he had the strength.

This then is the explanation of his silence; this the secret of his seclusion. When he went forth from the privacy of his tent and from the covert of his isolation, he returned to his autobiographical poetry in which he took a spiritual inventory of his life. Thus he turned also to the Biblical legend, in which he sought and found the roots of the national existence of his people. And, in truth, he converted the legend into something precious, a new poetic creation, a vine with deep roots and sweet wine.

III

In this new form of literary creation Bialik forsook the Biblical formalism characteristic of his predecessors and chose to go his own way, the royal road of the poet. He absorbed the fragrance and the spirit of the style of the Bible but he did not become enslaved to its crystallized and congealed form of expression. There are in many of his legends and especially in *The Legend of the Three and the Four* expressions and descriptions reminiscent of his poems, particularly, *The Scroll of Fire.* Here Bialik was not an imitator but an original creator. He poured the melody of his own style—and style is the soul—into the Biblical style. The manner of speech of the characters of his legends, the portrayal of their virtues and vices, the descriptions of nature, the methods of development of events are all given not skimpily but with largesse through all the blessed means granted to a twentieth-century poet-story-teller, even though he may treat of events and personalities of a much earlier era.

It was because of his great poetic ability and linguistic preeminence that he could completely free himself of Biblical formulas and break the fetters of the Biblical verses that had bound the hands of his predecessors. When one delves into his book, *And It Came To Pass,* he is aware of the gentle and peaceful atmosphere of the Bible, yet without being disturbed by the slightest trace of fragments of Biblical verses or expressions taken whole from the Biblical text and placed in the mouths of characters according to the whim and by the dictate of the author, standing behind them and compelling them so to speak.

The figures who live in these stories are living personalities, true to their times, their spirit and their proper character—no artificiality here. The poet-narrator, who walks along with them, recording their words, describing their deeds, tracing their movements and setting down their experiences in a book, is their comrade and cherished friend. He feels altogether like a habitué of that ancient but close world which is legendary and real at the same time.

Since the chief characters in these legends are kings and poets, renowned for both their wisdom and their poetry, the eminent poet of our era has an excellent opportunity to prompt the utterances of ancient sages and to cause the readers to savor something of the greatness of spirit and depth of understanding of two folk-heroes who accompany every Jew along the path of life and upon the byways of his imagination.

King Solomon, the principal subject and chief character of *The Legend of the Three and the Four,* appears in his classical impressive figure—"Divine wisdom lights up his countenance; his mouth utters words of understanding." When he speaks, it is with profound wisdom "of the ways of God and His dominion over the earth and of all the wonders of His doings." When the spirit rests upon him, he delivers a prophetic utterance even about "the stars of the heavens and their constellations, all the hosts on high that make their appearance by the command of God."

Only a wise poet could have written about a wise king as Bialik writes about Solomon. He does not disclose the king's words of wisdom until he first reveals his deeds of wisdom. Bialik can control the story-teller's spirit within himself and postpone things that beg to be written down until the propitious time come. For example, there is the dramatic scene when the kings of Tyre and Ammon, of Aram and Moab, guests at Solomon's banquet, utter words of foolish pride and envelop Solomon with thorny mockery, while their jealousy burns all the more within them. The rest of the kings invited to his palace, the major, the minor, the miniscule ones, "sensing the coming storm, exult with glee" and all their inward parts dance with joy in anticipation of the catastrophe soon to overtake the wise Hebrew king, so far superior to them. Their eyes are "all kinds of eyes, the eyes of dogs and hares, of foxes and hyenas, of snakes and monkeys, of falcons and owls." "They incite the king, flattering him, and, while all the time thirsty for the coming horror, encourage him with the words, 'Smite them, smite them, O King, crush their skulls!' " A powerful piercing reply can be expected from the wise and valiant king. But such is not the method of the poet-raconteur. With the peaceful calm that comes from the inner strength of an author certain of his way, Bialik, at this point, says, "But King Solomon paid no attention to any of them. He waited silently, putting his guests at their ease as they spoke. When they had vented their spleen, he then lifted his head like a young lion sure of his strength and in tranquillity and with majesty, he stated, 'When my words will be proven true (the words about woman, "that she, whether good or bad, is a divine gift granted to man according to his works"), then all of you shall go up, each man from his own place and his own land, and you shall come to the House which I have built for God on Zion and there shall you fall face downward upon the earth and lick its dust.' "

Solomon does not have the "we shall hearken" precede the "we shall do," the words before the action. He follows the way of the Torah and of Jewish life from of old. In the beginning comes the deed. At first there is the experience. Only afterwards come words of wisdom and understanding. That is a basic Hebrew concept and that is the way of the Hebrew king. And that too is the method of narration of this Hebrew poet and story-teller.

IV

Bialik wrote two versions of *The Tale of the Three and the Four,* one version concise and simple, the other more elaborate and profound.

In the first version he limited himself to the telling of the familiar Hebrew legend of Solomon and his daughter based upon the words of *Agur ben Yakeh* in the Book of Proverbs (30:18-19).

> "There are three things which are too wonderful for me,
> Yea, four which I know not:
> The way of an eagle in the air;
> The way of a serpent upon a rock;
> The way of a ship in the midst of the sea;
> And the way of a man with a young woman."

In brief, the story is this.

King Solomon has a beautiful daughter whom he loves more than self. But she worries him because of her strangeness and her desire to be alone. She is a dreamer; her eyes have a far-away stare. She wanders alone through the lanes of the vineyards. Princes come to woo her but she gives their words no heed. Her anxious father ascends to the palace roof to read the stars to see "who will be the prince destined by God for his daughter and when will he come. He examines the heavenly portents and behold, neither a king nor the son of a king has been fated by God for his daughter, but instead an indigent youth from among the poor of the people, such a one will come at the appointed time to wed her."

The king is sorely grieved at what he has seen in the stars "and he seeks a stratagem for the upsetting of heaven's plan." He decides to conceal the maiden until the heavenly decree will no longer be effective. He finds a solitary island in the midst of the sea upon which he builds a high tower, surrounded by a fortified wall. In this tower cut off from the world, he places his beloved daughter together with seventy eunuchs from among the Jewish elders to guard and serve her. He stores great amounts of provisions, all kinds of food and drink, every luxury—nothing is lacking. He then shuts up all the gates of the tower with iron bars and locks, making impossible any exit or entry, and says to himself, "Now I shall see what God can do, whether the prediction of the stars shall come true or not."

The stellar prophecy does come true.

"An impoverished youth, the son of good people and of a family of scribes, sets out from his native city, Acre, for his soul longs for distant places."

Thus he goes to and fro in the land, wandering through cities and villages, until one day nightfall finds him in a foresaken and desolate place. Hungry and thirsty, he lies down to sleep inside an ox's skeleton in the field. While he sleeps, a great and mighty eagle swoops down upon the skeleton and snatches it up, together with its contents, the indigent and famished lad from Acre.

The eagle carries its burden to the roof of the tower where Solomon's daughter dwells and there leaves it. Thus meet the two whom God has meant for each other and they plight their eternal troth.

"And the lad arises and pricks his hand and with his blood writes down the words of their troth in a document, inscribed and sealed, and weds her according to law, saying, 'The Lord be our witness and his angels, Michael and Gabriel.' "

When the time forecast by the stars has passed, Solomon comes to the tower and discovers the pair together. When he hears of the incredible but yet true occurrences, he understands that this indeed must be the poor youth revealed to him in the stars. Solomon admits, "Now I know that there is no wisdom, no intelligence, no design that can stand against the Lord."

This, in brief, is the legend in one version. But with this version the poet was not satisfied.

First of all, there is no development of all the four "ways," alluded to in the words of Proverbs. This version exploits only "the way of an eagle in the air" and "the way of a man with a young woman," but there is no reference to "the way of a serpent upon a rock" and "the way of a ship in the midst of the sea."

Secondly, even the "ways" that are found in this version, the way of the eagle and the way of the young man, are used in brief and simple fashion. The bounds of utter simplicity are never exceeded; no symbolism arises from the tale. It is a folk legend, based on two Biblical verses, told briefly and unaffectedly to prove a point and no more. If this be so, what does the poet succeed in accomplishing, coming, after a long period of about three thousand years and telling the same legend anew?

Bialik, therefore, could not rest content until he rewrote the legend, incorporating the emendations and improvements he sought, resulting in the second version of the tale. In his letter of April 2, 1933 to Doctor Jacob Nacht, he writes, "When I first wrote *The Legend of the Three and the Four,* I relied principally upon the abbreviated form of the legend as found in the introduction to Buber's edition of *Midrash Tanhuma* (Vilna, 1885, p. 136), and upon my supposition that this legend had been given birth to by the verses in Proverbs, 'There are three things which are too wonderful for me, etc.' This conjecture was fortified later when, by chance, I heard some additional details of the story from my wife. According to her version, which she as a child had heard from an old woman, a snake also played a part in that same legend. *Upon this basis I rewove the legend, giving it artistic completeness, so that it became an entire novella, full of action. I am not aware of any other sources for this legend.*"

The force of this second version and its innovation lie in the fact that the author here foresakes the narrow path of the folk legend, with its simplicity and naturalness, and sets forth upon the broad highway of epic creation, based upon the legend, but not enslaved to it, for it rises above it.

True, the story's rhythm and outward form are in the spirit of the Bible, without departing from its style, without doing the slightest violence to its simplicity, its clarity or its integrity—even the opening words of the story are the classical words, "And it came to pass." But into this framework, extended by Bialik, the poet poured a richness of imagination, a talent for description, a felicity of conception and a beauty of language whose compare is difficult to find.

The entire structure of the story is amazing both for its beauty and its completeness. Each chapter, and there are nineteen, has its own purpose, its own central idea, its own unity. Most of these chapters, if not all, can stand on their own feet; they are themselves stories or descriptions which, because of their content, form and abundance of charm shine forth with light of their own, glittering like emeralds.

The first line of each chapter foreshadows its entire contents. Each new chapter is joined to the previous one, developing the plot farther, ascending the scale higher and higher until the climax is reached and the vision seen by the poet in his imagination is fulfilled.

From the first sentence of the first chapter, "And it came to pass that the King, Solomon, made a great feast in his palace," until the two last chapters, wherein is described the second feast, the wedding feast of Natanyah and Ketsiah, there is unrolled the life's scroll of the young lovers in the lengthy and predestined fashion of two souls yearning for each other and despite many obstacles, finally reaching each other. The opening sentences of each chapter, that may be joined together to tell the story in brief, are the early notes of a symphony of wisdom and beauty directed by a wise poet singing the praises of a wise king. This story is a chef d'oeuvre of Hebrew creativity for in it are united the wisdom of past and present, while Judaism and humanity are fused together into one poetic harmony.

V

The greatest innovation in this second version of the legend is that the heroine, the instrumentality for the testing of man's fate and love's might, is no longer Solomon's daughter, but Ketsiah, the only daughter of the King of Aram. It was not without purpose that Bialik enlarged the *mise en scène* and made this aspect of the legend a subject for a universalistic story.

In the first version, built entirely upon the foundation of a folk legend, the Jewish king defies the stars and challenges fate, through his own daughter. Thus the theme remains a parochial one, a Jewish one. But just as Bialik was not content with the entire elementary structure of the first version, so too was he not satisfied with the setting placed between the national boundaries of the Kingdom of Judah. He, therefore, lifted the story's great challenge beyond these bounds, into the domain of the wide world itself.

For it was the poet's great aspiration to make of the legend's theme a broad humanitarian and universal one. It was not only the stars of fate that the Jewish king was testing but also the kings of the East and West in order to discern whether there yet lived in man's heart the great prophetic vision of the unity of mankind and the brotherhood of nations, the vision without which there could be neither order nor peace in the world.

It is for that reason that the prisoner in her symbolic tower is not a Jewish maiden but an Aramean. It is a Hebrew youth, Natanyah, son of Malkishua, whom the author brings to her in her tower of dreams and joins them together in a covenant of everlasting love. The fact of these two being united in love becomes all the more significant by the author's making of Malkishua and the King of Aram relatives by marriage in the end. For this very Malkishua, when he was young, strong and thirsty for adventure, had enlisted with the forces of Joab to wage war against Aram. In the hot and fierce battle that ensued, Malkishua shot an arrow straight to the heart of the brother of the King of Aram, the father of Ketsiah, and killed him. From that time on the King of Aram had carried in his heart a consuming hatred against Malkishua. Now fate appoints this same man to be his relative by marriage. And his only beloved daughter, who has borne her burden of loneliness and anxiety on the island tower, it is she whom fate gives as wife to Natanyah, the son of his enemy.

It is this novel though seemingly minor detail that contains the spark of dramatic action and that set Bialik's heart on fire. This he makes the paramount point at the feast and the chief burden of Solomon's lofty message on the brotherhood of nations and the love of man for his fellow. For the seed of this universal love, according to both the king and the poet, is the love between man and woman, which is the builder of life upon earth.

At the elaborate marriage feast, arranged by Solomon in honor of the bride and groom, at which are present the kings of the East and the West, who had all participated in the earlier feast at the beginning of the story, the King of Aram sits dejected, indignant, enraged, as though someone were raking hot coals upon his head and charring his living flesh (a favorite analogy of Bialik's). Why this anguish and fury? The explanation is a simple one—the great hatred he bears the Jew for having killed his brother in battle. That is the same ancient hatred kindled in the hearts of the nations of the earth from antiquity to our own day. And hatred begets hatred, envy begets envy and war begets war.

Thus does King Solomon speak to the King of Aram, to the other kings and to us too of this generation: "Are there not Sabbatical years even for wrongs committed? Shall a man nurse his hate in his bosom always, until he go down into the pit, even as the leper carries decay in his bones and the malignant plague in his flesh? Our ancestors hated each other and are no more. Their hate and their envy too perished with them. Shall then we, their descendants, continue to preserve their enmity forever?"

King Solomon knows full well that "Hate is as hard as *Sheol* and its fury is as the fury of cobras unto cruelty but love is yet stronger and mightier."

For "when love pours forth its spirit upon man, it returns him in a flash to his stature as of yore, as when God first fashioned him, and he no more seeks out old scores, large or small. The wall of enmity which the ancestors built layer upon layer, which they raised higher day by day with anger and animosity so as to separate nation from nation and man from his fellow, that wall would be razed to its foundations by their descendants, once the spirit of love would spread its wings over them but for a moment."

Thus the brotherhood of nations, the love of man for his fellowman, the love of man and woman, all are inseparable in Solomon's message and in Bialik's legend.

Love, in Bialik's poetry, was always something more than the love of man and woman, more than physical, sensual pleasure. In *The Scroll of Fire* and in all his love poetry, woman possesses a unique kind of beauty, distant and ethereal, spiritual and heavenly, for which the soul yearns more than the flesh. The figure of the beloved is that of the hind of the dawn. She is not alone the only one of his life, but she is also "the divine dwelling-place of his desires." She is "his heart's angel" who appears to him upon the peaks of cliffs beneath the wings of the dawn and the morning-star. She is "in appearance as the daughter of God." Most important of all, she is his redeemer. The poet prays to her with great tenderness,

"While yet there may be redemption for me,
Come redeem me and rule over my destiny."

In *The Legend of the Three and the Four* Natanyah, the lover, also appears as a redeemer and in the manner of the prayer in *The Scroll of Fire,* he asks, "Am I not the redeemer, even I? Is it not I whom God has appointed to bring deliverance to the maiden?"

Under this great pressure of sanctity and of redemption, love becomes in *The Legend of the Three and the Four* a mighty force, not only in the life of the individual, but also of all creation, a force that brooks no resistance. It smashes its way across the expanses of roaring seas. It is victorious over waste places, distant isles and prison walls. "For all of these together cannot stand before the might of love and the trumpet-blast of its power when, in its seemly but terrifying manner, full of God-given prowess, it storms its way to its gladsome goal and when, in spite of all obstacles, it carves out its mysterious path to its destination."

And if the walls of the lofty tower could not withstand the Jewish lad in his undaunted climb to the Aramean maiden, Solomon asks the King of Aram still nursing his wrath against Malkishua, the Jew, "How can you possibly think that the anger stemming from your picayunish heart will keep them apart? Is not the hind of Aram proper for the stag of Israel?"

Thus love fulfills a double mission. Not only does it unite two innocent spirits who yearn for each other, but it also spans the breach between two peoples, separated from each other through hate, the causeless hate dividing man from man, nation from nation. But "when love's voice rings clear," say the two, the king and the poet, "hate becomes utterly dumb." Love bears a healing salve for the wounded soul of the individual; it offers too a cure for the sick soul of the world. It "joins together persons far apart by ways past understanding" and "unites the separated by means of a mysterious wisdom." All this is in order to "blend together one blood with another, one fountain of life with another so as to make fruitful God's many fields and bring forth good produce upon the earth." This love comes from God for it quiets the hot blood of the man that longs for a woman's love and it redeems the blood spilled by fratricide. For it is not "the redemption of the blood," tribal revenge, indulged in by oriental peoples and of which the King of Aram dreams, that is true redemption. For, the Jewish sage remarks, "God will not place the means for redemption in the hands of Satan but in the good hands of his angels, in the hands of love. True, 'blood for blood and life for a life.' But not by the spilling of blood and by the cutting off of life does God redeem but by the creating of new life and by its multiplication upon earth, a newer and better life than the earlier."

Thus does the King of Judah speak to the King of Aram and with these words comforting him by showing that the redemption of his slain brother's blood, of which he has long dreamed, has actually come to pass. For that spilled blood has now found a peaceful redemption through the covenant of love between his daughter, Ketsiah, and Natanyah, son of Malkishua. Through this means is his brother's soul redeemed from the hate that has poisoned it for many years and instead of shedding additional blood to that already shed in war, there will come forth new blood, the blood of a new and rejoicing life which love will give to two families in Judah and Aram.

To Ketsiah, the redeemer of the blood of her uncle who fell in battle at the hands of her father-in-law, Malkishua, King Solomon, the wisest of all men, speaks in this manner, "And you, O innocent dove, daughter of Aram's king, because you have hearkened to the summons of destiny and to the call of your heart and have given your love to a Hebrew lad from afar, unknown to you before your meeting, be you blessed by the Lord! Fear not, nor be you cast down. Rejoice in the beloved of your youth and follow after him. Attach yourself to his father's house and to his family and cleave to their God and their ways. It has been predestined by God.

"Know this too and let your father be aware of it, that he may forget his wrath. You are not a foreign twig or an alien shoot to the tree of Judah. For although Aram was separated from Judah in ancient days, both have been carved out of the same rock. Our own early ancestors, our pillars of strength, all sprang forth from the loins of Aram and from the Aramean clan did they choose their wives. May then your origin be blessed, and blessed sevenfold be this day, your bridal day, as in the presence of all this multitude and of the elders of my people, you seek shelter under the wings of the God of Israel and to dwell in His shadow always. 'You are our sister. May you be the mother of thousands of ten thousands.' "

Thus the circle of humanity comes a full turn to the beginnings of Jewish history, to Abraham, Isaac and Jacob, who went back and forth between Canaan and Aram, and, too, to Sarah, Rebecca, Rachel and Leah, all the daughters of Aram. From this Canaanite-Aramean union came the Jewish people. Thus too was it with Israel and Moab, for from the union of Boaz, the Hebrew, and Ruth, the Moabitess, came the house of David.

And Solomon, the son of David, who, with his guests goes up to worship in the House of the Lord, offers seventy bullocks upon the altar according to the number of peoples upon the earth and on their behalf.

Such is the historic instruction, humanitarian and universal, that King Solomon offers to the guests at his banquet. To the reader it seems that not only are the Kings of the East and the West present at that banquet table but he is there as well. And the instructor is fitting for the instruction. For who can compare to King Solomon as a citizen of the world in the full meaning of that concept? Does not his very name, *Shlomo* (in the Hebrew) and the name of his beloved, *Shulamit,* point to the Jewish aspiration for the perfection (*shlemut* in the Hebrew) of humanity and the peace (*shalom* in the Hebrew) of the peoples of the world?

It was to give a new poetic expression to this ancient lofty idea that Bialik wrote *The Legend of the Three and the Four.* And he chose Solomon, the king-poet, the great citizen of the world, to be the director of this wonderful orchestra that blends together stirring music and profound wisdom into one perfect harmony.

VI

In the first version of the legend two of the four "ways," as cited in Proverbs, are missing: "the way of a serpent upon a rock" and "the way of a ship in the midst of the sea." In the second version Bialik fills the gap amply and with extraordinary poetic skill.

In two separate chapters, he describes Natanyah's voyage by ship, the storm that rages against it and the sad end that befalls most of the passengers who are cast into the depths of the sea. Only a few of the ship's passengers remain afloat on the surface of the tempestuous waves, among them Natanyah. But quickly the storm drives them apart and scatters them in every direction until they can no longer see each other. Natanyah drifts all alone on the angry waves until he is plucked up by Solomon's eagle who is bringing food to the maiden in the tower and thus he is brought to the island.

In these chapters that explain the words, "The way of a ship in the midst of the sea," Bialik adds a new dimension to the story—the breadth of the sea and its depth. All this points up the fact that in "the way of a man with a young woman," that is, in love's destined way with all its yearnings and humiliations, its obstacles and its hurts, there play a part all the forces of nature, all the powers in creation. For love is a cosmic force that turns the wheels of the universe and gives life to all living things.

Therefore, the wise allegorist seizes upon the phrase, "the three and the four." For the eagle symbolizes height; the ship, breadth and depth; the serpent, tortuous twisting downwards and upwards, horizontally and vertically; the man and the young woman two different forces, at times conflicting, but which fulfill each other so as to establish the human race that lives in the world and makes the world alive, that absorbs the richness of color in the universe, its echoes and its innermost secrets, converting them into drugs to stir up creation and to render it fruitful.

In order to round out this magic circle of the four "ways" that reach their climax in "the way of a man with a young woman," there is still one "way" more, the third one in the Biblical verse, "the way of a serpent upon a rock." The four chapters, ten through thirteen, in which the poet describes Natanyah's climb toward Ketsiah in the tower, aided by the big undulatory serpent, are a work of art of descriptive poetry whose like would be difficult to find. It is not for nothing that in Hebrew the serpent is called *nahash* for there is *nahash** in him, divination, magic. He casts a spell over the lad who dares to climb to his beloved even as the Hebrew poet too enchants his reader who is drawn after the bewitched youth as the latter follows after the serpent. In the symbolic figure of the serpent, the final beneficent instrument for the fulfillment of a great love, Bialik concentrates all of his poetic and linguistic talents. As in the supposed necromancy of Moses when his staff was changed into a snake and the snake back into the staff, so too here does the serpent discharge an important function, arousing one's admiration and wiping out the boundaries between imagination and reality, between the invertebrate creeping upon his belly and the sturdy vertebrate proud of his might.

There is a kind of colorful sport here between the pursued and the pursuer, between the serpent and the youth that excites the eye and stirs the heart. The two chapters, twelve and thirteen, are in the nature of a great challenge to a craftsman blessed by God who tests himself and his powers to see whether he is able to describe movement so realistically as to give the sensation of motion, whether his pen can convert a mocking vision into a glittering reality and a creative work of art.

The serpent with its magic arts leads the lad on to the hidden maiden. It is as cunning as the primeval serpent—seducer as it is faithful to its mission, the mission of love. It leads the bewildered astonished youth as though captive for it has stolen from him his emerald, his protector and surety for his love. In reality, however, it is not leading him captive for it is bringing him step by step closer and higher to his prize, climbing daringly up a tall oak, so straight and smooth that it affords no possibility for human hold, for "it has neither bough nor branch protruding."

Because of its original sin, the sin of the seduction of Eve in the Garden of Eden, the serpent had been sentenced to eternal creeping upon its belly. But now it has been made love's instrument by the Lord's commandment. It is exalted and lifted up, as it climbs the oak tree, taking with it the youth seeking his maiden. It too has merited its great moment, its hour of redemption.

---

* *Nahash* spelled with the two vowels, *kametz,* is "serpent"; but spelled with the two vowels, *patah,* the same word means "divination" or "enchantment."

The climbing of the oak tree by the serpent and the youth from the tree's base to its summit and then the stiffening of the flexible body of the serpent as it becomes a bridge over which the lover crosses to his beloved are the tokens and signs of the ascent of the poet to the heights of his powers and the climax of his abilities.

This is no mere serpent, but a royal sceptre, a rod of strength and might, "pierced through with all kinds of mysteries which a master magician has ferreted out." The master magician is the poet.

Just as he makes allegorical use of the serpent as a magic symbol, in similar fashion does he use the emerald that plays an important role in this legend and in the unfolding of the destiny of the youth and the girl.

The emerald is given to Natanyah as a gift by his father for the adornment of the sacred Ark when Natanyah would make a pilgrimage to Jerusalem. This very stone once shone as the morning-star upon the forehead of his mother on her wedding day. Now in the son's possession it becomes a star lighting up his path. The serpent steals it from him so that he is drawn after the two, the serpent and the emerald in its possession. The power of the emerald is the basal and mysterious power of love that passes from mother to beloved. And the youth yearning for the fulfillment of his fondest dreams moves on with a strength not his own to that which is still hidden from his eyes, to the heights of the tower where love lies waiting.

This gem, given to the lad by his father as a legacy from his mother, now fallen into the possession of the serpent which works magic with it, drawing the youth on to his destiny, is a gem of wizardry, a charm "in which lies hidden a mighty occult power." Never has its like been seen "for size, for brilliance of light, for scintillating color and for sparkling brightness."

"It is so cut," the poet adds, "that it is like a suspended tear-drop, a large full tear just about ready to fall."

When the lad gazes upon it, "he sees in it a vision of all the splendor and brilliance that a man's heart may summon forth or his spirit conjure up." This can be only because God must have concentrated within it a particle of every kind of His light, the essence of all the brilliances He created. With astonishment the lad asks, as in the language of the poet in *The Scroll of Fire,* "Is it the distillate of God's joy or the chief gem in His crown of salvation?"

This emerald, like its owner, eventually finds its mate, in the treasury of King Solomon and the two gems unite to shine brilliantly together on the Curtain in the Temple.

The king of all the serpents and master of all creeping things had given this second emerald as a gift to Solomon upon his accession to the throne. Solomon had hidden it until a propitious time would come. This was the propitious time—the moment of love's ripening, the moment of the great fulfillment. Now Solomon presents to the bride "the twin sister of the emerald" and the mates find each other, like finds its like.

"This can only be," says the king, "the hand of God which has joined together two living souls and which now brings together two precious stones, hitherto distant from each other."

"For," the wise king continues, "it is not only the human being alone whom God has created twain, male and female, but also all living creatures and all growing things. Why should the same not hold true for inorganic matter?"

At this point the king, and with him too the poet, unrolls the entire scroll of magnificent love as he has always conceived of it in his visions:

"Perhaps it is so too with all the enduring forces of the universe and the foundations of all existence, both the hidden as well as the revealed, the far and the near, the great and the small, from the hosts of the heavens to the dust of the earth, from the drops of rain to the winds and storms, all of them God made twain, male and female. In them all He planted the desire, the passion to be joined one to the other and to become one. From afar they are drawn to each other, they are attracted to each other, they are ever pursuing and being pursued, moving restlessly to and fro and they know no rest. For such is love, magnificent and conquering, implanted by a mighty God, the soul of every being and its living spirit, a fire pent up within the world's confines, filling all creation so that there is no place free of it—without end, without limit. . . ."

Such is love's great song, the song of divine love, whose wings always enfold Bialik. The story ends on a note of holiness, the holiness of the blending and the fusion of the two emeralds that sparkle on the sacred Curtain. This is the holiness of perfect love that comprehends both love of parents for children and the love of the lover for the beloved. Out of the seed of this love there grows the seedling of the future, of the hope for love between man and his fellow-man, between nation and nation.

It is this wonderful light, the light of the two emeralds—love and brotherhood—that Bialik kindles in his splendid tale, *The Legend of the Three and the Four*.

THE LEGEND OF THE THREE AND THE FOUR

King Solomon had a sweet and lovely daughter whose like was nowhere to be found. He loved her as his own soul and guarded her as the apple of his eye. But she was passing strange, differing from all other maidens of her years, disdaining the clamor of pleasure-houses and rather desiring to walk alone and silent through the gardens of the king; or to rise betimes and wander far and wide along the tracks that twined among the vineyards, her spirit absorbed and her eyes gazing far ahead; always did she seem to be dreaming while awake, and there was none that knew her heart. When her time came to be wed, princes from far and near arrived to entreat her from her father; but the king's daughter turned her face away from them and never paid heed to their words; so that they returned one and all, shamed with hanging heads, to their own countries.

Time passed; and when they saw that the maiden persisted in hardening her heart, the princes despaired of her and ceased entreating for her. By reason of this, the king was troubled in spirit on her account and went up to his roof by night to gaze at the stars and perceive who the prince might be that was designed of God for his daughter; and when he would come. He studied the signs of the heavens and discovered that neither king nor prince was matched by God with his daughter, but a poor and needy youth of honest stock would come to her at the appointed season, and take her to wife.

Now this vexed the king exceedingly, and he sought for a stratagem to foil the purpose of heaven. And he decided to hide the maiden away for a while, until the time foretold in the stars should be past and the decree of fate could no longer come about. So he sought him a lonely isle in the sea, far from the ways followed by the ships in their traffick; there he had a lofty castle built, with many a hall and many a chamber; and he ranged a buttressed wall around it on every side, and set his daughter in the castle with seventy

---

This is the first version of the legend referred to in the essay. The English translation of the second version may be found in And It Came To Pass, *translated by Herbert Danby, Hebrew Publishing Co., 1938, pp. 231-281.*

elders of Israel to keep watch and ward over her and serve her every desire; plentiful provision for them did he make, storing them all manner of food and drink and the delights of the world, nothing lacking. Then he closed all the main gates and postern gates and portals and doors of the castle from without with bars of iron and locks and seals so that none might enter or leave; and he said, "Now shall I see the feats of God and His deeds, and whether the intent foretold by the stars shall be brought about or no."

So the king's daughter dwelt within this castle, with the seventy elders mounting guard over her, keeping watch and ward day and night and hastening to satisfy the least as the greatest of her desires. She was permitted whatsoever pastime she might wish, for the king had ordered that she be amused that her loneliness might not oppress her. One thing alone was beyond their power; out of the gates of the castle she could not go since the castle was enclosed from every quarter, none entering and none leaving. If she felt strait and confined within the building she would ascend to the roof and take a turn to and fro in the open air; or would lean against the coping of the battlements, gazing at the width of waters round about and hearkening to the medley of the waves; and she would be eased.

On the wall stood a watchman night and day, his eyes wide on the sea round about, observing the isle lest any ship approach or any strange foot be set on its strand. Twice a day, morning and evening, a speedy skiff would come within bowshot of the isle, one sitting therein who was sent by the king to ask the weal of the maiden. The one in the skiff would wave the white cloth in his hand and ask whether all was well with the king's daughter. And in reply the watchman would wave a white cloth back, signifying that all was well. Then the skiff would straightway turn about and vanish on the horizon.

And the closer came the season which the king did fear, the more did the elders pay heed to their watch and their ward; they stayed awake at their posts by the sealed posterns and gates and portals, their eyes wide, their nostrils sniffing, their ears twitching, starting at the buzzing of a fly as it knocked against a pain of glass or at the scratching claws of a lynx striving to scale the wall; for they were good men and true, such as would not think to deceive while about the king's business.

II

Now a poor lad of good stock who belonged to a family of scribes forsook Acre his city, for he suddenly found that the home of his needy parents was too small for him; and he turned his face afar. He left his home with empty hands, carrying nothing with him save his staff and his body; nonetheless he had no concern and his spirits never fell, since his bones were springing with youth, and his heart bounded with visions and high hopes, and his locks curled and happiness thudded within him all the way, so that he sang as he went. Crossing the fields he watched the grasshopper hopping and the joyous birds at song and the cony of the rocks and the clambering, darting lizard. Every green tree attracted him, and every forgotten booth in a forsaken vineyard. He sustained himself as might a bird from his gleanings in the generous fields, and slept on the ground with a stone for pillow. And wandering wide, passing through villages and cities, he would lend his ears to the converse of the wayfarers, gathering traditions and parables from the people and the elders of the people and storing all such away in his memory; this comforted him in his poverty and restored his soul in his wanderings.

But one day the sun set upon him while he was alone in a desolate, foresaken spot; the evening was rainy and cold, the lad was hungry and thirsty and naked and barefoot, so that frost consumed him and his strength all but vanished. In this plight he saw the carcass of an ox near by and rejoiced, saying: "Blest be God who hath revealed me a couch in this place; lying therein, I shall grow warmer maybe." So he crept between the ribs of the skeleton, curled himself up and fell asleep.

During his sleep a huge eagle descended, picked up the skeleton in its beak together with him sleeping within it, flew off and set them down on the roof of the princess' castle, where it began picking the little that was left of the carrion from the bones. Then the youth came out and drove it away, afterwards sitting on the roof all night long, weary and trembling by reason of the cold and the rains.

Morning came and the heavens cleared. The king's daughter mounted to the roof as was her daily custom, saw the strange youth, stood at a distance and asked:

"Who are you and who has brought you hither?"

And he replied very simply:

"Prithee fear not, O maiden, and be not angered with me. An Hebrew am I, a son of poor folk who dwell at Acre; last night the rain caught me in the fields in my hunger and my thirst, with never a garment to cover my flesh; so I lay me down in that skeleton yonder, and the eagle flew away with me and set it down here. Now I do not know the fashion after which I can depart hence, for there is nothing but the sea round about and never a ship in sight!"

The king's daughter pitying him, brought him in secret to her bower, where she bathed him and garbed him and gave him to eat and to drink; and thereupon the brightness of his countenance returned to him with his high spirits. She gazed at him, found him handsome and pleasant, rejoiced in him exceedingly and was fain that he should be her companion. So she concealed him in her chambers and the elders knew nothing, since she had not revealed his coming to them and they would not venture to enter her chambers saving if they were summoned. Thenceforward she went forth twice a day to them to report her weal; and the elders paid no attention, thinking it but a whim. And they remained diligent and wakeful about their charges, each remaining in his position as he had been ordered, his eyes darting hither and thither, his ears wide to catch a stirring, his nostrils quivering to sniff; for the men were exceeding, exceeding faithful, doing the king's behest with faith and an entire heart.

III

The king's daughter perceived the wisdom of the poor youth, his good understanding and his pureness of heart, and loved him with all her heart and all her soul. And there came a day when she said to him:

"Am I fitting in thine eyes to be taken for thy wife?"

And the youth rejoined:

"Wherefore dost thou ask? I am thy slave to wash thy feet."

Then the maiden told how great her love was for him; how he was more desirable and precious to her than all the princes in the world; how God Himself had brought him thither on the wings of the eagle; how from the moment she saw him her soul did cleave to him; how in his lack her life would not be a life. Many such words did she utter from her ardent heart, and he answered her with the like, seventy and seven fold; and they made them a covenant of eternal love. The youth arose, let blood from his arm, and wrote with his blood the matter of the covenant on a scroll, signed and sealed, betrothing her according to law, saying: "Witness be the Lord, and witnesses His angels, Michael and Gabriel."

And meanwhile the elders knew of all these matters neither much nor little, though there were none such as they, honest and upright men who turned night into day and remained awake and exceedingly watchful at their posts.

When the season revealed to Solomon by the stars had gone by, he bethought him of his daughter shut into the castle; and he resolved to bring her home again. So he went down to the sea in a ship and came to the isle with its castle; he examined the bars of iron and the locks and the seals on the gates and the posterns and the portals, and found that none had tampered with them and they were whole; so he ordered them to be hacked through and the gates and the portals swung open. Thereupon he entered the castle and the elders sprang up before him, then made obeisance and greeted him with peace.

And the king asked: "Is all well with my daughter? And where is she?"

And the elders replied: "All is well with her, O lord king, and she is within her bower."

Then the king proceeded to the maiden's bower, the elders following. They opened the door; and there was a handsome youth there facing them. And the elders quivered and quaked, and their hearts perished within them. And the king turned his eyes on them and asked:

"Who is this?"

But the elders could not make any answer, for they were so astonished that they might have turned to stone. They stood silent and pale, their heads drooping.

Then the king stamped his foot and cried in fury:

"Answer, or you shall be cut down one and all and hewn in pieces!"

The elders fell on their faces before him and answered in fear and trembling:

"Alas, our lord king. What is there to say and how shall we speak: As God lives we have kept watch and ward over the king's daughter with all our might; we do not know the fashion in which this lad is come hither."

The king turned to the maiden, breathing hard with anger as he asked:

"Wanton, say what this lad is doing here. Who brought him hither?"

The maiden fell at his feet, replying:

"Not in thy wrath, my lord and father! For this thing is come about only from God. He sent His messenger the eagle to bring me this youth my beloved, whose wife I am become. Take him and bless him, O my father!"

Then the king asked the youth:

"Who art thou? And after what fashion art thou come hither?"

And the young man stood erect before the king and answered without fear, relating all that had befallen him. The king observed how fine a youth he was and treated him in friendly fashion, conversing with him and finding him versed in all wisdom and parables more than all the scribes in his entire kingdom. So he enquired his name, his city and the house of his parents; and the young man answered directly and truthfully to all his questions telling him of his poverty and his wanderings, and the wonderful manner in which the eagle had brought him to the roof of the castle, and how the maiden had pitied him and taken him to her, entreating him graciously. And he produced the scroll which he had written and signed with his blood and showed it to the king, in token of the eternal love existing between him and the king's daughter. And Solomon hearkened to all these wonders and understood that he must be the poor youth of whom he had been forewarned in his star-gazing; and he said:

"Now indeed do I know that there is no wisdom nor understanding nor counsel that shall withstand the Lord."

When the elders perceived that the king was no longer in a fury their spirits returned; and they rose from the ground and raised their hands aloft to heaven, saying, "Blest be the Lord Who giveth a man a wife."

V

Then Solomon brought his daughter and her husband to Jerusalem, where he made them a seven-day feast and rejoiced with them greatly. When the feast had come to an end Solomon said to his son-in-law:

"See, thou art the son-in-law of the king, and my domains spread far and wide. Choose thou whatsoever high office thy heart may desire and it shall be thine!"

But the youth replied:

"My lord king! Since my childhood I have been but a poor man of letters; my forefathers were scribes and learned of the Lord one and all, never aspiring to greatness nor acquainting themselves with pleasure-houses. Therefore if I find favor in thine eyes, let thy servant be given a secluded home on the seashore, where I may dwell with my spouse, conning the works of God and studying His ways like my fathers before me."

The king granted his request, setting him in charge of the royal scribes. So he dwelt in his home and gathered together all the words of wisdom, proverbs and parables, which Solomon uttered from time to time, and recorded them in a book. Further, the king's son-in-law wrote down some little of his own wisdom, which he had learnt or had fashioned in his meditations; adding them after the proverbs of Solomon the king; these being the words of Agur son of Yakeh.

And among his sayings is to be found:

> There are three too wonderful for me,
>   Four and I know them not.
> The way of an eagle in the heavens,
>   The way of a serpent along the rock,
> The way of a ship in the heart of the sea
>   And the way of a man with a maid.

Saul Tchernihovsky, Poet of Paganism

The Hebrew poet laureate after the death of Bialik, Saul Tchernihovsky was born in Russia in 1875 and died in 1943 in the city of Tel Aviv. His education was more modern than that of most Hebrew writers of his day. He did not begin to study Hebrew until he was seven, which was unusual for those times. Instead of Yiddish, his mother tongue was Russian. He never attended the traditional *heder* or *yeshiva,* but was privately tutored and was taught modern Hebrew literature in addition to the usual classical texts.

A precocious child, he read avidly and was familiar with the poetry of Lebenson and Dolitzky and the works of the first great modern Hebrew novelist, Abraham Mapu. When he was twelve he wrote a long Biblical poem, *Uriah the Hittite,* illustrating it himself. At high school in Odessa he distinguished himself in languages, mastering English, German, French and the classical languages.

In 1899 he began his study of medicine at Heidelberg, continuing at the university in Lausanne where he received his doctorate in medicine in 1907. He also studied philosophy and the history of religions and acquired the knowledge of still another language, Italian. But all during his student days he never forgot his first love, poetry, and he continued writing poems through the years.

His first published poem was written when he was seventeen and, strangely enough, was printed in an American Hebrew weekly, *Hapisgah,* issued then in Baltimore. Its title, *By the Might of My Spirit,* was indicative of the poet's future approach to his work. He sounded a new, strong note in Hebrew poetry, voicing contempt for ghetto life and demanding retaliation for Jewish suffering. His first book of poems, *Visions and Melodies,* was published in Warsaw in 1898.

Upon the completion of his medical studies, he returned to Russia and for the next three years served as physician in the province of Harkov. Afterwards he engaged in practice in St. Petersburg where he was an assistant in the Royal Institute of Medicine. During the First World War he served in the Russian army and after the war in various military hospitals. In his poetry he gave expression to the suffering he had witnessed.

In 1922 he left Russia for Constantinople and shortly afterward established his residence in Berlin. He travelled extensively, visiting the United States and, in 1925, was present at the opening ceremonies of the Hebrew University in Jerusalem. After working for a brief while, at the Kupat Holim Hospital, he returned to Germany. In 1931 he took up permanent residence in Palestine and was appointed physician for the city schools of Tel Aviv which also named him an honorary citizen.

His second volume of poems appeared several years after his first and under the same title, *Hezyonot Umanginot.* In 1911 he published a book of collected poems. Eleven years later in Berlin there appeared his *Mahberet Hasonnetot* (Sheaf of Sonnets) and *Sefer Ha'idilyot* (Book of Idylls); in 1924 in Leipzig, *Shirim Hadashim* (New Poems). The year before, he published a book of children's poems, *Hehalil* (The Flute).

In 1932, upon the fortieth anniversary of the publication of his first poem, his collected works were issued in a ten-volume edition by a jubilee committee in Tel Aviv and Berlin. A special one-volume edition appeared in 1937 and three years later a new book of his poetry, *Re'i Adamah* (Behold, O Earth), was awarded the Bialik Prize. He received honors also from the Finnish government and the Academy of Athens and an honorary doctorate from the Jewish Institute of Religion in New York. Shortly after his death another volume of poems, *Kokhvei Shamayim Rehokim* (Stars of Distant Skies) was issued.

Tchernihovsky wrote some five hundred poems and much prose, including *Immanuel of Rome,* philological studies and short stories. He translated widely from world literature: Homer's *Iliad* and the *Odyssey,* the Babylonian epic, *Gilgamesh,* the Finnish saga, *Kalevala,* Longfellow's *Hiawatha,* Anacreon's poems, Plato's *The Symposium,* Sophocles' *King Oedipus,* Shakespeare's *Macbeth* and *Twelfth Night* and selections from the works of Horace, Molière, Goethe, Heine, Pushkin and Alfred de Musset. He wrote monographs on the subject of botany, edited a Hebrew-Latin-English medical dictionary and contributed to several encyclopedias.

English translations of his poetry have been done by L. V. Snowman (London, 1929), by Maurice Samuel in *The Jewish Anthology* (Fleg, New York, 1940) and by Harry Fein in *Harvest of Hebrew Verse* (Boston, 1934) and *Titans of Hebrew Verse* (Boston, 1936).

His poems have also been translated into French, German, Italian and Russian.

I

In one of his poems Tchernihovsky asks, "Did I come before my time, or was God late in creating me?" There was good reason for his query, for he remained a stranger at the gates of Hebrew literature for many years. Unlike other Hebrew poets, he did not stem from the *yeshiva,* but from the wide-open fields of the Crimea and from the wild steppes of the Ukraine. His path, compared with that of other Hebrew writers, was therefore a strange one.

He never had to break with the old hoary traditions; he was free of them from the start. His background was not that of most Jewish intellectuals who had studied in the traditional Talmudic academies and then broken away from their parochial influence.

His was an unusual personality for the Jewish era into which he was born, a time of serious self-searching and re-evaluation. He came upon the literary scene together with Bialik. But in their conceptions and reactions they were separated by a wide chasm. They represented two different worlds. Bialik felt the suffering of his generation in a personal as well as a national sense. Enveloped by the shadows of the synagogue and the tradition, impelled by an unceasing unrest to find light, life and salvation, he wrote great poetry which found an immediate response in the hearts of his contemporaries. His generation sensed that he was *its* poet and crowned him poet laureate. But Tchernihovsky was different both in background and nature and so his early verse did not meet with the same response. It was simple, unsophisticated, and not particularly Jewish in either form or content.

As a poet, he is strongly masculine. He seeks to command, never succumbing to vague emotions or moods of doubt. He uses the Hebrew language with economy and his sentences are crisp and compact. But his reserve is external only. He hesitates to give free rein to his inner drives.

> "At times my words are cold,
> While I am consumed by mighty flames.
> Lean are the phrases I utter
> But the Song of Songs is in my heart."

Tchernihovsky draws strength from the primitive in nature. He knows no boundaries, no lines of demarcation. There is but one humanity, one God, one great cosmos. The brook and the wave speak to the poet and though he may not understand their message, he responds to their voices. In them he recognizes his own personality. He understands the language of the forest and in the trembling branches he recognizes his brothers from whom he parted long ago.

In *Nocturne* he speaks profoundly of the primeval night. He sees it covering the branches of the trees in the dark forest. The elements have met and the poet feels himself part of them. Chaos breaks up into its constituent parts. Eternity shuts its gates. What should the poet do with the forces within himself? In his soul he is aware of a striving toward creation and out of the fragments of chaos the poet finds new life and faith. Man does not stand alone. He is part of the cosmos. When the storm of life has been stilled and the present forms of human existence have ceased to be, life will not end. Only the forms will change. For life itself remains eternal. And the poet feels that he too will be a thread in the mighty fabric of the universal canvas.

Because of his conception of nature, Tchernihovsky is called the "Greek" poet in modern Hebrew literature, the poet of paganism. He is not concerned with formal moral problems. Because he seeks only beauty he occupies a unique place in Hebrew literature. His worldly refinement, culture and gaiety strike an altogether new note. Secular and free, he is also disciplined. Since his poetry first appeared in an atmosphere dominated by the ghetto spirit, it is not at all strange that he was considered a "pagan."

He is deeply intuitive but he refines his vision by subjecting it to reason. When shaken by unrest, he exercises self-control so as to change his mood from restlessness to calm. As an artist concerned with form and striving always for beauty, he is truly representative of the Greek spirit.

In Jewish life, which considered education and learning praiseworthy above all else, his paganism is the exception. Bialik prepared his readers for his love poetry by first writing poems of "suffering and anger." Tchernihovsky avoids all such references. His love songs are simple and natural, full of the spirit of youth, of stolen kisses, of sweet promises and of broken hearts. Flowers, stars, brooks and forests are frequent subjects of his poems. As a happy young student intoxicated with love, he has no compunctions about dancing with the beautiful girls of Heidelberg or giving his love to non-Jewish women. The daughters of Israel are inhibited and do not have the child-like spirit of the non-Jewish women.

He understands love not only as a relationship between man and woman, but also between man and the world. The love that exists in the world inspires him. He suffers with the wounded of all generations. He would feed all the hungry and give drink to all the thirsty. He believes in charity but he knows he will be laughed at because many people believe that altruism and faith are futile.

"Laugh, laugh at my dreams,
This is a dreamer speaking now.
Laugh because I believe in man.
Because I still believe in you."

As a dreamer, he believes in humanity, in friendship, in happiness and in the future. And he expresses his faith forcefully and gracefully.

He hears man sing many songs of suffering, of love and of longing for the unattainable. The song of the farmer rises quietly over the fields—the song of human freedom. From the temples there is heard the song of the faithful adoring the greatness of God. But still more beautiful is the song of the blacksmith, the song of strength and of the hammer, the song of revenge. The whir of the sword being sharpened is the song of those who rule the earth.

Man is lord and ruler. A great, rich world is at his command. He understands the language of animals and birds, of plants and of moving waters. For everything lives and sings in harmonious melody. Man searches for reason and beauty in all existing things and he himself stands at the summit of all creation. Those who turn to God and proclaim Him the only ruler do so out of weakness, according to the poet. By creating an abstract, moral God, man underestimates his own strength. Tchernihovsky will not rely upon nebulous concepts.

"Were you to ask me of my God:
'Where is He that we may praise Him with song?'
He too is upon earth, the heavens are not for Him,
And the earth He has given to man."

God is with us and within us. In a tree, a fertile field, a high mountain—wherever there is life, God can be found. He is not a

God of spirit; He is a God of emotion. He has become fused with man. Such is Tchernihovsky's pantheism.

He called this group of his poems *Visions of a False Prophet,* for the traditional true prophets of Israel had seen other visions. He writes of the "truth" which for centuries the Jews have rejected. He is representative of the rebellious spirits in Jewish history. He is a Jew, but not of the post-exilic type. He belongs to another period, to the age of heroes, to the era of glorious deeds. He is a descendant of the rulers of the earth. Because he cannot bear to watch the progressive decline of the generations, he seeks escape in Apollo, but he knows he is on foreign ground. An age-old conflict separates him from Apollo and the poet returns to his own people. But this people has grown old and its God, too, has aged—an intolerable situation.

His use of Greek concepts sounds foreign in Hebrew because Judaism is monotheistic in spirit as well as in form. The concept of a sun god is non-Jewish; Astarte, the goddess of love and procreation, is pagan. But these Greek terms, paradoxically enough, added to his contribution to Hebrew literature. They enriched his imagery and gave his poetic expression a greater freshness and vigor. They helped him mold new concepts of human values and new forms of Hebrew poetry. He rejected the ready-made formulae and created his own language and style to attain his poetic ends. And his economy of words made for a radiant style with the glitter and hardness of steel.

In *The Song of Astarte and Bal* he sings of life and growth, of love and procreation. He calls forth hidden desires,

"Come out from your lairs,
From heaps of bitter leaves
And hollow stumps of trees
And cracks in hidden rocks!
Clear a path for joy!
Pave the way for happiness!"

He goes on to say—I will throw a handful of grain in your face. Each kernel contains a mystery, the secret of eternal life. Let this mystery enter your blood. Arise and go! Be strong! Desire is the command of life. The earth carries the burden of many generations of grass. The seed of life, the seed of Bal, comes from the sun. The sea within its depths carries the weight of eternal birth.

This is a cosmic concept. Generations of life have awakened to glorify human existence. Hence the poet speaks with such passion of the growth of the plant that absorbs the rays of the sun, that blooms, ripens and bends under the weight of its seed.

II

In one of his most revealing poems, entitled *Man Is Nothing But . . .* Tchernihovsky declares,

> "Man is nothing but the soil of a little land.
> Man is nothing but the image of his native landscape,
> Nothing but that which his ear heard while still alert,
> Nothing but that which his eye saw before it grew jaded."

It is obvious that he speaks of himself, for the second stanza starts with the line, "In that corner of the land where I was born." Much can be learned about the poet from this confessional poem.

In that corner of the earth, on that expanse of colorful wasteland, altars of the heathen stand dreaming over mysterious graves, pagan idols covered with the dust of generations gaze into the far distance. Wild eagles dwell there, "giants with weighty wings." Sometimes, when an eagle swoops down from the skies on a main highway, a man stares at it from afar and ponders, "What is this? It resembles the hill of a tomb, and yet it is not a tomb; it looks like a bird, yet it is not a bird." And when the eagle emits his wild and piercing scream, the sound dies in the wasteland for his cry is barren. "There is no heart to absorb it and it has no echo in the wilderness."

In that corner of the earth there is an everlasting wanderer—the wind. There is no field which it does not pass, no path which it does not touch. Sometimes it slowly steers clouds heavy as lead and sometimes it goes on a rampage over the horizons. At its whim it may raise clouds of dust to darken the mid-day sun, or it may wildly romp among mountains of snow—and nothing can restrain it. Only when it makes for the great southern sea is it obstructed by ancient rocky mountains.

His own life follows the pattern of this corner of the world, the poet tells us. In the same way his own destiny in life is revealed. "With a free, unblemished soul and with a heart fully in tune with the world's harmony, I wandered alone among my people, burdened with the blessing and the curse of the graves of the great."

"And my song is foreign, my song is strange to the heart of
my people,
Barren it was when it appeared and barren will it be when
it departs,
With no heart to absorb it and no echo to reverberate,
With the same scream of the lonely eagle—a wild scream,
And with the same wind which wanders forever,
I wandered from sea to sea all the days of my life.
And when I wanted to reach the southern sea,
The mountains hedged me about . . .
Where then shall I build my nest?"

This feeling of being a stranger and outsider was ever with him. In 1897, at the very beginning of his career, he ends one of his songs with the poignant line, "And strange is the singer and his song." In his group of sonnets, *To the Sun,* written in 1919, he asks "Did I come before my time or was God late in creating me?" And in his poem, *The Anemone Bloomed,* written some time between 1924 and 1929, he sings plaintively,

"There is no one besides me—no brother to sing,
In all the sun's land and under the blue heavens,
And the twig I would send as a token is bare.
I have nothing at all, nothing to my sorrow. . . .
In the land of my fathers, there is naught!"

In Palestine in 1936, he writes in the poem, *In the Hour of Darkness,*

"Behold yourself, Zion, amidst your holy ruins,
In the glory of your proud, destroyed places!
Where are you, my exalted and enchanting dreamland,
The dream of my dreams, where are you? . . .
Who muted my violin? Who darkened the brilliance of
my song?

I know not—and if I knew, what matter?
The lightening of her eye is not for me,
Neither the dream of her nights,
Nor the magic which blooms upon her lips."

This feeling of being a stranger in his own land, though cause for his sadness, is a blessing in disguise for the poet. It is this very alien quality of Tchernihovsky which struck a new note in Hebrew literature at the time. True, today after the revolutionary changes in Jewish national life and the contemporary renaissance in Hebrew literature, there is no longer any novelty in Tchernihovsky's poetry. But when it was first published, there was in it something exotic, refreshing and intriguing. He was "The Greek." He sang about Apollo and nights before idols; he saw the visions of the false prophets; he sang to Astarte and to Bal. For his work of translation he harked back to the Greek and Persian epics. He went back to the poetry of the Babylonians, for the *Songs of the Idol Worshippers*. When he wanted to delve into the mystery of his own descent, he asked, "Who are you, turbulent blood within me?" And he answered characteristically, "It is not the blood of the Chmielnicki martyrs of the Ukraine, nor that of the victims of the Spanish Inquisition, nor the blood of those who died at the hands of the Romans with 'The Lord is One' upon their lips, nor that of the Maccabees—but the blood of the desert generation, the conquerors of Canaan."

He is not always easy to understand and his poetry requires more than one reading. There is a sort of veil separating him from his reader and even the poet himself from his own poetry. For the poet is always the Hebrew poet, while the poem may not be in the Hebrew spirit. He struggles with each poem and each image and sometimes with every line and every word. It is as though in the dark recesses of his mind the words were conceived in another language and only through the deep pains of creation were they delivered in Hebrew. These difficulties do not have their roots in the language, as such, but in the essence of his poetry. The contradictions peculiar to his poetry are to be found within his own soul. For in addition to the struggle between Judaism and paganism in his poetry, there is the conflict between primitive civilization and the modern culture of which he is the exemplar. It is not easy for the poet of modernity to breathe the musty air of the ancients.

His feeling for the present is just as strong as that for the past. He faces issues with a healthy, almost sensuous, attitude. He is of the earth. For that reason, he will not uproot his reader from the present world to transport him on the wings of inspiration to past horizons. On the contrary, he changes the order of events. He uproots the distant and the dark past to bring it to the people of the present.

Thus in his ballads and historical poems he uses not the past, but the present tense. So, for example, in *En Dor,* King Saul appears and speaks his lines to the witch:

> "Are you a witch? 'Yes, my lord, I am.'
> Then use your magic powers,
> Show me the shadow of the seer!"

In the *Three Crowns,* where philosophical thought is blended with poetry, there is no way of telling until well in the middle of the poem, which historical era is involved or who the characters are.

Here the sun of mid-day turns toward the west and blue waves dash against the shore. Soft winds blow toward the green groves. Birds spread their wings over the crags of the coast. And behold:

> "The healthy and the sick
> Have come through devious paths,
> Through alleys and wide market places,
> They have come in droves on a tiring journey,
> Sick, weary from heat and sweat,
> To bathe in the waters near the rock."

Can the scent of the distant past be sensed here? Not as yet. It seems to be a description of some city or town in the Ukraine. Even the rhythm is reminiscent of his well known poem, *The Rounds of the Torah.* And who are the people who figure in the poem, who go to bathe in the waters near the rock? They are a wholesale provision dealer with sore feet, an asthmatic baker, a pot-bellied bartender bathed in sweat, a near-sighted clerk, a scribe, a yellowed and consumptive tailor whose legs are crooked from too much sitting, a farmer with a painful shoulder, a pale shoemaker with a sunken chest, together with a strange-looking camel. The line of marchers continues. Farmers with crooked legs and a grimy carpenter with deformed hands. Some are vulgar and some tipsy. And there are scholars, petty officials, teachers, weavers, drummers, a potter, a goldsmith, a tanner, a porter, "each man with his pain and each with his deformity."

The eye of Tchernihovsky, the physician, and that of Tchernihovsky, the satirist, are sharp and penetrating. They see every disease and symptom of pain, all the filth and deformity of that dark and ugly multitude, those "whose filthy clothes offend the nostrils of man and beast," who flee from the heat and the dust to enjoy the cool refreshing water.

He tears the veil from off the past and with rich imagery vividly portrays the common people as they lived week in and week out in ancient days, even as they do now.

But the physician and the satirist in him do not dominate him for long. The poet in him seeks its own and attains it. The stirring picture of the marchers to the water emphasizes and enhances by contrast, the physical prowess and beauty of the few exceptional ones who bathe with the rest.

"There was one there who seemed to be cast in bronze. He was tanned by the desert sun and the winds of the sea. Cool waters had caressed his mighty muscles. His high and magnificent chest stood out, and his curly beard was coal black and well shaped."

Who was he "whose wide chest split the waters, whose eyes blazed fearlessly?" Who is the man before whom "everybody turned aside to allow him the right of way?" He is none other than the famous Resh Lakish (who in ancient times, before becoming a renowned Talmudist, had been a wrestler and highwayman).

There is another man. He is "straight and of noble bearing. He is like an ivory statue and his eyes are powerful. His face reflects the strength of princes and the glory of God's chosen ones. He resembles a delicate young deer that had gone forth from its lair and descended toward the light." They turned aside from him also and allowed him the right of way. He is Rabbi Yohanan.

"The rabbi and the highwayman approached each other,
And each is enthused at the other,
Both are moved.
'Your beauty belongs to women'
The highwayman scoffs at the rabbi.
The rabbi looks at the highwayman,
Admiring his magnificent physique and replies,
'Your strength should be devoted to the study of Torah!' "

This strange encounter between the two remarkable men under such strange circumstances is indeed an original approach to hallowed characters in Jewish history. But that which is strange and new to the Hebrew reader is not so to the poet. To him it is quite logical that these two men who represent opposing worlds—one of physical strength and the other of spiritual beauty—should find their synthesis in his poetry.

He casts his favorite poems in the form of sonnets, of the never-ending circle. The last line of one sonnet is the first line of the next. And all fourteen sonnets interlace their lines in the braid of the fifteenth—all like a magic circle.

So the beginning of *Three Crowns* is, with slight change, also the end of the poem.

"There are three crowns in the world,
Each with its own splendor;
The crown of physical might,
The crown of learning
And the crown of fair beauty.
Hail to the crown of might in the world!
Praise to the crown of learning in the world!
And as for the crown of beauty,
Who can esteem its value?"

By such repetition, which accentuates the rhythm and deepens the feeling, the poet seeks to enmesh the reader in the circular form of his poetry.

Thus he goes on:

"There are three truths in the world,
Each with its own splendor:
The truth of the individual, which is the truth of might,
The truth of learning, which is the truth of the many,
And the truth of beauty which is the truth of all.
The truth of the individual can possess insolence,
The truth of the many, accursed can be,
But the truth of beauty ascends ever upward."

These thoughts run like a scarlet thread through all his works.

III

In 1940 Tchernihovsky received the Bialik Prize of the municipality of Tel Aviv for his book, *See, O Earth.* In this modest and charming book the poet gathered his latest poems and the translations entitled *From the Poetry of all Nations,* together with four well-known poems omitted in error from his *Collected Works.* In the section devoted to translations there are eighteen poems of Horace, five from the Serbian folk epic and eight others by Goethe, Pushkin, Francis Thompson and others.

From this book one obtains a clear picture of Tchernihovsky. In his translations, as well as in his original poetry, he follows his natural inclination toward the primitive and the elemental in the ancient folk epic of various peoples, still a source of the world's culture. He is drawn, too, toward the classics in which lie the roots of contemporary poetry. From time to time he savors the wayward charm of shorter poems written by great poets indulging in lighter moods.

His original poems retain the same refreshing quality, the exuberance and vigor characteristic of his earlier poetry. Though some of the themes are familiar, his poems are not repetitious.

He sings, as is his wont, with a wholesome sensuality about nature and love, conflict and victory, wickedness and righteousness, self and other, the diaspora and Palestine. But in no poem will the reader be offended by redundance of language or triteness of description, by heavy tread or dim vision.

This book bears the title of its first poem and its echo is heard in all the Palestinian poems in the book. The poet sees Palestine in the period of its preordained trial, in the hour "when your people wallows in its own blood" and "you, my land, are very drunk and young . . . and yet you sing!"

The land can sing because "she is young and brimming with power and her stars are little suns; there is an unworldly joy and there is no tomorrow and no yesterday." So too the poet himself is imbued with this conquering spirit.

Yet he knows in the depths of his soul that there is great profligacy. The blood of Israel's sons and daughters is poured forth abundantly. In the bosom of the land, which should be the storehouse of all blessing, there was not planted the seed of spelt and wheat or a grain of barley or a sheaf of oats. In these years the seed that was planted was that of humanity itself.

"Here, take the best of our sons, the youths whose dreams
are pure,
Strong of heart and clean of hands, as yet uncontaminated
by earthliness,
Their tapestry is still unwarped—a tapestry of hope for a
future day,
We have no better than these. Have you then seen any?
Where?"

And these sons and daughters, the flower of Israel's youth, kissed by the first rays of the sun, were planted in the earth.

"And you shall cover up all these, and let the harvest come
up in its time,
To them a hundred-fold measure of glory and power,
for holy are they to their people.
Blessed is their sacrifice in the assemblage of the dead,
and atonement in glory for our lives . . .
See, O Earth, we have been great profligates!"

This conception of things makes man a part of the life-giving force, a thread in the web of creation. Heartache is softened, weeping stilled. For no drop of blood is spilled in vain, no revelation of life lost in oblivion. The earth covers them up, but the harvest will come up in its time. And there shall then be a hundred-fold measure of glory and power.

For the sake of this glory, and for the sake of a continuing creativity, Jews suffer and fall and die. Holy seed is planted in the eternal land, destined to blossom with flowers of splendor.

This optimism is reflected in the poetry of Tchernihovsky always and shines particularly through his Palestinian poems.

Tchernihovsky pays tribute to the *halutz* with the hoe. It is no wonder that the hoe with which the *halutz* tilled the earth irrigated the soil for his saplings, uprooted weeds, dug a well and hewed a cornerstone for his fence—that with this very hoe "we also dug his grave and quietly we hewed an eternal edifice."

> "In our eternal home, which looks out in all directions,
> There is no tear, no trembling of the hand,
> No hostile eye can see our mishap.
> Thus we dig here the grave of a friend
> With a hoe."

And the truth to be learned is

> "A land is gotten by sweat and blood!"

This truth is not only absorbed by adult minds, but it is impressed upon the delicate soul of the infant rocked to sleep with a mother's lullaby.

In days gone by Jewish mothers would sing their babies to sleep with a lullaby about a little pure white goat. But the Jewish pioneer woman in modern Palestine puts her baby to sleep with a different kind of cradle song. It is thus the mother sings to her infant:

> "A little child was given me,
> Conceived as wails of jackals sound,
> Born as bombs crash to the ground,
> The son of parents, *halutzim,*
> Sleep, O sleep, my love."

This child, born while bombs were exploding and immediately orphaned of his father, is commanded to gather strength to face the great day ahead when he is destined to become

"A helping and a needed hand,
Skilled and faithful to the land."

The strength that leads to glory underlies all these poems, a strength required not only of the individual, but of the people as a whole. With a poetic sense Tchernihovsky sets his message to the people in a framework of ancient history. In a direct message dealing only with the present there is the danger of rhetoric, but the use of historic example provides the possibility of both wisdom and poetry. And the object lesson can be learned with greater force as well.

For example, there is his poem, *Thus Was It In Israel In Time of War.* When war broke out in ancient Israel, the priest would ascend the platform to pray for the people in the fields or on guard. In his prayer he would ask God to implant strength and understanding in the missile so that it not betray him who shot it nor hit an innocent person. "And may the hand of our enemies weaken and delay; may it grow weary in the fray and its iron strength crumble."

And he would pray for more to the God who knew the afflictions of the people and their inner decay, the God who knew the misdeeds of the statesmen and the sins of the priests:

"From our hearts remove poverty and pettiness,
Speak, so that Satan will not dance among us,
So that armies will not smite us again and again,
Bringing joy to our foes, their eyes rejoicing,
They despise one another and brothers are foes
Speaking no word to one another, to the hardened of heart."

The poet implores God to purify his people, to renew their youthfulness, and to remove from the fold the "moth-eaten man and the unworthy among the congregation who drinks the blood of the poor in his over-sized goblet, who causes inflation, brings ruination, rejoices at famine and is concerned only with his own fleshpots and his own skin."

In his poems dealing with the internal conditions of Jewish life he makes use of parable and prayer, while in his poems dealing with public affairs he employs satire and scorn.

Thus he derides a British governmental commission in his clever poem, *Three Ukranian Peasants Who Went Forth.* In the poem,

Grandmother Used to Say he lashes out satirically against the 1937 proposal to partition Palestine. Grandmother, may she rest in peace, used to advise her grandchild never to be part of a group who divide money among themselves, "Because you will receive nothing, my dear." Nor should he join those who quarrel among themselves, "for if they come to blows, you will be their butt!"

"And I am sure that even now, when the Arabs and the British
Divide our ancient heritage, we shall receive,
As my aged grandma said: Less than nothing in a tiny cup."

His good humor not only brightens his idylls written with so much love. It also softens the poems written with hatred for the enemy.

IV

To a certain degree, Tchernihovsky's entire poetic personality is reflected in this last small book. Here the reader will discover poems dealing with the themes of love and nature, physical strength and pain. There are also charming and exhilarating idylls and stirring, terrifying poems like *The Martyrs of Dortmund*—a worthy successor to *Barukh of Magentza.* Here, too, are philosophical and autobiographical poems such as *As For Myself, I Have Nothing* (in the style of *Man Is Nothing But . . .*) and *A Stray Bird. Lesson On Anatomy* deals with the waywardness of youth struggling with the cleverness of mature man. A song of love and desire breaks through a lesson in surgery given by a doctor who knows all about the mysteries of the body, the movements of the limbs and the folds of the skin. Lyric strains are interwoven with earthy, physical portrayals by an artist who laughs, sings and cries. The grace of Tchernihovsky's humor is sharpened by the cutting edge of his satire. In *A Passover of Oppression* the evil in man's heart is bared in all its cruelty. The same theme runs through *And It Was Evening, and It Was Morning,* and with greater emphasis in *The Martyrs of Dortmund.* But together with all this, there is also a glowing description of nature in all its beauty. The voice of poetry is audible throughout. It eases the difficulty and the agony of life so poignantly projected in this book.

In *A Passover of Oppression* there is described in great detail—for Tchernihovsky is a master of descriptive detail—the fear of a pogrom in a Russian village on the eve of Passover. As in his idylls, two aspects of his creative talents are combined, the poetic and the narrative, in order to present a moving portrayal of the environment and its people, of both the spiritual and physical milieu. To underscore the horror of the situation, the poet at first assumes a peaceful guise and, in idyllic vein, describes the days preceding the Passover holiday. Spring is awakening, nature rejoices. As a backdrop to the events to follow, the poet describes the gentle rain, the delicate scents that give rise to day-dreaming, hidden groves filled with wonderful, full-blossomed flowers and happy, romping spirits "pursuing delicate, fluffy white clouds."

It is as if the poet himself would forget and make the reader oblivious to the horror soon to come. Exhilarated, he enjoys the rich pictures of nature replete with the strength and joy of living.

After this colorful description of nature he goes on to the human element. There are heard the characteristic sounds in the Jewish home on the eve of Passover: the crackling of the dry matzah in the folds of its linen covering; the whisper of the iron and the sizzling of the stones; the creaking of the table boards and the "tinkling of tiny teacups tied together on one holder." The metallic ring of silverware fills the air. The poet makes good use of alliteration for his sound effects.

Then the sudden denouement! A Jew returns from the big city and begins to relate the rumors he has heard. A shudder goes through the village. People begin to talk in whispers, eyes are filled with fear and hearts beat with panic, remembering the association of the Christian Easter with the usual season of attacks upon Jews. Gentile neighbors take on a new appearance. Those who were friendly but yesterday may be among the attackers tomorrow. There is an increased sense of unity among the Jews, for they have become brothers in misfortune. But most to be pitied are the children who see and hear, but do not understand. That concealed fear—the Jewish fear—is in their eyes too. It becomes intensified when they see a gang of gentiles go by in great uproar, shouting and drawing their hands across their throats—the sign of slaughter!

The eve of Passover approaches and there is need to prepare for the holiness of the festival and to rejoice in it. But fear of the pogrom wins out and the mothers flee with their children. "There is no wild beast in the world that will not have pity on a child," says the grandfather in his naive optimism. Nevertheless, the children flee.

But it is forbidden to refrain from rejoicing on a festival and the grandfather who remains in the village with a quorum of other elders prepares for the *seder*. And even more. He carries out the tradition of children playing with nuts in order to make up for the absence of his little grandchildren. Tears stream down from his eyes as he plays with the nuts and mutters, "For the sake of little Jewish children, the offspring of innocent mothers! For the sake of your holy flock! The enemies of Israel will never, no, never, live to see a Jewish home without a *seder,* a Jewish home where there will not be children happily at play!"

So did it often happen in Czarist Russia. But though the great fear was always there, the calamity did not always follow and here too it ends only with the sense of terror and nothing more. The priest, although an inveterate anti-Semite, placates the rabble with his ikons and crosses and disperses the crowd. Only the windows of Jewish homes are broken by youngsters and peace settles down once more upon the village. The days go on as before.

But such was not the case in the poem, *Martyrs of Dortmund.* Unlike *Barukh of Magentza* here the poet's words are spoken more softly. And for this very reason the events described are more heartrending, their tragedy more poignant.

At the beginning of the poem, the poet wisely states, "These are the events of a story of horror, a story partially true, but not altogether. For there are events which a man can neither hear nor tell until he be somewhat out of his mind."

This is the story of the madness of the killer's personality and the double slaying of an unfortunate Jew. It was not enough for the murderers to kill the Jew once; they had to exhume him from the grave in which they had buried him alive to kill him a second time. Thus was profaned "the hour that was portentous, holy, awe-inspiring and glorified—to which there was never a compare."

The story is of a Jew, his wife and two daughters who flee from their Christian tormentors. They hide in the woods for many days and nights, suffer hunger and thirst until their pursuers find them and bring them back. The entire community comes out to greet them; the men, the women, old and young, the priest, the merchants, the city officials, the servants, the artisans and their apprentices. They all spit into their faces and shout ominously, "Death to the cursed Jews, the enemies of the Redeemer!"

Like the martyred Jews of old, they face death calmly with the pride of believers, descendants of believers. For theirs is the steadfast faith that God would remember the souls of all those who love and sanctify His holy Name—all the slaughtered, the burned and the drowned; all the tortured, the hung, the strangled and the buried alive.

In that spirit, the Martyrs of Dortmund face their destiny. The mother and daughters are privileged to die a quick death. They are brought into a church, thrown down a steep flight of stairs and killed. But the father, "his throat cut by a butcher's knife used on pigs stumbles and faints away while his blood flows—and he does not die. In his condition he is ordered to dig a grave for his beloved wife and daughters and for himself.

He does as he is told. He places his beloved wife at his right, wipes the blood and dirt from her face, straightens out her clothes and kisses her forehead. He does the same for his daughters—removes the dirt and blood from their faces, arranges their clothes, kisses their foreheads and places their innocent bodies at his left.

It is quiet, a terrible, grim silence. Then the mob yells, "Get down, stretch out!" He descends into the grave and lies between his wife and two daughters. He recites the *Shema* and the murderous rabble cover the grave with earth. In the grave there are three dead women and one live man and all night his voice is heard.

In the morning the "heroic" mob gathers again to exhume the Jew from the grave and to poke fun at him. The believers in Christ hope that the cursed Jew will realize after all that their God is stronger than his and he may yet reform.

But the blood-drenched Jew, who has escaped death only to be derided, does not reform. He cannot believe in any Redeemer. He does not now believe in anything. "Is it possible that God is at a loss for an answer? Is it not in His power to perform miracles? Is there no mercy left in Him?

The skeptical prayer of the half-dead Jew chills one's blood. The figure of the blood-splattered, dying man, thirsting for water, is a terrifying spectacle. He has left off being human and he has no further need for belief in God. Satan steers the world according to his whim. What need has this Jew for the life the "religious" gentiles propose for him?

When a man sees his wife and daughters slain and buries them with his own hands, what savor can there be in life? What interest can he have in mankind? What can faith offer? He would rather turn into a wild wolf, to tear and devour the so-called human beings around him. Not he, but the mob has turned into a wolf. He is the devoured and not the devourer; he is the slain and not the slayer.

The mad mob waits until the morrow when they plan to exhume the Jew again from his grave—the Jew who lives and does not live, who has died but is not dead.

There is in this epic poem something symbolic of Jewish fate, and even more, something symbolic of the insanity and barbarism of our era. Therefore, it has more significance than *Barukh of Magentza,* set in the time of the Crusades.

When the latter poem was written, the poet was young and the world still had faith. It was a powerful poem, but of events of long ago. The poet with youthful vigor, roared like a lion because he still believed in the efficacy of protest and the world's willingness to listen.

But now men are more mature and "wiser." The times are confused and people with them. The sane have become insane and a simple, believing world has become bestial. The poet, who now understands the calamity that has befallen both man and his world, does not protest as he did in his youth. The impression he leaves is stronger because his insight is far deeper and, therefore, the tragedy is greater.

The later poem, like its own chief character, burns itself into the reader's consciousness, a never-to-be-forgotten symbol of the cruelty of our day. And in its light it is easier to understand the meaningful personal poem, *As For Myself, I Have Nothing.*

The poet, who has wandered abroad all his life, knows that for him there will be neither settled home nor planted vineyard, for "immovable property is not for the wanderer, not for me." All that he asks is one little corner for himself and a table. And on the table, "one statue, of marble or of wood."

What will the statue offer him? All the symbols he has sought in life, the fantasies he has envisioned in his poems, the dreams he has dreamed either awake or asleep—all these things he seeks to incarnate in this one statue.

He wants a statue of basalt, out of which shall be hewn the image of humanity's greatest law-giver, he who saw God face to face, the giant among all visionaries, the ideal of his youth, the prophet of the desert of Paran and of Sinai—the man whose name is Moses.

He wants an ancient copper statue of the blind dreamer, "the man who poured out words like melodies from tinkling silver bells"—the man called Homer.

He wants a statue of the marble of Panthlicon which will give form to him "who grasped the idea that truth is beauty and beauty truth"—the master-thinker, Plato.

He wants a statue of oak from the Odenwald from which shall be carved the image of the poet who was beautiful in spirit as well as in body, "a glorious man," he "who held the universe in his arms, who loved the mystery of the planets, who interpreted the message of the waves, who spoke the language of the trees"—the man who was Goethe.

He wants a statue of dull cast-iron that will reveal the image of the bard whose heart was awake "to sorrow and to joy, to happiness and to pain, to love and to scorn, to hate and to pity," to the entire gamut of emotions in the heart of king or jester, murderer or roisterer, queen or prostitute, prince or persecuted Jew; the man without compare—none other than Shakespeare.

But more than all this, he wants a statue carved from the stone of Judea that will be "as hard as flint and bathed in blood," from which will shine forth the prophet who was "intoxicated with the vision of righteousness conquering all," who was like a volcano gushing forth a hail of precious stones of wisdom, who "masterfully blended enchanting words with flaming thoughts, himself faint from the thunder that issued from his holy mouth, he who was the noblest of seers," the comforter of his people—Isaiah, son of Amoz.

In the end he wants an ivory statue from ancient India which will incorporate the image of Astarte, "completely draped, for no man can look upon her and live. Every fold, a vibrant hint; every line, a breath of fire, and her loins and thighs kindling unbridled lust, an evil spirit lurking therein. She stands strong and consecrated in all the glory of her beauty, receiving her worshippers during the pagan holiday."

> "But as for myself, I have nothing,
> Not even a table . . .!"

It would seem that in this poem he concentrates his faith in the spirit of man and in its greatest exemplars. He blends into one precious unity the glory of poetry and the secrets of wisdom, the spirit of culture and the beauty of art, prophecy and vision, law and science—all the enduring phenomena emanating from man, who is constantly struggling and ever rising, who can sing and have faith. This is his charge to a lost and confused generation.

And in his poem, *On the Way to Timnah,* through the character of Samson, he emphasizes this thought:

> "Man, why fear the wrath of the jungle lion?
> Tear him apart!
> A savage beast has never obstructed the path of man."

Faith wins out in the heart of the believer. Mighty poetry is triumphant over tragic and cruel reality.

Tchernihovsky's writing is that of a monolithic spirit playing with the many colors of the rainbow. He is a self-restrained poet submerged in his own personality. His creative cycle begins with himself and, in the end, returns to himself. It is difficult at first to grasp his concepts, but once the spirit of his writing is caught and the basic tone of his work felt, the reader is won over. One marvels at his clear reasoning, never upset by emotion. He created a graceful Jewish idyll against a Ukrainian and Crimean backdrop. And he was the first to enrich Hebrew poetry with the sonnet.

At first a stranger in Hebrew literary circles, Tchernihovsky found it difficult to capture his audience. But his natural gifts and his forceful personality triumphed in the end. He became one of the most beloved of Hebrew poets. His yearning for beauty, his purity and moral approach, his love of nature and humanity and his belief in man's basic goodness endeared him to the new generations of young men and women. Slowly and quietly, he attained his goal.

CREDO

Laugh at all my dreams, my dearest;
  Laugh, and I repeat anew
That I still believe in man—
  As I still believe in you.

For my soul is not yet unsold
  To the golden calf of scorn
And I still believe in man
  And the spirit in him born.

By the passion of his spirit
  Shall his ancient bonds be shed.
Let the soul be given freedom,
  Let the body have its bread!

Laugh, for I believe in friendship,
  And in one I still believe,
One whose heart shall beat with my heart
  And with mine rejoice and grieve.

Let the time be dark with hatred,
  I believe in years beyond
Love at last shall bind the peoples
  In an everlasting bond.

In that day shall my own people
  Rooted in its soil arise,
Shake the yoke from off its shoulders
  And the darkness from its eyes.

Life and love and strength and action
  In their heart and blood shall beat,
And their hopes shall be both heaven
  And the earth beneath their feet.

Then a new song shall be lifted
  To the young, the free, the brave,
And the wreath to crown the singer
  Shall be gathered from my grave.

BEFORE THE STATUE OF APOLLO

To thee I come, O long-abandoned god
Of early moons and unremembered days,
To thee, whose reign was in a greener world
Among a race of men divine with youth,
Strong generations of the sons of earth:
To thee, whose right arm broke the bound of heaven
To set on thrones therein thy strongest sons,
Whose proud brows with victorious bays were crowned.
Amongst the gods of old thou wert a god,
Bringing for increase to the mighty earth
A race of demigods, instinct with life,
Strange to the children of the house of pain.
A boy-god, passionate and beautiful,
Whose mastery was over the bright sun
And over the dark mysteries of life,
The golden shadow–treasuries of song,
The music of innumerable seas–
A god of joyousness and fresh delight,
Of vigour and the ecstasy of life.

I am the Jew. Does thou remember me?
Between us there is enmity for ever!
Not all the multitudes of ocean's waters,
Storm-linking continent with continent,
Could fill the dark abyss between us yawning.
The heavens and the boundless wildernesses
Were short to bridge the wideness set between
My fathers' children and thy worshippers.
And yet behold me! I have wandered far,
By crooked ways, from those there were before me,
And others after me shall know this path.
But amongst those that will return to thee
I was the first to free my soul that groaned
Beneath the agony of generations;
For a day came I would endure no more,
And on that day my spirit burst its chains
And turned again towards the living earth.

The people and its God have aged together!
Passions which strengthlessness had laid to sleep
Start into sudden life again, and break
Their prison of a hundred generations.
The light of God, the light of God is mine!
My blood is clamorous with desire of life!
My limbs, my nerves, my veins, triumphant shout
For life and sunlight.

And I come to thee,

And here before thy pedestal I kneel
Because thy symbol is the burning sun,
I kneel to thee, the noble and the true,
Whose strength is in the fulness of the earth,
Whose will is in the fulness of creation,
Whose throne is on the secret founts of being.
I kneel to life, to beauty and to strength,
I kneel to all the passionate desires
Which they, the dead-in-life, the bloodless ones,
The sick, have stifled in the living God,
The God of wonders of the wilderness,
The God of gods, Who took Canaan with storm
Before they bound Him in phylacteries.

SAMSON

On the way from Timnath Karath, near Zareach by the valley,
A vineyard to this side and that. On the slope gleam
The white bones of a youngling lion,
its sinews still holding toegther.
One magnificent bone by the others, wondrous their vigour.
A swarm of bees at their work, buzzing, humming and singing
Their sacred song over every flower and plant and tree,
While from the midst of the carcass lifts out honeycomb
The man who has smitten the lion;
for sweetness comes forth out of strength.
A youngling lion had met him, a youngling lion and he smote it.
A youngling lion of beasts, a youngling lion of men.
Man, why fear the wrath of a desert lion? Come rend it.
Ne'er has the savage and brute withstood the true man.

BARUKH OF MAYENCE

Here are the graves. And here is thy grave too.
Three days ago their bloody sacrifices
Were brought here to be thrust into the earth.
Thou too are buried here, my dearest one!
Not even a Star of Zion marks the spot.
Yet I have found thee. . . . Secretly I came,
And not one living eye has seen my coming.
I came to tell thee all that chanced to me
Since the dread day whereon I met my death. . . .
For I am dead! And I who speak to thee—
I am no longer I. . . . I am another. . . .

Does thou remember yet the desolate day,
The day of wrath, when God abandoned me?
On that day all the bells throughout the land
Woke storm and tumult with their evil tidings.
And wild one bell unto the other called,
"Woe to the daughter of the House of Jacob!"
And in the streets the thronging multitudes,
Peasant and soldier, artisan and priest,
Gathered like famished wolves about their prey—
Deaf to the weeping of the children, deaf
To the moaning of the mothers, blind and deaf
To age and sickness. And about the victims,
Spattered with foulness, driven torn and bleeding,
They howled like wolves for blood, for blood, for
slaughter!
And suddenly a poignard flashed before me,
A band was gathered round me, and one voice
Above the others howled the question at me.
I saw their wild-beast faces. And I saw
The hand outstretched, the poignard at my throat.
And I made answer in a stifled voice,
And what I answered I remember not.
But I remember now their house of prayer,
The pealing of the organ, candle-lights. . . .
A multitude of voices like a sea,

The priests, the cowls, the singing of the monks—
And in me the bewilderment of death.

. . . .

And then I cursed my people and my God.
I cursed the breasts that once had suckled me.
And all that had been sacred to my fathers,
I spat upon; pronounced anathema
Against the hopes and longings that had been
Until that day the dearest of my life.
Yea, I denied my people and my God,
The God of holiness.

Then suddenly
My childhood rose to life before my eyes.
And I was young again. I was a boy
Awaiting my *Bar-mitzvah,* and again
For the first time I bound upon my arm
The *Tephilin;* and I saw my father's face
Shining with happiness. And through my flesh
There ran a thrill of joy and holy pride.
For I was now a man, and on my shoulders
Rested the sacred burden of the Law,
The *Torah* of my Maker and Redeemer.
What strength was in my soul! In all the world
That day, there was no happiness like mine.
And as I bound the *Tephilin* on my arm
I counted: One, two, three . . . and seven times
I wound them on my flesh, and drew them tight
Until the skin beneath was flecked with blood.
"Behold I bind thee unto Me forever!"
And I had shamed the bond God made with me.
"I bind thee unto me in faithfulness!"
And I was faithless in the day of trial.

. . . .

Listen, dear heart; listen, my dearest one,
For now thou wakest. I have brought with me
Tidings of horror. Listen, dearest one,
And I will whisper to thee. Dost thou know?

Our children, our two daughters, now are free. . . .
My hand gave back the freedom to their souls.
Miriam rebelled at first, and Zipporah
Clung to her sister and looked long at me
As if imploring mercy. . . . She was first.
I could not bear the pleading in her eyes. . . .
My daughters, O my daughters, turn from me!
Mine eyes are seared. One vision like a flame
Burns up my brain, and withers with its fury
My heart, my blood, my strength.

. . . .

I am the man, the father, who
With his own hand his daughters slew.
The knife was firm and trembled not
Until the hilt with blood was hot.
The lives which God to gladness gave
I have imprisoned in the grave:
I could not, dared not let them live,
Their young and stainless spirits give
A prey to those whose hands were red
With bloody guilt of human dead. . . .
O well for thee, in darkness set!
Rememberest thou thy daughters yet?
O my daughters, my daughters, my daughters!

. . . .

Accursed be thou for ever, cruel race!
Accursed for ever be they evil name!
The wrath of God shall dwell with thee for ever.
The blood that thou hast sacrificed, the tears,
The moaning of thy victims, shall arise
In one wild flood against thee, and the sound
Shall be a horror in the stormy night.

. . . .

Ha! How fearful is the night!
    Here in the dark I feel
The cold that cuts into my heart
    Like driven steel.

But through the town are crimson flames
    As from a furnace blown.
And the hand that lit the furnace there
    Was mine alone.
Look! The dull-growing clouds of smoke
    Roll further, higher.
The monastery burns and wraps
    The town in fire.
When I had lit the funeral pile
    I lingered there
And joy was in my heart to watch
    Their fierce despair!
How good, how good, to mark the bitter tears
    The holy fathers shed!
To hear the wailing and the wild lamenting
    For the dead!
I laughed to see one man wrapped up
    In flames as in a mesh,
Screaming he ran, and as he ran
    The fire devoured his flesh.
Oh, long I laughed remembering
    The horrible eyes,
The terror and the flight, the prayers,
    The dying cries.

And when the altar was prepared
    Then did I bring
Two daughters for a sacrifice—
    A burnt offering.
Then from the town I came to thee.
Arise, dear heart, return with me.
The flames I lit are burning bright,
Arise, and we will walk in light.
And where the flames the fiercest burn,
Thy daughters wait for thy return. . . .

MARTYRS OF DORTMUND

(An excerpt)

He looked at the speaker and smiled:
"Right you are! God triumphed over god.
There is no God, there isn't. That's it.
There is no God. Neither Jewish nor Christian.
Cannot God answer?
Cannot God have mercy?
Cannot God work a miracle?
And when my lungs, hungry for
A whiff of air, burst with pain,
And when I gnawed at my fingers with my teeth,
So that pain might still pain,
So as to quench my thirst with my blood,
Where was He? Where—the Omnipotent?

. . . .

There is no God! There is Satan alone!
He guides the world in his insanity,
He rules over all the sons of Satan,
The monsters. You offer me life—
Life for what?
Only that I, too, become
Among you, like you, a beast breaking loose. . . .
Oh, slaughter me right now, immediately—
Else I, too, shall become a wolf,
A mad dog among leprous dogs,
Human filth, all foul.
There is no God. Perhaps
There is no Satan, either, and there is . . . there is
In the world—woe is me!—falsehood alone,
It, great falsehood only.
Man that is vanity, and no more, forever."

THIS IS THE HOE

This is the hoe that has worked into the hand
Hardness of horn and scaling of skin
Both when you make the runnels and plant
And when to uproot and to weed you begin.
When you dig a seedling pit in the ground
Or for a stake in the fence make a hollow—
This is the hoe.

This was the hoe when we dug the graves
Silently hewed out the dwellings for ever
In our graveyard where they face in all ways . . .
Tears? Ne'er a tear; and the hand did not quiver.
No foreman's eye will e'er spy us shaken.
Our comrades' graves are still there to show—
This is the hoe.

This is the hoe when we deeped the trench
As a fence for the group just gone up on the land.
The ground moans and groans to each heave and wrench,
The rock spits its sparks at each blow from our hand.
Land that is won by sweat and by blood.
Praise ye the tool that pierces below—
Praise ye the hoe.

This is the hoe to drive straight to the sun
Furrows that race when the future is found,
While fadeless, on paths that are not yet begun,
Rise our seed in the fields without any bound
Along all the tracks in our strength we can level.
Towards this unsleeping future we go—
With this same hoe.

BEHOLD, O EARTH

Behold, O Earth, what spendthrifts we are indeed!
Where blessing swells, in your hidden lap, we have buried seed. . . .
Not grains of heavy wheat, pearls of spelt with glossy coats,
No gold-sheathed barley seed, nor timid ears of oats.

Behold, O Earth, what spendthrifts we are indeed!
In you we have hid our choicest flowers, most splendid of the breed,
Kissed by the sun's first kiss, concealing still
Their grace on lovely stalks, cups of incense ready to fill.
Before they could know their noon, at innocent sorrow's core,
Or drain the dew for dreams of light that their sprouting bore.

Take you the best of our sons, youth's visions of purest worth,
Pure of heart, clean of hands, not soiled with filth of earth,
The fabric of their lives still weaving, with hopes of a day more fair.
We have none that are better than these. Have you? Then where?

And you shall cover all these. May the plant arise at length!
To its homeland's people sacred, in hundred fold splendor and strength!
Blest be their offering of death, by whose glory our lives are freed . . .
Behold, O Earth, what spendthrifts we are indeed!

LULLABY

Unto me a child is born
Where the jackal howls ere morn,
Coming to me from the womb
With the bursting of the bomb.
Lulla lullaby, lulla lullaby.

Sleep when I am here by day,
Sleep; and mother, sleep away.
She is weary, she is worn,
She must watch until the dawn.
Lulla lullaby, lulla lullaby.

Sheep are sick and fowls are flown,
Watchmen peer with hand on gun,
We are poor but hope withal,
Son of mine, grow strong and tall.
Lulla lullaby, lulla lullaby.

In the cradle kick and crawl
While the fox and jackal howl
And outside explodes the bomb
And we guard you in the room.
Lulla lullaby, lulla lullaby.

Sleep and grow and gather strength
Till the great day comes at length.
We shall need your helping hand
To defend and build the land.
Lulla lullaby, lulla lullaby.

Zalman Shneur, Poet of Passion

Zalman Shneur, one of the titans of modern Hebrew literature, was born of a notable Hasidic family in 1887 in Shklov, Russia. At the age of 13 he left home and finally came to Odessa, then the center of Hebrew culture and the home of Bialik, Mendele Mokher Sefarim and Ravnitzky. Bialik recognized his talents and predicted a fruitful literary career for the young man.

His first poems were published in 1903. The year before he had come to Warsaw where he worked in a publishing house and as secretary to the great Yiddish author, J. L. Peretz. Here he met David Frischman who became his life-long friend and literary advisor. Shortly afterward he moved to Vilna where he began to write in Yiddish as well as Hebrew.

In 1906 he published his first volume of poems, *Im Shekiat Hahamah*. In the same year he left Russia, first living in Switzerland and later in Paris. Here he continued his university studies, begun at the Universities of Warsaw, Vilna and Geneva. After having been interned as an enemy alien in Germany during the First World War, he went to Copenhagen, then to America, back to Germany and in 1924 settled again in Paris where he lived until 1940, when he came to New York. He died there on February 20, 1959, after several years' sojourn in Israel.

His works include *Min Hahayyim Vehamavet,* a collection of stories, 1910; *Shirim Ufoemot,* poems, 1914; *Bametzar,* stories, 1923; *Gesharim,* poems, 1924; *Hezyonot,* poems, 1924; *Leyaldei Yisrael,* children's poems, 1933; *Pirkei Yaar,* poems, 1933; *Noah Pandre,* a novel, 1936; *Noah Pandre's Village,* a novel, 1938; *Kaiser und Rebbe,* a five volume historical novel of the Napoleonic period, written in Yiddish and translated into Hebrew; *Anshei Shklov,* a novel, 1944; *Downfall,* a novel, 1944; *Song of the Dnieper,* a novel, 1945; *Pandre Hagibor,* a novel, 1945; *Luhot Genuzim,* poems, 1951; *Bialik Uvnei Doro,* literary essays, 1953. An edition of his collected works has recently appeared.

Selected works of his poetry and prose have been translated into English, French, Spanish and Polish. Novels in English translation include *Noah Pandre, Noah Pandre's Village, Downfall* and *Song of the Dnieper.*

He was awarded the Bialik Prize in 1951 and the Louis LaMed Prize and an honorary doctorate by the Jewish Institute of Religion.

I

The three master-builders of modern Hebrew poetry are Bialik, Tchernihovsky and Shneur. They are its pride and glory, the prophets and pioneers of its rejuvenation, an achievement made possible by their revolutionary transformation of the Hebrew language. They form the true advance guard of Israel's renascence. With their coming, Hebrew literature underwent a complete creative change.

Of these three writers, Shneur is the most impetuous and daring. His youthful ardor and volcanic temperament burst suddenly upon Hebrew literature. Bialik regarded him as a young Samson, newly come forth from the wilderness. Like Samson, Shneur took hold of the pillars of the temple of sacred concepts and time-honored traditions and shook them so that they were well-nigh overthrown.

He is a poet-revolutionary. He rebels against everything: against society and its injustice, against sanctimonious virtues, against that pretentious humaneness which is inevitably cruel towards the weak. He rebels against gentile brutality towards the Jew, at the same time aiming a blow at what he terms the fossilized institutions and moth-eaten sanctities of ancient Judaism. He assails the very universe.

Hunger and thirst—these are the instinctual drives in Shneur's soul. In his very first poem, *If Not for My Hopes* (1900), he writes of his hunger for the sensual joys of passion. And in *Thirsty We Go Out in the Morning* (1903), he sings, "Thirsty we go out in the morning, thirsty for sunshine, and we would fain swallow the sun of heaven in our tremendous hunger." These early poems are but a foreshadowing of the passion to follow.

He defies fences and marked-off flower-beds. In his hunger he refuses to listen to the mumblings of invalids, for the fruit of life is ripe and ready for the taking. Senile guardians of laws and boundaries know only one refrain—"Don't! It is forbidden!" He hates the venerable and the respectable bourgeois mannikins and precious little souls. He insists on collecting what is due him from life—joy and love.

When he talks of joy and love, he is not indulging in poetic metaphors. His heart's desire is to be found in the joy of youth, human happiness and earthly love. Even the mountains that he loves are cold without the touch of youth. And without love even the boundless universe becomes confining. Therefore, he would call every woman to life with the command, "Love!" In the bosom of the daughters of Eve, in the lips of women, there lies hidden that of which he was deprived in his youth.

As soon as he touches upon the subject of woman, Shneur's poetry becomes a consuming flame, a glowing eroticism that, when it first appeared, was not only new but daring in Hebrew literature. Only the Hebrew language, itself enkindled in the East and embodying the ancient strength and might of the early Israelites, could bridle and restrain the fiery outburst of this virile poet who sings with the intoxication of youth.

Therefore, Shneur the modernist, the poet of culture and the big city, the poet of today and tomorrow, is at the same time the poet of distant yesterdays and of primitive man. He does not neglect any opportunity to contrast the frail, enervated specimen of modern man with the mighty savage of the primeval desert. His symbol of the true man is Adam, his embodiment of essential woman is Eve. He longs for the freedom of the desert and the jungle and dreams of the time when naked, sun-drenched Eve would wander abroad in quest of her mate.

> "Blessed be thou unto me, O free Savagery
> Of a period of deserts and forests!
> Then would a daughter of Eve, unclad, sun-burned
> Seek her lover in the mountains."

When he contrasts the sacrifice made upon the altar by the savage with the offerings of the modern artist, as in his poem, *Epochs,* he asserts that the former was a powerful expression of primitive faith, fear, love and consuming ecstasy. For the sake of the Sun-God, wife, child, pangs of hunger are all forgotten. The latter is the offering of a refined gentleman, pampering himself with his yearning for beauty, but who can thrust a beautiful sunset behind him when he hears the ring of the hotel dinner bell.

"The God of light was mortified," says the poet. He bitterly hates all hypocrisy and sham. He delights in tearing away veil and disguise. The very sight of a mask or a cloak arouses the destructive instinct within him. He strives after nakedness both of body and of spirit. "Rend the garment and the riddle will out!"

All this does not suffice him. For he finds every man, even primitive man too soft. To find true prowess, nature's might, unbridled passion, one must go back to the unspoiled beasts, faithful preservers of uncontaminated instincts and impulses. As the poet stands in the zoological garden, watching the love-play between lion and lioness, he is for a moment transported back to the jungle, the true home of devouring love and consuming passion. The lioness is possessed of feminine tenderness; affection flows through her limbs. She yields to her love, surrendering her majesty to the eternal feminine. She seems to beg for love as a prisoner begs for a drop of water to moisten his parched throat. But the lion, though caged, proudly paces back and forth in his narrow confines, a still unsubdued force, his paws and his nostrils, his nose and his eyes, his muscles and his mane, all proclaiming the desert, where he is lord.

II

Seemingly the male animal is lord; actually he is the slave. The deepest, most perplexing problem in Shneur's poetic world is woman. She dominates all his dreams, she is the focus of all his visions. Like a cobweb, gossamer-like and intricate, she has enmeshed his whole being in the web of her domination. One might imagine that it is he who lords it over her—he, the virile, aggressive male. But the truth is that he is her captive, caught in her net.

In her and through her does he behold the world. It is through her that he would revive the "glory" that is gone. She is the source of inspiration, the origin of life. She alone is real truth, the golden window opening out on all existence. And if in a moment of agitation, he calls out, "Women are no mystery to me, but for the riddle of my youth there is no solution! . . ." then there come other moments when he whispers into the ears of his beloved, "Mother, eternal foe, and yet sweetheart! There is neither end nor limit, O woman, to the enslavement of the man who loves you and there is no end to his lust for domination."

Here lies the key to the poet's relationship with woman. He is enslaved to her and yet lusts to dominate her.

In order to escape the heavy burden he attempts to tread a slippery path. He splits his being into two—"the soul to God and the body to the Devil." Both seek their fulfillment in woman. Thus he consoles his sweetheart against whom he has sinned in having embraced another woman, "Thy hand is so tender. If thy heart be as tender as thy hand, thou wilt surely forgive me, for when my arms embraced *her,* my soul embraced *thee.*"

Life is a riddle and woman is the very vortex of the enigma. He would wrench the lid off the secret whose name is woman but he cannot; hence he hates her, the cause of his suffering. He does not love her, he desires her. He is a Samson fettered by the braids of dark and blond Delilahs. And he often confesses, "I have frequently scoffed at her, at the woman who has neither memory nor past, whose heart and whose dream depart with her sleep and when she arises she is left with nothing. I have hated the celebrated enigma clad in a mysterious silken dress which rustlingly whispers, 'Arise and rip the garment and uncover the secret!' "

And again he admits that in his love affairs he would always conceal within the web of his songs and sighs an effigy of Mephisto. He would whisper, "I am thy slave," yet all the while he is king and she a servant among servants, and behold the outcome—he stands trembling over the last crumbs of his love, soft, bitter and full of green envy, hating the girl fiercely, yet wanting her. His poem, *Prayer,* he closes with the words:

"I stand before her bed as before an open grave.
Upon her pillow there flame the poppies of her sweet lips.
Oh, my God, powerful and wise, into thy hands let me fall.
But not into these embracing arms of marble!"

Too late! His prayer is of no avail. Already he has fallen into her hands.

III

Shneur is a poet of heresy. The sentimental, the dreamy, are not his genre. In another poet, heresy and mockery might have become a source of tragic conflict and divisiveness. It might have completely blocked the way to creativity; for generally, that is the way of faith and of tenderness. But Shneur's way is to build through destruction and negation. His whole creative process is an insistent striving to lay bare and to bring to light the concealed. He is disillusioned, but fond of his disillusionment and so would disillusion others. His is not song for song's sake. He is never intoxicated by external beauty, by purposeless sparkle and glitter. Such glitter would dazzle into blindness, and he is not interested in blinding. On the contrary, his purpose is to uncover, to ferret out the very kernel, even if the kernel be decayed. If anything does intoxicate him, it is his own audaciousness, the ferment of his own insurgence. He is the poet of the effervescent idea. The world of ideas is the world in which he lives and breathes, but his ideas are not abstract concepts, the fruit of cerebration. His ideas scald and burn. His whole being trembles in these poems. He either loves or hates, and more often he hates. Destruction is his way of building; hatred is his way of loving; and he loves with passion. With a unique relish he keeps on repeating, "I love" and "I hate" in one breath. "Why, with my very blood, do I crave all, and in my heart I love naught?" he asks.

Passion is the seal of his being, the wing of his daring. He does not refine passion, he does not sublimate it so that it be dissolved in a quiet, unearthly love. On the contrary, he fans it, until his entire being is caught in its flames. That is why he is always so tinglingly alive, so unfrugal in expression, untamed and unbridled.

In his poems he is constantly addressing an audience. He mocks, exhorts, reprimands, complains, predicts and serves warning. His creations demand a listening ear and seek an object upon which to wreak their effect. He seldom withdraws into solitude to hold communion with himself. Full-throated, he shouts out his wrath, his pessimism, his thirst for love, so that all may hear. And he spares no one.

Nothing is sacred to him. Even the holy madonnas of *Notre Dame de Paris* stir in him sinful thoughts. Their white throats glistening out of misty purple, their full breasts, their big almond eyes, are a call to carnal desire. . . . Faiths die in a generation, and Shneur will not keep silent to spare the feelings of the elders. The gods are dead, he says, and man has not yet come to life.

His epicurean skepticism became evident very early. In a poem published in 1905, when he was only nineteen years of age, bearing the title, *In a Night of Passion,* a poem still elemental in form but forceful in expression, he writes as one over-satiated with experience in jaded metropolitan life. He longs for love but for a healthy, primitive love. Man has abandoned the fields and has imprisoned himself amidst the stony cages of the city. Woman is drawn to man but they are ashamed. They mask their true selves and wait—what are they waiting for? . . .

IV

With all the poet's youthful exuberance, he was mature at his first appearance. In one of his earliest poems *From Morning to Morning,* he tells how he orders his hours, how he lives from day to day. He never sees the sunrise, because, weary and lazy, he sleeps too late. When he arises at last, the day has already lost some of its beauty. The sun has turned yellow, the world is sad, the heavens are overcast. The spirit of the forever lost sunrise plaintively pursues him, seeking at least some recognition in his poetry, but in vain. For in his poetry there is room only for the day's end, for the sunset. With preciseness he describes the sunset, the funeral of day. He bemoans the setting of the sun, mourns for it until the third watch of the night. And in the morning, he again misses the sunrise.

Yet it would be wrong to call him a poet of sunset and decline. If he does not sing of the dawn, it is because it is mild and gentle, pure and peaceful. And he cannot abide quietude. He finds no charm in the subdued sounds of the early morning. Yet he is far from being the poet of dying day. He maintains that his "sunset is also a dawn," and like the dawn, has a red glow of its own.

The poet is fond of putting himself, the individual, in antithesis to society. For he finds himself in direct opposition to it. "Contempt" is one of his favorite words, which, like a spear, he flings at his opponents on every occasion. For "he" and "they," the poet and society, are mutually contradictory worlds.

He is conscious of his uniqueness and superiority. "I have sinned against mankind. I was born full-statured." Rockingly, he beats his breast in penance. "I have sinned in height, I am guilty of depth." He portrays a tree as a striking contrast to man. Man's feet are on the ground and his hands are in the air, while the tree has its head within the earth and thrusts its limbed branches out towards the sky. In his descriptions of the tree he writes, "It is dying, it is asphyxiated in the stifling air like a Leviathan cast upon the dry land." He himself is like that Leviathan. And the dwellers upon the dry land are busy regimenting life according to the rules. They are the inveterate foes of the individual, of him who differs, of the searching soul. Their intention is to chill the fire of the individual, to extinguish his unique light. They fear every new idea. They dread every daring step. In every attempt to create, to reveal, they see blasphemy and sacrilege.

This is his reason for enmity and revolt against them. His is a searching soul. His enemies, the multitude who fail to understand him, are enamored of dead scrolls. Their professions of faith deal with musty, stagnant sanctities; he seeks the living God. They are engaged in preparing themselves for the future; he wants the desirable, the lovable—now. They dream of a world to come, while he seeks to grasp the world to come *now,* in this world. They keep on waiting for love, for happiness, for joy, while the poet has only contempt for them who wait. They have abandoned the fields of Nature and have shut themselves up within the iron walls of the city. Men and women with false modesty and pretense delay taking their joy till it is too late and their desires have died out. "For when are you delaying happiness?" asks the poet with wrath and impatience.

"Once upon a time"—thus the petty, terror-stricken mannikins of today seek consolation for their own weakness in the heroic deeds of the past. If that be not sufficient to induce complete complacency, they comfortingly bolster up their lives with visions of a satisfying future, with that which is to come "in the end of days." But has the present no claims of its own?

Has the power of creation departed from us? Has God's blessing deserted us? Was it given only to our forefathers to engrave laws, to carve patterns? Or, on the other hand, has posterity alone the right to happiness, while we are to bear the curse of sterility? And in many of his longer poems, *Under the Strains of the Mandolin, On the Shores of the Seine, In the End of Days, The Vision of Silence, I Shall Never Forgive, Epochs, Songs of Destiny,* he rises to the full stature of a Prometheus who wrestles both with man and with God Himself for the sake of man and of God.

Such is he, "the hater of mankind," who is consumed by his love for mankind. Therefore, he cannot tolerate their pettiness, their cowardice, their abjectness. Hence his untiring rebukes. If only they were not such herded sheep!

For Shneur admires strength and despises those who allow themselves to be devoured. His sympathies are with the lions, the leopards, the wolves, the panthers. He shares their contempt for the innocent creatures, the sheep, the lambs, the kids, whose ultimate destiny it is to be rent and swallowed by the strong. Even thoughts and ideas he divides into two categories, wolf-ideas and sheep-ideas.

He lauds Spartacus for having aroused to action the apathetic slaves who were ready to die the death of rats in a trap. If not for such as Spartacus in every generation and among every people, who knows where he, the poet, descendant of a vanquished people, would be today? He depicts a world characterized by cruelty and destruction, hatred and annihilation—a universal arena where, instead of gladiators, there are artists fighting for bread, pale geniuses desperately striving for a scanty foothold. The choice seats in the arena have already been seized by the pot-bellied, false-hearted persons. Their folds of fat gently quivering, they point with fat fingers, bedecked with diamonds, to the combatants—this one has won, that one has lost!

In this same arena there sit weary harlots, the nations of the world, who watch, as unarmed peoples, and among them, the Jews, battle for their existence. They watch and they sigh with false pity.

How admirable, therefore, how hope-inspiring, was the emergence of an incorrigible insurgent figure like Spartacus who lifted a banner with the watchword, "Revolt!"

For revolt is the secret drive behind all of man's yearning and spiritual hunger. One must not be static. Every idea is but a way-station for generations in transit. Every truth is but a flimsy tent for the wanderers through the universe. And for him who seeks the way, the poet has the following exhortation: "Get thee a night-lodging in one of truth's temporary tents. And on the morrow arise with the dawn, leave the tent behind thee, and hasten onward, until thou reach a second resting-place, and then—to a third, and onward, onward. . . ."

V

An analysis of his style, its vocabulary and rhythm, its imagery and rich suggestiveness, its earthiness and resonance, show Shneur to be a poet of the first magnitude.

Nothing can restrain him, nothing confine him; he is all restlessness, disturbing and penetrating. He is never abstract. He is the most vital and earthbound of the poets in modern Hebrew literature. His world is a world of flesh and blood and his images are three-dimensional. His forms are aquiver with life, with reality. Even the philosophic element in his poetry, so important a factor, is colorful and alive. He bristles with ideas, but his ideas are clothed and made luminous with form and feeling. Thus it is that even in *The Mountains,* where the ethereal predominates over the earthly, his human bonds keep him from being lost in metaphysical clouds.

He is a man of many conflicts. As an individual, he is in conflict with society. As modern man, he is in conflict with Judaism. The heretic is at odds with God. Man is at war with woman. Hate contends with love. The old would choke out the new, while the new carps at the old. Iron makes inroads into the wildwood and hacks at ancient roots to tear them out of the earth.

Foremost of the struggles is that of the craftsman, the artisan, the artist, grappling with inchoate Nature to solve its mysteries and to bring to light something of value to man.

The gold-digger penetrates to the depths of the mine. He would wrest the source of wealth from the bowels of the earth. The pearl-diver plunges to the bottom of the sea to gain his pearl.

The man of spirit, the poet and seeker, searches avidly for knowledge and understanding, in his limitless yearning for life's secret. He would find a solution to the riddles of life and death.

All things strive and suffer, bloom and wither, live and die. This eternal strife, which has neither beginning nor end, has found in Shneur its great seer and singer. Constant quest is the destiny of man, and Shneur is the poet of this destiny.

His trilogy, *Songs of Destiny,* shows with characteristic insight and clarity the poet's grasp of his role.

The gold-digger knows that his lot is to dig in the dark to find gold for others. Rocky cave-roofs are his heavens, dark catacombs his horizons; the lantern at his belt is his sun, the chop of his pickaxe his song. Even as above on the green earth, so here below in the mine—there is a struggle for every slice of bread, every cubit of earth, each bit of happiness. Every move means a new danger, every step a new struggle. It is a harsh, cold, black world in the bowels of Mother Earth.

With scientific accuracy and verbal mastery, the poet, now the gold-digger, leads us through the dark subterranean labyrinths, challenging primal titan powers to bouts of strength. Actually the gold-digger is only a poor workingman, anxious to earn a living for himself and his family; it is for this reason that he has crawled into the depths of the earth. But Shneur's song knows no slave, for to him slaves have little right to existence. The slave forthwith becomes master and conqueror of the realms of darkness.

The King of the Underground, locked within rock-strata, grits flinty teeth, weeps water-rills and pleads with the worker who has come to disturb his rest. "Go away, man-child! Go out of this confusion. This is the Kingdom of Satan, his the gold and the darkness; he reigns over both and has commingled both, deep darkness with pure gold. Fear thou to break his locks! . . . These rock-layers are thy Mother's cloth-wraps, Mother Earth's garments, her manifold blouses, which she puts on and off for untold aeons. Rend them not, sin not, reveal not her nakedness. Go forth unto the clear upper world. There thou wilt find gleams and grasses, whispering silk dresses, fluttering garden-breezes, laughing, lusting eyes!"

But the gold-haunted orphan-child hacks his way into the hard bones of the ancient Mother. He tears pieces of her wrinkled flesh, because he thirsts mightily not for gold alone; he would master the secrets of her heart. Like a worm eating its way into a fruit, he covets *the seed at the core!* It is for this he has deserted the surface of the earth, so beloved of him—the glorious sunsets, the colorful dawns, dew and green bushes, children and kittens playing in the sun, cherry-trees and the arms of maidens who offer ripe fruit and satisfying love. All these he has abandoned for the quest of the secret hidden in the heart of Mother-Earth.

He does not rely on his strength alone. He also has recourse to prayer. He, the struggler, "the wrestler and heretic," is also a believer. "O, Mother," he pleads, "harden not thy heart unto thy youngest son. Thy last-born, thy best, is knocking at thy doors!—See! I am orphaned of God and of Man, and naked I strive with these rocks. Reveal to me thy soul, thy tear-drop petrified to crystal, open up they heart!"

At last he reaches his goal. He conquers the terrible miserly King of the underground. He vanquishes the Mother who would treat him in stepmotherly fashion. Sparks fly, gold glistens. The man-child has triumphed. Eternity has unveiled its face. Earth has yielded her secret.

Of course, this is but parable and metaphor. It is not mere gold that the poet has sought. He would conquer the very dead who have taken all the ancient riches with them into the grave and who endeavor to frighten us with superstitions and taboos. We, however, must continue to dig and seek and uncover.

He will not rest until he will have opened all cellars and uncovered all hidden treasures of tradition laid away by fathers and uncles and grand-dames. He will crack the age-old rocks until the treasures appear.

He needs this yellow symbol of wealth for the happiness of mankind—gold for sacred temples, gold for wedding-rings, gold for royal crowns, gold for returning triumphant generals. It is to inspire faith and arouse love, to develop intellect and promote valor, to bring pleasure and joy to human beings, that he seeks for gold in the bowels of the earth. These recesses of dead traditions and mummified heritages are not lacking in that which he seeks to bring to mankind.

No less powerful or profound are the other two poems in the trilogy, describing the pearl-diver and the Man of Spirit. Like the miner, they too probe obscure recesses to find wealth that is rightly man's, to solve mysteries that are man's proper prize.

In form, this trilogy, *Songs of Destiny,* is among the most daring attempts in all contemporary poetry. It is a great work stylistically and of far-reaching philosophic import. Pregnant with a deep and varied symbolism, it reveals a profound intuition of man's fate. The experiences of the pearl-diver at the bottom of the sea amidst its strange flora and fauna, his intense passion for discovery that drives him to enter the unearthly realm of water and fish and crustacea, reveal something of the greater mysteries of the deep. The poem of the pearl-diver is another illustration of the poet combatting obdurate titans to compel them to yield their wealth unto man. Here, as elsewhere, the poet-fighter faces Nature challengingly, though he himself is whirled on the spokes of a fateful wheel.

The stronger wins. The pearl-diver, who has dared the wrath of the God of the Sea, at last has the fruit of victory within his hand. He slowly rises to the surface, with the triumphant knowledge that he possesses the pearl destined to brighten and adorn human life.

The plunge into the sea is the poet's fate; his songs are the pearls he wrests from the deep as his reward.

Another man of destiny is the Man of Spirit. His lot is more tragic than that of his two fellow seekers, the gold-digger and the pearl-diver, because he is prouder than they, and the more gifted. He thus bears witness concerning himself:

> "I am the lonely Light
> Who warmeth others, himself ever cold,
> Who illuminates paths for wanderers,
> Himself ever wandering roadless."

He inspires men to brotherhood and mutual endearment, while he himself is full of bitterness and hatred. With his right hand he strokes a wounded bird's head in pity and love; with his left he would choke it, but pity holds him back. The weak always arouses his contempt, even his latent brutality. This is another of the contradictions characteristic of the poet. And not only the Man of Spirit, not only the poet, is subject to inner conflicts; the universe at large is full of them.

Conflict is part of Nature's rhythmic movement. What were the sacred without the profane, light without darkness, justice without criminality, redemption without slavery? What were God's Image without the figure of Satan? Was there ever a mountain without its valley? Hear the poet singing to the chime of bells in the Swiss mountains:

> "Who lieth there alone, in silence?
> A man, a man.
> And what is his thought?
> Death.
> Ha-la! Ring-ting!

There is no death, there is no life,
The balance is even,
The account is just.
Where death ends,
There life begins;
Where leaf-mould rots,
There poppies redden:
Naught knows a bound—
Let the chimes attest:
Ring, ting, gong.
Round, round
Are the routes,
Roundabout, roundabout
Without pain—no joy,
Without darkness—no meaning to light,
Ring!
The seed wanteth the fruit's rotting,
Peace yearneth for war and rebellion,
The most ravishing melody—for silence;
Behold now, it cometh and ariseth
  with the evening . . .
Ring, ting, ring!"

VI

In his poems there is neither pure white, nor raven black. His true color is red, the red of lust and of blood, and both are his elements. He has written an excellent poem called *Poppies,* a singular expression of these two motifs. The poppy blossoms are congealed cries of passion that have burst forth from the breast of the earth. Tongues of flame lap the green of the grass but the green is not consumed. And he stands like a taller, darker poppy among the scarlet flower-flames that dance all about him. Earth's blood is seething. Through these flames the neglected Earth cries out to her faraway lover, the Sun. Earth yearns for Sun, and the poppies are the notes of her song of desire. The world, caught in a swirl of passion, exclaims, "Long live evil! Away with innocence!" Contempt for holiness, for every emotion that hampers freedom!

Straightway a racial feeling is aroused in the poet. In his red bacchanal he inhales something of the fragrance of the East, he beholds something of Oriental splendor. These poppies remind him of scarlet, turbaned Arabs, of Hebrews of Mohammed's day. He falls to dreaming of the zealots of old who raised the red flag of revolt against the Romans. The poppies are flecks of blood upon their garments. He thinks of red-cloaked toreadors teasing the bloody-eyed bulls in the arena. Then, again, the poppies are his own glowing desires, come alive in the field. In the red flaming field he meets his love. Two races melt into one; he, the dark son of the Orient, embraces a gentle, fair-haired daughter of the Occident. Here are fused in liquid fire love, passion, blood and race and over all, the craving for life.

But after the poppy blossoms, its fire is extinguished and the poet feels disenchanted and deceived. The desiccated, rattling poppy flowers filled with dark, ticking seeds are no longer his. They remind him of the charity boxes that keep rattling in the beadle's hands at every funeral. "Ye have deceived me, O poppies! Beneath your flame, ye have nourished a fruit for the future. Outwardly, ye pretend to despise, but inwardly ye yearned for sated Autumn with its decay and its gold. All the passion of those red, glowing flowers was merely a preparation for these dry, prosaic poppy-seeds, fit flavoring for bulky Sabbath loaves."

This disillusioning consummation of all of our dreams gives rise in Shneur to the most withering contempt. It gives edge to the shafts of his ruthless satire. Hence there is no gloom in his autumn. After the inebriate season of love and satiety there is neither apathy for him nor melancholy, but the wise, keen sense of satire. He did what he was bound to do, what he was destined to do. Such was the dictate of his desires. He had followed an unerring, infallible intelligence and he was right. Now, when awakening comes, the stark pallor of sobriety, he remains as confident and as daring as ever before and it is here, perhaps, that one finds the secret of his power. He ranges from horizon to horizon, from shore to shore, and does not grow tired nor does he surrender. Often one gets the impression that all this frothy foam, all the bloody impulses and the over-indulgence in mockery and heresy are the result of a superabundance of strength, an overflow of youthful exuberance. His pessimism stems not from weakness, but is rather like a sea swept beyond its boundaries.

He dislikes limits and ends for they set up confining borders. He loses his patience whenever he reaches a goal that would impede further progress. This is the reason for his tireless pursuit. His road has no terminus and he casts bridges *(Bridges* is the name of one of his volumes of poetry) to join end to beginning.

Shneur is the enemy of respectability, of bourgeois attitudes, for they spell mediocrity, which to him is intolerable. He rails at bourgeois comfort for such marks the end of struggle. Yet at times he too must comply with the conventions he hates, for he must earn his daily bread.

So he tells *The Legend of the Duck,* a species which once had powerful wings and could engage in long flights. But their stomachs had betrayed them and they had become earth-bound in their struggle for existence. Hunger had deprived the ducks of their ability to fly.

Shneur often plunges into the abyss of doubt. Then his fire is extinguished, his pathos subsides and he bares a sombre cold nook of his soul. These are the grey moments of existence. The poet's lagging sentiments seem to drone on devoid of will and purpose and without sense of direction. "Neither does the fog move, nor does the rain pour; there is neither wind nor storm, no pale morning, no sunset; there is no joy and no sorrow; the heart craves nothing, neither the embrace of a girl nor yet to be alone; you dream of no tomorrows, you forget the past." One merely desires to sleep a dull torpid sleep untroubled by dreams until awakened by a blazing summer sun or a savage snowstorm.

Such were the quiet interludes of his creative life. His first twilight songs breathe with singular charm. He knows not whither to go or what to choose. One half of his soul is given over to darkness, the other still dipped in sunlight. Of which should he sing, which should he celebrate? Night is so terrifying and so bewitching is the burning west. Should he sing of the lurid light or greet the gathering shadows?

This pleasant winging in the dappled spaces of light and shadow is natural and genuine with him, but in his later poems this not unblushing playfulness is wanting. He knows now but one color, red, but one voice, that of the blood. He harbors but one desire—

sin. This is his affirmation, his yes! He thunders against the accepted forms prescribed by respectability and conformity. His poem, *In the End of Days,* sounds like a bitter travesty of Isaiah. He scoffs without mercy at the beatific vision of the coming millennium. For then everything will fall into desuetude. All men will be equal and all alike in usefulness. Evil will be no more and cruelty will disappear. While the wolf will dwell with the lamb, the green phosphorus will die in his wolfish eyes and the smell of the stable will be sweet unto his nostrils as the smell of the forest. And the lion will eat straw and chew the cud with touching docility. His roar will no longer cause the desert cliffs to tremble. A peasant boy will condescendingly stroke his feeble mane, reprimanding him, "Oh, you lazy lion, you don't deserve the straw that you are chewing."

A team of panthers will submissively be harnessed to the plough and patiently await their mushy bran at the trough. Snakes will no longer be venomous. Barefoot urchins will play with them and regale them with a generous dose of grandpa's snuff. The snakes will sneeze good-naturedly and mumble, "Oh, naughty boys that you are!" Leopards will nestle like pampered cats in the lap of old spinsters. The eagle and the cock will forage for food in the same garbage heap and the eagle, all eager for peace, will flatter his barnyard comrade, "Fellow rooster, what a beautiful headpiece you are wearing."

All will then be alike. All will wallow in universal equality, leveling both the dwarf and the colossus. The Hannibals and the Napoleons will march on foot, lost amidst their military phalanxes. There will be neither great nor small, neither high nor low. If a man is born taller he will be told to bend low, lest he violate the universal equality. Indeed the sun will be forbidden to be too hot; it will have to be mildly lukewarm. The ocean will have to flow softly. The whole world will cloy with sweetness and time itself will grow mellow and saccharine. If by chance anyone will wax angry, his anger will be quickly subdued—he will be brought down like a fly caught in molasses.

In that day useless flower-gardens will be converted into pastures; fountains sparkling like emeralds will be made to turn a mill-wheel; museums holding idols and carven heroes will be cleared out to make room for soup-kitchens for the old and weak; artists' paintings will be used as fuel for a huge bonfire to bake potatoes at a democratic feast. Spears will be beaten into pruning-hooks.

Worst of all on that day will be the lot of the Evil One, "this salt of existence, this pepper of creation." He, who would mingle the blood of the just in intermarriage with the blood of the wicked, who gave zest to love, who filled poets and artists with unrest and gave them creative power, who reigned over the world despite all Gods of Mercy and Kindness, the arouser of passions, the instigator of wars and hatreds, will meet a bitter end on that day of honey, flax and pruning-hooks. He will be publicly slaughtered as a disturber of the peace. His slaughterers will then dip themselves in the ocean to rid themselves of the blood-stains—the last blood to be shed on earth—and will come out to bask in eternal purity.

Just as Shneur's passion for woman, in the course of his development, is sublimated into the desire to pry into the secrets of Nature and the mysteries of being, so too is his proud fighting ego sublimated into and identified with the ego of the Hebrew race, the historic personality of Israel.

In his long national poem, *Under the Strains of the Mandolin* (more particularly in the second canto, *Chants of Israel*), he, a man of Judea, argues the case of his people against a sun-ripened, lovely daughter of Rome. He begins in typical fashion, with love and youth, color and light. The young Italian girl is not merely an allegorical figure or the embodiment of an idea. She is a voluptuous creature with small hands, dimpled elbows, alluring limbs; her cheek is a ripe fruit which one might bite into with laughing white teeth. She wears a red sash about her waist, the color of youth and revolt, which angers wild bulls and turkeys and frightens kings on their thrones.

Thus Shneur leads us into her world, into *his* world of sparkling youth. "Thou art," he says to her, "a ladder standing in Hell whose top is in the Heavens."

Under the spell of her melody he falls to dreaming—the dream of one thirsting and who sees cool streams. He dreams of the beauty that is departed, of the glory that is no more He laments the death of the gods. He, the mighty rebellious one, yearns for ancient days, when man was young and wild, untamed and triumphant, one with Nature and his own instincts, ere yet he succumbed to a false, benumbing civilization. Even as he dreams half-awake, the glory of Greece and Rome too falls off as a mask. Between him and this daughter of the Romans the image of Jerusalem arises. All of a sudden, the mandolin in the girl's hands becomes the dead head of a Jewish martyr. The thin strings of the instrument become the veins of tormented brothers and sisters in Israel—they tremble under her fingers! The very melody undergoes a change. It begins to sob to the traditional tune of *Lamentations*. The poet-lover becomes a changed person. Now all communion is lost between him and her. She is a grandchild of those who crushed his homeland and his temple. He is a Jew, a scion of the Zealots of Jerusalem. "Look into my eyes," he says, "see, you will find in them something of Simon Ben Giora's fire. Look again, do you not see in them a spark of the vengeance that raged in the breast of Johanan of Gush-Halav?"

The love between the son of Judea and the daughter of Rome is changed into a war generations old, a conflict between two cultures, a life-and-death struggle between two worlds.

True, one sun once lit the eyes of both Palestine and Rome, one blue sea once lapped their shores, but the same treacherous sea was not ashamed to bear into exile over its waves the young lads and maidens of Judea. Our sons were thrown into the arena unarmed to fight with lions and to be devoured by them. Our daughters, the innocent and lovely, were forced to become maidservants to their defilers and tormenters.

But the sea that did not mercifully overturn the ships bearing our children into slavery carried the praises of our great God to the shore-cities founded by Rome and His might shattered the idols of Phoenicia and Greece to which the Roman Empire was subject.

My zealot-warriors, says the poet in pursuing his argument with the daughter of Rome, were powerless to avenge the blood shed by my brothers and sisters in the Roman world; but my spirit has avenged itself sevenfold. Go forth and see: Where is the land which my God has not imprinted with the seal of my race, the imprint of its mentality and the beauty of my Galilee? Where is there any sacred book in which the rushing of Jordan's waters and the rustling of the Lebanon forest are not heard? Where is the temple or shrine which does not resound with the echoes of Moses' speech, of David's hymns? All the world's great art-works—do they not tell, without word or voice, the grandeur and holiness of our prophets' visions and dreams?

The dawn-dew of Creation which moistens the book of Genesis, the beauty and sadness of autumn which pervades the scroll of Ecclesiastes, the joy of youth and the fragrance of vineyards which arise from the Song of Songs, the mystic light that plays over the later prophetic writings, these have become a profound influence and powerful formative current in the consciousness of mankind.

> "Like a delicate citrus smell, the breath of my soul
> Drips into the odors of earth-flowers,
> Every Gentile nose inhales it—and knows it not."

This is the vengeance of the Jew, a vengeance of the spirit. The Gentile pagan world set out to destroy Jews and Judaism, but in the end, it was itself conquered by Judaism. Therefore, are we so hated and persecuted. The victor, overcome by the vanquished, is wroth.

Now the son of Judea comes with his bills before the world for payment. The bills are written on parchment, stained with the blood and tears of our fathers. God Himself has signed them by the hand of His secretary, Moses. Jesus and Mohammed are co-signers and witnesses. They, the Gentile nations, have robbed us of our heritage but being bankrupt, they cannot repay. They have taken over all our cultural possessions in their own names and in the names of strange gods and in foreign languages and have left us in our destitution, like impoverished aristocrats who have not even a sword left. Now all belongs to them, the earth and sky, the air and water, war and peace, might and right, *everything*. And I, the Jew, have become the stepchild of the world, seeking a share in my own wealth, demanding part of my own rightful possession, unrecognized and spurned by all.

The poet, so skilled in tearing off hypocritical masks, forces his way into the Holy of Holies of Christian churches, and there recognizes in the images and ikons the faces of our fathers who have been robbed from us by Gentile bandits. They have set up our dead fathers and ancestors as their own saints, but us, the living children and grandchildren, they have driven away, unacknowledged paupers.

VII

We have given to an ungrateful world the blessings of our genius. Now, the poet adds, we may also give it our curse and show our contempt, no longer as beggars, but as self-reliant, self-chosen creators. Now he stands up in a new light, endowed with new power. He appears as a national Hebrew bard, thundering with the voice of Ariel, lion of the tribe of Judah; he calls with the accents of chastising prophets; he sings as a son of Judea resurrected.

The Ukrainian pogroms at the close of World War I draw from him an outpouring of scalding wrath in a series of songs and sonnets. Even before the War, at the time of the Beilis trial, he had burst forth with his prophecy, *Behold, the Middle Ages Are Coming!* How truthfully he foresaw the return of barbarism and fanaticism, the Jew's plight, the world's shame. He could take no joy in the promised bliss of the "End of Days," for he sensed the coming recrudescence of medievalism. Not in a spirit of "I told you so!" but in sorrow, he now declares in a sonnet, "And the Middle Ages have returned. . . . "

In *Maasei Slav* (*Travels of the Slav,* which is an allusion to *Maasei Tzlav—Travels of the Cross,* i.e., the Crusades) Shneur tells of the new pillages, auto-da-fés and crucifixions of Jews perpetrated in the name of Jesus in the post-war Ukraine. As far as the persecution of Jews is concerned, the Church is no better than Islam; the Cross kisses the Crescent. This corrupt cowardly civilization has undertaken to destroy us: "A thousand huge Gentiles chase after one small Jew."

All the horror of the Ukrainian pogroms, the tales of degraded drunkenness and savage cruelty on the one hand and of noble martyrdom and spiritual valor on the other, pass in review in these poems. Moreover, the poet realizes bitterly that no salvation awaits Israel from the much-heralded Russian Revolution. "The Cross will never mate with the Shield of David," exclaims the poet, no matter what new outward symbols that Cross has as its disguise. It is the fact, not the name or emblem, that speaks.

With his renewed, turbulent consciousness of national feeling, the poet turns upon his own brethren. He would have them eradicate from themselves every vestige of weakness, meekness and cowardice.

In *The Night of Hanukkah,* the poet sees Judah the Maccabee run after an Old Woman intending to stab her. The Old Woman symbolizes the traditional form of Judaism in Exile. She pleads with the warrior, "Spare me, do not desecrate the holiday of my children who now rejoice by the light of thy Hanukkah candles."

But Judah does not recognize his children. Their song of joy over the miracles of Hanukkah sound to his ears like the lament, "How Doth She Sit Solitary . . . " which the orthodox intone on the Ninth of Ab, the anniversary day of the destruction of the Temple.

The Old Woman continues to plead, "Do not disturb them, Judah. It is not with thy might, the might of the sword and of revolt, that they have endured these centuries of Exile and have reached this day. When from inquisition-fires they screamed, 'Hear O Israel. . . .' it was I who screamed with them. When their faces were spat upon, yet they were not insulted, for it was I who wiped the spittle from their cheeks. Let them alone! Away with thy revolt and thy revenge! Thou dost not understand the soul of the tormented and the beaten. But I love and understand them like a mother. Move softly, slowly. Remember the Law says that these Hanukkah candles were not made for utilitarian purpose. One must not kindle world-fires and flames of hatred with them."

But the spirit of Judah the Maccabee abhors these weak grandchildren of a proud tribe, who cherish their small candle-flames, who make much of a martyr-psychology (*Kiddush Hashem* they call it), who have a unique talent for being hunted down and devoured.

So now he has come from his distant village of Modin to the Russian Jewish Pale to slaughter the ancient Mother, her and her devotees. He announces himself, "I am the Murderer and the Redeemer." Let only one of ten thousand remain alive, provided that he be not imbued with the spirit of Exile and not bow down to kiss the Exile Shame, as once a weak Hebrew bowed down and kissed the feet of the *Baal.*

On the very night of Hanukkah, upon the glistening snow of the Russian Pale, he slays the Exile Mother.

When the poet, heir of the warriors of Judea, comes to modern Israel, walks through the reborn Emek and treads the new paved highways, he bursts forth in song together with the *halutzim.* He chants,

"Clear a way, tread a path,
Wait not for the Messiah!
He showeth his face to all the nations,
His own people hath he deserted."

Universal schemes of salvation may help others; they will not help Jews. The *halutzim* must themselves undertake the messianic task of breaking through a road for themselves and for all their brothers.

The many-sided literary activity of Shneur cannot be dealt with here, for he has written Hebrew prose and many Yiddish volumes, some successfully translated into English. This essay deals only with Shneur the poet. Truly, his poetic works in the Hebrew language are among the highest achievements of its national renaissance.

THE KISS

No, my darling, my dove, thou knowest not yet the kiss that we call a kiss . . .
Close-pressed unto breathlessness, close-pressed until self is confounded,
Breast grown to breast till thou know not thy heart from the heart of thy lover,
Lip to lip molten in purple flame,
And each from the other draws out youth and the ichor of youth,
Draws out the ichor of spring, and renders the passion of summer . . .
The kiss that we call a kiss.

S-s-t! Body is melted and gone, and only the souls, the spirits remain.
Man and the world of man are no more, there is only the world of vision,
Earth from beneath us is vanished, vanished are limits and walls:
The universe hangs on a kiss, exists in the hold of a kiss:
Woe if the kiss be broken, lest the universe fall into dust . . .
The kiss that we call a kiss.

Mine is not the blame, my darling, if the lightning is locked in my eye,
If my arms and my lips were made for embraces and kisses,
Kisses that know not beginning or end . . .
There is a fire that burns in our veins, and if, trembling, it be not spilled.
In the lap of clear-eyed women, pure-ringleted girls,
It will burst from its channels, consume the heart within.
And God, the great God of love will never, oh, never, forgive us
If the fire of our love should waste, should be lost in the frozen mists of life,
Should consume in the ice of the north,
If our hearts to the hungry be scattered
And our heat swallowed up by the earth. . . .

YEA, EVEN WHEN MY COURSE IS RUN . . .

Yea, even when my course is run
And I am dying on my bed,
My seething blood congealing slow
Beneath a breast that's withered—
Yea, even then thou wilt not weep;
With frozen gaze thou'lt me behold;
Thine heart replete with reverence,
No moan or plaint will it unfold.

My death thou wilt not understand
Just as my life was strange to thee,
While my warm heart was dreaming dreams
And fervid kisses gav'st thou me.
My death thou wilt not understand,
My parting will appear to thee
As great as was my flame of life—
Therein doth lie my victory.

Man doth the flower mourn which bloomed
Imprisoned 'neath a bowl of glass,
And withered like an orphan pale,
Sans sunshine and sans dew, alas!
Man doth the bird lament which from
Its lofty nest to ground did fall,
Still featherless and frail and blind,
To cruel fate a helpless thrall.

Man doth not mourn the mighty rock,
An offspring of eternity,
Which towereth above all in pride,
In solitude and majesty—
Which suddenly quaked and split and fell
When thunder struck it mockingly,
And left a ravine wide and deep
Of darkness and of mystery.

LIFE

Oh, empty is Life with its tumult and beauty
  Unto the great dreamer who yearns all his life,
And wherever he turns, he forever finds wanting
  A goal that will quench his desire and strife!

Consumed is his heart in the flame of his passion,
  And aged he grows, and finds strewn at his feet
The treasures he sought but could never discover,
  The treasures with light and with roses replete.

But void is his heart from the flaming old passion.
  Compassionate, weary he gazes in pain,
Rememb'ring desires that vanished like shadows,
  And wistful and saddened, he yearns once again.

Then merciful Death comes to man and he aids him
  And silently lulls his great longings to sleep.
A heap of cold earth swiftly fills then his world
  That was ever more empty and void than the deep.

UNDER THE HAMMER

Thud! Thud! The hammer in the hands of Time
Beats on my heart beneath its thunderous rhyme.
Hoary and dumb is he, but on his arm
With life and swing the rolling muscles swarm.
His beard upon his bosom trembling lies,
And strength has veiled its secret in his eyes.

The days with all their sorrows pass like ghosts,
And with the hammer beats the march of hosts.
So changed beneath the tireless fall and rise,
'Tis not my heart that on the anvil lies—
So vacant and so wan, so void of dreams,
And once resplendent with a thousand gleams. . . .

'Tis not my heart, my heart of passions vain,
The plaything of the daughters of disdain,
The slave of every wandering ray of grace,
Bribed with the laughter in a girlish face,
'Tis not my heart since I have made my vow—
To you, blind smith, it is abandoned now.

Smite hard, old smith, smite hard and do not spare;
My heart has paid with weeping and despair.
Smite on the weaknesses that still remain!
Smite hard, until the heart is mute to pain!
A heart of dreams and weakness is not meet
In days of greed, of softness and deceit. . . .

And where the heart is bruised with love or hate,
There ply the hammer fiercest. I will wait
Until, responseless as thrice-molten steel,
Nor love, nor hate, nor hope can make it feel.
And when of smiting I have had my fill,
I'll take my heart again to work my will.

I will arise and cry "Ye valiant men!
I came with dreams once, and you scorned me then.
My tears you met with the contempt of might,
But now I come to weep not, but to smite. . . .
Woe to the hearts which laughed at all I dreamt!
Yours be the tears now—mine be the contempt. . . .

"And you, my golden visions and my dreams,
And hopes resplendent with a thousand gleams:
In vain you gather round my heart, in vain
You raven for the gates to ope again;
Enough that once your seeds were scattered there,
For all I reaped was folly and despair.

"And you, my pretty ones, the days are gone,
When, flesh and blood for you to feed upon,
My heart was with eternal want accurst—
And yours be now the hunger and the thirst. . . .
Bite on my heart now, as you did of yore,
And break your teeth upon the iron core."

THERE ARE TIMES

There is a time for the silence of sorrow—
Not for loud weeping for a people who died—
Butchered like beasts, entrapped in their lair. . . .

Ascend unto the mountain
Made high by our dead.
Scorn and spurn
The promises of a brave new world
Which holds such wonder in it!
So lying tongues proclaim.
No brave new world
Without repentance from the old;
No wonders bloom
Where conscience is debased.
No scent of rose or myrtle
Can sweeten the foulness of the jackal's den
Or add a clean aroma to the stench
Of child-devouring haunts.

Ascend again
Upon the hill of death.
Spurn and scorn
The long peace-mongering procession
Of politicians, leaders, diplomats—
This long black-coated crew with white cravats;
And all the smart-attired generals
Bloated with honors like sated cannibals,
For whom the bones of our martyrs
Were a fortress of defense.

Sooner, later,
Will your scorn
And the groan of all our dead,
Like a cloud-burst fall upon them
With a rain of lead.
Brave new world of base deceivers
Lusting for the blood of men.

And you our saintly grandsires,
The *Book of Lamentations* close;
The *Yahrzeit* light extinguish.
Fall upon the ground—
The silent witness of our latest *Tishah Be-Av,*
When temples in their thousands fell in flames,
And Warsaw, Wilna, Cracow,
Lublin and Minsk and Kovno
Were devastated like Jerusalem

Arise!
And blow upon the *Shofar*
The ban of excommunication
To the four corners of this earth,
Till the sound shall stab each Jewish ear
And reverberating mingle with timeless tomorrows.

The murderer's vintage, made rich upon our ashes,
No Jewish lips shall taste;
Not for us to share his golden corn
Springing from soil by Jewish blood enriched,
Not for us his luscious fruit
Made sweet by Jewish pain;

His tongue not of our speaking,
His songs not of our singing.
Not for us his fine fabrics
Interwoven with the hair of our daughters.
No smile of ours shall ever light upon his babes
Conceived in vilest evil;
The light within their eyes is but the sparkle
Of their fathers' murderous knives.

Unclean their violence and crime;
Unclean their degradation;
Unclean their humiliation and their doom;
Unclean to the end of time shall even their
 repentance be.

Tekiah, Teruah, Tekiah Gedolah
Blow the *Shofar* loud!
Proclaim the sole revenge of a living people—
Eternality!
A people pledged to life—
Pledged to the uprooting of the evil within life.

AGAIN THE DARK AGES DRAW NIGH

(Excerpts)

Again the Dark Ages draw nigh! Do you hearken, O man, do you sense it—
The whirling and swirling of dust and the sulphurous scent in the distance?
The air is with omens impregnate, with omens grim evil foreboding:
Eclipsed is the radiant sun, the houses are ashen and crumbling,
The azure clear skies are like lead, the terrified oxen are lowing,
The grass and the leaves have turned pallid like foliage growing in cellars,
And faces are numb and grotesque as if covered with masks cold and waxen.
The ancient black cloud has returned from the distant Dark Ages long vanished,
As rivers return to the sea and the sun to the clouds in the westside.
The ancient grim wheel is rotating and creaking with rust of the ages;
The deluge of blood stirred its spokes, as a river o'erflows and surprises
The wheel of a desolate mill—an abode for stray ravens and demons.
Not moistened enough is the axle; with dryness it creaks and it curses,
And from its cleft spokes soar aloft the dried dust of the victims primeval.
The darkness of Ghettos arises with terrors and flames spread to heaven.
A people ill-fated are we! Our woes are in cycles repeated;
Each message of springtide is followed by seven thick squalls and fierce tempests.

The conquering nations fell heir to the wealth of the countries they vanquished;
Both sunlight and darkness are theirs and cyclical summers and winters;
Of love and of hate they are masters, now cunning, now artless appearing . . .
Inclement next winter will be; too long the gay summer has tarried—
Again the Dark Ages draw nigh! . . .

If destruction is fated, my people;
If the tyrannous wheel, drawing nigher and nigher, is ready to snatch you,
And grind you to bits with its teeth and grease with your bloodstream its axle;
If murderous nations conspire to drag you to deserts unpeopled,
Determined to crush you before you can finish on earth your great drama—
What have you then to do with peace? Come, hasten the world's last sunset!
Come, seize with your teeth the rotating wheel and cling with your nails unto it,
As the leopard clings to the reindeer which strives in wild frenzy to butt it.
Be like the destructive acid corroding iron and copper!
Vent your wrath on the wheel, avenge your shame and the shame of your fathers.
Let its worn out teeth fall out with a furious shrieking and creaking,
Till naught but its twisted crushed axle remain, still rotating, though twisted,
In the midst of the ruinous heaps of temples, idols, and garlands.
Then dance ye, the only immaculate humans, around the loath axle
A last dance of freedom, a last dance macabre . . .

Ah, long have you died saintly deaths, and bequeathed
 the world to the godless—
Now die the sweet death of creators who finish their task
 and vanish
That a new generation more perfect the fruits of their toil
 may inherit.
Abstain from the saintly and holy! Come, learn to be
 warriors valiant . . .
Again the Dark Ages draw nigh!

EXALTED AND SANCTIFIED

O'er the sepulcher of a nation chained
To its traditions a new free nation prays:
Exalted and sanctified be His great name!
Who led a people out from a house of bondage
To teach them freedom's law in the wilderness,
But sold them as eternal slaves
To countless lords, both east and west—
Exalted and sanctified be He!

Who heaped on them the weighty load of mountains—
Sinai, Mecca, and Golgotha—
That they might bear them as gifts in formless paths
To infant-slayers on the heights;
Who filled their sacks with precepts ethereal
Food for eternal life,
As the air fills broken leather-flasks;
Who ordered them to guard these precepts well
Through fire, water, war and pestilence—
Exalted and sanctified be He!

Who strew his shrines and prophets
O'er savage lands and isles of cannibals,
Llike pearls torn from a string;
Who ordered thus his chosen race:
"Press forward, go and gather the dispersed
To one Jerusalem and one Messiah,
To a world-redemption in the last days! . . ."

And when these deeds were done, He cast this tribe
In northern snows like a withered twig—
Exalted and sanctified be He!

Who planted gardens of great nations
White and black, yellow and red,
And made His tribe eternal manure,
Sanguine manure, in deserted nooks o'ergrown with nettles,
To fertilize each resurrected tribe,
Each vassal-folk inheriting its master
And flourishing on heaps of ruins—
Exalted and sanctified be He!

Who created sires for this nation to wail,
And gave them comely daughters to be shamed,
Sons for bereavement, fiery eyes to be hollowed,
Sharp tongues to be plucked, creative hands
To be chopped with axes,
And a heart within the body to quiver
On every pyre, in each confusion and distress—
Exalted and sanctified be He!
O'er the sepulcher of a nation dying beneath
Its burdens, thus prays a new free nation.

David Shimoni, Idyllic Poet

David Shimoni (born Shiminowitz) was one of the major contemporary Hebrew poets. He was born in Bobruisk, Russia, in 1886. At the age of fifteen he began his literary career. He continued his studies in the universities of Berlin, Heidelberg and Wurzberg. In 1911 he published his first book of poems, *Yeshimon,* a second book, *Saar Udemamah,* appearing the following year.

After settling in Palestine as a manual worker and watchman at Rehovot and Petah Tikva, he became a teacher of Hebrew language and literature at the Herzlia Gymnasium in Tel Aviv.

His published books include the following: Collected Works, 1925-1932 in four volumes; *Sefer Haidyliot,* 1944; *Eshet Iyov; Ahavat Shlomo; Armilus Harasha,* 1945; *Bahashai,* 1945; *Bishvilei Habevar,* 1946; *Moledet,* 1946; *Havlo shel Mashiah,* 1952.

He has translated into Hebrew many poems by Lermontov and Pushkin, Heine's *Die Harzreise,* Tolstoy's *Hadji Murad* and *The Cossacks.*

A jubilee volume was published in his honor by the Friends of the Hebrew University to mark his sixtieth birthday. He was awarded the Bialik Prize in 1936, the Ussishkin Prize in 1944 and the Aharonovitz Prize in 1946. He died in 1956.

I

David Shimoni is a prolific poet of sturdy mettle. In his ripest works, his idylls and narrative poems of Palestine, he achieves great spiritual lucidity. But it would be erroneous to regard these portrayals of pioneer life in Palestine as being in the classically epic mood, even as it would be wrong to see in his earlier poems nothing but storm and stress. The truth is that restlessness is the very essence of his soul. His is a dynamic spirit addicted to eternal *wanderlust*. His blood hearkens to the call of ranging distances. He does not love the earth as an anchorage, but as an object of eternal desire. The desert is his coveted destination; but not as a place where his spirit may be at home and howl with the jackals. Rather does he have the painful urge to flash through the desert like a sandstorm to carry back with him its blazing heat and fury, its vastness and its loneliness.

The world is large and spacious. Life is complex and taxing and human powers ludicrously limited. Not only does the body hinder and tether, but age and place, man and milieu are in league against us, to dwarf us into insignificance and an intolerable transiency. And so the poet would constantly be on the wing, changing site and scene, both in body and in spirit, in reality and in vision. He defies time and space and like time itself, he will not stand still. He wanders like a homeless spirit, a cloud adrift amidst clouds.

It often seems that he purposely ranges over far-flung distances in order to veer back and enjoy the abandon of his rebound even as he does the flight itself. When he is in the north, of which he sings, so rapturously, it is the east that beckons to him; when he is in the east, which he loves so passionately, he hears the call of the "daughter of the north." When in the valley, it is the mountain that lures him and from the mountain top he is drawn to the valley.

Shimoni is often called the "Poet of the Desert" because of his love for its endless wastes, its rolling sand dunes, its interminable desolation.

The sands of the desert lie white-hot and scorched in the heat of the afternoon. In the midst of this wilderness there trudges a heat-weary wanderer, a slave of the desert. His lips are parched from thirst and his entire being is consumed by a passion for rest and drink. He prays, "Spring up, spring up my well!"

But the well does not spring up. Its waters continue to flow underground into the distance. A mirage of peaceful waters calls, but all about him there is only the dry and burning wilderness. The lonely wanderer, singed by the heat and consumed by thirst continues on his way but does not reach his goal.

"Where are the morning winds? Where dewy night?
Who sees my pain? Where is God that I might cry to him?
The night is far away and morning has passed,
The burning heat of noon is with us,
There is no relief in sight."

A flaming intensity bursts from this song of sorrow, telling of white-hot, enervating afternoons in the wide and endless wilderness, an intensity typical of Shimoni.

But not only does the desert attract him. He loves the ocean just as profoundly because of its unfathomable depths and its haunting secretiveness. The ocean with its turbulence attracts him as it did Byron and Swinburne and Masefield. But while on the ocean, rocked by its towering waves, a homesickness for terrestrial silence and steadiness assails him. He longs for *terra firma,* but then only for a short while—a mere glimpse and no more. Like Noah's dove, he soars over a land submerged by the deluge, finding no resting place because he chooses not to find one. This is the better way—to be on the wing, and while winging from pole to pole to catch a glimpse of light, to hear the rustle of a leaf, flying on and on into ever higher spirals. At the sight of the crashing waves and the ponderous mountains of water rising in wild fury, only to crash down again into a fathomless abyss, the poet's soul expands and he sings,

"I hunger to walk upon desolate shores
With eye and heart wolfishly prowling,
Till sated are heart and eye with the ocean,
Where billow rides billow a-howling."

Shimoni's preoccupation with the desert and the ocean, with bottomless depths and summitless altitudes, leads him constantly to invoke images that symbolize prodigious strength and ferocity. The lion and the wolf are his kin. There is a bond of sympathy between him and the sphinxes whom he apostrophizes, for he, too, is but a sphinx transplanted from some uncharted distance. In snow-bound Petrograd on the shore of the Neva he accosts them, these fossilized children of the Orient, and in the blue dusk of the wintry moon he reveals their own secret to them. For the secret of their existence is the secret of his own.

The root of his own existence is in antiquity. He comes from ancient stock and he still seems to walk in the shadow of hoary ages. His roots are lost in the mazes of eras long past. He is a son of the past, living in a world in which he

> "Wanders open-eyed, yet does not see,
> His ears are open, yet he does not hear,
> He sees only the mysteries of years long forgotten.
> He hears only the chords of generations that have
> passed.
> And in a dead forgotten tongue
> His lonely life he utters in a song."

The historicity of his people is for him not a rhetorical phrase, but an actual inner experience. It is not of the brain, but of his very blood. His home is one of the geologic fastnesses; here he is a mere guest, a wayfarer, a transient.

> "I am a stranger on this soil,
> An unfamiliar intruder.
> The whole earth is my trek
> But I nowhere belong.
> Who can plumb the depth
> Of my innermost spirit,
> The root of my dream
> And the source of my song?"

He is a stranger upon this soil, an intruder in this world. He has stood upon earth's furthermost rims, but he does not know where he belongs. The truth is that he belongs to an ancient world and he is astray in the desert of the ages. From the actual root of his being to his own age, millennia intervene. He has come from prehistoric distances so what matters the care of a day or the sorrow of a life span? He is above it, beyond it. He is free. He folds his tent and goes light-heartedly.

Hence, too, the illusion of his own prodigious strength. He is not merely strong; he is a Samson who does not fear Delilah, nor can Shulamith be his foil. They will not bind him; they will not enslave him. "You may bind him with flaxen rope, bind him with silken thread, he hears the call of the open road upon which he must tread."

The here and the now are handicaps. They sap man's stamina; they clip his wings; they bend his spirit. But the remote past and the realm of imagination give man a new lease on freedom. *Here* man is slave; *there* he is king. *Here* he can merely grumble plaintively; *there* he can roar like a lion:

"Here my voice is sad and faint,
There in fierceness I shall roar,
When at night on icy deserts
With the wolves I shall explore,
There in fierceness I shall roar."

His strength must find an outlet. Too many storms are pent up within him and he must give vent to them.

He thirsts for battle, not against man, but against the blind and mighty forces of nature. He must settle old accounts to save his name. So he loves iron and strength. Soft silky couches are strange to him. "It is not for me to know joy, not for me softness and pleasant caresses."

He despises the falsehood of softness. He abhors the weakness of refinement. He hates the ease that goes with lack of strength.

"I cannot tolerate
Triumphs without sacrifice.
I love the sea when it is stormy."

More than once he was chained by trivialities and held prisoner in the confining prison of life, but like a wounded lion he stormed the walls of bondage and escaped the trap life had set for him.

This inner strength, these hidden tempests he must express. For strength is a heavy burden to carry. This turbulent overabundance accidently bestowed by God destroy the poet's peace. His power hounds him like the insect that harassed Titus. He calls upon "all those who pound and thunderously beat their hammers. Come armed with axes and anvils, beat the iron till the sparks fly, till the rock is crushed to bits—maybe you will drown out the great torment in my mind."

Strength thus becomes a curse robbing the poet of his peace. Samson too suffered from an overabundance of strength. He tore apart a lion with his hands in an attempt to discharge his strength. But he failed. The exuberance of life seethed on in his blood. In Samson's eyes there was sadness—

"The flames have consumed the grain,
And the Philistines are smitten,
Yet am I burdened with my strength,
Overcome with power inhuman."

Such is the suffering due to abnormal strength. It is more than man can bear. The strong man does not seek more power. He wants to rid himself of that which he already has. He goes to battle with the secret hope of losing his burden, but instead every victory intoxicates him and he remains a slave to the force which governs and subdues him. The ruler over others is slave to his own might. "Great and boundless is my strength, but I know not where to spend it. Clear and fresh strength I possess, but to whom shall I bequeath it?"

Whence so much power? And the poet himself answers:

"Double freedom, twice the storm
The Creator granted me,
And since then He looks with envy,
And insists upon being doubly paid."

Shimoni's *wanderlust* is not always convincing. If the here and the now are too narrow and unattractive, his vision of the beyond is too new and too lonely. He is a spark in search of its flame; nevertheless, one wonders whether the plaint of his loneliness is indeed justifiable. There is always a brother's eye to watch him on his flights away from himself and back. His very aloofness and sense of self-appreciation make him nearer and dearer to us. He may never sing the praises of his people, but his people see in him not only a poet of universal scope and import, but a truly Jewish poet. His temperament and universality, his will to power and his pride in isolation, his imaginative flights and his visions, are characteristics common to his people. And when he sings a paean of praise to the Hebrew tongue, the medium of his song, the Jewish people sing with him,

> "Oh, tongue of my muse, thou Hebrew of old,
> We are one in the blood, indivisible twin,
> Worlds long forgotten in both of us spin,
> Ancient of stock and abandoned of kin,
> Mysterious echoes of ages untold."

II

This blood relationship, this racial at-oneness with his tongue, binds him to his people. Now his lines become tender and measured. The storm passes and is followed by the soft sadness of twilight that he had previously disdained. He hides his face in the mane of the lion, his brother—"Away with lover and friend; the fiery lion dies in silence." He is ready to listen to the song of the swan. On a coal-black night the swan floats upon the waters seeking a trace of whiteness. But all is black and the swan sings the song of birth and death in the great darkness. The song ends and there is only the darkness and silence.

When storms rage in the poet's soul, there is the brightness of day. When the storm subsides, night descends. The flame flickers and dies. All the paths are lost in the darkness and the heart turns homeward, toward the quiet corner, toward a mother's hidden sigh.

For days and years the poet has roved the seas and on the wings of storm was carried over deserts and wilderness. Suddenly he finds himself without ground and roots. He almost loses sight of his goal. There is desire, but what is its aim? There are many boundaries, but where is the end of the road? It is twilight hour—the twilight of pride and strength. His poems no longer exude the freshness of mountain air or the mighty breath of the giant. The eagle's wings are trimmed. The man of battle and of victory now knocks at the door of a modest house. He would enter and he prays wearily,

"How I long for home . . .
My father is now an old man,
My mother an aged woman.
Many days have passed
Since they heard of me last."

These are simple unsophisticated lines, the elemental song of an orphan who wants to be a dutiful son and brother.

"You are tired, my son,
Weary of foreign lands;
The samovar on the table
Hums a welcoming refrain."

At such twilight hours the poet conjures up various incarnations of loneliness: a sick angel abandoned by God, a bird wandering in the night, a pale rose of the valley, a single cloud drifting in the sky, a brook weeping its way through the rocks, a palm tree lying broken in the snow, a crystal palace in the desert, a lion pursued by hunters, a wild cataract spewing its scorn to the stars, a tempest among dark cliffs. And of all these one image stands out:

"A hidden sadness slumbers in my soul—
The desert lion is pursued by hunters."

But weariness and twilight moods do not necessarily spell danger for a poet. There is a weariness preceding the new strength of a morrow, a sunset anticipating a new dawn. Such changes in the life of a poet may be good omens. There are potential blessings in his turning to new hues and tones. The brilliance gives place to half-tones, the light of day is no longer blinding nor is the darkness of night so oppressive. Man rests after his toil and the flame "neither flares up nor dies, but rests." This is neither wakefulness nor sleep, but a state of dreaming. The heart is alert, though the poet does not see. He trembles at the edge of the abyss.

> "The spring air is transfused with haze,
> In deep slumber the world stands revealed,
> As if not the pulsing life about me
> But its inner mystery do I see."

It was 1921 when Shimoni wrote such poems, when his life was marked by restful calm and a clear perception. He had experienced storm and gale and now it was necessary that calm succeed them. During the white-heat of day he had wandered faint in the heat and now it was good to rest upon the shore like a fisherman at noon. "How sweet the sunlight! How wonderful is rest! White clouds drift beneath the high blue vault . . ."

Wearness and slumber pass. A wave splashes. A fish darts about in the water, its glistening scales reflecting the light, and bubbles rise to the surface.

> "Fisherman, awake, spread your net!
> Though rest be so sweet on a clear afternoon."

Shimoni's storms have died down. "On the sea-shore, on the shore of my life, I enjoy the silence. Thoughts come like clouds in the sky; dreams rise and fall like fish within the waves." He speaks in intelligible similes. Not only is the sea quiet, but the poet too is calm as he dreams. The storm has subsided into a peaceful restful afternoon.

Was it time or place that induced this calm? Was it the maturity and understanding of the poet that brought on this new mood or was it the peace that he found in the motherland? Did the wanderer finally find real rest or was the lion only caged?

His luminous idylls of the new life in Palestine are assuredly a product of the new environment. In these narrative poems the daring dreamers of Israel's redemption cast their imposing shadows, sad but sturdy, bent but buoyant, upon a wasteland that sings under their heavy steps. In the Hebrew literature of our time these idylls are the first efforts in the creation of an indigenous Israeli literature in the saga of Jewish revival. Together with the *halutz* Shimoni worked at re-creating the genius of his people. With him the poet celebrated the return to the soil. Not only does Shimoni know the *halutz,* not only does he understand him and appreciate him, but he loves him. Like a brother, hand on shoulder, he walks with him behind the plow, lengthening the furrows and sowing the seeds in the soil of the new Judea.

After the period of storm and defeat, days of strength followed by days of weakness, these idylls mark the beginning of a new process of clarification and synthesis.

III

Shimoni journeyed twice to Palestine. His first trip, in 1909, was like the quick visit of a young poet of twenty-three who had come to see his yearning bride. His second trip was a real return to The Land. The first visit lasted only a little over a year; the second was to be for permanent stay.

He begins his Palestinian poems by asking, How shall one sing about his land and what form shall he give her? Shall he describe the purity of her air and the brilliancy of her skies, or shall he tell about the glory of her rugged mountains and the deep melancholy of her destroyed places? But poets before him had already written about these themes. They had sung, each according to his powers and his mood, about the "enchanting folds of her rising vapors, the mystic softness of her clouds, the hidden and incomprehensible magic emanating from every tree, every rock, every line of her wonderful heights." They had sung too of "the voice of God, the voice of wonders" heard among the hills, in the valleys and along the pathways of the Land of Israel, the land of eternity. The spell of ancient, exalted visions of glory still hovers over its quiet streams, over the crags of its desolate mountains, the wide expanses of its fields and deserts bathed in dew or scorched by heat. The poets had sung about everything: about the hopes and consolations which sprout like modest flowers among the rocks, about the Divine Spirit which appears in every corner of the land, about the *Galil* and the *Sharon,* about the days and nights of Judea. Ruefully he asks, "And who am I to sing their song anew?"

But Shimoni does have something new to say and he says it in an original manner. Although a lyric poet, he is the first to describe the new life in Palestine by means of the idyll. He was willing to suppress his own natural tendencies in order to be original and not to repeat the lyrical work of his predecessors.

In 1907, he wrote *Jordania,* the first of his idylls. It has little plot and there is nothing about the struggles or the accomplishments of the pioneers. But from it arise the pleasant aroma of the land and the charm of wholesome and sincere poetic expression.

With his second idyll, *In the Woods of Hedera,* written in 1914, he begins to introduce living personalities. But, as yet, the poet does not feel at one with his heroes. Nor are the characters in the idyll united with their environment. They are not rooted in the land as is the tree in the field. The strong attachment binding the Jew to his country had not yet come to Shimoni.

In his next idylls, *The Struggle Between Judea and Galilee, Karmit* and *On the Shore of the Sea at Jaffa,* he introduces a delightfully playful spirit into his poetry. A youthful exuberance is blended with rich poetic imagery. He portrays the true beauty of the Palestinian landscape, with its transparent air, pure blue skies, the silence of its almond groves, its golden fields and melancholy streams. One hears the rustle of hurrying lizards, the swish of branches, the howl of jackals and the songs of the men on guard.

Shimoni finally becomes part of the soul and soil of Palestine. Only in this way is it possible for a poet to integrate himself within a land. He has to be born anew, to fit his personality within the setting of his environment.

IV

When Shimoni went to Palestine to settle, he did not go alone. He was accompanied by an army of *halutzim,* saved from the upheaval of the First World War and the revolution which came in its wake. From that moment onward he accompanied his comrades everywhere. The song of their lives was his song and their struggle to conquer the soil was his.

From the day he boarded the ship which brought the *halutzim* to Palestine, he was possessed by a new spirit. He loved his oppressed, suffering and tempest-tossed brothers who still retained a spark of youth, hope and faith in their eyes, and "whose power to live could not be suppressed by plague, sword or hunger."

In *Halutzim,* his first major idyll, Shimoni steps out of the narrow bounds of the individual and enters the wide terrain of the community. He describes the passengers aboard ship: a *yeshiva bahur* from Lithuania, a doctor of jurisprudence from Leipzig, a singer from Vienna, a young man with a scar on his neck, a frail woman and her child, a sweet young lady from Vilna and a Jew who combined the pursuits of Hebrew teacher, marriage broker and business man. There were skilled workmen, accountants, students, teachers, dentists from various lands. "Each country was represented with its language and its songs, but there was only one common aim and slogan for all—Palestine, work and freedom!"

He sees these individuals as the scattered remnants of a crumbling society. This world, in which Cain is always killing Abel, is drawn in its true colors, and the Jew striving for redemption and deliverance finds their symbols in these fugitives from violence and the sword, the embodiments of high ideals and lofty visions.

The sons who return to their motherland become the builders of the country and the rebuilders of their own lives. For these people had fled from "a hateful, deteriorated and impure world." These *halutzim* had fled to Palestine from an accursed diaspora that had destroyed the "dwelling places of Jacob."

The *halutz,* Reuben, who scrubs the ship's deck in this idyll, had been compelled in a Ukrainian pogrom to dig a grave in which he was to have been buried alive, but he had escaped to become a farmer in Palestine. In the old country he had dug a grave for himself; here he digs the soil for seeding and planting. He works hard on barren plots of ground, in the fields, in the mud. He splits rocks and crumbles clods of earth. Through work his spirit is healed. In digging the soil of his motherland he takes revenge upon the diaspora which had compelled him to dig a grave for himself. He sees the people of Israel as a corpse risen from the dead to renewed life, even as was true of him. This is the secret of Israel, the mystery of a people descending into the grave and coming up alive; a people struck down and trodden upon, but which had lifted itself up to self-emancipation.

The heroes of Shimoni's idylls are workers, watchmen and poets—innocent and simple men. They are strong in spirit, glorious in their faith, great in their love and wonderful in their devotion. They are themselves all true poets.

When distinguished guests come to the various settlements and lavishly praise the young builders, the innocent *halutzim* stand amazed and ask, "Why this praise? What is the miracle or the mystery they see in us?"

But their admirers say:

"Tell us, if you will,
Are such miraculous deeds possible among any other people?
Is there another nation in the world whose sons suddenly go berserk,
Leave their dwelling places and wander off to rocky desolations,
To crumble heavy masses by the sweat of their brows,
And while so doing, to sing as if a great privilege were theirs?
Behold, we are such a unique people in The Land! And Lombroso was right
When he said that insanity and glory dwell under one roof. . . .
But there is majesty and resplendence in this colossal insanity of ours,
With it we shall build an eternal culture.
Long live this holy insanity!"

But Kasriel, "The Anonymous *Halutz,*" who possesses a sort of sanctified simplicity, is shocked by the display of oratory. He does not see any greatness or insanity in his work or in that of his friends who have settled in the mountainous terrain. He asks,

"Is it true that only we and nobody else
Split rocks, dry swamps and rebuild ruins?
Otherwise, should we not be like grasshoppers in comparison with other peoples
Who dig in the depths of the earth,
Who construct highways in waste places,
Who conquer oceans, search out the mysteries of the depths and the heights,

Who connect sea to sea, climb the highest mountain peaks,
And, in great simplicity, bring forth bread from the earth?
These people too are not an angelic host, neither are they performers of miracles,
Down their noses the sweat runs too and their backs break with hard work,
Even if paeans of praise are not sung to them daily as to our *halutzim* . . ."

Kasriel is one of the most inspiring and wonderful characters created by Shimoni. He is filled with love, kindliness, grace and delicacy. He and his wife pour forth their sweat upon the ground, watering it and making it fertile. They are satisfied with little. They eat the bread of affliction, saving every penny to bring more of their friends to the Land.

But fate does not decree happiness for the honest couple. Kasriel's wife dies in childbirth. He decides to erect a monument on the grave of his wife. It must be of marble, for she deserves it. But marble is expensive, and where can a *halutz* get the money to pay for it? He sells the chickens, pays off the debts incurred during his wife's illness, closes his vineyard and farm and looks for work in the city. By chance he meets a friend who tells him of a job as a night watchman in one of the large orange groves. He takes the job. One stormy night while making his rounds among the trees, he hears the neighing of a camel. He investigates and sees two Bedouins loading sacks of fruit on the animal. He attempts to retrieve the stolen goods but is shot. All night long he lies in a pool of water that slowly reddens with his blood.

In the morning the other workers find him. A doctor and his friend, Zebulon, are called, but Kasriel is beyond all hope. An otherworldly light shines from his eyes. The same strange and wonderful expression that had covered his face when he had come to Palestine, suffuses it now that he is leaving the Land. Zebulon says, "A mysterious combination of suffering and ethereal joy, as if he were seeing a vision, appeared on his face, and it suddenly occurred to me that he looked like a prodigal son returning to his mother's house."

On his deathbed, Kasriel dictates his last will and testament to his friend and to his entire generation. In his quiet, dying voice he whispers to Zebulon, "You taught me the *Torah of Eretz Yisrael:* to unite and possess the land, to be satisfied with little, to persevere. Above all to persevere! To turn neither to the right or left. But I, Kasriel, have turned aside from the proper path."

He had turned aside from the proper path because he had broken the commandment to be satisfied with little. Instead of a simple monument for his wife he had wanted one of marble. And one broken commandment leads to another. So he had forsaken his plot of land and thus had broken the commandment to persevere. And if one man could do so, and a second, and a third, what would become of us?

Before he dies, he asks Zebulon to give away his farm to someone who would pledge to work it, preferably to the head of a large family. Zebulon is to take the money he has earned as a watchman to buy chickens for the farm and to erect a monument on his wife's grave, an extremely simple one. Upon his own grave there is to be no monument at all.

"I beg of you . . . let the grave be covered with grass . . .
Even without grass it will be good . . . dust . . . just the dust
of the earth . . .
For the earth is good and it is good to be within it,
To fuse with it, so that nothing remain. . . ."

So "The Anonymous *Halutz*" became one with the good earth which he had tilled with a holy love. And although no monument marks his grave, one exists none the less. It is a monument of the spirit, whose image is engraved upon the soul of the people and the memory of the Land.

Not all the *halutzim* were like Kasriel, nor did the others leave only intangible monuments of the spirit. They married, had children, created a generation of heirs and builders, of fighters and victors—the dream of the fathers realized.

Judah, the watchman of *Resisei Lailah (Dewdrops in the Night)*, who came to Palestine with the second wave of immigrants, sees the fulfillment of his dreams in his son, Gideon, the soldier.

Judah goes on guard and Gideon, not yet 18, goes to a colony into the danger zone in order to follow in his father's footsteps. Judah had been a watchman in the early days of that same colony in Galilee. Now, thirty years later, his son goes there. "Don't worry about me, mother," says Gideon, "How fitting for the wife of a watchman to be too the mother of a watchman."

And thus two generations of Jewish watchmen go on their rounds: one in Judea, and the other in Galilee. While on guard in the darkness of night the father dreams of the redemption of the Land and of mankind. This is the most precious attribute of the *halutzim:* they combine their Jewishness with a feeling for humanity. At a time when Arabs burn trees in fields, a Jewish watchman walks his guard, dreaming of love for fellow man, for all men. All the atrocities and all the evils that he had experienced could not prevent the holy seed of love for humanity from sprouting in his heart.

He knows full well that the world's conscience is asleep. But Judah, the Jew, believes that ultimately that conscience will awaken and redeem mankind from its unclean and shameful bondage. He is a man of faith, a believer, a Jew whose innermost being is bound up with humanity. From his childhood days he has carried with him his dreams of redemption, the vision of Isaiah. The filth and poverty of the European village of his birth were pierced through by the rays of light emitted by the yearning for the Messiah. From that village and its inhabitants, poor in material things but rich in things of the spirit, he had received his faith and his hope. Those he has brought to his Land, the land of prophets and seers.

And like the father, so the son. Gideon, too, is a sensitive dreamer although born not in a dark Russian village, but amidst the light of Judea and the hills of Galilee. But like his father, he lives "in a hateful, despicable and impure world." At eighteen he is a watchman in Galilee, guarding vineyards and fields against Arab arsonists. Shortly afterward he joins the British Army, to fight against the forces of Satan, who has unsheathed his sword against the world.

In his childhood and in his youth, in days of peace and time of war, Gideon carries on the tradition of his father, the tradition of a people waiting for the awakening of the world's conscience. And the son-disciple becomes in the end his father's teacher, for a while later Judah follows in Gideon's footsteps and enlists also in the fighting forces.

The poem, *A Letter to Someone Out There,* continues the narrative of *Dewdrops in the Night.*

Gideon goes to war. The sensitive, dreamy child becomes a man among men and a strapping soldier. But the seed planted in his soul during his childhood is not lost. After much journeying on the seas and the North African desert, he remains the same dreamy child of the Palestinian colony. When he writes to his parents in Judea, he tells poetically of the expanse of the desert, the majesty of the mountains, the sunrise over the ocean and his secret longing for his native land, the valley of the bees and honeycombs.

He does not write of the bursting shells or of the bombs exploding in flaming fires or clouds of smoke. He surely does not tell of his wounded leg and his protracted illness. But of the twinkling stars shooting in the heavens he writes in detail. It is as if he is not on the battlefield, but in some pleasant pasture land. When he writes home, he wants to know about every little thing happening there, about every garden-bed and tree in his village, every bird's nest, foal and calf in the neighborhood and the founding of the new colony on "the site so majestically beautiful." The same gentle dreaming lad, the same tender lyric man!

And the father, replying, now turns from teacher to disciple. For he had reached his limit, beyond which there could be nothing more. True, he had been a man of faith, who had always believed that only the good is permanent, the evil of brief moment. Even when the Polish ghettos were erected and the House of Israel became an object of scorn and desecration, he still had hoped for the triumph of the good. And when the reports had reached him of the unity of the Jews even in the pit of hell, he had been overcome with emotion by that extraordinary spirituality, that invincible faith in the good. But when the horrible reports of destruction continued, his world turned dark and the beauty of heaven and earth were blacked out. A barrier arose between him and the world. First came the pain of disillusion and then there came a consuming wrath; but even that left him with a small crevice through which to peep at the four cubits of space about him.

But in the end came disgust.

> "Such a hateful, contemptible world,
> Which exists on the blood of an enslaved people,
> A world of murder, barbarism, lies and deceit!"

This detestable world, with all its impurity and abomination, entered his blood. His bowels, his muscles, his limbs writhed in agony at the pain. He wanted to vomit. The man whose ear was attuned to the whispered mystery of the soil and to the secret stirrings of the seed of life within it; the man who not only saw the green grass of the valley and the mountain, but who also listened to the rustling of the grass as it penetrated the hard surface of the rocks; the man who had clung to nature and loved all living things—this man now seemed to be ejected from the world. For the impure and hateful world had penetrated his heart and his eyes and his ears had shut tight.

At a time when his brother Jews were convulsed by the poisonous fumes in the gas chambers, and his sisters were put to shame by human beasts, and living infants were thrown into mass graves it seemed to be an unforgivable sin to go on living and breathing the fresh air of the fields. Faith died in the man of faith and the light of the sun was obliterated—the sun that had brightened his life and had led him through the fields and vineyards, and had given him the strength and faith to build a new home and establish a new generation.

He dreamed about a Messiah who would redeem the world from slavery, from filth, and from sin. But he asks, "Will such a world accept the Messiah?"

> "Can the King, the Messiah appear
> On such an earth, drenched in tears and blood,
> Which did not quiver, move or writhe,
> Which did not uproot those who defiled it?
> Can the King, the Messiah appear
> Neath such a sky which saw everything
> And which did not diminish in the least its azure light?
> Is it possible to wash away the filth of such a world?
> Is it possible to drain off the impurity of its blood?
> Such a world! So disgusting!
> And how do I breathe its air and absorb its light?"

The world had become loathsome to him; he even hated himself. He was sick with nausea. Broken was the attachment between him and his soil, between him and his sky. The enchantment of life had fled.

But his son, who was fighting somewhere "out there," rescues his father from total destruction. He cures him of his sickness with his soothing letters written between battles. For between Gideon and the world there was no barrier. His spirit remained alive. The world was not blacked out for him because he had gone out to fight its battle, determined to improve it. The world is not given on a platter. One has to fight for it. And Gideon was fighting.

So now it becomes the father's turn to follow in the footsteps of his son. And he too volunteers for the army. Just as Gideon had once said to his mother, "Don't worry about me, mother. It is fitting for the wife of a watchman to be the mother of a watchman"—so Judah now says to his wife, "Don't worry about me, Deborah. It is fitting that the mother of a devoted soldier should be the wife of a soldier . . . "

Once this happens, he is cured. His eyes again open to behold the world, to enjoy the sight of a billowing cloud, a newly ploughed field, a tree. Of course his fiery wrath is not quenched, it never will be. But the disgust leaves him. Life takes on interest once more. The vineyard and the field, the furrow and the grass plot, the bush and the blossom, summer and spring, which had been estranged to him, now recognize him even as he sees them afresh. Just when he had thought he had finished with them, they return to him.

He had come to Palestine to find the solution for the riddle of his life and peace for his soul. But now all the world was united in the flaming desire to cleanse itself of pollution, to save man himself. And the man of Palestine, rooted though he had become in his land, is not a stranger in this world. He is in it and of it. And when its cry now reaches him, he goes forth to war for this world gone mad. He leaves the land he had helped redeem, but it is sealed in his heart as he goes on his way to battle and to victory.

In the quiet of night he hears a voice from above, from these heavens which had always accompanied him and which had deepened the meaning of his life on earth. The voice whispers to him,

"Don't you see how busy we all are,—
The heavens, earth, winds and clouds?
On mysterious and exalted missions,
To renew endless worlds,
To renew the works of creation,
To shift the autumn and the spring seasons—
And yet you would impose upon us a task that is yours,
The task of humanity: to combat evil!
We go to change the seasons,
We go to bring the snows,
We go to bring forth grass upon dry lands,
We go to fill the oceans,
We go wherever we are sent.
Go you too upon your own mission,
To your own destiny . . ."

The father listens to the voice and goes forth upon his destined path. And the poet who has accompanied his *halutzim* on their journey to The Land and their conquest of its soil, now goes forth with them, fathers and sons, on this new and great journey to distant horizons for the redemption of mankind.

MOURN NOT!

Mourn not, weep not at a time like this,
Nor bow your head.
Work! Work! Plow, O Plowman!
Sower, sow your seed!
In time of stress, redouble your toil;
Dig, and then plant; clear and fence.
Level and cast up the highway of freedom
Toward a new day of light.
For on the path of pain, redemption comes,
And the blood drawn by the tyrant's lash
Cries out to the soul of the people:
"Bestir yourself and work!
Be redeemed! Set others free!"

IN THE WOODS OF HEDERA

(An excerpt)

. . . Crimson the forest treetops, whispering the afternoon prayer
As the wind of evening woke up. The western horizon flashed
In springtide and transparent flickers caressing and hanging on
nothing,
Speedily poured forth and fading in the widths of the dark evening
blue
And passing as swift as its coming . . . And Reb Pinhas looked to
the west,
And gazed there a moment or two, and then turned his face to the
east,
And leaned on a tree; and he prayed . . . He knew that as the west
flickered
So his weary life flickered away . . . The axe had already been slipping
From his weak weary hand more than once . . . His heart was tired
out with dreams
While his legs had grown doughy with wandering and rest was still
long delayed,
And rest is a good thing . . . Yet his heart was still restlessly thudding

At his ample and unquenched yearnings . . . The eagle pinions still lifted
To magical radiant heights . . . But sadly they lowered again.
Under his wings his chicks did not hide, they had scattered
To all the four winds, and forsaken the rocks of the homeland . . .
Grass had grown and withered again, and again the slight earth and mound
Where the wife of his youth was concealed . . . No proud eagle daughter was she
But a quiet submissive dove. The quiver of her gentle wings
Had held back the beat of his mighty pinions forever . . .
Silently Pinhas stood as though joined to the tree
And his full height seemed to bow low . . . Had God accepted his offering . . . ?
Had the flame of his furtive tears made fruitful the desolate rocks,
Those tears no man had yet seen? Did the blood of his silent dove
Not rest on his weary head? . . . And he forcefully shook his head
As starting from out of a nightmare, then opened both his eyes wide
And gazed round about him, restored: For who had borne and raised these?
Who had poured the iron in their blood? Who lit up the laugh in their eyes,
Or taught them the confidence tried?
Clouds in the west still quivered,
A chain of transparent bubbles with heady juices within them,
One running over with dark red juice of the cherry,
Wine golden-pink in another, a third milky clear and flashing
With a gentle radiance, quivering, pink . . . And joined by an unseen conduit,
Were all those magical bubbles, and one liquor mixed with another
And color poured into color . . . The row of them arched out and rounded.
Above the thick of the forest, and a crimson radiance fell
On the trunks of the trees arranged white in clump after clump,
And all of the band had arisen and prepared themselves for the way,
One seeking his coat in the brush, one whetting his axe as an extra,
Another getting branches and brush for a gift to the kitchen
While somebody in the right mood took a running jump, and he landed

Upon the donkey's back all of a sudden while the beast was quietly grazing.
Then Naphtali stood up and silenced the cheerful noise of his comrades
And lifted his hand aloft, in sign they should pay him attention
And then he began: "Whereas the name of wood-chopper
Is not held in esteem in Israel ever since Gibeonite days,
And whereas the maidens in Judah and Galilee are refined
And always exhibit their preference for writers and teachers,
With your permission I therefore proclaim our Wood-chopper Party
Is a Lofty and leading Party; and the head thereof is Reb Pinhas—
So comrades, three cheers!" And the forest thundered as they all roared:
"Hurrah! Long live Reb Pinhas and long live the Wood-chopper Party!
And long live every lad with an arm to swing up and bring down the axe!
And long live Galilee and her mountains, and long live Judah the proud,
And the Shefela and Sharon, every hill, each valley and brook!"
Still they were cheering in force and the forest was cheering them back
While silently darkened the skies, when Naphtali thundered again:
"Let us gravely remember, brethren, the peerless Hedera heroes,
Consumed of malarial vapours and slain by the sword and the bullet . . ."
Naphtali's voice was trembling, there was no more laughter about him,
And the sunburnt young fellows were suddenly silent and stern,
Till Reb Pinhas thrust himself forward and stood in their midst and said:
"Now is no time for sadness. We shall not crown their memory by grief.
Let us labor with gladness and joy, for by gladness and joy we reward them.
And then, seeing day turns to evening and we are all of us here together,
Come let us make up a ring, and hallow our day with some dances . . ."

Then, all of the gang together, each with his axe in his girdle,
Each arm-in-arm with the next lad, they began to whirl round in a circle,
Beating against the tree-stumps and held back by the brushwood
Yet how light their feet were . . . The eyes of Reb Pinhas grew bright
And his own legs also lost weight . . . The cracked shoes began to flash
In the air and vanished again, the jackets they spread far and wide,
While the broad-brimmed straw hats slipped down and off the heads of the wearers,
Some still miraculously hanging while others had fallen to earth,
And the dance grew more and more lively . . . The tune it was lilting and strong
And though the voices did not harmonize, they came from a dozen true hearts
And a distant echo responded . . .
Galilee lofty they praised,
Lauding labor and strength with a roar of lusty fresh youth
That coursed like the torrents of spring . . . And the donkey of chunky Berel
Loaded with empty tins and ready to start back home
Rubbed in wonder against a tree, pricking his long ears up high
And wondering what had happened to gentle, pedantic Berel
To go whirling round in a ring and forget his donkey its crib!
And a nightbird shrieked in the distance, silently fell the dews
While the clouds in the west grew pallid, and drained off the last of their gold.

TONGUE OF MY MUSIC

(An excerpt)

O tongue of my music, Hebrew tongue!
How close we are, true twins we are . . .
Forgotten worlds both me and you enflare,
Both of us ancient, far, bereft,
Both of us—wonder-echoes from forgotten moons.

THE JUBILEE OF COACHMEN

(An excerpt)

Long was my soul low-bent from the day I had come
to the land.
Nature unrolled her book, but I could not read:
Strange the script was, and new; new were, and
strange, its syllabications.
The mystery of the charactery held me spellbound;
I felt its secret fascination,
But my heart had not learned how, without knowing,
To leap in response to its call,
As does a bird into its nest. . . .

Thus I first understood that I still was in exile.
Gazing at the glorious palm, I yearned for the
wistful white birch of the northland;
A blossoming winter contrived to entice me,
But I dreamed of the deserts of snow.
Long was my soul low-bent, and little, indeed, did
I then comprehend
That nature ne'er hastes to cast off its veil in
the sight of a stranger
Who will not, who cannot approach it more closely. . . .

CHILDREN FROM NOWHERE

(Excerpt from the idyll *Resisei Lailah, Dewdrops in the Night*)

"Dear Gideon" . . . and a wave of warm emotion swept over the
heart of Judah. . . .
He recalled how wonderful and strange the child appeared
Lisping Hebrew, as if that was his tongue from generations back . . .
Little Sir Impudence . . . to speak Hebrew . . . so simply,
As if it were not the Holy Tongue in days gone by . . .
To express in Hebrew: "Father," "Mother," "Bread," "Camel,"
"Horse," and "Toy,"—
As if to say: "This is my language! Who dares to gainsay that?
If I wish, I speak it!"

And when Deborah burst out laughing at Judah's ecstasy,
He would try to explain to her that this was a deep subject,
"Deeper than you think," he said. "Try to understand, for example,
The Hebrew words: 'Bread,' 'Donkey,' 'Onion'—there is no sharp distinction
Between all these concepts and the little haughty person who pronounces them;
It's really as if he was the prophet Isaiah himself,
And as if I, who did not speak Hebrew as a child,
Can never experience that blessed earthiness,
That elemental directness which Isaiah and Gideon have in common . . .
How shall I not admire him, this little Rabbi Huzpit?*
He has attained a wonderfully high standard in Hebrew,
Which Bialik and Judah Halevi never achieved."

Thus Judah tried to clarify his thoughts to Deborah,
But she laughed louder, tapped him on the lips and said "Silly!"
Judah also laughed and said: "What can I do about the limited mentality of a woman?"
And with secret admiration and trembling expectation
He continued to feast his eyes on Gideon and his little friends, and he thought:

"This is a blessed, pioneer generation—exuberant and unspoiled,
A generation which is suckled directly from the roots of our culture,
Not through round-about, blind, or involved channels,
Somehow, I must pay tribute to those wonderful channels
Which brought life-giving forces from the well of secret wisdom—
A well dug by princes and the most noble minds of our people;
These channels brought life-giving forces to an uncharted wilderness,
They bridged the hills of darkness and pierced the mountains of ignorance,
To reach those who were parched with thirst in the wilderness,
Those who went astray in the desert of nations. . . .
But in the cloudiness of the eras, in the dreariness of generations,
Rust appeared upon the surface of the channels,
And it mixed with the life-giving waters and dried up their flavor. . . .

* Literally, "Rabbi Impudence." Actually a rabbi of the Talmud.

But now a new generation flourishes, and it crawls upon its belly,
Laps up the water which flows from the blessed ancient well,
And the soul of those who drink it is restored. . . ."

On these and many more things did Judah meditate
As he watched Gideon and his playmates,
As he listened to their conversation and observed
The free and easy manner in which they enjoyed their pranks
At home or in the fields.
It is true, that after the children grew up
And Judah became accustomed to their "blessed earthiness and elemental directness,"
Something resembling a feeling of disappointment overcame him,
Sharp doubts began to oppress his heart in secret:
"Perhaps—and I hope I am wrong—these free children of the modern cultural rebirth
Are more tainted in their souls than the oppressed ones of the diaspora,
Perhaps they lack the depth that only children of suffering have,
Those yearnings for light that they who dwell in darkness know,
Those longings for redemption which have no equal in the sweetness of their intensity.
Which have nurtured countless generations in the heroism of martyrdom—
In the aspiration for sanctity and purity, and for loftiness in living,
This modern generation lacks the respect and that inspired acumen
Which always characterized the children of Israel in exile;
They are too shallow and light-minded, their spiritual horizons how narrow . . ."

But when Judah followed the footsteps of the children with a loving and watchful eye,
As he saw them threading their way among the clods of earth and rock piles of Kefar Sela,
(This time, not only in play, but with intent on hard labor)
His doubts evaporated and he was ashamed of himself.
"This boy who kneels underneath the cow's udders,
Who scrubs the walls of the chicken coop and weeds the garden,
Who carries full, burdensome pails of milk on his frail shoulders,

Who rakes up the stubborn and parched earth . . .
(All vie with each other to ease the burdens of their tired parents)
This boy who knows the name of every plant and flower of the village,
Who battles with the hornets to prevent them from harming the saplings,
Who fearlessly wanders through the mountains and explores their caves,
Who is friendly with every clod of earth, every bush of his native village—
Is he not a true branch of the ancient stock of stalwart Hebrews
Who knew how to defend their land with supreme courage,
They who threshed their wheat and cultivated their fig trees—
Did they not give their people everlasting redeemers and prophets?
It is true that our sons will not bend their backs over books,
(Their backs hurt enough from the yoke of hard labor)
It is true that they will not uproot mountains
To grind them to dust in heated discussion of traditional law.
But did we not pray for this?— that a new generation should arise,
Hebraic in spirit, in expression, in the outlook of its literary leaders,
Who would love toil and its tribulations,
Who would hear the language of the earth, which is deeper and more exalted than seventy languages—
A generation which would be wholesome, strong and straight of back, of heart and of mentality? . . .
And as for depth and all the other noble ideals
And yearnings for the exalted in life—
Why, unexpected depth and idealism are revealed at the oddest moments. . . ."

While meditating thus, Judah recalled a strange and wonderful experience:
He was quite sick and depressed at the time, steeped in pain and doubts,
Examining every dream of his life and wondering whether it was not all in vain.
In his delirium he beheld the structure of the cultural rebirth floating in air;
There was wickedness outside, disunity and frustration within;

Suddenly he became conscious of Gideon sitting and eating at the table.
The boy was perspired and fatigued, gobbling up his food ravenously,
Just like Esau in his day . . .
And Judah turned to his son and said:
"What is the matter with you, Gideon,
Why are you so exhausted and famished?"
And the fourteen-year old boy mumbled with a full mouth:
"It was your turn to plow today, father, and I plowed for you,
And the furrows and the hills straightened themselves out for me too. . . . "
He answered his father and stuck his head again into his steaming plate.
At the mumbled utterance of "I plowed", which issued from the mouth of his tired and hungry son,
A wave of brilliant light seemed to illumine the soul of Judah;
An all-embracing sun seemed to split the dark and threatening clouds;
Though it wore a crown of dark clouds, the sun's bright smile
Was soft and deep, like some secret unexplained tidings . . .
And a mystic voice whispered to Judah's heart:
"Do you remember when you were a boy
Of Gideon's age . . . in exile . . . and your soul went out to Zion. . . . ?
Your father brought you an illustrated map of Palestine
Issued by the Hovevei Zion Committee.
There were pictures of the colonies on the map:
Rishon-le-Zion, Gedera, Rosh Pinah and Petah Tikvah . . .
You saw low houses nestling among trees, vineyards on the hilltops and fields. . . .
The sun arose in the east and in the first rays of dawn
A Jew was plowing his field.
The fringes of his praying shawl were swaying in the morning breeze,
But your eyes were chained to the all important figure
Of a little boy who was helping his father.
He wore a big straw hat on his head,
In his hand were the reins of the animal he was driving,
Behind him were plowed fields and confronting him,
Uncultivated fields awaiting their turn for the plow.
The bluish mountains of Israel were on the horizon . . .

How you envied the boy, and how much time you spent dreaming:
If only you were privileged to have such exalted happiness—
To work on the earth of Israel, to plow the fields of Judea!
Now look—here is the solution!
The dream was realized in your son!"

That day Judah was confused and his mind wandered.
Before the tired and dim eye of his soul
There stirred scenes of ancient days and he heard echoes of ancient sounds.
Figures encircled with a new light were praising God with new songs. . . .
But dark and dispirited was the prophet imprisoned in the dungeon,
Prophecying coming terrors, events of approaching horror and confusion.
And behold the word of God came to Hananel ben Shalum:
"Buy my field which is in Anathoth, and you will have redemption. . . ."
. . . A Jew was plowing his field and an Arab passed by and said:
"Leave your cow, Jew, and leave your plow,
I just learned from the lowing of your cow that your temple was destroyed. . . ."
The cow lowed again, and the Arab spoke a second time:
"Jew, Jew, take hold of your cow and your plowshare,
From the lowing of your cow I just learned that your Messiah was born!"

Judah was taken aback that despite the hour of weakness and depression,
Gideon said to him in all simplicity, "I plowed,"
But he was more astonished that these ordinary words
Should suddenly ring out in his soul
Like the song of wells in a parched desert,
Something like a revelation, a hint of wonderful distant lands. . . .

"Dear Gideon . . . dear Gideons . . . blessed boys"—
Judah continued to meditate,
And in the cool mountain breeze,
He felt that his body became suffused from the flame within his soul.
"Depth . . . acumen . . . ideals" . . . oh well! They will come in time.

Days will come which will demand all your strength,
Fateful days, with big doings, which I can see are not far off . . .
Days in which all the dew of your youth,
All your light, all the delights of your innocent lives,
Will be offered by you lovingly and in all simplicity
As something which is self-understood.
In the same way you go about cultivating your parched earth
You will sow, reap, milk your cows, clean coops and stables!
In days to come as well as in the present day
People will speak of you with respect,
Yes, with true recognition and with fear and trepidation!
My heart trembles as I remember all the difficulty,
All the exalted significance of the task imposed on your shoulders
By the Almighty God, dear sons and brothers!
The broken bridge of eternity (one end of it is in the past,
And the other—in the mystic clouds of the future,
But the wrenched arches are suspended limply
Over the tempestuous present,
Which seeks to swallow them and undermine the foundations)—
This everlasting bridge which was broken,
Will be mended by you with mighty effort,
With superhuman strength you will raise the chariot of redemption
Which was caught between narrow straits of adversity,
And you will set it on the main highway . . .
You will not do this amid lavish praises accorded to pathfinders in
a desert,
Not with any of the fanfare given to an admired, privileged few,
Not with the intoxicating enthusiasm of the pioneer,
Not with the self-esteem of the martyr sacrificing his life—
But with the simple feeling of everyday peasant folk,
The feeling of 'this is my own, my native land' present in a
generation
Which built up the land with bare hands,
A feeling as natural to you as your heart beat, as the circulation of
the blood in your veins!
Thus a bird guards its nest, and thus the oak is held by its roots
In the soil, should a storm arise to uproot it;
The four-square feet of earth in which it was planted

Has become a house of life for the tree,
It derives its strength from this earth and it has no other place to live but that . . .
It is true that to those who left Egypt, the land of their bondage,
There still remained a path to return,
And in days of trouble and helplessness,
They thought sinful thoughts,
Some rebelled openly and muttered:
'Let us turn around and go back!'
And now, to their descendants—to you, dear Gideons—
The paths to the house of bondage are closed,
In fact they are not even known to you—you children from nowhere!"

And Judah smiled to himself in the dark,
He even waved his right hand in the air
As if to give a loving pat on the back to the dear and blessed boys. . . .
As he did so, his hand touched the gun leaning on the rock,
Whereupon he hurried to get up, take his weapon,
And continue his rounds as a night watchman. . . .

SLEEPLESSNESS

(Excerpts)

What joy I have in wandering on waste seashores
When mighty breakers roar and rage,
Oh how my heart exults when sea-expanses heave,
A groaning in their swell and fall. . . .

A stranger I am upon this Earth, a foreigner for aye,
I measured all her boundaries, but no place I call my own.
Where may the searcher be, will sound and read my thought?
Where the interpreter, will know my dream's behest?

Here my moan is sad and feeble,
There I roar the killer's roar;
When in night on prairies frozen
Swift I run with wolves of darkness,
There I roar the killer's roar.

Jacob Fichman, Lyric Poet

Jacob Fichman, poet, critic, editor and pedagogue, was born in 1881 in Belczi, Bessarabia, Russia. Until 1912 he worked as an editor and teacher in various parts of the Russian Empire, in Warsaw, Kishinev, Liova and Vilna.

In 1912 he arrived in Palestine and was among the founders of the Hebrew Writers Association. At various times he was the editor of *Moledet, Maabarot, Hashiloah, Moznayim* and other literary journals.

He began writing poetry at an early age and in 1911 published his first collection, *Givolim.* His later volumes of poems include *Aravah,* 1922; *Yemei Shemesh,* 1934; *Tzelalim al Sadot,* 1935; *Aviv Beshomron,* 1943; *Peat Sadeh,* 1943; *Demuyot Kedumim,* 1948. Some of the most exquisite sonnets in modern Hebrew are to be found in these poems. He also translated Hebbel's drama, *Herod and Mariamne* and many poems.

He is equally distinguished as a literary critic. His studies of a number of Biblical books and of a series of modern Hebrew writers from Moses Hayyim Luzzatto to Bialik are outstanding in their field. His essays in literary criticism are *Anshei Besora,* 1938; *Shirat Bialik,* 1946; *Amat Habinyan,* 1951; and *Ruhot Menagnot,* 1952.

As a former teacher in Jewish normal schools in Warsaw, Odessa and Tel Aviv he filled the gap of much needed Hebrew textbooks by publishing such volumes as *Perakim Rishonim, Shivilim, Lashon Vasefer* in five volumes, *Sefer Haadam* and *Maanit.*

He was a frequent contributor to the daily and literary press in Israel. He was honored with the Aharonivitz Prize in 1941, the Bialik Prize in 1943 and 1954 and the Ussishkin Prize in 1946. He died in Tel Aviv on May 18, 1958.

I

Jacob Fichman has made a double contribution to modern Hebrew letters. He has given us delicate and tender lyrics, as well as refined, lucid prose.

These two forms of expression represent a single aspect of Fichman's genius, deriving their inspiration from the same source. In each is foreshadowed both the art of the discerning poet and the lyric critic. Such a combination of powers is indeed rare.

For there are great poets who lose much of their talents when they turn to prose. And, of course, one need not speak of masters of prose who find themselves helpless when they attempt poetry. But Fichman is one of the few whose abilities are magnificently displayed in both poetry and prose. His prose, especially his literary criticism, is imbued with a poetic spirit. And he has refined modern Hebrew prose, giving it an inner musical quality. He has broadened its color range and deepened its tones. An essay by Fichman is as rhythmic as a poem.

His poem *Ruth* shimmers with an idyllic beauty. Yet this is not the only Biblical theme he has graced with spiritual tenderness, subtle observation and original manner of expression. In *The Sorrow of David, Joab* and *Samson in Gaza* as well as in his essays on *Job, Ecclesiastes* and *The Song of Songs,* Fichman sparkles at his alluring best, reflecting the qualities of tenderness of spirit, acuteness of observation and poetic expression.

Yet it must not be mistakenly supposed that there is no difference between Fichman's poetry and his prose. For were there no difference, there would be no need for the two modes of expression. It would have been enough for the man to be poet and no more. But Fichman's prose, close though it be to his poetry has a mission all its own and, therefore, a right to a separate existence.

In poetry his talent is best expressed in his short lyrical works. They rise above the golden field of his poetry like swaying stalks of grain, charming in their delicacy. With their slow and gentle movement, they play upon the heart-strings of the poet and reader alike. In the vertical line of the slender stalk, the poet can perceive the never-ending circle of nature's beauty. The shadow passing over the field is enough to give him the feeling of nature's mystery. The lonely butterfly, quickly flitting by, is sufficient to stir up a sadness within him and to fill his being with deep yearning.

For the birth of a poem one lone crystalline drop suffices.

But not so with prose. Its scope is greater; its horizons broader. Therefore, it permits of greater freedom. But with its greater freedom, it imposes limitations. Prose is structurally more complicated. It requires another mood, a different kind of effort. It demands the sobriety of the craftsman, the skill of the architect. And these are the qualities displayed by Fichman in his essays. For although he has written several major biblical epics, yet it is still true that in poetry Fichman has shown his greatest ability in his briefer lyrical poems. While in prose, his longer works are his best efforts.

And another distinction. In his poetry he is most successful with description of nature and moods. There are neither persons nor events and there is almost no room for "the other." For even in his Biblical poems the historical personalities are the extensions of his own personality. For it is the soul of the poet himself that sings forth from out of a dream-like world, a world marked by landscape, whiteness and sadness.

But in his prose, particularly in his critical works, he seeks to penetrate to the soul of his fellow-man, to feel the pulse of a kindred spirit. Yet here too, in prose the essential character of Fichman the poet holds sway. If people appear more gentle when touched by his magic wand, it is to be expected; for a delicate poet-critic reveals the image of people as the poet sees it. Yet, as a critic, he strives for an objective insight into the writer he discusses.

In his critical essays Fichman always searches for the mystery and power of the creative personality. External circumstances do not interest him. He is not concerned with social factors. He looks for the inner quality, the hidden forces of the soul, the distinctive aspects of personality. For him the principal matter is that which separates the individual from society rather than that which unites the two.

In his poetry Fichman becomes one with the world through the medium of nature. In his prose he becomes one with man through the union of the human soul.

II

Fichman is the poet of landscapes. In the introduction to his book, *Yemei Shemesh* (*Sunlit Days*) he states, "I have always considered the landscape to be the foundation and the essence of the world." His book, *Shadows on the Fields,* is full of the beauty and the sadness of the landscape.

What is the character of Fichman's landscapes? Let him speak for himself:

"So has the gentle autumn landscape allured me,
The yearning it created whitening my heart;
Like sad butterflies, leaves strayed
And sorrow rose, and the heart understood it not."

This stanza, so Fichman-like, serves as an example of the main elements of his landscape artistry. *Gentleness, autumn, allure, yearning, whiteness, sad butterflies, stray leaves*—and you feel a sadness rising and the heart understands it not. Of all the emotions that attract him, he is drawn most after tenderness. Of all the seasons he likes best the autumn, with his next favorite the winter. Of all the colors, he prefers white, the second best, blue. Of the moods of the spirit, sadness and yearning; in the world of sound, muteness and stillness. Of winged creatures, birds and butterflies.

If this does not suffice to grasp the threads with which he weaves his poetry one need only turn the pages of his books and, like doves from a thicket, there come flying forth expressions and word-pictures such as these: *mists of mystery, shadows of magic, moonlight visions, deep canopy of night, anticipation, mysterious shore, singing springs, forgiveness, longing of the soul, perplexing riddle, gracious hand, chill and desolate evening breeze, spots of light, feminine charm, secret joy, sorrowful beauty, sheaves and stalks, weariness of brooding steppes, crystal drops of grace and sadness, fields pure in their stillness, silver song, nets of wondering light, white sadness, pallid fog.* All this is but a minute portion of the treasure trove of color and sound in Fichman's poetry but enough to introduce us to his world and to catch something of his outlook. He likes the incorporeal and the intangible, the not easily grasped and the constantly mobile.

Such material in other hands could easily have become too evanescent. But Fichman seemingly was created for this type of writing and his forms are exactly appropriate for the material.

He has been accused, by some, of monotony. Such an accusation, on the surface, sounds plausible—but only on the surface. For while it is true that Fichman has one basic tone, it is not true that he constantly repeats it without variation to the point of monotony. On the contrary, one is constantly surprised by his ability to be ever fresh and new in what seems to be such a still and static world. Many of his poems have similar titles: *The Blessing of Summer, Summer Night, Summer's Last Storm,* or *Early Fall, Fall, Singing Autumn,* and too, *On a Winter's Eve, A Winter's Journey, Winter, Winter's End,* and *Snow Fell This Night,* but there is a new approach and fresh emotion in every poem, just as each summer storm is different from the preceding and every snowfall is a wonderful new creation in itself.

Of course, he accomplishes much by a skillful use of the Hebrew language, which is his loyal servant even as he is its loving master. With its many nuances and shades of meaning it unfolds something new in every additional poem albeit the theme is the same. But it is not a matter of language alone, but also a keen perception of the manner in which nature reveals itself. To Fichman landscape is the "seed of the world." And what does the seed do? It gives rise to flowers and fruit which, in turn, produce seed that will give birth to new flowers and fruit. Thus the cycle never ends. For this is nature's way—not repetition, but renewal, not monotony, but growth. And this is the way of the poet.

III

Of all the nature-images, the flower-stalk predominates in Fichman's poetry. His first book of poems is called *Givolim* (*Stalks*). Years later also, when his talents had fully ripened and "shadows had fallen upon the fields," the stalk is still seen nodding sorrowfully in the golden fields of his verse.

Thus, he whispers in *The Heart's Prayer*:

"Watch over me!
I am but a trembling stalk,
Alone, exposed to the winds,
My head bends low
Under the weight of dreams,
Caressing the earth
Like a bush at night."

The stalk rules over his field. But this image does not sate him. He seeks out others to satisfy his poetic craving, and such as *delicate sun-struck plant, dewy grass, calm waves,* until finally he kneels *like an ear of grain, heavy with happiness.* For together with his self-identification with the slender stalk, there comes the mood of calm surrender.

Fichman's most complete and rounded poems are those in which he describes moments of transition between day and night, light and darkness, storm and calm. At such moments it is as though the world stops in its course to look at itself in puzzlement. It is a time of wonder, a moment of suspension and "in an instant the earth vanishes as though it were no more and there remains only a white curtain overcast with soft light."

In his vision of morning and noon he sees "flocks of delicate white clouds" hanging like "drifts of pure snow after a storm." No one knows whence they came and whither they are going but it is evident that "they are absorbed in themselves, they shine for themselves, and they drink avidly of the glowing light."

At night the "wilting grass exudes its incense" and gay stars move to and fro between the clouds. Swayed by mystery, the poet follows the night and walks beside it. He can simply step out of the night and walk beside it, even as he can step out of the world and surrender all claim to it. "When not a ripple bestirs the lakes, when the world itself is held captive by its own stillness," he is capable of leaving reality and regarding the world as an observer from above. At night he does not raise his eyes towards the heavens, but his hair "feels the swift running of the cloud." At midnight the slumbering grasses bend their little heads, hands under cheeks, and dream.

"In a narrow field a weary traveler kneels.
In the meadow a horse raises its head in wonder."

"At that moment a man stretches out his hand over the earth and all moving creatures come to a halt . . . And a strange mysterious light plays upon the darkened earth."

What force stirs the poet's soul? Stillness. Of it he says,

"It is wonderful; it stirs my soul so."

In another poem, he says, "Here is the boundary of the world, beyond it no one can go."

He then invokes the evening wind bringing rest from afar.

"Evening wind of kindly hand,
Here stay and rest awhile!
Rests each bush, rests each tree,
Rests the rowboat by the shore."

Is there any wonder then, that his favorite counsel is *Rest?*

Even after Fichman had come to Palestine, and had burst forth in songs of exultation to the new land and its beauty, he still cautioned, "Let us walk carefully and in silence" and "let us not crush its tender plants." And he added, "Nay, I will not raise my voice."

"I shall hearken only to the blossoming of the blue valley,
Tranquil and white is my path."

IV

Tranquil and white is his path. Tranquillity is sensed in all his poems, a tranquillity arising from surrender to fate. In *Before the Storm,* the storm has not yet broken; only the grass trembles, only the clouds move swiftly. Then the earth quickly bows "under the shadow and surrenders." Again in *Tishri*—"the earth in its surrender justifies the divine decree." And even before any portent of storm, while "the winds are still far off and no cloud plans evil against another, the earth hastens to stretch itself out in calm submission." What great happiness there is in this world of Fichman—to be still and to surrender.

Not only is the world itself so. So too is "the seed"—the landscape—and so too is the soul of the landscape—the spirit of the poet. Both the evil and the good he accepts with resignation. Even when, in spite of himself, the flame of good fortune shoots high, like a brilliant comet through his sky, he sings,

"I bowed my head before it . . . Come!
To my soul I softly said . . . Bless its coming!"

For such moods of stillness and resignation, what colors could be better than white and blue? And indeed, these are the colors in Fichman's poetry.

"Like a blue corn-flower amid the white grain," does Ruth appear. In her image Fichman concentrates all the beauty and tenderness of his poetry. A strange, white, delicate bud blooms on his path through life. He knows whence comes this whiteness: "It is the sorrow of the world, that has become a restful melody of vision; it is the whiteness of the field that remains when the blossom of happiness has vanished."

This then is his soul's song—sorrow rather than joy, the whiteness of resignation rather than the struggle for happiness. Through this whiteness, interwoven with threads of blue, he sees everything—himself, his world, his love and his visions.

"Between me and thee rests a world of virgin soil;
Like God's flower, eternal whitness blooms within
its bound."

To Fichman, autumn sings "a white song," and the almond tree appears to him in a snowy "vision of white." Bluish shadows steal between the white clouds. In the springtime he sees bluish-white flowers. In the Jordan Valley he feels "a white drought." Upon the tomb of Rachel, that "gleams like a white altar," "night falls—a night heavy with the dew of grace and the blueness of the stars." "The shadow of a white happiness" follows him throughout life.

These white and blue effects manifest themselves in all of Fichman's poems, even when not specifically mentioned. They spring from within himself and merge with the deep harmony of his soul's song. They are its essence and its color.

V

For a color so gentle and plaintive, the appropriate mood is sadness. For the poet there is no greater joy than sorrow. There is hardly a poem of his which does not contain something of sorrow. As early as 1901, the first year of his creative work, he called sorrow the only full cup offered by life. He invoked the spring of his sorrow, to sing out, "If a brother dies, if a friend betrays, your waters, as always, shall never fail." He finally calls sorrow "the most precious rose of the world." It is this rose which blossoms on all his paths and fills his heart with happiness and song. For poets know many kinds of happiness.

There is the poet who loves life without questioning it. He loves it and enjoys it; he sings and exults. He blossoms with the springtime and ripens with the summer. He rejoices in the revelation of his power. He uproots mountains and becomes intoxicated with light. From morning to morning he lives with gusto. All the rainbow's colors are reflected in his life and in his poetry. His happiness lies in being happy.

Another poet loves passion and blood, conflict and storm, crime and punishment. Such a poet chooses red as his color and the strong arm, the climb and the fall. His happiness lies in his unhappiness.

Still another poet despairs of everything. He sees only darkness and evil. The sun is hidden from him; love denies him its joys. He has no friend or lover; he knows no dawn and no hope. Such a poet chooses black as his color. His unhappiness lies in his happiness. And this is not all.

For there is another poet, who is neither bold nor daring. He does not uproot mountains, neither is he exultant. He is neither bellicose nor arrogant. But neither does he dwell in darkness nor does he see only gloom. He certainly knows no despair nor is his goal the abyss. He drinks not from the cup of bitterness, but from the cup of sweet melancholy. He is fond of gentle and pure landscapes. He is an unencumbered wanderer over the earth's fields, absorbing their hidden beauty. In the autumn he sees the soul of the world revealing itself. The bluish-white hue soothes his eye and softens his mood. He seizes upon phenomena in their purity. His happiness lies in his melancholy. And such a poet is Fichman.

He loves a world bathed in light; he loves the golden autumn fields and the sadness in which they are wrapped. When the charm of autumn overcomes him, he asks,

"What is the meaning of this sweet trembling
Which has again so suddenly trapped your heart?"

The question is enough; for it contains its own answer.

Sadly murmuring rain at night—that is to Fichman's taste. And in the city he sees sad forlorn reflections. "What of the forest? It is an empty hall with sad gold in its bosom." At sundown "the sorrows of the world slumber"; the evening wind comes "with the mystery of night and its sad dreams" and " 'neath its wind there is secret sorrow." "And the heart's melancholy quietly sings at sundown." And, "As I have grown, my sorrow has grown with me."

From this mood comes a love for longing itself, and the desire for separation. Because Fichman wants to long for something, he loves to wander, since only from a distance can one long for dear ones left at home. "There is no sweeter pain on earth than the pain of parting." Therefore, he cherishes loneliness. He isolates himself in his own world and weaves the golden web of his wandering song. But "at night, when the wide world cries out for help, my song is left deserted, like a flower clinging to the heart of my beloved."

When Fichman sees the world in its bareness, he is not saddened. A great joy seizes him, for

"From all this space robbed of its veil of mystery,
Even from this empty falling of the leaves,
The glory of existence will not deceive me."

This glory of existence that will not deceive him is not that glory of which many dream. Perhaps some will not see it, feel it or understand it; it is so delicate and insubstantial. Yet for Fichman it is the greatest reality of all. He clings to it, seeking in it his salvation. Ruth, who often serves as a vehicle for Fichman's ideas, says,

"He who forsakes his sadness
May lose the noblest visions of his life."

But Fichman never forsakes his sadness, for a poet cannot afford to lose the noblest visions of his life.

VI

In clear calm fields, sown with slender stalks, in a world full of shadows, and covered with haze, in a maze of wondrous light and amidst the singing of hidden fountains—what shape does love assume?

To the poet it assumes the same white tender form in which he sees all phenomena embodied. Even at the most trying moments, when "the heart which has forgotten youth cries out again for friendship" and "the very stone in the road cries out for love," even then the poet remains true to himself.

Day in and day out the poet goes to the home of the girl he loves. A word trembles upon his lips, but "the word is not yet said and who knows if it ever will be spoken?" Each day in the secret garden of his heart the blossom of his love first grows red then pale and yet "Day in and day out I go to your home, and no inkling of it has reached you."

He describes himself wandering in *Those Nights* through the throbbing city streets and remembering that somewhere there is a lonely house enclosed by a garden. In the house there is a white room (Fichman's habitual *white*) and from its window his love peers into the silent darkness. She awaits the storm and fears its coming.

As for him—what is his desire?

> "In these hot and silent nights, pregnant with storm,
> I would fan your burning forehead with my song.
> I would waft a breeze of rest and vision,
> Then secretly return to my distant mountains."

In *Memories* Fichman lives with the memory of the moment when, at the setting of a summer's sun, she (his beloved) came from out of nowhere toward him. "With the innocence of a maiden and the charm of a child, eyes frightened and shy," she stood confused, smiling at "this unexpected encounter, this first miraculous occurrence, and without a word, lowered her eyes." All the splendor of her charm smote his heart and, overwhelmed by happiness, the words all tender and passionate that he had rehearsed to himself during sleepless nights were suddenly forgotten. He stood before her speechless. Although he knows that she will never be his young wife, the mother of his child, the light of his habitation, it matters not. He will carry forever her memory with him to faraway lands.

Memory of distant things is as potent as vision of the nearby. Indeed he is satisfied with the image of the faraway that is revealed to him.

And in one of his most delicately fashioned love poems, *Yearnings,* he declares,

> "It is a great happiness to know
> That thou art mine, though the day be distant.
> There is but one wonder hour cometh on a day,
> And when it cometh, it partaketh not of normal
> life, so alien to it."

The poet can time the coming of his happy hour, but his heart trembles no longer at its approach.

> "In my room, unseen, thou wilt appear,
> Thy soft hand wilt thou place
> Over my eyes and heart,
> When thou art not here,
> Thou art wholly with me, my dear."

In this and other like poems, the essence of Fichman's poetry is revealed most clearly. Thus in another poem, he says, "The farther I go from thee, O maiden, the more clearly doth thine image shine within me."

The love of the flesh and the throbbing of the blood are not the messengers of his love; it is the sweet veiled premonition of love to come, the image perceived as purified from every tittle of sin. So, he speaks clearly in his poem, *Allusion:*

> "Now that thou hast granted me
> The gold of thy purity,
> The dear mysteries of thy youth,
> Those beloved treasuries of blessing
> Whose magic my boldest dream dared not divine,
> Today are all mine.
> But even now I read in thee
> A secret sign

Of greater days and moments yet to come.
Thou art, all of thee, a portent until now
Of future happiness yet to come."

Thus, in woman as well as in landscape, Fichman seeks and finds the clear and the pure, the inner grace and the *white* happiness, the hidden charm and the sad glory. For in his love songs more splendidly than elsewhere there shines forth the strange and wonderful light of his poetry—the poetry of one enchanted by the calm beauty and autumn-like sadness poured out over the universe.

SAMARIAN NIGHTS

Beyond the cypress unexpected drifts
A ripened moon; kissing the face of homes
All faded with its warming gold, it wafts
The ruddy grass and stirs the crests of palms.

Among the sheaves across the threshing-floor,
The night rests blue and calm, we at its edge;
Now drowsy scents that from the grain-ears soar
Our ripe, contented universe submerge.

Yet midnight's splendour, wonder-struck and red
Deep in our cells and blood is now inbred,
And every sparkling grape stunned by the moon.

Each finely woven bush, each reed, how slight,
Will be remembered after years with gloom,
Mysterious as a primeval night.

SAMARIA

The sea at midnight moves sometimes, rock-pine
With boughs aquiver answering its address;
Yet on the slope there's scent of ripened grain,
And silence shuts the garden's duskiness.

Far floats the moon and whitens olive-leaf
With wonders of reflection—grass, stone
While taciturn, the heavy carobs weave
Their mingled shadows, aloof, alone.

How fair thou art, Samaria, when light
Pours through each garden entry, overwhelms
The tiny grass and cypress with wide streams.

Then give me day's soft soil all furrowed bright,
Where every kernel in the sun drips warmth
Forgotten to the burning heart of earth.

HARVEST

A time to sing, a time to gather. Day
By day the wind trails joyously along.
So take a fork and scatter off its prong
Dead leaves accumulated on your way.

The dreary heap, go onward spray,
And down the evening road, tread upright, strong!
Sing with your fullest voice the marching-song
And gather on and never cease or stay.

Great is the day of harvest. Let your eye
Be ever clear. Not all that grows up high
And blossoms fair is homeward brought to store.

Look down its dusky bosom. All amass
In which the summer burning gold did pour.
And thus preserve your goodness. Be stronger thus.

HERMON

Beyond all tracks and solitary, ripped
From the terrestrial core, your crest shows white,
With chequered wreaths bedecked, strange as old script,
With coloured shawls, by giant hands bedight.

Ungrounded, as the wind's suspended lair,
Hermon, you quake on earth's unfathomed deep,
And through your merry veins send with a roar
A thousand noisy streams down slope and steep.

The ways of earth are sorrowful. And heat
Heavy with many days of vapour laves
The peaks invisible from our retreat.

Yet when the sight is clear, past the world's dust,
We who distinguish in affluent waves
Your limpid presence, never more are lost.

IN PRAISE OF JERUSALEM

You are the capital city. Your name has the loftiest sound.
There is no kingdom to which you can be compared,
Nor is there any mountain soil as bright as yours,
Nor splendor on the earth that can dim you
For you are glad with secrets, holding within you ease;
You are the rock to which all precious things have clung,
And those who trample you will seek to hold you fast.
Whoever fires upon you
Will kneel down in your ashes, begging forgiveness;
For you contain both peace and the angry roar of the lion.
When a night of terror descends upon the heads of your people,
Both blossoming and compassion are in you.

You have been judged in fire again, oh city of hills!
But this time it was not the powerful boots of Rome
That mounted your sacred walls;
It was with heartless insolence that you were conspired against
And your gates were opened to the enemy.
You were sold as a merchant sells his wares,
From an exalted seat,
And the eyes of the nations froze,
Watching and keeping still;
And no one raised his voice at the impiety
To see a people robbed of its last majesty.

But you shall be the holy of holies forever, the loftiest place.
For you were built for your people; your people built you up:
For you the wakeful heart breathed out laments
Through centuries of nights;
Nor has your crown been darkened, nor your voice been stilled,
Despite the worlds that rose, the worlds that were destroyed,
And underneath your ruins and your grief
An unimagined beauty lies concealed.

IN THE OLD CITY

In the white of noon-day's brightness the city seems blotted out.
Silence. Heat. Forgetfulness. Only a pigeon-flock plunges
into woven tree-tops, noisily sowing yearning, and a palm-tree,
like a green remnant of life, floats in the heart of the blue.

And see, in the heat's heart, like a wave of wonders, movement,
and the whole City is borne, overflows, and seems to tremble,
as if something is clasping every crumbling tier of stones,
and even every ruin is caught by the web of a hidden festival.

There is glory of much-meaning in the whitening City of God,
and the moment it is revealed, this grief sheds its grace
on the heart, like a secret gift, like reward and recompense.

Not mine to explain. Not for me. Unknowing did God
lead me into this world, and his cup of sad enchantments
hold out to me, and it thus far still sounds and is flowing.

RUTH

(An excerpt)

Upon these fields of night, serenely pure,
My feet tread lightly and securely, as if upon
A soil most native, sacred from the day
When first my star began to guide me hither.
How friendly are the wings of night! My eye
Distinguishes each bush, each rock, each clod,
As if a good and loyal hand were leading me.
Few are the days I have been here;
Yet like a grain of seed, untouched by frost,
This land so strange absorbed me lovingly . . .
As if all that I knew and loved, from days
Of childhood rich in mystery till now,
Had ever sought but this one land of peace
Where my soul would be revealed to me
And where God's face would whitely glimmer forth.

REMEMBER, MY HEART

Remember, my heart, that besides the beasts of prey,
Who vision the fall of man,
There still are millions of hearts that love,
That struggle in the surging billows of blood;
    Remember those who have joined battle for man.

Remember, my heart, all those who stand
In the flames facing the foul foe—
All who have rushed forth to save those that may perish,
All whose heart has not remained silent in the dark;
    Remember those who have joined battle for man.

Remember those who trudge in the scorching sands,
Who leave their traces in deep, heavy waters;
For the noble hearts that still are there
Remembering them—let us pray for them.
    They are the ones who have joined battle for man.

Sh. Shalom, Mystic Poet

Shalom, best known for his poetry, although he has also written dramas, novels and short stories, was born in 1904 in Parczew in the Galician part of Poland, the scion of a well known Hassidic rabbinical dynasty. His name originally was Shalom Joseph Shapira. It later became Shalom Joseph Shalom, but his literary pseudonym is simply *Shin* (the Hebrew letter *sh*) Shalom.

He fled to Vienna with his family upon the outbreak of the First World War. In Vienna he attended the local *gymnasium* and was active in the Zionist and Hebrew movements. He began to write poetry in German at the age of thirteen.

He settled in Palestine in 1922 in Kfar Hassidim. Later he attended the Mizrachi Teachers Seminary in Jerusalem and then taught in that city, in Rosh Pina and Hadera. He continued his education at the University of Erlangen in 1930 and 1931 and so was a witness to the rise of Hitlerism.

His works include the following: *Belev Haolam,* 1927; *Mi?* 1930; *Yoman Bagalil,* 1932; *Mitokh Halahavot,* 1936; *Shirim,* 1939; *Safer Hashirim Vehasonnetot,* 1940; *Panim el Panim,* 1941; *Hayad Hashniah,* 1942, a novel; *Shabbat Haolam,* 1944-45; *Olam Belehavot; Ilan Bakhut,* 1946; *Shirim,* 1949; *Adama Ushmei Shamayim,* 1949; *Haner Lo Khavah,* 1952; libretto for the opera, *Dan Hashomer; Shaul Melekh Yisrael* and *Adama,* both plays; *Hayinu Keholmim,* 1954; *Mivhar Shirim,* 1956; *Bein Tekhelet Lelavan,* 1957; *Shirei Komemut Yisrael,* 1958. A number of his poems have been set to music. He displayed his great love for children in his book of children's poems, *Hag Li Hayom.*

He was awarded the Bialik Prize for *Panim el Panim* in 1941, the Brenner Prize for *Shirim* in 1949 and the Tchernikhovsky Prize for his translation of Shakespeare's sonnets. He now makes his home in Haifa.

I

Shalom, who uses the Hebrew letter, *Shin,* as a first name, is one of the greatest of contemporary Hebrew poets. His work has gained a foremost place in modern Hebrew literature because of its never-ending freshness and dynamism. From his early adolescent poems to the later more mature ones, there is evident a sense of blessed unrest and fertile discontent which lend a mood of youthfulness to his work, the *wanderlust* of a nomad eager for new worlds.

Shalom's path is beset by obstacles and hindrances, the path of a man caught between two worlds that differ from each other in form as well as in content.

On the realistic, conscious level, on the plane of autobiography, his is the path of the modern, bewildered Jew, uprooted from the dying Eastern European world, who is tossed hither and yon until he reaches the shores of the homeland, Israel. There he again experiences the transformation and the terrors that have pursued him from childhood until, finally, he himself attains that which his people have achieved in its renewal of its life on its own soil.

But in addition to this level there is also another. There can be spiritual as well as physical odysseys. The real world in which the poet lives and suffers is but a half-world and a reflection of another world of mystery and imagination. (The Hebrew word for "world" is closely related to "mystery.") This is the "other world" in which the spirits of poets dwell and weave their fabric to clothe the body of reality on earth.

Wandering between these two worlds, Shalom takes his readers along into the mysterious labyrinth of sensations and experiences of which only echoes and shadows can be grasped. He is blessed with a talent for coining new poetic images that possess external beauty and evoke an inner echoing response.

His well-formed stanzas have a musical quality all their own, but the reader soon realizes that they contain more than the momentary delight that one derives from the reading of beautiful lines. Beneath the obvious there lurk allusions and implied images, the true essence of his poetry.

His autobiographical poem he named *On ben Pele* thus, by association, evoking the symbolism of *On ben Pele,* one of the desert rebels against Moses. This clever and meaningful name points to the contemporary rebellion taking place in the wilderness characteristic of the world in which we live. Even more does it symbolize the personality of the poet and his conception of his own poetry. He thirsts for *On,* "strength," the virile strength of youth, but he recognizes that such strength is the product, the *ben,* the "son," of *Pele,* of "mystery," of One who is lofty and mysterious.

The name also symbolizes the two aspects of human personality, the real and the imaginary. *On,* "strength," represents the real "I," while *Pele,* "mystery," stands for the imaginary "I." The real always appears as *I,* whereas the other aspect, the imaginary, is referred to in the third person since it continues to exist outside the real first person and transcends it.

Hence the duality in everything Shalom visualizes. The entire world is dual—a world of reality and a world of imagination, this world and the other world, "other" not in the sense of time but in dimension. And since the world is dual, man is particularly so. There is the physical, material, visible person as well as the other mysterious existence of the same person, which can be discerned only by the eye of the poet as he wanders in the borderland between the two worlds of reality and imagination. The first is subject to the laws of human logic and reason because it is part of society, bearing its burden and participating in its struggles. But the second, unreal personality is free from the laws of logic. It is a metaphysical being wandering through the various planes of existence and seeking poetic-philosophic expression on the part of people who can live in two worlds, who build their life out of the fibers of thought and the strands of poetry.

This question of the "I" occupies a central place in Shalom's poetry. Not only does it clarify his own place in the world, but its definition provides the clue to the world itself, the world in which he and his generation live. Indeed, the first series of poems with which his collected poetry begins is entitled *Who?* the implication being, "Who am I?"

The answer to this question given in the various poems presents the picture of a personality split into two or even more phases that at times are integrated and at other times contend with each other. One phase lives in the present, another in the past, or else they are separated in space or in degree of awareness. A group of poems is entitled *Camps,* for different camps war in his soul. He rises in the morning yet lights a candle in bright daylight because while one part of him lives by daylight another part is still in the dark of night. "I was not asleep, I was awake–yet about me was the dream." When asked concerning the reason for the candle at daylight, he replies, "My blood cries out, but about me is the dream."

As a teacher, he goes to his classes to teach Torah to Jewish children. The bell rings. But is it the school bell that he hears ringing? Outwardly that is so. Schools have bells and they ring to summon the pupils to their classes. But the poet of the split personality hears other bells, sirens announcing fires and floods, and village bells from the far away past of childhood. The two individuals within the same person respond to different bells that are removed in time and space, the bell calling children to class and the mysterious bell of the second "I," that tolls the alarm over the coming of "legions of turbulent fate, the clarion call of destruction."

With one phase of his personality he sees a child in the fifth row striking his classmate, while his alter ego flees the burning forest where his dream carries him away from "the world with its hungry crying for bread." A little girl in the class takes fright and begins to cry. But in actuality it is not only a little girl crying. Somewhere among these rows before him another sits weeping, a mother mourning the loss of her sons. One part of the poet sees the child, the rest of him beholds the mourner.

The teacher is tossed and torn between two worlds. The class is unruly. "Why all the noise, children, why do you shout to no purpose? Open the book and read in it: 'In the beginning God created heaven and earth and the earth was unformed and void' and man wanders still between the unformed and the void and wonders, 'When will my right time come? To what end do I travail? Where am I in this world?' "

The two halves of his being are thus closely intertwined, like the ram's horns caught in the bushes in the Biblical story of the sacrifice of Isaac. But in his wonderful ballad, *Help!* in which are heard echoes from Dante, this split personality is presented in another and unique manner. Through the door of his house bursts the cry, "Help!" He is deeply stirred by the call, in fact the whole world seems to be aroused by it. Even the furniture which hitherto had stood in inanimate indifference now asks:

"How can you sit here with arms folded?
While there, somewhere in darkness unknown,
Whether in the heavens above or the depths beneath
A soul perishes, a soul drowns,
And with last breath, moans, calls, Help!"

The bewildered man goes out to the rescue. But rescue whom? The drowning, perishing soul, calling for help. But where find it? Its location is unknown. The cry came both from above and below. Nevertheless, driven by the lash of compassion, ready for darkness, tempest and destruction, he pursues the fleeing cry.

"He searches, pursues every object, each wind,
Presses his ear against the loose sand.
Disregarding every hurt, overlooking fatigue,
Losing sight of time, of the minutes and hours:
'Be you human or God, woman or man—
O voice, where are you, amidst such pain calling?'
From above, from below, from every direction
Comes the answer from that soul, its hope gone: 'Help!' "

He madly runs after the cry until he reaches the sea and, paying no attention to the water, "he plunges into its turbulent blackness until his knees." Soon the waves reach his neck. Only then, as he begins to sink like a heavy stone in the water does it come to him. He knows now. He understands. It is his own soul that is perishing, his own soul that has called to him out of its straits for help. And the cry for help is muffled only by the waters as he sinks into its depths.

With such poetic imagery, so powerfully moving, does Shalom give sharp and lucid expression to the sense of dualism that grips him.

II

Even greater evidence of this dualism is found in his volume, *Panim el Panim (Face to Face)*, which treats of the mystery of life and death. The first mentioned volume begins with the question, "Who?" this one with the word, "He." "He" is but another manifestation of the "I." It is but the "I" divested of matter, a concretization of his philosophical mysticism. In the words of the poet:

"Between me and the world stands one who waits,
Among the sea's mist he stands or in the forest,
And yet like a brother is he unto me.
Within me I hear constantly the beating of his heart.
His step accompanies mine like a tune from a world
forgotten.
I want to speak to him—but I lack the language.
I want to touch him—but my hand cannot reach him.
Only a great silence spreads its wing over us,
And I know that he is near,
As near as is a tree to its shadow."

Such a poetic perception would be appropriate for a religious man speaking of his God. The "He" of Shalom would be more easily understandable as that "He," lofty and awe-inspiring, before whom man kneels in the torment of his searching, of his not knowing. And indeed in some stanzas there are truly prayerful overtones: "All the years of my life, to Him shall I direct my heart"; and "My strength, my worry, my secret, I shall offer to Him upon the inner altar"; again, "I write a psalm for one who trembles, a prayer in mystic allusion." But the mysterious "He" of the poet does not attain the level of Godhead but remains the abstract image of the split personality which had succeeded in detaching himself from the earth of reality without reaching the heavens of divinity. "I am—He; And He is—also you." Thus Shalom tries to define the identity of his "he."

This is the most involved part of Shalom's poetry, which is otherwise so clear and vivid. Generally, his language is richly descriptive and can endow any image with life. But in his book *Face to Face* he transcends the real world and walks in thick darkness. Thus he testifies in his poem, *Let There Be Man:*

"A ladder I found in my wanderings at night
Amidst emptiness never-ending.
I climbed it—and the bright skies darkened,
Lost were the heavens and lost the earth—
And I became heaven and earth."

But he was still pursued by the chief problem of his existence—"Who am I?" In many poems he tries to answer this question and the answers vary: "I am the child that was born." And "I am the train going through the forest of my childhood." "I am the cry on the sea." "I am the star breaking its heart for the night that is gone." "I am the blood spurting from the wound." Also, "the wave that sees, that sinks." And "brothers am I" (several in one). And even more revealing, "I know that I went away from myself to myself."

Shalom was aware of the vagueness of this chapter of his work and in the introduction to *Face to Face* he apologizes for it, trying to explain some of the more mystifying passages in the following manner: "Is there a gate of mystery to the sobriety of existence? Perhaps. We cling too much to the obvious. We believe too hard in the tangible without realizing that it is but a momentary reflection of eternity, the light of a remote star, the mirror of a mysterious existence, an external symbol of what goes on within. My poem tries to penetrate to that which is suggested within. Such is the way of the Jew of the twentieth century; only from within can he be understood. Everything that has happened to him is but a symbol and is described as such."

Then he proceeds to give clues to other vague passages—his childhood, his leaving his own identity, the eternal "I," in order to set forth on man's journey through this life. In the end he hints of a solution in terms of self-integration, that man will yet see in reality what he has been shown in a vision. In moments of despair he finds consolation in the faith that there exists a loyal "stoker" firing the vessel of his life, who diligently keeps at his work and who sleeps not. He explains that there are forces hindering the union of man with himself, Israel with its redemption, mankind with its appointed destiny. These forces are "the enemy" which must be sought out, unveiled and fought. But this "enemy" is within us. He is the wall "that separates the lover from his beloved, the striving from its fulfillment, the song from its rendition."

How break down this barrier? How, the poet asks, can man reach himself, Israel its redemption, the world its destiny?

To this he answers: "From within, through immersion in one's own soul. Were one to go there without fear and weariness, one would discover himself, his salvation and destiny; one would discover the forgotten "He" standing on the bridge of childhood. By facing oneself thus, the path to the final effort, to the union of the desired and the realized, the union of the "I" and the "He," is no longer so dark, though it still be distant."

Aware of the vagueness which hides the meaning of his poetry, Shalow attempts to translate into prose the images that pursue him and to illumine them with the light of logic. He tries to reveal what he beholds with his inner eye. But poetic symbols must be instantly and intuitively grasped by the reader through his emotion and imagination without recourse to interpretation. Such is the very strength of poetic imagery, that it elevates the humdrum and the everyday to the heights of vision and, lighting up the darkness, opens the eye to the deeper and loftier significance of things, to the seeing of things whole. But this deeper significance must be conveyed through concrete images that can be quickly comprehended by the eye and ear, almost as tangible as real objects themselves.

In this respect the autobiographical poem, *On ben Pele,* serves as a better guide to *Face to Face* than the prose explanations. It is a truer interpretation because it is a poetic interpretation, springing out of the very life of the poet and his surroundings. This reinforces the conviction that the poetic personality of any poet is more potent than his philosophy. Shalom is no exception to this rule.

In this poem Shalom speaks in straightforward, measured and musical strophes of his journey from the diaspora to the Land of Israel, of the utter reality which was revealed by the miraculous light of a people's vision of rebirth, of Jerusalem rebuilt and the Emek reclaimed—works in which he personally participated.

He begins with his childhood, the water of whose springs flowed far away in time into the haze of the future. And now, when the future has become the present, he knows that his entire life has been molded in that early framework and that the child already knew everything that was to happen, just "as the chord is hidden in the string."

Man's way in life is hinted at in childhood and its visions contain the visions of the later poet:

"Since then all my life is but a book
Whose every page is the writing of God.
And man and his vision, flame and ashes—
Are but symbols for my erring senses."

Here too he describes the journey of man toward himself, but now the description is natural, understandable and clear. It is the path of the Jew going to his sources, to his past and to his land.

"I go to myself, to an ancient land,
I go to my past that is dead.
I know that it is all a dream—
And yet I know that it is all true."

Here also there is the inner conflict of the two "I"'s, the split personality. But now this conflict is resolved along simple lines—the "I" of the diaspora Jew dies and the "I" of the Jew in the Land of Israel comes to new life.

"Open the gates!" cries the stirring "I" on his way to redemption —"the waking hour is at hand." But the other "I," still hibernating, is too weary to be aware of the passing hours, too lethargic to awaken. When the first "I" asks

"Hast thou forgotten that thou art—the wonder,
Thou—the light, thou—the universe?"

The other replies,

"The bones of my dead dwell with me in the pit,
For whom shall I awaken?
O, let be . . . I am a mourner . . . "

But in the end it is the new "I" that has the final say, the awakened "I" of the Land of Israel.

"I'll not allow it—I cried out—I will not!
Thou art I, and I crave life!
Through tempest and tears came I here,
To redeem thee from the vale of death.
And though thou buriest thyself ever so deep in the grave,
Thence shall I bring thee forth into the light."

III

It is natural that a poet with a split personality should find that his world is equally split. The duality of the person presupposes the duality of the world.

Sh. Shalom's world is thus a compound of two different worlds, the world as it is and the world as it is to be, the one in a state of chaos, the other in the process of creation.

In this unfinished world there flit about lost souls and the sparks of unrealized beings. There is something about this view of the world that reminds one of the Kabbalistic concept of non-existence, out of which develops future being. It is a world of vague moonlight and the language of dreams. Its motion is that of a cosmic pendulum. In it,

"The days flow on slowly, and I along with them, as in a dream,
Nothing is there to lean upon and the earth is like the cloud above,
Houses, sounds, movements are like pictures on a moving tapestry.
I am a shadow among shadows, pleasant in their confused appearance.
At times I am not sure of the walls, the chair, the coat, the shoe.
I know not whether I sit or stand, or float aloft in blurred space.
I gaze in wonder at the lamp that it shines, at the clock, that it ticks.
At times I cannot perceive what it is that my cup contains—
Is it wine, or is it poison?"

This world of the poet is one of twilight, of quiet sunsets and silent expectations of a new sunrise, of half-tones and the whisperings of sleep. In the words of the poet, "I know that the world is a dream." In this dream world the poet implores the void, "Become a path! Be a light amidst the chaos!"

"Along such a path and for such a light have we been created; we have set forth to find ourselves." And from that time to this, we have been searching for ourselves and the world. We try everything. We throw bridges over the abysses in our frantic desire to grasp the world. But "the world flees" and is not to be caught up with. All the knocking on the door is in vain for one knows that "one goes from nothing to nowhere," that "we lift our eyes in vain" and "our desires will never come true."

Even when the poet wanders about in the wide world, as well as when he walks the paths of the homeland, he has the strange feeling of another existence in another world. Whether he speaks in the first or third person, in the singular or plural, his words have a moonlight quality suggestive of another world.

He ascends a mountain together with a group of others, but in the midst of day, darkness sets in, the paths vanish and the weary climbers lose their way. "Where are we?" they ask of themselves and of the world, but no answer is forthcoming. "From the abyss a whisper, in the night a hand, silence crying to the heights." The moon floats in a solitude of blackness and "we continue our ascent between mountain and abyss."

Thus they wander in the eternal forests of chaos with no light cast "upon paths that are not there." Who are these wanderers?

"We who have neither tears nor voice
To weep for the buds of our youth, now covered by the sand.
No sanctuary for our life's song, no mother to comfort us—
All alone we stray in these forests."

Such is the plaint of the poet amidst the paths of the homeland, even where his "I" is accompanied by the other "I"s of the colony. And such is his song in the great cities of the world where the Hebrew poet wanders all alone. There, cast forth from home, native city and his people, alone he climbs the rungs of the ladder and all about him is thick darkness. His is "the story of a man born in some unnamed city to some unidentified people who no sooner opens his eyes upon the world than he realizes that he has been deceived, but he dares not return." In the course of his wanderings through the great cities on his way to his true home he is not like some identifiable refugee from a certain city or a particular people, but rather like one of the legendary giants fallen from another world, borne along like a spark from a primeval flame that had flickered out and dropped into the abyss. In between moments of despondence and rebellion he has mellower moods during which he warms himself by the fire of the strange realization that there is nothing better or sweeter than the sadness of "burning like a bush and to be consumed, utterly consumed." Whither should he go when all the roads are obscured, and to whom turn, when no one is left? He fully realizes that "man is like a voice crying out, a stretched out hand in a world searching its way out of confusion," and that "our life is not life yet die will we not."

But enslaved to his yearning he must proceed along his appointed path and he shoulders his "pack which contains nothing" and "goes to explore a city without a name."

But poetic yearnings, as long as they are genuine, are a source of strength and inevitably lead from the negative to the positive. For this type of yearning is the poet's way to himself and to the world, a path through the wreckage of chaos toward the creative light of life. Every creative person has his chapter of Genesis through which he must pass. He cannot escape the allure of the hidden and the mysterious, the light hidden in the darkness, through which he must pass on the way to self-realization, to the moment of self-conquest and his integration into the world.

And though there exists no logical sequence in poetry and a poet can skip from one perception to another, from one experience to another, the flow of his poetry will land him, from time to time, at one of his destinations. At such times he sings of the wonders that have suddenly been revealed to him and of the reality that has been laid bare, one that he can actually feel and experience.

Thus he exclaims in his group of poems entitled *Pele G'ma:* "Drink deep of wonder, oh my heart, drink deep of wonder . . . Each touch is a revelation, each image a vision."

Suddenly the very contact with things, all things, somehow turns into revelation and simple images become visions. We are reminded of the Psalmist who wrote, "The Lord is my shepherd." Even though he walks in the valley of the shadow of death he fears no evil and senses no despair. All of a sudden he beholds the vision of green pastures and still waters and The Great Shepherd, who shows man the light of creation, restoring his soul and filling his heart with song. And the poet wandering in a vague dream-world suddenly bursts into a paean to life:

"Break forth into song, o my heart, break forth into song,
To light that is infinite, to splendour endless.

Lift the cup and drink to joy and to sadness,
Rejoice in the face of life!
And rejoice in the presence of death!"

The song emerges from the inchoate gloom, from the forests of darkness, and even death becomes a companion of life and a subject for a hymn to strength and victory.

"There are indeed heights and glory
And the sea's depth,
And more wonderful than the dream is man."

Man is indeed more wonderful than the dream for he is the dreamer. He creates the dream in his own image, in the image of his own desires. The dreamer stamps his own personality on his dreams. In them he lays bare the secret desires of his heart as he sends ahead his shadowy dream-being to explore the path he may use later when awake. And just as the dreamer precedes the dream, so does the dream precede reality. For it hints at the future even more than it reflects the past. The seers and visionaries of old first beheld their visions in dreams of night. Job phrases it thus:

"In a dream in a vision of the night,
When deep sleep falleth upon men."

So did the dreamers see their visions and hear their voices, as the Book of Numbers states, " . . . if there be a prophet among you, I the Lord do make Myself known to him in a vision, I do speak with him in a dream." Only after they awoke did they interpret their dreams in terms of reality, in the language of prophecy for the education and inspiration of the people. The dream is thus a sign and portent, proclaiming a new life and affirming its possibilities.

The dreamer wandering between the two worlds of imagination and reality does not dream only his personal visions, but those pertaining to mankind as a whole. His personal "I" is but a symbol of the collective "I" and any poet deserving the name sings not only of himself but of man in general. His own dreams and visions are his gateway through which he enters broad life to become the interpreter of the heart of mankind seeking its way in the wilderness of life.

Sh. Shalom's poems in which he deals with himself, with his personal "I"—both those mentioned in this essay as well as many not mentioned—give the impression that he is trapped in the closed magic circle of his individuality and cannot escape from it. Hence the questions he poses to himself: Why is he confronted face to face with the mystery of life? Whence has he come? And where is the morrow? "Where has yesterday fled? And who, in dream, guides the foot-step of house and window, of stone and lamp?" Hence his strange desire to be silent in the dark and to hearken to matter, as one listens to a sea-shell.

Even more he pleads:

"Let forgetfulness draw near, stretch itself over me
  from all sides,
Spread over me its coverlet, I would fain sleep.
I would upturn my earth into a grave,
Let the grasses grow upon it, sorrow and anxiety."

But the tolerance of the dreamer of the split personality has here reached its limits beyond which there must either be an awakening or death. Yet it is in the nature of every dream as of every poetic yearning to culminate in awakening if the sleep is not to be eternal. This also happened to the poet-dreamer who had desired to sleep and to upturn his earth into a grave. The pounding noises of life gave him no rest, permitted no sleep. They disturbed the dream, aroused him, and compelled him to realize that "in vain you seek to flee to a nothingness shut off from the world."

"In vain do you lie down. The blood does not forget
Whence it has spurted and where it is to be spilled.
For an eternal fire burns upon the world's altar—
If you will not be a flaming light, your fate will be ashes."

Thus he escapes from "a nothingness shut off from the world" to the open existence of the world, from the danger of turning into ashes to the bright road of living man. Then he integrates his dream into reality and his individual ego into the collectivity of mankind, and particularly into the collectivity of his people.

Thus from his *On ben Pele* he comes to his collections of poems entitled *World in Flames, Weeping Willow* and *The World's Sabbath.*

The opening poem in *World in Flames* was written on the eve of Rosh Hashanah, 1948, the first year of the state of Israel. It is characteristically entitled, *I Dreamed a Dream.*

> "I dreamed a dream
> That suddenly we were redeemed
> From slavery and exile."

And it goes on to conclude:

> "And, disturbed, I wept,
> Am I still only dreaming?
> It is all really here, not an illusion. . . .
> Brothers, lend a hand,
> I cannot all alone
> Bear this miracle, this splendor."

IV

The two collections of poems, *World in Flames* and *Weeping Willow,* were written during the years 1936-48, the most critical and fateful in Jewish history. In these poems the Jewish national spirit found powerful expression. Shalom's great talents that had stood him in good stead in his earlier difficult wanderings from one world to another (both geographical and spiritual), now underwent a process of clarification on the soil of the homeland in the midst of his own people. Simplicity and directness mark these poems, combined with depth of perception and great love for Israel, so that they constitute one of the highest attainments reached by Hebrew poetry in this generation.

He merges his individual poetic personality with the national ego. Step by step he follows the *halutzim,* the guards, the soldiers who wrested the land from strangers to transform it into the state of Israel, and the martyrs and heroes in the hell-hole of Europe who gave their lives to sanctify God's name and in order that there might be a remnant left to Israel. Many of these poems have become popular folk songs, such as *Five, Hanita* and others.

For every great era in history is accompanied by song, giving expression to the great moments of heroism and sanctity. This particular period too has its own song, its own poetry, both in Hebrew and Yiddish. And Shalom's contribution to the Hebrew poetry of this generation that has witnessed both destruction and redemption merits a special blessing. It has profound emotion and the modesty and integrity of the simple son of his people who wants to be "a brother among brothers on guard." In one of his poems he expresses his desire to speak "a language simple as in the face of death." For when a man speaks of or to himself and is preoccupied with the problems of his own ego he may indulge in vanity or self-satisfaction, as the muse moves him. But the moment he enters the Holy of Holies of his people's life, where burn the sacred flames of suffering and hope, of death's sanctity and life's heroism, he must bow his head in reverence. Then he stands on the sacred ground of a great and ancient people and his poem borders on prayer. Therefore, Shalom says that "when the lots of destiny are cast in the dark shadows" he wants to "merit life or death together with my people, Israel." For he is aware of his origins and his proud lineage. He is "the son of those fiery Jews whose spirits dared challenge the heavens, while their hearts gently exuded love."

"When our ancestors set sail on the sea of wondrous destiny,
They drew their strength from the heart-beat of their brethren in captivity."

In other words, even those chosen spirits to whom it was given to ascend the mountain of thought and vision and who were swallowed up by the thick clouds, remained rooted in the masses of the people at the foot of the mountain drawing their strength from the collective strength of their brothers sharing the same covenant.

"There was one in our world who ascended on high
Only to return to see that all God's people are prophets.
And the deeper they probed and the further they went—
They would yet measure their soul by the light of the 'simple Jew.' "

Popular Hassidism here supplants the aristocratic mysteries of Kabbalism. Shalom is a descendant of Hasidic rabbis and everything he learned in his father's house during his childhood and in his native village, as well as his experiences in the Emek colony of Kfar Hasidim in the Land of Israel, were purified and exalted when the hour struck to sing for land and people. His forebears in Hasidic manner spoke in understandable terms when simple Jews came to them for some sign that might lighten their dreary lives and bring them nearer to God. They would use simple similes to cast light on matters mysterious. Even so did their offspring, the poet Shalom, know no rest until he found exactly the right words for his laboring brother for whom he wrote.

Even when he would be wrapped in "the clouds of creativity," his poetic visions would be accompanied always by the awareness of the laborer's yearnings. The more he isolated himself, the more he lifted his eyes to the masses. His long wandering through the shadowy esoteric world of the "I" and of "non-existence" now strengthened his desire to join with the masses, with the simple folk, those ordinary people building a homeland for him. He offers a modest prayer:

> "May it be His will that I be found worthy
> To follow my path to its end,
> And that I hearken not to the seductive voice
> Of the heart of the market-place.
> And when my soul expires upon the altar,
> And my eyes behold the mystery of God—
> May I be the offering of atonement
> For some worker ploughing Israel's soil."

Shalom's poems of Israel are not peaceful idylls for he is the son of a turbulent generation and a restless time, the period of Israel's struggle for liberation. The poems are characterized by the feverishness of one ready for battle. Their very rhythm conveys a mood of protest and rebellion. One can sense in them the soldier's measured tread even before there was an official Jewish army. His lines are short and decisive, terse questions are asked and quick answers given, like exclamations of military command. In his poem, *Voices in the Night,* this rhythm is particularly evident.

"Are you prepared?
Asked the voice
In the still of night.

I am prepared,
Replied the voice
In the still of night.

Can you leave
House and hold
Friend and fold?

I can leave
House and hold,
Friend and fold

Could you tread
Far ahead
Without dread?

I could tread
Far ahead
Without dread.

Then take the light in hand,
And go on as far as you can,
Never return! Never recant!

I take the light in hand,
I go on as far, as far as I can.
Never to return, never to recant.

In this poem the answers are a literal repetition of the questions. In this very simplicity lies its force, in the slight change of punctuation and of personal pronoun. In time of war there is no place for lengthy conversation or complicated phraseology. A military brevity is demanded, quick and to the point.

Shalom employs an identical technique in his poem, *Hanita.*

"What of the night in Hanita?
In Hanita what of the night?
Darkness wherever I look,
A great slaughter in Israel.

Lo, all is lost and yet
Shall we not even here be rebuilt?

O Lord, Thou knowest,
God, answer Thou!

Have you not seen even the faintest sign,
Some portent of the Redeemer?
Yet they stand guard in Hanita
All through the night,
All through the night."

Shalom's brief poems of this period, like *Hanita, Sounds at Night, Our Nights Under Siege, They Are Called Brothers at Night, In the Holy City–Tiberias, Five* and others constitute a cultural treasure-trove. There is much of the night and darkness in these poems because they are songs of siege, of men battling alone for their very lives, for every inch of the ground. But the night is not altogether black nor is it without the light of moon and stars, the light of faith.

It is true that it was a time of siege and many went forth to battle and did not return. But above the poet's lament, there rings his melody of faith in ultimate victory. Life goes on. And the moon floating in the heavens above is a symbolic comrade of those astonishing men of the night-watch, who have faith and who fight even as they sow their fields. The poet, speaking for them, addresses himself to the moon, "Move slowly, O moon, slowly. For we are sowing the fields of Galilee for the food we need. Slowly, slowly, O moon, and fear not our peaceful shadows. We are Hebrews sowing our fields at night . . . so that our children may eat their full and bless their fathers."

So there is heard amidst the very days of battle and the nights of siege *The Song of Blessing* in praise of the toilers of the fields.

"From above the blessing flows,
The desert has become fruitful field.
A people has found its homeland,
And man has returned to his soil."

The people had struck roots in the soil and had become part of it while raising their eyes heavenward. *Earth and High Heaven* is the name of one of Shalom's more recent books. And this is his constant refrain, earth and also heaven. The ladder standing on earth and reaching the heavens–this is the worker's toil. And above is the star of labor. Labor is more than mere toil; it is the glorious dream of a people that has not known Mother Earth for two thousand years. From the earth of the homeland, once again being tilled, comes the call for a renewed covenant between man, animal and earth.

Therefore, the poet sings not only of Jewish nationalism, but also of that universalism of which the Hebrew prophets spoke of old.

So the lines of Sh. Shalom read:

"For the equality of all men everywhere,
For the redemption of a sinning world,
When no more shall a child be born to battle
And every sword shall be destroyed . . .
Every man is born in the Image,
He is brother to all creation.
Together let us plough the furrow
To equality and redemption."

But the Arab-kindled flames that consumed the fields of Palestine from 1936 to 1939 were not those of the final conflagration to be followed by the beating of swords into ploughshares. It was rather a fiery introduction to the great world conflagration in which six million Jews were consumed. In his volume, *Weeping Willow,* Shalom joins the chorus of other Hebrew poets mourning the great destruction.

"How can my lips utter song?" he asks in his poem, *Harvest Time on Earth.* In the face of the unprecedented calamity, words would not come. The poetic muse languished. The very attempt to give literary or artistic expression to the apocalyptic destruction of all ethical and moral values, to the burning alive of people in crematoria and their suffocation in gas chambers, seemed like a profanation of the sacred. It was simply impossible, above and beyond man's power. But the very poets who could not open their lips with song could not remain silent either. They did what they could do, what they were inwardly compelled to do. They cried out and they wrote their poems even as they squirmed in pain.

These poems, depicting the horrors of the time and drawing the portraits of saints and martyrs, cannot yet be properly evaluated because we are still too close to the gruesome facts themselves to appreciate their poetic reflections. In time they will, perhaps, take their place in the spiritual treasure-house of the nation. The poets themselves were too deeply shocked by the events to be able to think clearly and rationally. Only isolated outcries, shadows of images, emerged from that inferno of Europe to be clothed in words during that period when the world went mad.

Shalom calls the whole world to judgment for having stood by silently and at ease while Jews were led to death. "How can you clear yourself, O world?" he asks. But of what avail are questions when no answers come, "when poisonous grief gnaws away at the heart," with the realization that the whole world is guilty of sin and there can be neither vengeance nor atonement.

Thus the wounded Hebrew poet perforce skips from one mood to another, from despairing cry to death-like silence, from protest to lamentation. Only when it becomes a matter of commemorating those who had been and are now no more does his voice become clearer. Pain has a more concrete reality to seize upon.

Thus there arise the living suffering personalities of Reb Mendel, brother of the Rabbi of Gur, of Reb Aaron, of the town rabbi, with Aunt Feigele, Leizer the teacher, Tevel the blacksmith, Keile the good soul and the other Jews of his native village who bravely met their death. In these people, who also symbolize all the other martyrs, we behold the sacred beauty that shone on their faces to their last moment on Europe's defiled earth. Their stray gestures, their casual remarks, their last words, reveal that which was uniquely Jewish in their lives. So they remain living personalities even after their death.

Reb Mendel of Gur in his last moments cried out like a man fainting, "A glass of water! Jews, a glass of water!" He died with a smile on his lips because a Jewish tailor, himself bound in chains, dragged himself over with the water with which Reb Mendel could properly wash his hands before reciting the *Vidui,* the last confessional. He died with a smile because it was given to him in his dying moments to see that even in the last stages of hopelessness there was still "a Jew who dared to sanctify God's name through self-sacrifice"—for the tailor paid with his life for his act. He saw a Jew who loved his brother and who, even at the moment of death, was stronger than wickedness and evil.

And how did the town rabbi go to meet his death? His brow wrinkled, a Torah in his arms, all the while trying stubbornly to solve a difficult Talmudic problem that had bothered him all his life.

And Aunt Feigele, how did she meet her death?

> "Her garment of silk, her eyes shining with
> loving-kindness,
> Tear following tear upon her cheeks."

She spread a veil of dreams over her fear. She saw herself, at that very moment, as a bride walking to the wedding canopy.

They all summoned up from their forgotten past all that was holy and pure, gentle and fine. At the moment of their farewell to life, a heavenly light shone upon the faces of these humble and pious folk who had sanctified God's name with their life and were now sanctifying it with their death.

"How did our town go to meet death?
Pious women with a prayer on their lips.
Men with a glorious tear on their cheeks.
Lovely young girls with the wonder of sadness.
School children with a stormy outburst."

And the poet asks:

"Do you not hear their song from the ends of the earth?
Do you not see how the heavens do open?
Thus did our town go to meet death."

Thus died the native town in the far away lands of the diaspora. But as a counterpoint to this terrible procession of death, Shalom describes a different and unique kind of procession. Those very martyrs who walked in the death march are now seen to be going to Israel.

In his poem, *The Vision,* he sees the Congregation of the Dead, the Lost Remnant, whose only emigration had been by the sword unto slaughter, now marching gaily as on a festival and at the head of the procession—the light-giving Torah. The elders and rabbis carry it with reverence while all the men and women of the sacred congregation accompany it with song. Joy and exultation are cast over the roads and fields and

"A mysterious sun places crowns upon
The heads of the dead who march in the caravan. . . .
And byway joins highway and a great tumult is heard,
From every village and town the precious, sacred congregation
Comes dancing and singing as before the bridegroom and bride."

This is a vision of the resurrection. From every corner of Poland they come streaming from their graves. The gates of Israel open wide before them and they are met with love and blessing. So does the song of destruction merge into the song of new life.

The splendor of the diaspora that was merges with the new splendor of Israel. The song of reconstruction overpowers the broken orphaned songs of yesteryear. For the survivor who drinks in the wonder of cultivated fields and blossoming gardens, of the landscape of the homeland, the sound of Hebrew song, the sirens of Jewish ships, the roar of Israeli planes and the marching steps of the legions of the Israeli army—all the wonder of the new Jewish state and the renewal of its people's life—now exults in the song of the new day. It is the day "when the vision of the people has come to pass."

In Shalom's hymn, *The New Day,* there are concentrated all the desires and visions of the Jew on his way from the dark depths of slavery to the light of freedom. It is a hymn of praise to the victorious Israeli youth, who stood alone against seven countries and triumphed. "They wanted it, so it was not a mere legend."

In his poetry inspired by the birth of the State of Israel, the poet, who had wandered with divided personality in the thickets of mysticism, now bursts forth with a great love for Israel. He appeals to the Rock of Israel to teach him prayer and song, how to bear the crown of freedom, how to carry the new pure *menorah* into the destroyed temple. Upon this sacred candelabrum he engraves in glowing letters the name of one of the poet-sons of the people—"Shin Shalom, son of Jacob and Esther of blessed memory, one of the many thousands whose souls have been seared in the flames."

ON THE WATCHTOWER

(From *On ben Pele*)

I am lost in the stillness and lost in the sound,
Lost in the storm that bursts out from within;
What am I? What my life? What my people? My Land?
The Rider of Infinity gallops wildly through my regions.

Who struggles with whom? It is I with myself!
The sea with the wave! The There with the Here!
I have seized on the Now as a red thread of hope,
But the hand of the past casts a threatening shade.

Master-Sorcerer of the Deep, mass your hosts,
My heart is cut sharp on the flint of despair;
The beam will not falter or fade in my hand,
God's war lurking in life is my battle.

I sought to bind the infinite fast in my hand,
In a clod of this earth, in paths close by.
My garments I wished to wear like a man,
While every vein was consumed with wondrous fire.

To me! Unto me! From horizons is borne
The light of a breach in the dim, opaque wall.
O brother, my brother in generations still distant,
I cried out to you from the heart of the mist.

ABOARD SHIP

(From *On ben Pele*)

Who are these who whisper at night in the wind?
Hush! Seal your lips! For these are the dead . . .
The dead of Israel whose hearts cannot rest,
Skeletons of the Exiles, borne by the hawks.

They sailed in the stillness, they travel unseen,
But with us, beside us, is their icy hand.
Thus the seamen strain at their harsh toil;
As the ship is approaching the region of storms.

Do you hear their song, solitary as Eternity?
They sing of the glory of martyrs who leaped
On the pyre to sanctify God, of the slain
Of generations without end, ever unchanging.

MAN IS A PARABLE

Man is a parable. So is the sound and the sight.
We are fed on fanciful tales: we never existed at all.
Books are written in vain, in vain the years pass withal
The unreal bags are devoid of happiness, pain and blight.

Earth is not fashioned of clay nor heaven of azure light.
All our wisdom is merely the stutter of dwarfs in the squall.
The heretical mime is a fool, a fool—the creature of gall.
Words and words without end, and silence governs in might.

Calling on you in distress, I am only a whirl in the wind,
A sound that was torn from its source and suddenly found its palls.
The pall of flesh and desire, the pall of sorrow and sin.

Until you open the window that faces the halls
Of the deep—and my being return to the fount and sink in the stalls
Of chaos, I'll not comprehend—like a prophet until he begin.

MIDNIGHT

The night is still.
I stand in the long and empty street
And weep my fill.
I weep
For knives are sharpened once again,
I weep for somewhere men are slain.
In the world there is so much that is not good
And there is no end to poverty and pain,
I weep my fill
Because the night is still,

The night is still.
Against dark windows behind bar and lock
I raise my fist
And knock.
I knock
For hearts within are sleeping.
Without the spears are leaping
To damn and destroy
Through history
Bond and free,
Bondage and freedom
Blood.
Ye topers in the midwife's arms, arise,
Today I prepare a funeral
For man the wise.
Upon all fours I crouch and crawl
And thrust my nails in the earth 'neath
the pall
And dig.
I dig
Perhaps the treasure to unearth
Perhaps the dead will come to birth,
I dig a grave for my flesh that fades
and fails
A grave for my voice that storms and
rails
And weeps my fill.
And the night is still
The night is still.

WHEN A MAN DIES

When a man dies in the valley of Esdraelon,
The ears of corn are still.
The Holy of Holies is the valley of Esdraelon.
No man weeps in the Holy of Holies.

When night descends upon the valley of Esdraelon,
The stars tremble.
They are the candles for the dead in the valley of
Esdraelon
For those who have no *kaddish.*

REB MENDEL, BROTHER OF THE RABBI OF GER

(An excerpt)

In this ballad Rabbi Mendel, together with his Hasidim, stands surrounded by a German firing squad. Other Jewish prisoners, arrayed in long rows, dig the common grave for the condemned rabbi and his adherents.

Rabbi Mendel observes them:

Despair, destitution, the shadow of death,
Have completely quenched the light in their eyes—
Their only awareness is death.
Is there still room for the uplifting of their souls?
Rabbi Mendel is sorrowfully silent.

Then suddenly he cries out, as if swooning with thirst:

"A glass of water, O Jews, a glass of water!
Half my portion in the world to come
To anyone that takes his life in his hands."
But none stirs, not a man responds—
Doom and hopelessness in all eyes.

"A glass of water," Rabbi Mendel cries. "Isn't there
anyone?"
And ashamed he is to have broken with speech
That silence of desperation and misery
Forever stamped upon them by enslavement.
But look! A prisoner there has broken forth
Hobbling through the rows of trained gun-barrels.

A mere Jewish tailor he was, a simple pious man,
Running in his chains to the well.
A glass of water he brought, paying in blood.
Rabbi Mendel performed the oblation,
And began the confession to the Creator of all worlds;
"Amen," the endless spaces responded.

And when the cruel lieutenant gave the order to fire,
Rabbi Mendel smiled to the Highest—
For in the realm of ultimate despair there still was
A Jew sanctifying the name of the Deity,
A Jew loving his fellow, and triumphant,
Even in death, over viciousness and evil.

ON GUARD

Tonight, I want to stir up the dust of the roads,
To move the yet unsullied air of the summits.
I want to stand a brother among brothers
On guard.

Tonight, I want to speak in the simple tongue
With which one speaks of death or the day yet unborn.
All about us is fear, collapse and
No refuge still.

Silent and tense I commune with myself
While lots are cast in the dark mists beyond.
My soul seeks merit of life or immortal death, with
My people, Israel.

FIVE

Five went forth to build a land,
Five;
Leaving behind mother and sister,
Infant and wife.

Hammers pounding in the hills resounding,
Hammers;
There stood the five, dreaming, paving
Byways and roads.

Suddenly, the morning was pierced by shots—
Shots!
And they fell, with hammers in hand,
Five bodies fell . . .

Then they arose!
On the hills when fires are kindled in the night,
Again five hammers pounded with might,
Since never ceasing.

And at times one hears the moan
And whisper of the five;
Leaving behind mother and sister,
Infant and wife.

Not for a moment rests the hand . . .
Five went forth to build a land,
Five . . .

REDEMPTION HAS COME

Now redemption is come, a wonder newborn
Whose course is blood-hallowed by ages dismayed—
With weary eyes waiting in horror long-drawn,
And whose souls yearned and prayed.
Yet you as of old remain hucksters, shopworn,
Turning coins in your fingers, this way and that,
Debating and prating of thistle and thorn.
And your fork-tongue venom you spat.

At your tall markets, with seats rising high
Eternities rush surging by.

The shofar has sounded, the shofar doth roar
For all who are left after furnace and cell.
A thousand a day come here to the shore,
Scorched to the heart and smoke-salted as well.
They stretch their arms out, they offer their souls
For a brother's embrace, for a nation grown great—
Yet you drag their tatters down into mud-holes,
And into their faces you spit your sick hate.

On Ephrata road Rachel gazes today,
And just as of old, she weeps without stay.

The day darkens over, clouds gather and frown.
Upon every side now rallies the foe
And deep in a sea of red flame he would drown
The fluttering banner, the dance and the glow.
And winds offer warning, the fields lie outflung
For the salvaging plough and the fort on the rise—
Yet you still divide, and you spit and give tongue
And signal and sign to our foes and their spies.

While round your heads hover, hover and beat
The wings of the night-hawk, the screech-owl
and bat.

Avigdor Hameiri, Poet and Novelist

Avigdor Hameiri (Feierstein), poet, novelist and short story writer, was born in Bereg in the Carpathian section of Russia in 1886. He graduated from the Rabbinical Seminary in Budapest and served as an officer in the Hungarian army during the First World War. In 1916 he was taken prisoner by the Russians. After the war he worked as a journalist, editor and translator in Kiev and Odessa.

In 1921 he settled in Palestine where he wrote for *Haaretz,* the daily newspaper, and later served as literary editor of the daily *Doar Hayom.* He founded and directed the first satirical theater in Palestine, the *Kumkum,* in 1927. He is now the co-editor of *Divrei Knesset,* the official record of the Israeli parliament, and honorary supervisor of the official documents of the government of Israel.

His first volume of collected poems was published in 1912. His books include the following: *Kibbutz Galuyot,* 1923; *Tahat Shamayim Adumim,* 1925; *Halav Haem,* 1925; *Keshet Yaakov,* 1926; *Beshem Rabbi Yeshua Minatzeret,* 1928; *Hashigaon Hagadol,* 1929; *Bein Shinei Haadam,* 1929; *Massa Beeiropa Haprait,* 1936; *Begeihinom shel Mata,* 1932; *Massada* (play), 1932; *Hokhmat Habehemot,* 1933; *Sefer Hashirim,* 1933; *Tnuva,* 1935; *Shirat Hadamim,* 1936; *Haivri Hakadmon,* 1942; *Hamoked Haran,* 1944; *Halomot shel Bet Rabban,* 1944; *Pinocchio Beeretz Israel,* 1945; *Sodo shel Sokrates.*

In addition, he has enriched Hebrew literature with many translations of works by Max Brod and Stefan Zweig, *The Travels of Baron Munchhausen,* plays for the theater and others.

He was the recipient of the Bialik Literary Prize in 1936 and the Nordau Prize eight years later.

His novel, *Hashigaon Hagadol,* was translated into English under the title of *The Great Madness* by Jacob Freedman and published by Vantage Press in 1952.

I.

In Budapest in 1912 the Hungarian Zionist organization published a Hebrew book entitled *Poems of Avigdor Feierstein, First Collection.*

The book was something of a novelty because until that time Hungarian Jewry had made no contribution to modern Hebrew poetry nor, indeed, to any branch of modern Hebrew literature. In addition, in these poems of the then unknown poet there was a felicity of style altogether new in Hebrew poetry. It was evident that the young poet had emerged from a different world and that he had not breathed the air of Russia, Poland or Lithuania where modern Hebrew literature had developed. True, though his language was not rich, it was warm, perhaps even overly so. His feeling for his people burned within him. His youthful emotions bubbled over. But with all this, there was something in him of the distant brother, of the foreign visitor whose training and way of life differed from the mainstream of Jewry, as it flowed within the Russian empire. That which was natural and acceptable to them was to him new, radical and revolutionary. To use his own expression, he had in himself a little of the old *payytan,* the liturgical poet, not of the *Haskalah,* but of the medieval period.

His first book of poems was divided into four sections: *With the Kiss of Dawn, Son of the Future, Heart of My Mother* and *Of Fruits and Good Tidings.* These very titles were an omen of the fact that a new spokesman had arisen, a man kissed by the dawn and a son of the future, a son sprung from his mother's heart who would prophesy of future fruits and good tidings.

Indeed, the opening words of the book are those of the young poet "prophesying within the camp." In his prefatory poem he writes,

> "The hoary film of blindness of two thousand years
> I shall tear from your eyes, and ask in my rage,
> Hear ye now, my masters, judges and learned ones,
> Will you not yet unloose life and set it free?"

And at the poem's end he proclaims,

> "Lift up your eyes. Do you see something wonderful?
> Like Ezekiel's flaming chariot drawing nigh.
> Open your ears, do you hear the piercing song
> Rising up from our desolate world?"

But these prefatory lines of poetry did not suffice him. He felt compelled to write a prose introduction as well. In it he writes as follows: "Let me be but one spark from a fissure in the mountain of our strength, its flame burning everlastingly from of old. With my own eyes have I seen the God of our life in His fresh and fruitful return and into His eye have I poured my soul—to receive our ancient spirit's blessing, the spirit now groping for the light of a new dawn." Later, in his introduction to the first section he offers it as "a living gift to Old Israel which has now lovingly entered into a covenant with the fruit of our homeland in the East."

There is much of the innocence of youth in all this. The lofty figures of speech and overflowing metaphors seem odd and almost archaic, especially now when the days of youth are long past. But Feierstein did not suceed in freeing himself of this style even after he had changed his name to Hameiri and had already rooted himself in the national homeland and in the soil of Hebrew literature. The same contrariness of spirit and inner exultation and the same style of hyperbole—he rightly calls Bar Bar Hana, the legendary Talmudic master of exaggeration, "my father"—all these characterize his poetry to this day. His most common themes throughout his poetry are return and fruit (he calls one of his novels *Fruit*), the kiss and the bite, raging fury and its appeasement, the outburst of hatred and its conquest through love, the brewing of hopelessness and the awakening of faith.

For even after he had come from afar to join the Hebrew literary family, there was no change. If one opens the book containing his poems written from 1906, when he was 20 to 1932, when he was past 40, Avigdor Hameiri is seen to be the same original Avigdor Feierstein. Here too, with even greater emphasis and joy, he calls the groups of his poems by the titles so dear to him and so characteristic: *Mother's Milk, Son of the Future, From Out of the Jewish Straits, Amidst Great Perplexity, The Flaming Marble Statue, Seething Sinai, Dreams of the Old School, Source of Our Sleeping Fruits, Ruler of Tomorrow, In the Garden of Sorrow, Dream of the Desert.*

Of course, much of this is figure of speech, but there are in it also clear indications of the poet's outlook and perception, guide-posts to his style. We are drawn into the garden of sorrow to savor of the taste of death that was his during his life in a strange land, in wartime and captivity. We accompany him along his way in the desert to the seething Sinai and to the coveted and promised homeland. We feel his great sorrow, the sorrow of disillusionment. Reality has deceived him and has not fulfilled his dream. Out of the Jewish straits we hear his voice calling for enlargement and freedom.

More than all else, we hear his voice. For his is not poetry for the eye, of scenes and colors reflecting the world of nature. His is rather poetry for the ear, of sounds and echos, voices rising from the depths of man's soul. Whether because of his special Hungarian education or for other reasons—his having been orphaned at an early age, his grandfather's influence, the environment—he pays little attention to landscape and spectacles of nature. He devotes all his heart and soul to the problems of man, especially to the problems of the Jew, in a world alien and cold, evil and false, a world that has rejected its sanctities and emptied itself of its dreams. So his voice is heard crying out of the straits, from a strange land, from out of the desert, to hearts far away, to brothers of yesteryear. Perhaps they will hear, maybe they will answer, perhaps an echo will reply.

He sees himself chiefly as a son of the *Seething Sinai,* as a descendant of prophets and priests and, therefore, as a strange Jew in a foreign land weeping because of the exile of God's presence and yearning for redemption. Perhaps for this very reason he denies himself the enjoyment of life and nature even though he is so sensitive and emotional a poet and dedicates himself to the problems of Israel, then and now.

Indeed there is no doubt that Hameiri knew, even when he was still called Feierstein, the secret of pure, lyric poetry, simple and direct, casting the readers into a mood of mirth or sadness. No further proof is needed than such pleasant exulting poems of his as *After the Rain, Purity, On the Way, Midnight, Short Prayer, Now, Insanity, Whence to Where* and *Love's Dedication.* Such poems show that the usually heavy-browed poet can also be merry-eyed. He too loves "to embrace the clouds and the pure heavens" and "to gather breath-taking blossoms and to drink in the dew of dawn and to wreath with laurel of love the messengers of glad tidings." And even more. He can also water the grass and dry clods with tears of joy and, with sad prayer, overwhelm even the ears of God. To kiss all existence and to shout aloud and sing, to sing, to sing . . .

In truth, he can "sing, sing, sing" of the beauty in nature and "kiss all existence," but, nevertheless, he sets himself apart from all this "alien" beauty. For himself he decrees a different kind of beauty, the beauty of the poem Jewish in aim, the poem serving an ethnic national purpose.

For he sees himself as an offspring of the priests of the Lord, who look upon the face of God. Therefore, he chooses for his light that of the Eternal Lamp. Instead of the variegated, enticing colors of the poets of other peoples—and of such Hebrew poets as walk in their footsteps—his color is red, the color of his blood that he spills upon the wounds of the victims of the exile. He too yearns for beauty and glory, but for him the glory is "the glory of God hovering over him from between the outspread wings of the Holy of Holies." The breath-taking wonders that reveal themselves to him are "the wonders of holiness." And if his heart is filled with love, he knows in truth that that heart of his is "the breastplate of love, engraved with the names of the Children of Israel." "The rod of his poetry" blossoms at twilight when beyond the Curtain (of the Ark) he gives ear to the words of God.

Thus did the priest of ancient times sing in the temple of the Lord. And thus does his poet-descendant sing in the literature of our times. Just like his ancient ancestor so does he affirm that when he waves the censer of hot coals over the altar he offers up too his own flesh, himself, and in such a sacrifice "there shall be no alien fire." When the anger of the God of Vengeance bursts forth, he sings "the song of life—and the plague is stilled." And although the whole house of Israel weeps because of the plague's results, he, the poet-priest, scatters "a comforting light in every direction so that death come not between the horns of the altar and the light of the Eternal Lamp be not darkened." For his life is "a round of festivals, Sabbaths and new moons" and he is "a lad of the stock of the priests of the Lord."

So Hameiri becomes a poet crying out in the wilderness, not disdaining to make use of current events, what some would term journalistic matters, in the building and strengthening of his poetic structure. This practice bothers not only the reader, but the poet himself. For if publicistic matters give added force to a poem, it is but for the moment, a temporary experience, an ephemeral emotion. When the moment passes and the event is no longer current, the force it propels is spent. Only what remains is the real poetic essence.

Perhaps here lies the root of the poet's deep discontent which gives him no rest, a sense of aloneness accompanying him from his early days. "The inclination of the heart of the Jew," he writes in one of his poems, "is mournful from his childhood onward." Such an emotion has characterized him always.

When he was young and his heart yearned to enter the inner camp of the Hebrew renaissance, to be one with the poets, writers and activists in modern Hebrew culture in Russia, then he poured his fury upon the older Jewish generation in his native land, Hungary. He would tear from their eyes "the hoary film of blindness of two thousand years." Much later, when he becomes one of the leading figures in contemporary Hebrew poetry in Palestine, he strains to leave the camp and to return to the diaspora of his mother's grave and the memory of his grandfather, the diaspora where in his childhood he had dreamed of Old Israel and of the future redemption. Just as formerly he had vented his wrath against the Jewish elders in the diaspora, now he does so against his people dwelling in Zion, the very ones who are fulfilling the dream of redemption that he had dreamed in his birthplace in the diaspora.

For now that he has achieved maturity through experience and understanding, he perceives that great dreams are not easily or quickly realized. Their very attraction lies in their distance, whether they be far off in the past or in the distant future, whether behind us in our childhood or far ahead in utopia.

Knowing this now, he becomes all the more sorrowful. The dreamer who would be the warrior lifts his voice to his people all the more, the voice of the lonely poet who cannot abide his loneliness. Like the observant Jew reciting a blessing before eating, so does the poet utter his blessing over the fruit of the tree of sorrow that he eats in the garden of his woe. And he himself is "the fruit of the tree of woe." Indeed, says the poet, his people is misshapen, weak and small, but what can he do, since his own frail body blossoms within this people like a garden bursting into bud, thirsting for the dew of heaven. As a part of this people, ill and unattractive though it be, all his senses spring to life. Without it, he is "a sick beggar, an orphan." Without this people, feeble and miniscule though it be, spring is not spring, summer not summer. For then in the spring there is no Passover song of redemption and in the summer no chant of *Lamentations* and during Elul no Indian summer. Of what good are God's lovely creations to an unhappy soul if there be no inner Jewish feeling of "blessed sadness"? Without that holy Jewish sense of sorrow, "there is no hope for us, no vision of Isaiah, no divine madness of the son of Buzi." It is this sense of sorrow that atones for God's great sin "of having created us." This Jewish sense of sorrow is our great creative force, our *élan vital*. "All, everything, stems from it—heaven and hell." And blessed is he who bathes himself in his own tears before he succumbs.

True, his people is misshapen, rejected, frail—

> "But what can I do and how cease
> Being what I am: fruit of the tree of sorrow
> Under the skies."

II

A man's childhood dreams are the starting threads of his life's fabric. With Hameiri this is especially true. They are the very foundations of his poetry. In these dreams and in his poems based on them he succeeds more than elsewhere in catching the spark of purity and innocence. In his childhood Garden of Eden where he had dreamed those dreams, two principal images had walked with him—his grandfather and his mother, particularly the latter.

His grandfather had taught him Torah and introduced him to Judaism. His mother had nursed him with the milk of love and implanted within him a Jewish heart, as his two dedications to her testify. His dedication of the third section of his first book (1912) was entitled *Heart of My Mother;* that of the first section of his collected poems (1932), *Mother's Milk*. That heart inspired him wherever he walked in life. The milk nourished him all his days.

These two personalities, of his grandfather and mother, live and sing through so many of his poems, particularly in the group called *Dreams of the Old School* and *In the Garden of Sorrow*. In the image of his grandfather there is revealed to him the embodiment of Old Israel that he had seen in his visions of childhood. The more the historic sense develops within him and the appreciation of Old

Israel, the more precious to him is the recollection of the mother's father, who had given him his first guidance in the world of the spirit and the imagination. He is more than the embodiment of Old Israel. In the poet's imaginative mind he is also the Ruler of the Earth who commands the fruits of the field. (Again the theme of *fruits*). Through his half-closed thick eye-lashes he saw "scattered prophecies." And even more. The poet sees him in the figure of Boaz, a man of noble lineage before whom the stalks of corn bow their heads, as though he be the Ruler of Earth and the Master of Nature.

But not even this will suffice the poet and he raises his grandfather's image still higher. He sees him as sweetening every sorrow, healing every pain. He is "the refuge for Israel, the servant, and a rod unto the nations." For he is not just an ordinary Jew holding his little grandson's hand and leading him by the still waters of Torah and knowledge. He is also "the builder of worlds and he causes the forgetful land to bear fruit." His face—a vision, his look—the fiery sun. He is "the king over life, the ruler over death." In parentheses, as though whispering a secret, the poet adds:

> "(and at night in a dream revealing mysteries
> I sense my grandfather's secret:
> He was the Prince of Summers,
> A prophet . . .)"

To such heights does he elevate his grandfather's image.

In like manner does he treat the image of his mother who had died in his childhood, magnifying it into the prototype of all Jewish mothers.

The Jewish mother, he says in his poem by that name, is a very sad person, altogether sad, but she keeps on dreaming until the dawn. "Her heart-beat is like a mysterious psalm, her eyes two songs, her spirit a bright light, but very sad is the Jewish mother, very sad indeed." She is sad and pure, as pure "as a snow-white dove in a dream . . . and she is enveloped in love, compassion and innocence." The Jewish mother is very beautiful, her beauty combined with purity. "She is full of wonder, the Jewish mother, and she floats about like a melody in the East, all the while preparing her son for his destined land—for she is a daughter of the eastern dawn, full of wonder and mystery."

His mother's name was Hadassah (Myrtle) and it was she who fashioned her son into "a young myrtle laughing in the light . . . a tender flower craving the light, a Jewish blossom, the joyous object of every generation. Hadassah—that was my blessed mother's name and I am a young myrtle laughing in the light."

"Hadassah—that was my beautiful mother
And upon me she cast her fragrant influence;
The warm sun of the East,
The sun of Judah, the beneficence of the Lord,
Hadassah—that was my beautiful mother,
And upon me she cast her fragrant influence."

This lofty image of his mother becomes interwoven, together with that of his grandfather, into the fabric of his Jewish nationalism. The light of her spirit is poured into his poetry. Her eye is not only that of the good and kindly mother, but also "the eye of the Judean sun and the eye of the Lord." For she and her father brought him within that palace where lies hidden the mystery of God, the mystery of Jerusalem, of Zion. In his memoirs the poet tells that his mother had revealed to him this mystery, received by her from his grandfather who "had found it in an ancient hidden copy of the *Mekhilta*." And this is the way it went. In a certain palace concealed from all eyes, "a palace built by master craftsmen of glistening white marble, sit very young souls in its Holy of Holies. Surrounded by fiery celestial awe-inspiring beings, these spirits of school children" engage in the study of Torah. But this Torah is neither *halakha* nor *agadah*, neither law nor legend, neither research nor liturgy, for it is study without words. "There is heard only a song, no more than a tune, an ancient melody emanating from heaven and its name—Jerusalem." The city, Jerusalem, "Like a candle each letter so fair; but, alas, there are only six candles, not seven—the *yud*, the *yud* is not there!" *

This mother who gave him both life itself and Jewish life as well, who brought him into the world and revealed to him the mystery of

* In the Bible Jerusalem is spelled without the second *Yud* as in modern Hebrew, with six letters instead of seven. *Yud* also means "Jew."

Jerusalem—this mother he sees as the virgin Daughter of Israel. In time of calamity and concern he lifts his eyes to her.

When he remembers her, he lowers his voice and stills the stormy rage that seethes in so many of his poems. For he knows that his mother has handed down to him an ancient heritage. In "blood and stillness" did she leave him "a Judaism of quietude" and "the holiness of silence." He has betrayed his heritage or it him, for, as he confesses, "the heavy silence burst forth from my heart and I have become as one of the young prophets. Thou hast left me a heart full of secrets in my safekeeping but, like a drunkard, I have babbled it away all over town."

This is a further indication of the inner conflict within him, as between the poet who would concern himself with life's themes and the descendant of prophets whose people's destiny gives him no rest.

In order to appease his poetic sense and to give his Jewishness the quietude depicted for him by his mother, he writes his poems of childhood, *School-Day Dreams*. Their style is marked by a gentle and delicate lyric quality, by tender yearning. The narrative poem becomes the singing poem. The past becomes the present, but a perceptive present flooded by its own light, dream-like and poetical. This light overpowers the harshness of reality that imprisons the spirit and binds the imagination. Here there are the simple love of childhood and the great love of life, the love of nature in all its aspects, the play of light and shadow, the baring of man's dual personality, the longing for the far-away, the yearning for the moonlight and the strong attraction of death whose seed lies hidden in life itself.

Of course, it is to be expected that these poems touch upon all the themes that used to be so dear to Jewish children, all the tales and legends told by our mothers and grandmothers in the quiet evening hours. But interwoven with them are other luminous threads —scenes of nature, childish fancies and the first experiences of love and longing and of the heart's yearning for the distant and the near, the visible and the invisible—in other words, all that makes poetry out of life.

And how is poetry revealed in life? By the leafy top of a tree on a hill rustling in summer days and all silent in winter. By its vigorous sap bubbling and piercing its way through the tree's length

—that is like the sap of life bubbling and penetrating through the words of a poem. And there are many others like unto these: a light-strewn rain, a smiling sun, gathering clouds, nature's grace in all growing things, a shepherd bedding down his flock, a fountain spouting forth fresh water, twittering birds, whispering breezes, the enchantment of distant horizons and the scent of spring and summer—all these and many more are the revelations of poetry. They are also life's distinguishing marks.

Over it all is spread a thin curtain of sadness. For the visible and the revealed are followed by the shadow of the invisible and the concealed. To the joyous and exulting there is added the sequel of the sorrowful and the tristful. For life has a companion always at its side—death.

Death had deprived him of the most precious of all, his mother. And the young grieving son keeps telling himself, now it is mother who has gone far away, tomorrow it will be I. Tomorrow the clock will stop and the white angel will come and wink to him: Come, mortal man! He will not rebel nor lift his voice in protest. It will suffice for the white angel but to mention his mother's name. At once he will understand and he will follow the angel to her.

Besides, not only had his mother been taken thither. Three others had died, his good friend, Joey the parrot, lovely Mary who would smile through her tears and little Peter, the son of his kind nurse.

Little Peter, upon whose forehead there had always been the mark of death, was fashioned of unearthly stuff. He would dream of some primitive forest whither he would some day go, never to return. But for the time being until the call came he would spend his days amidst the trees keeping company with the birds who, understanding his language, would obey him. When he commanded them to sing, they would chirp; when he decreed silence, they would be still. The sick boy was also ruler over the worms and the frogs, the dogs and cats. When his time came to depart this life, he came to his young Jewish friend, later to be the poet, and whispered into his ear in his childish babble, for he could not speak clearly, "I am going home to the everlasting forests." At night he died.

Afterwards sweet Mary went, the orphan of the court-yard whom he secretly loved. She was as pale as the reflection of the moon and when she would look deep down into his heart, he would feel that he was melting away. And all the while that he loved her with the unspoken love of childhood, she got steadily more ill. Before she spat out her last drop of blood she whispered to her beloved, "I shall put on wings and fly to the heavens and from there I shall enfold you with dark clouds." As she spoke, she laughed out toward the woods and died.

She was followed by Joey the parrot who kept on grieving for Peter. "I calmed him. 'Joey, what is the matter with you?'

"He would just reply, 'Peter gone.' I gave him a sweet and fern leaves, but he would not stop, 'Peter gone.'

" 'My little Joey, be still, do not grieve.'

"But he would screech, 'Peter gone!'

" 'My dear little Joey, we must calm ourselves, if you too will leave me, I shall go mad. Tonight Peter will return and will whistle at you again.'

"But his only response was 'Peter gone.' "

Joey the parrot could not speak very much, but in those two words that he did utter, "Peter gone," were concentrated all the inexpressible woe of one mourning for a departed devoted friend. So the parrot kept on repeating his two words of mourning until he grew silent, fell from his bar and was killed. And the childish poet was left all alone in the big world.

From that time onward orphanhood made a home for itself in his heart and governed his life, as he testifies in one of his poems:

> "Whilst yet a tender child, a son of sorrow, without strength,
> And already had my God anointed me king of the orphans."

Hence his preoccupation with orphanhood, a theme found in many of his poems. In almost every one of his love poems the beloved appears as an orphan. And because she is an orphan he loves her all the more, as he confesses in one of his poems of childhood:

> "I have a beloved whom my heart desires,
> An orphan am I and my beloved an orphan too."

Can there be a match better suited, more harmonious? It is no surprise then that the young lad, anointed by God as king of the orphans, now anoints his orphaned beloved as queen.

"Yesterday at eventide I saw her alone,
And today amidst the throng I anointed her queen.
I whispered to her, 'Gentle art thou and young,
Shed thy tear for all the world's sadness,
On my forehead the mark of nothingness,
But my heart gives rise to song,
And thou—be thou blessed unto me
O queen of the orphans.' "

This theme of orphanhood runs through Hameiri's poetry from its earliest phase. Its shadow is cast over everything, even over the moon. He sees the pale moon as "the great orphan," as "the orphan of all orphans wandering through the vast expanse, home of the heavenly angels, cooing like a dove amidst the planets, asking for justice." If you look at her but once, he says, you are lost. For wherever you may go, she is there, for everywhere there is orphanhood. You wish to flee from her, to forget her, to erase her from your heart, but she, the great orphan in whom all the world's loneliness is concentrated, will not permit it. She floats after you, pleading for your protection, for the mercy of your love, for she is alone, she is an orphan. And during the long dark night, at an hour when sleep is especially desirable and you pray for kind spirits and sweet dreams, she comes out from behind the clouds and "casts upon you the image of her cold face, her icy light, her lonely orphanhood, her muted cry, and your soul quivers with her dying woe as she asks for justice."

So do the sorrow of orphanhood and the demand for satisfaction rise from the poetry of Hameiri who was driven forth from the Garden of Eden of childish dreams into the cruel and alien world of exile, of war and captivity.

III

The First World War radically changed the course of Hameiri's life. He was called up to military service in the Austro-Hungarian army as an officer. On the battlefield he was captured by the Russians and sent to a prisoner of war camp in Siberia.

One can easily imagine what war can do to the soul of a dreamer-poet who long before had been driven forth from his Garden of Eden of childhood fantasies. But with Hameiri something else happened in addition to his military draft and service. Not only did the war lay bare for him the soul of the sick world, of murderous man, of The Great Madness, but it also brought him to Russia, the land of the Jewish masses and of the renaissance of Hebrew literature. There he came face to face with a deep-rooted Judaism, vital and creative, thirsting for something new and fresh, for a veritable revolution that would wipe out the old darkness and kindle a new flame in Jewish hearts.

This writer well remembers those days when the dreamers of a Hebrew revival had their little centers in Moscow and Kiev, legally or not, and planted in inhospitable soil the first tender shoots of Hebrew education, Hebrew journalism, and modern Hebrew literature. On one of those days the news reached us that a Hebrew poet, this same Avigdor Feierstein, a brother in his ambitions and creativity, had been captured on the Austro-Hungarian front and was being taken to Siberia. Only a few years before, his first literary appearance had caused some excitement because of his new and unusual talent and had been discussed in the Hebrew journals of Russia. In the *Hashiloah,* a young poet had essayed his first venture in literary criticism by writing an article on Feierstein's book.* Rabbi Jacob Mazo hastened to arrange a meeting with the prisoner and to see what could be done to free him. He did not succeed at first and the poet was transported to Siberia. Only after he had suffered some time there was he released. He got to Kiev where he quickly became one of the family of Hebrew writers of the Ukraine and Russia.

This brief excursion into personal recollections serves to point up the radical turn of events in the life of Feierstein, before he became Hameiri, which so greatly affected his literary career.

But of course greater than the effect upon him of his new contact with Russian Jewry was the effect of the war itself and his captivity. The war struck him like a bolt of lightning, shattering his world. Not only was he an orphan; all the world was an orphan. Hundreds, thousands, millions of young men, as simple and innocent as children, were wrenched from their parents' homes and cast into the fiery mouth of Moloch, into "an earthly Gehenna" whence their rescue came only through agony and death. The world was re-

* Translator's note—Ribalow here has reference to himself.

vealed in all its barbaric cruelty to these young dreamers. They may have come from poor homes, they may have been orphans, but with all their hearts they had believed that life possessed beauty, enchantment, hope. Now came The Great Madness and with it their great awakening, their great disillusionment.

In days to come, the young poet would pour out his heart's indignation in bitter and violent prose. His mind was already then spinning the scarlet threads that would later be woven into the tales of terror of his books, *The Great Madness, In the Earthly Gehenna, In the Name of Jesus of Nazareth, Beneath Crimson Skies* and others. But for the time being, in his poetry he was like a lost child, still holding on to his past, to his tradition, to that which was left him by his grandfather, his mother and his early Jewish environment. There still burned within him the visions and prophecies of the son of Amoz, the son of Hilkiah, the son of Buzi, and they fortified him against all that might occur. It is interesting to note, in passing, that he would call the prophets not by their own names, Isaiah, Jeremiah, Ezekiel, but by their father's names, Amoz, Hilkiah, Buzi, perhaps a reflection of his own orphanhood yearning for a father.

With all his might he held fast to his origins, to home and legends of childhood. Although he knew full well that in this new world of his he might at any moment suddenly be swallowed up in darkness, yet he soared aloft on the wings of the future. Although he was aware of the fact that along the painful path being trodden by his comrades and himself graves lay waiting, yet he could walk the path and sing,

> "Blessed is he who can carry to his grave
> Together with his pain, the laugh of an infant,
> Mother's milk, a lullaby."

Even when the taste of death is in his mouth, it is difficult for him to wipe the infant's laugh from his face or the mother's milk from his lips and to forget the lullaby whose echo still rings in his heart.

With childish, poetic naiveté, he prays, "Let me be a glittering butterfly consumed in an instant by a flame at noonday." Like the prophet Elijah who ascended to the heavens in a whirlwind, he too would forego the "boon" of death at the hands of man and would ascend straightway from the earthly Gehenna to the heavenly paradise.

He would die like Elijah not only because he does not want to be killed, but also because he does not want to, nor can he, kill. In his *Prayer,* he asks, "My God, my God, my God, whither hast Thou sent thy child, the tender blossom?"

He had been the kind who would open the window for a fly buzzing on it or help an ant in its heavy labors. "The warm glow of gentle love" would melt his strength. The desire for world peace had long gripped him. Therefore, he asks Elijah,

> "And shall I slay? Shall I draw the sword?
> My God, my God, my God!
> And what shall I do with the Jew within me?"

Here there is something more than the normal fear of death or of killing. There is something loftier here—the fear of the abasement of man, the human degradation involved in killing or in being killed at the hands of one's fellow man. Man created in God's image, how can he slay or be slain by his fellow?

He still retains within himself the integrity of his childhood; nor has he forgotten the Torah he had studied. So the death of his dreams pains him as much as the death of men. His aesthetic sense, his ethical sense rebel against man's defilement by war, against the profanation of the sanctity given him by the Lord. The man driven forth from the Garden of Eden seeks to preserve one precious spark from that lost Garden.

The fury in the heart, the indignation, the contempt, the abhorrence he feels for man's low state and his bestial cruelty—all this he pours into his works of prose. In his famous war stories he becomes a harsh realist even at the price of aesthetic and artistic standards. Cruel man deserves only a cruel reflection and so he wrote the kind of prose he did. But in his poetry, as much as possible, he maintains the standards of poetic taste so that not infrequently his poetry will border on prayer.

But this too within limits, for it is not Hameiri's way to cramp himself or to be sparing with words. Since he is a poet of sound rather than of sight, he lifts up his voice in order to be heard. He waxes loud to strengthen his effect. He always needs ears into which he may speak his message. If there be no human ears to listen, he will use the ears of an animal as his receptacle. So he calls to his dog, his friend walking beside him—and we recall that in his childhood too he had had a dog, his companion, Hector, the subject of a number of beautiful lines in *Dreams of the Old School.* He asks his dog to sit beside him and to be his comrade. "Do not call me master, my dog, my good friend, for I am like you. I am a barking prophet, barking unto the generations—and one common fate awaits us . . . Like you I too have bayed at the cold moon in the dark of night. Like a caged bird we both have voiced a hymn to freedom."

There is something alien and strange-sounding to the Hebrew ear in this conversation between a descendant of the prophets and a mere dog. But amidst the war's great madness when all the barriers separating man from beasts are torn down, when dreams of beauty and nobility are wiped out, why wonder about such a conversation with a dog? Even more so, after the Second World War, when disillusion is far greater, do such mundane and prosaic things become quite natural. The proof can be found in contemporary literature which rips away the curtain from every Sacred Ark.

This was one of Hameiri's novelties in Hebrew literature, to ride rough-shod over the innocence and the sanctity that had characterized Hebrew poetry. And all because of the war and his captivity. What the former had failed to do, the latter completed.

The sights he saw on the battlefield he described in his prose for poetry could not contain them. The experiences of his captivity he put down in poems. But even though their form was poetical, the nature of these latter experiences remained what it was: filth and loathsomeness, meanness and corruption, ruthlessness and murder. The prisoners, the poet among them, were brought to a prison camp in Harbin, their quarters a dung-hill in a stable. Twenty men arrived. Almost at once, two died, one of hunger, the other of cold. Is this the stuff of poetry? Certainly not. But something else is here—death. And the poet, aware of the fact that in narrating such a tale he is not fulfilling his poetic mission, adds a line parenthetically in mocking manner, "How lovely is the twilight." This, as it were, is all that remains of the true poetry.

Then the story continues. Three more die and then the rest, one after the other, from leprosy, malaria, the plague, by hanging and execution. Of the twenty, two remain, a gypsy and a Jew. The gypsy laughs and says to the Jew, "If you go first, little brother, save a piece of earth for me."

The two of them embrace and fall asleep in each other's arms. When the Jew awakes, he finds himself in the embrace of a corpse. He is left all alone now. What more remains to be told in poetry? Only one line more: "How bitter is the cold!"

Fortunately, the narrator was saved from execution and with him his story. But he was not spared from suffering and his early innocence was gone forever, that gentle innocence of his childhood dreams, of the visions he had seen long ago. The crickets and spiders, the bedbugs and the lice, the mice and the weasels and the other vermin and crawling things had befouled his spirit and had stopped up the poetical impulse.

If, at times, his spirit would wax proud and confident in its unsophisticated innocence, then the man of experience within himself, he who had walked amidst the horrors of war and who had dwelt in the dark valley of captivity, would remind himself, "Bare not your arm against the Lord. Show your strength against this miniscule creature, this vermin, that gnaws at your proud flesh even while you yet live."

This tiny vermin sucking his blood and biting his flesh conquered his pride and opened his eyes to man's worthless estate and to his utter hopelessness. This was the lesson taught by war and imprisonment to the man who had been driven forth from his childhood Garden of Eden. This was the mark of Cain they branded on his forehead for all time to come.

Yet, in spite of it all, his faith did not die altogether nor the poetic urge. In a letter he writes while a prisoner of war to his mother, still alive for him, he returns to poetry in all its tenderness, gentleness and purity. For poetry is to him as prayer. Whenever he would return to his source, to himself, he can do it only by returning to his mother. It was she who had held him in her lap, she who had placed him too in the lap of God. She had impressed the melody of her prayers upon his heart and mind. She it was who had implanted within him divine visions. She had poured into him "her pure

Jewishness whose arms embraced all creation." For him her eyes were the primeval heavenly bodies, her shining forehead the heavenly firmament. When her hands caressed him, he sensed the hands of the compassionate God and the kindly light on her face was to him like the light from heavenly constellations.

To her, the eternal God-like mother, he cries from out of his straits, from his foul and filthy prison cell, that he may be delivered from the pit of captivity and brought forth to freedom.

True, he prays and pleads for small favors: for a dry bed and clean linen, a little clear water to wash his ears and a clean handkerchief to dry his eyes. He prays to his mother that she intercede on his behalf with God up there in the heavens so that no creeping thing come upon him and cause him to profane his sacred heritage with cursing. But with all this, there still lives in his heart the dream of great things. He wants to go back to the source of his belief in God and man, to the fountain of an as yet undeveloped humanity. The light filtering through the window of his loathsome cell becomes suddenly a precious illumination; the squeak of a mouse, the song of all creation. His heart and mind, full of an eternal people's prayers from the days of his childhood, with pain and anxiety begin to pray for the reawakening of all peoples' compassion. In a time when so much blood was being poured out on the battlefields he gives voice to a poetic plea for pity and mercy.

Years later, when he will know life better, he will look upon death as "the temple of peace and quiet" where the weary find rest. But now in the time of his youth, just "the taste of death" is more than enough. In the very days of *The Great Madness,* whose fury and ugliness he describes in his stories, poetic creativity does not cease for the young dreamer suddenly uprooted from his childhood Garden of Eden and thrust into life's Gehenna.

IV

The First World War, the days of *The Great Madness,* came to an end and the world slowly returned to normalcy. The Jewish world too awoke from its nightmare of war, revolutions and persecutions to behold a new vision of national rebirth, of the reconstruction of its homeland. The Balfour Declaration was followed by the bestowal of the mandate on Great Britain. Those were days of great hope, of a new-found pride, of a vibrant pioneering movement of *halutzim*. This pioneering movement fulfilled a great historic role in the self-redemption of the Jewish people. It became a powerful creative flame that kindled the imaginations of Hebrew writers and poets. Some, accompanying the pioneers to Palestine, were themselves forcefully drawn into the midst of this movement of national regeneration that had within it more than a little of the fervor of religion and the creative joy of Hassidism. Its light began to be reflected in Hebrew literature, especially in poetry.

The poets who came to Palestine from Russia and Poland brought with them, in addition to their pioneering fervor, something of the revolutionary drive and the unbridled utterance characteristic of the "barefoot" and "raggedy" literature that had risen to ascendancy in Bolshevik Russia.

Abraham Shlonsky, who was filled with the spirit of the new Russian literature and especially influenced by Alexander Blok, together with Uri Zvi Greenberg from Poland, where the poetry of the "barefoot" had grown strong, were the chief spokesmen for the Hebrew revolutionaries in Palestine. With much noise and fanfare they exerted all their strength to change the paths of Hebrew poetry and literary expression. They raised the flag of rebellion against the enthroned literary powers of the time. But more important than these revolutionary antics of theirs was the fact that they personally joined the ranks of the *halutzim* and pioneered in the actual work of rebuilding and redeeming the homeland. Like prophets in the camp these young men walked among the excited people caught up by the fever of rebuilding and gave poetic expression to their joy of creation blended with the aches and pains of construction. In the Valley of Jezreel and the other areas where the pioneers settled, these "barefoot" and "raggedy" two moved about, but now their style was different from what it had been in the diaspora. From negativists they became positivists. Then, to affirmants of the old, old story of the rebirth of an ancient people and its redemption in the land of its predicted future.

Avigdor Hameiri, who was neither Russian nor Pole, also joined this camp of writers and poets and became one of them. He went to Palestine at that time and like the other revolutionary poets began to sing the song of the pioneers, the song of national intoxication. The pioneering *halutzim,* who were both happy and sad at the same time, who danced their *hora* until all strength was gone, seemed to the poet to be seized by a kind of religious ecstasy through which they sought to cleave to their Creator unto the last breath. This, undoubtedly, was the magnetic force that attracted both the poets and the dancers, binding their souls together.

Hameiri, like the others, wrote many songs of the *halutzim* which became popular in the collective settlements and, in recordings, made their way to Jews in distant lands. They are certainly not the best of his poetry but they are the best reflection of the great and unique historic event then taking place. They are simple poems, as folk-songs usually are, like the songs of grown-up children. But their very simplicity and forthrightness evoke within us even now a warm nostalgia. It is easy to imagine what appeal they must have had in those days.

"My coat is shabby, torn,
My hair is wind-blown in the night
My heart is wounded to bleeding—
Hey, my friend,
Can you tell me why all this, why?

My spirit is restless as the sea,
My head a copper sphere,
I have no home, no garment—
Hey, my friend,
Can you tell me where is God, and where truth?

There is hope—but it is waning,
There is song—but it grows hoarse,
And the soul with cold is trembling—
Hey, my friend,
Can you tell me the meaning of this word, 'Homeland'?"

This is the entire poem, the song of the *halutz,* sung by the pioneer for whom it was written. It was sung then too in America, as were others like it. They were simple songs, one might almost say "bare" songs. But there are some songs that are life itself, not literature. These songs grow out of life and help fashion a way of life.

The naively uttered questions in this poem begin to bother the poet himself and when they become not the *halutz'* questions, but his own, they are all the more bitter and perplexing.

Something strange happens to him. All his life he has yearned for the homeland. The vision of Jerusalem has been before his mind's eye always. Its holiness he drank in with his mother's milk. Palestine was for him "his mother, she who has conceived him." And when he finally succeeds in reaching the land, he would have her but kiss away the blemishes. "No request have I of thee, my land, my mother, my conceiver." It is enough for him that he can stretch out in her grassy fields and with closed eyes pray for rain. So he tells us in his poem, *My Land That Conceived Me.*

But before long his pen writes new poems, different and sad. Before the echoes of his *halutz* song die away, he is aroused to write a poem expressive not of the *halutz,* but of himself. In this poem, entitled *O, Why Should It Be So?* he asks bluntly and bitterly, Why should it be that our sun-kissed hope . . . "as soon as it is clothed in the skin and flesh of reality, becomes sickened, wretched, accursed"? And "What curse is this that the sea of our blood whose waves have struck at the very heart of the heavens, as soon as it approaches the shore of reality turns into water and vapor?" And "Why is it so that our stock, the stock of the burning bush . . . as soon as it touches the grassy soil, withers and dies like a fallen leaf? O, why is it so?"

Yet, this is the land he had panted for, to which he has sung endless songs of love and yearning. How does he portray it now that he has at long last come to it as a son and builder?

This is the land, he says in his poem by the same title, a land of madness, at which "even God is astonished in mournful dream." This is the land where the sacred is profaned, upon whose Mount Tabor Ezekiel stands, desperately seeking to pierce God's mystery concerning the fate of the individual and the people—Who is destined for life eternal and who for abhorrence? This is the land, the land of the prophets, upon which God gazes and sees "a camp of lepers, all of them the sons of the heavens, who with half-shut eyes look toward the past across thousands of miles, thousands of generations."

But yet with all this, this land is still the soil of Akiba's descendants, "whose every clod grows with the Lord's blessing." He calls to his brother wandering in alien lands, whose soul is enslaved in foreign chains, to come hither and see "with open eyes the God of Sinai's wilderness." "Stand at night," he tells him, "and look upon the everlasting stars and feel your soul dissolve within you, your blood purified. You will become a new person as you surrender yourself into the hands of the living God for punishment and reward."

"This is the land, it is your land, O Jew,
Every clod here in valley and mountain, an altar.
Blessed be you if you can feel the heavenly flame,
And seven-fold woe unto you,
Seven-fold woe, if you feel nothing."

This is a land of madness, completely upsetting the Jew who, from afar, saw it as a holy sanctuary, but, at close range, finds in it the very opposite. From far off he saw it, not with the eye of reality, but with his mind's eye. Hence, what was seen was a vision of perfection. Everything that his heart desired, that his imagination pictured, that his soul yearned for, he saw in it.

But now, having arrived in the land, having become part of it and living its life as one among many, it is difficult to reconcile the reality with the dream. He turns sad, bitter, critical and reproving, without surcease and without compassion. In this land, he says in his poem, *We Have Everything,* what do we not possess? A blessed land, blue skies and God above, a two thousand year old hope and abundant prophecies fulfilled—we have everything.

"But one thing we lack—ourselves,
And to the sanctuary in our hearts, the door is locked.
Locked is the door."

We, ourselves—in the plural. But the many is composed of individuals. One of the individuals is, undoubtedly, the poet himself who feels himself "punished" because of the vast divide separating the reality from his distant childhood.

He did dream. For Hameiri who delights in playing the role of the rebel, "the defiler of the sacred," the mocker of simple dreamers, is himself basically a child of simplicity who cannot exchange dream for reality, for reality has not yet caught up with the dream in its freedom, in its flight of imagination.

Therefore, his seeming contradiction in his Palestinian poems. At one moment he falls to the ground, comforts its sacred soil, pours into its lap the song of his soul. At the next moment he attacks it with all the bitterness of his spirit and his overflowing disillusionment.

He stands in Jerusalem and in his poem, *An Orphan of Jerusalem,* he sees that all is pain and scar, scab and a choking.

"Here all is God, here all is death." Here is the garden of eternal suffering where everything happens with murderous force.

> "Here suffering is the flower, sorrow the secret,
> To pain seven times over, to pain is eternal."

He remembers, as do we, his orphanhood in his mother's home and his childish love for the moon. Now the orphaned moon casts its light also upon this orphan of Jerusalem and by it he goes to seek the soul of Jerusalem, his mother.

Jerusalem, his mother, the source of his life and his dreams, his visions of the past and future and the place where dwells his Judaism, "so beautiful and warming." To it he comes now to find that denied him until now. He pleads with its band of faithful, the priests of suffering, the carriers of the burden, the guardians of the sanctuary, "O ye faithful to Jerusalem, take me into your midst!"

When Passover comes to Jerusalem the thousands of spring seasons of the past come to life in the son who used to visit his mother on Passovers of yore. With all his strength he sings,

> "Blessed be you, O breezes, messengers of the God of
> fruitful fields,
> Today I await, I await at such a time
> The Messiah, or the seducer—for someone to come,
> Only that he come.
> Today is Passover and to belief there is no end."

Is there then no difference between Messiah and seducer? Of course there is, but because of excitement and exhilaration caused in the poet by the scent of eternity wafted by Jerusalem, the mother, he has become so confused that he cares little who will come. Only that he come—be he Messiah or seducer!

But we well know that he is eager not for the seducer but for the Messiah. To this many of his poems testify. Perhaps it is just because he is so eager for the Messiah that he is so bitter, turning what should be a song of rejoicing at the redemption, or, at least, the beginning of the redemption, into a sad song of the exile, a song yearning for his brother of yesteryear, "a dream of the wilderness."

For all that he now sees *here* is less than what had been shown him *there,* in the wilderness of the exile. He had wanted to see his people in its land with the Lord's eyes. "From the heights, generations and future without end." To see "the way of tomorrow and the day after" as does a pure heavenly creature, without sight of blood or stain, tear or pain.

> "Our soul shall I see as we have wished it,
> As we have pictured it in the joy of our creation.
> Let its blood be like the dawn's purple
> Lighting up our faces
> With the light of strength
> Of creation eternal."

He would make of the desolate land a garland for his head that would sparkle as with the heavenly stars while he would look down from above and pour forth a divinely inspired joy upon the nation and the individual alike.

But not all that the poet desires or dreams of is immediately realized. Redemption pains are as severe as birth pains, if not worse. And the man who is essentially a dreamer despises the ugly grey reality. He berates his brothers with a vitriolic fury, those who are content to accept reality as it is, with its greatness and its pettiness, the sting of the bee with the honey.

All the bitterness, the fury and the hatred accumulated in the heart of the orphaned poet during the war and his period of captivity, when the world was smitten with *The Great Madness,* when all the world became an earthly Gehenna, all this he poured forth now on the heads of the settlers in Zion who had turned the magnificent dream of a King Messiah into such a bitter and picayune reality.

"How wonderful was the mystery that dwelled in Zion—its hidden wonder bathed us with its light." And see what had happened to it! Blurred had become "every dream, every excellence, every height, in its disillusion with both God and man." The poet had dreamed that "every Mendel and Yankel would become a son of the Messiah" and now, the same old petty business, the shrewdness, the sating of the stomach—the same "leprosy attacking the brain and the blood."

There is no doubt that the poet was greatly depressed by the general evils of the times, the speculation for profits and the fratricidal rivalries among the political parties that reached their climax in the murder of Hayyim Arlosoroff, to whom he dedicated his poem, *Worshippers of Satan.* No less was he upset by the troubles besetting the individual. It is not difficult to recall what the plight of the Hebrew writer was then, especially that of the poet, in those troubled days of the early redemption of Israel.

Hunger was their portion, and that of Hameiri as well. If he did not write much or explicitly about it in his poems, there are ample allusions to this wretched condition. In his poem *My Brother, Tubal-Cain,* dedicated to Bialik, he writes,

"Who will give a flagon of wine to my father, worker in brass,
My father, player on the harp, to whom shall he turn for bread? . . .
Who has dulled our teeth with such poverty,
We who forge the harvest sickle and the winter song?
And in our old age
They who harvested our life's joy turn their backs on us."

They who reap the harvest grown from the creativity of others go forth to dance to the music of the poet's harp and the sculptor's hammer. But the poet and the sculptor go forth to beg amidst the dancers.

It is even more explicit in his poem, *My Brother, Sacred Poverty.* His brother is "gasping poverty, the empty stomach dying for a piece of bread." Although he is aware, better than all others, that "there are dreams of magic in the colors of the rainbow," he also knows, he and his brother, poverty, that "the greatest of all happiness is to gasp silently, in pain and in trembling," for

"This is the meaning of happiness—to give from that which
we do not have;
To dream till evening come, hungry and dull-eyed
Of the white roll on the king's table."

To give and to give again, such is the portion of the poet. He gives of his heart's blood, the essence of his spirit, of his very life. All that he has, he gives, uplifting man's spirit, purifying his soul toward an appreciation of a new life. But the land so long dreamed of has cast upon the poet the double burden, the suffering both of the spirit and the body and even the shame of hunger. He must make free-will offerings material as well as spiritual. Always must he keep on giving. "Like a mother with dried-up breasts giving her tender infant her watery milk. And to look upon a friend chewing his piece of bread and to forget that there is hunger in the world."

To give and again to give, without receiving anything in return, to suffer loneliness and hunger in the land of dreams and expectations, all this was undoubtedly the principal cause for the bitter disillusionment running through Hameiri's poems of Palestine. That is why in his book, *The Singing Hearth (Hamoked Haran),* he has a section of Palestinian poems called *Land of Blindness* and *Land of Naught.* That too is the reason for his return to poems of longing for the days of the wilderness of the exile, for his stretching out of his hand to his brothers of yesteryear. Hence also his hard words, that the exile of Palestine is more bitter than the exile of Egypt and Babylonia together. Therefore, he was ultimately led to lift up his eyes to the heavens, "toward the empty skies."

In this poem, *Toward the Empty Skies,* his poetry plumbs new depths of despair, beyond which there can be only emptiness, nothingness. It would seem that the limits have been reached of any interest in living, of any further ability to write poetry. Here the poet is seen sitting on a mountain in upper Galilee, looking upward toward the face of God. What does he see? Nothing at all. True, all about him is spread the land of Galilee and "exulting, it pants to warm the slumbering blood of the parched fields to produce their yield . . . and the sea sings and autumn wafts its aroma." All is as it should be, with rhyme and meter and delightful expression. But for him there is neither fruit nor sap, neither root nor foliage, neither whispering of leaves nor beauty of blossom, not even poem or meter or rhythm—only the stillness of death.

There is an echo here of the poems of Judah L. Gordon and of M. M. Dolitzky in which the poetry of the *Haskalah* period reached its outermost limits of hopelessness, bordering upon the end of reality, vision and poetry itself.

Like them, our poet in his despondency and desperation, cries out from his straits,

> "A poem! Give me a poem!
> But whence a poem, if my heart detests itself?
> Whence a spark of light, if a worm gnaws at my brain?
> Whence any delight, if every part of me pains to the breaking point of sanity?
> Whence a poem, if I have no heaven
> To which I can lift up my hands?"

What is the explanation for this deadly despair, what its source? It is all due to the conflict between dream and reality, to the lack of fulfillment of those beautiful visions dreamed in his parents' home. The poet tells us in his memoirs that he came to Palestine in accordance with the dictate of his grandfather "who, all aglow, would lift up his eyes from the pages of his Talmud" and weep at midnight because of the exile of the *Shekhinah,* of God's presence, who would look forward "with God-filled heart and a pure soul to some sign of the coming of Elijah the prophet, himself ready at any moment to rise and go (to the Promised Land) to crown the King of Judah on the Temple Mount."

The faithful grandson of this believing grandfather came to the ancestral land, himself filled with belief. Indeed, at the beginning he saw "God in every eye," "Heaven and earth kissing." He saw brothers and blessing and boundless love. He saw fields like "tables prepared for the family sacrifice," villages like "bunches of flowers for bride and bridegroom," mountains like "companies of Levites in sacred tones bursting forth with the hymn of redemption." Seeing all this, he too prepared "a quiet lullaby, a song for the offspring of my mother, the *Shekhinah,* for the baby Messiah." He was all ready for the coming of Judgment Day, as soon as the sign would be given, to weave a garland of all the sighs, the tears, the drops of blood, the prayers and the pleas and with it to crown "the infant Messiah" and with overflowing heart "to roar rejoicingly to the four winds, 'The King who sitteth upon the throne of David, lofty and exalted!' "

The poet was in complete readiness for the Messiah. What happened then to this mood? What shattered the dream?

His mother, the *Shekhinah,* although enthusiastic *halutzah,* became terrified at the coming of the moment of destiny and gave birth to a still-born child. The poet ends his poem with lines of mourning and lamentation which have in them something of the piercing cry of the prophet,

> "This land is soil fertile not for poem
> Nor for Messiah. It is Canaanite still,
> For the traitor, for the alien,
> For the foe attacking the fortress of Judah,
> For him who would blind the eyes of others,
> For the seller of the fortress of David
> For a pair of shoes."

His spirit, bitter and disillusioned, he rips the purple from off the sons of Zion and cries out to them,

> "Zealous am I for the Lord, God of hosts,
> Israel's sceptre shall be torn away for downward flight—
> And with the coming of Judgment Day, when the sign
> will be given,
> Your children, orphaned of God, shall be scattered
> by man
> To Moscow and to Rome."

It is quite evident that this latest disillusionment is the most severe of all. His earlier disappointments had come during his wandering across the desert of the exile, during war and imprisonment. With the blossoming again of belief, it was possible to see them as signs and portents preparing the Jew for his future, setting his steps on "the highway across the wilderness to our God." But this last disillusionment had happened to him here in Jerusalem, in the midst of the Land of Israel. What meaning could it have? What message could it bear for the future, if there still could be a future?

When one speaks of poets, particularly of perplexed and wondering poets, dreamers and rebels, their questions, difficult though they be, do not always require answers. We understand that the questions are no less important than the answers, if not more so. Particularly, when we deal with a poet who considers himself a lineal descendant of Bar Bar Hana (known in the Talmud for his exaggerations), must we not take him literally. This ancient ancestor of his, when the time came for him to leave this world, said to his twelve sons,

> "Through the sun-lit skies, sowers of dreams,
> Your father soared, wandering in their light,
> There he plowed, there he sowed
> Lofty overstatements."

Should it not, therefore, be permissible for his descendant to plough and sow some "lofty overstatements"?

If proof be needed that even the disillusioned poet, striking in all directions with the rod of his anger, has not foresworn all hope, it is enough to remember his poems in which belief becomes full-blown again. They are scattered here and there in the general section of his poetry called *Seething Sinai* and in the sub-divisions, *This Is the Land, Children of My Rebellious Joy* and *Delights of Summer.*

Here, immediately after the poems, *My Brother, Sacred Poverty* and *My Brother, Tubal-Cain* come two poems, *I Believe Again* and *Fruit of the Tree of Troubles.* The sun casts its blinding rays upon him. The scent of jasmine delights him—and he believes again. The blue sea smiles at him like an infant and at once he knows again that "it is worthwhile existing upon earth." And once again the houses of Tel Aviv dance before him like the palaces in the old legend. When he hears from afar the hoot of the immigrant-laden ship, the golden sand of the seashore sings to him. From the high heavens God's face smiles again. Once more the old belief captures all his being and the past is forgotten.

For when a person merits being recaptured anew by faith and love, his people, small, poor and rejected though it be, becomes precious and beloved. His own stricken being begins to blossom again like a garden in response to the very defects of his people as though they were the dew of heaven. For without his people, what is he, its son and its poet, if not *A Sick and Orphaned Beggar?* And how can he cease *Being What I Am?*

Indeed, he does not cease being what he is. He does not stop singing the song destined for him from his birth, from offering *A Prayer to the Light of the Burning Bush,* even though the Messiah has not yet come.

For Sinai still seethes.
And the poet's flame still burns.

THE HUT

Fruit of the goodly tree, leaves of the palm tree,
Branch of the myrtle, and willows of the stream—
God of every fearful hour,
In this forest of horrors, guard Thou my hut,
Hut of young shoots, hut of creativity,
From the conjurings of men, and men that come of lions.

Fruit of the goodly tree, branch of the myrtle,
Willows of the stream, and leaves of the palm tree—
God of every pleasant hour,
In this forest of horrors, never fete for victory,
No exulting over spoils, and no paean after battle;
Here in the straits, guard Thou this hut of mine.

Fruit of the goodly tree, willows of the stream,
Leaves of the palm tree, and branches of myrtle—
God of each eternal hour,
In this forest of horrors, only this coign is for me,
In all of the earth, and in all of heaven.
Perhaps, perhaps, perhaps, Thou'll not move me again?

IN THE DAY'S RADIANCE

Yesterday the sun stood still in the valley of Giveon,
A sevenfold light glowed in the depth of the evening
And an arrow tipped with eternity's poison lodged in my blood.
Press me against thy breast, O divine presence,
And whisper into my ears continually:
Have no fear; be not afraid.

Ah, fate holds an ancient fear for me
And there is a dark terror within every flare-up of joy,
Leaving behind it a hell of weariness.
This radiant graciousness is more than fitting;
This day of fitness is too blessed
Not to be a dream.

This sacrifice of blood is too desirable;
Each drop of it has become another planet,
Or the sun rising above the darkest graves;
And blessed above all light also is the sudden wonder:
The first fruits of our generation falling like leaves:
Our sons, our children.

Our sons, our children. Who dreamed of them *then*
During the bridal night, while the seraphim made songs?
Desire of despair is more than prophetic hope,
The hope of those whose death-cries are as healing as these,
Who drink unto life from the poisoned cup:
Long live those who come after us!

Our sons, our children. Divine presence, close my eyes;
Let me draw their radiance deep into my blood;
Let me pass through it into the comet's heart.
In their radiance the dream of Isaiah came true;
In their purple fire the comet's tail
Shall be turned to red.

Soothe my sorrow for an infinite moment,
That I may believe with closed eyes
That the hidden hero of Israel
Will not cause us to sleep by reason of his pledge.
When the heavens are finally split asunder,
So that we may slumber again.

This I believe: the end of days has come,
And the globe of the earth is split into two,
Between yesterday's curse and tomorrow's blessing;
And he who looks backward at Sodom quaking
Will find that his eyeballs are frozen stiff
For eternity.

JERUSALEM

From the summit of Mount Scopus,
I bow me down before thee,
From the summit of Mount Scopus,
Jerusalem, I greet thee,
A hundred generations I have dreamt of thee,
Hoping once more thy face to see.

Jerusalem, Jerusalem,
Shine forth upon thy son!
Thy ruins, O Jerusalem,
I will rebuild, each one.

From the summit of Mount Scopus,
Jerusalem, I greet thee.
Thousands of exiles from afar.
Lift up their eyes to thee.
A thousand blessings we will sing,
City and Temple of our King.

Jerusalem, Jerusalem,
I will not stir from here!
Jerusalem, Jerusalem,
Come, O Messiah, come near!

GO FORWARD, SAMSON

Go forward, Samson, against the Philistines,
Go forward with feet of steel,
And break down every fortress, every wall.
Go forward, army of a desperate nation,
Suffering defeat in silence—
We have nothing left to lose!
And take the oath!

Once for all we have determined,
There must be an end to pain!
To the world we cry aloud:
Enough this time! Enough!

If we must die—this is the Homeland,
Honorable grave,
And if to live, a life of beauty,
We shall live in this our land.

There in Hell a myriad brethren
Live in torment in the dark,
And they cry out for salvation.
We will not recoil nor rest now,
Either we will bring Messiah
Or we here will breath our last.

Once for all we have determined,
There must be an end to pain!
To the world we cry aloud:
Enough this time! Enough!

If we die—this is the Homeland,
Honorable grave,
And if to live, a life of beauty,
We shall live in this our land.

KINNERET

Blue of the skies draws me to the heights,
A secret inscrutable draws me to the depths
All grief and all gladness—and joy full of fear.
On the waves of Kinneret to float without end,
In thee be reflected, to love and to love,
To pour out my soul in rejoicing and weeping,

Kinneret, Kinneret! Thou marvel of marvels,
The God of Eternity lives in thy depths,
Under thy skies to live and to die!
Thou marvel of all the marvels of earth.

EPIGRAM

In the Bible Jerusalem is spelt without the second letter "Yud." In this epigram, written over twenty years ago, Hameiri comments on the weakness of the Jewish element ("Yud" also means Jew) in the Holy City.

Jerusalem, Jerusalem!
Like a candle each letter so fair;
But, alas! There are only *six* candles, not seven–
And the "Yud"–and the "Yud" isn't there!

Samuel Joseph Agnon, Major Novelist of Yesterday and Today

Samuel Joseph Agnon, one of the ablest of contemporary Hebrew novelists and short story writers, was born in August, 1888 in Buczacz, Galicia, then a part of the Austro-Hungarian empire. His parents were Shalom and Esther Czaczkes; his father, descended from a prominent family, was a merchant and a man of learning. He first went to Palestine in 1909 where he was the first secretary of the Jewish court in Jaffa, as well as secretary of the national Jewish council. In 1913 he went to Germany where he was a lecturer in Hebrew literature and a tutor in Hebrew. Among his pupils were the family of Walter Rathenau. He returned to Palestine in 1924 to make his permanent residence in Jerusalem.

The Jewish Theological Seminary of America bestowed upon him the honorary degree of Doctor of Hebrew Literature in 1936. The following year he received the Bialik Prize for Literature given by the city of Tel Aviv, the highest literary distinction in Israel, and of which he was the recipient for a second time several years ago. In 1950 the Ussishkin Prize was awarded him.

Utilizing vast sources of midrashic, hasidic and folk literature, he created a unique Hebrew prose style. His work links historic Jewish piety and martyrdom with the longing for Palestine. He is the portrayer *par excellence* of the saintliness and simplicity of Eastern European traditional Jewish life before the advent of the modern temper. In recent years he has been preoccupied with the epic of Jewish rebirth in the land of Israel.

His works include the following: *Agunot,* 1909; *Vehaya Heakov Lemishor,* 1912; *Mahmat Hamatzik,* 1919; *Giv'at Hahol,* 1919; *Besod Yesharim; Al Kapot Haman'ul; Polin; Hanidah,* 1926; *Hakhnasat Kalah,* 1937 (English translation entitled *The Bridal Canopy* by I. M. Lask, 1937); *Oreah Nata Lalun,* 1937; *Elu Vaelu; Meaz Umeata; Beshuva Uvenahat; Sippur Pashut; Tmol Shilshom,* 1950; *Samukh Venir'eh; Ad Hena,* 1953; *Sippurei Ahavim.*

He is a contributor to the daily newspaper, *Haaretz,* literary magazines, yearbooks and anthologies.

His selected works have been translated into fifteen languages. In English translation, in addition to *The Bridal Canopy,* there are *The Heart of the Seas,* 1948, and *Days of Awe,* 1948, a treasury of traditions, legends and commentaries concerning the High Holidays, and *Hemda,* 1952.

I

When Samuel Joseph Agnon began to write, the new chapter of modern Hebrew literature was dominated by the general European spirit. Jewish life seemed to be entering a new era and a new hope for the future characterized all the Hebrew writers of the times. There was reflected in their works a sharp controversy between "Jewishness" and universalism, not infrequently to the disparagement of the former.

The young passionate poets were anxious to forget the Jewish village together with the traditions of their fathers and to become part of European civilization. They extolled man, the human being, and not the Jew within him. Burning love poems set young hearts aflame. And nature, which for so many centuries had been a forbidden garden to the Jew, now burst upon the Hebrew writer with all its beauty. It beckoned enticingly to the newly-liberated children of the ghetto, calling them to a new life and a new creativity.

Berditchevsky, the Nietzschean, fought his battle against Ahad Ha'am, and against spirituality and the tradition of "the book." Tchernihovsky, the "Greek," sang to Apollo and to "the false prophets," and stormed against the phylactery straps that tightly bound the arms and the thought of the modern Jew. Shneur kindled the flames of passion with his impetuous love poems and his paeans to nature. The same is true of Jacob Cahan, Jacob Fichman, David Shimoni and Jacob Steinberg. They used the national tongue, Hebrew, but the song they sang was a universal one. They were all possessed by a common desire—to capture outposts in a newly opened world, to become equal partners in universal human attainments, to create values that would command respect in world literature—but to do so in the language of the Jewish renaissance, in Hebrew. Their Jewishness they would assert by the language in which they wrote, their universalism through its content. In such a manner were they preparing the final synthesis of Judaism and universalism, of the Jew and the human being.

Briefly described, this was the European revolution in Hebrew literature. Frischman began it with his critique. His friends and disciples continued it with essay, story and poem.

Agnon appeared on the scene and began a counter-revolution. He reversed the trend from Europe homeward again, from alien ways back to the native road. He did not burst upon the scene in stormy fashion. He brought no theories or arguments with him. He said not a single word *pro* or *contra*. He simply began to write in a different manner, different from all other Hebrew writers of that time. His novelty lay in his old-fashionedness. His uniqueness consisted in his return to the old sources, to the folk-character and its traits of simplicity and sincerity, purity and piety.

Like the other authors of his generation he had drunk deep of the wells of European culture and had sipped the wine of world literature but he had not become intoxicated. He remained sober and unaffected. His entry on the scene of Hebrew literature was an event of major importance.

With Agnon the Hebrew short story reaches artistic heights. He has the secret of the perfect blend of content and form, style and rhythm, inner beauty and outer grace. He has tapped new sources of Jewish ethical and esthetic values, revealing the spiritual grandeur in Jewish life. He has done what others have sought in vain to do: to convert simplicity and folk-naiveté into a thing of consummate art and beauty. To the jangled nerves of this troubled generation, Agnon's stories bring balm and comfort.

In the serenity of Agnon's world, "the weariness, the fever and the fret" of living are forgotten. The piety and simplicity of his hasidic style had led many to believe mistakenly that his is merely an imitative technique. But one entering Agnon's world is caught by the spell of his narrative and touched by something more pervasive and more deep-rooted than mere stylistic novelty. While it is true that his literary style is graceful, his real power lies in his vision. This is manifested in his character portrayals. His style is not a question of "literature" but of "life." It mirrors the very soul of his characters. It radiates the mild and kindly humor of brotherly understanding and forgiveness, the humor of an artist who is at one with his characters, their suffering, their faith and hope, their silent study and their fervent prayers.

Only one who denies the basic truth underlying all creative art could suspect Agnon of creating a "style for style's sake." If naiveté were not a genuine and integral part of his characters, he would not have been able to portray with such consistent infallibility the inner state of their minds, their inevitable reactions and their particular speech. But even were one to insist that Agnon consciously stylizes his narratives, playing only the part of a weaver of tales, projecting himself with conscious effort into the role of his heroes, one would still have to admit that Agnon is an unusually brilliant artist.

However, careful observation of Agnon's creative technique shows that his true greatness lies in his knowledge of Jewish folk-life. The delicate and deep-lying humor characterizing Agnon's works springs out of the traditional Jewish faith and trust in God that are identifying marks of his leading characters. Because they possess this faith, his poverty-stricken and hapless men and women never become embittered. The clear light of their greatness of soul shines through the woes of their daily life. Their utter lack of envy, their passive suffering, their quiet hope lift them to the level of saintliness. Of course poverty is a trial. Certainly it is a cruel humiliation to have to witness a Jewish child begging for bread—but God is a Father and one must believe that in due time He will have compassion upon His children. In the meantime one must have faith.

Thus do Agnon's characters accept their trials and suffering with love. They are quiet and humble people, good and pious *hasidim,* full of mercy and kindness. The healing power of Hassidism lay in the fact that it sublimated grey reality, illuminating it with the bright light of faith. It poured into the lives of the poor the richness of the spirit and, in this world, gave them a taste of the world to come.

Agnon is a *hasid* writing about *hasidim.* That is why he idealizes his characters so much. Their faith and trust, their goodness and humility make them men of high calibre. Like his characters Agnon himself is a simple and upright man of faith. When he depicts the life of his people, it is his own life that he is portraying.

Who else could have created such a simple-hearted person as Reb Yudel of *The Bridal Canopy*? The author states that among a thousand simple folk you will not find one that can equal Yudel, who is the artist's idea of a noble soul. That is why Agnon has lavished upon him all his imagination. In Yudel, Agnon delineates what he conceives to be the paragon of human virtue and upon him he brings to bear all the radiance of his own creative powers.

Agnon's art is uniquely Jewish. In this respect he has achieved an enviable independence such as no other Hebrew writer enjoys. He has probed the emotional depths of his people and, extracting the essence of the Jewish conception of things, has united the Hebrew tale and its sources. He has resurrected obsolete and long-forgotten devices in story-telling and has made them the instruments of artistic expression. Biblical phrases and Talmudic parables, ordinarily unassimilable in modern Hebrew, are a harmonious part of his art.

Numerous quotations scattered throughout his works, together with sources and references unparalleled in modern fiction, serve to heighten the effect and to throw into bold relief the characters he portrays. When he adds "even as the Midrash says," or "as the Zohar has it" or "as it is written," it is not a mannerism used to embellish the story but an organic part of the tale, in which are mirrored the life-pattern and the world-outlook both of characters and creator.

The titles of the stories and the names of the chapters are typically Jewish. The first and second volumes of his works are called *The Bridal Canopy* and *Marriage* respectively. As an explanatory key to the first title he adds, "The Wonders of Yudel of Brod and his Three Virtuous Daughters, and the tale which tells of the greatness of the holy assembly of Israel who have pitched their tents and dwell in the land of our great emperor, may his glory increase."

In his book, *From Then to Now,* he begins the story *And The Crooked Shall Be Straight* with the following words: "A story of a man whose name was Menasseh Haim, a citizen of the holy community of Buczacz, may its tribe increase, who was afflicted with poverty and whom this affliction of poverty led astray from the path of righteousness. He besmirched the good name of our holy people and dwelt long in exile and in dire suffering, and in the end was privileged to leave after him a name and a remnant (as is told at length in the pages of the book; it is concerning him and his like that the Bible says: 'And then their sins shall be favored,' and as the Commentary has it: 'And then their sins shall be atoned by their suffering'). Composed and recorded by S. J. Agnon."

Another feature of Agnon's technique is the story within a story. Each time a new character is introduced, Agnon abandons the major protagonist and has the newly introduced hero tell of his exploits. Thus one reads the adventures of Reb Yudel and Reb Note. Their journey is not as long as it appears to be in the reading but the impression is that it lasts very long. In every roadside or village inn there are wayfarers, each of whom has a story to tell. Story is linked to story and thus the skein grows.

Because of this technique, the thread of the main story is often temporarily abandoned. The major characters are side-tracked but that is of little concern to the author. He is interested in unrolling before our eyes a broad and variegated canvas of Jewish life. Even if the central figure of the story disappears for a time, the story is not really interrupted. The narrative goes on. It is merely taken over by another. Life's spinning never ceases and God's loving-kindness is constantly being revealed to us.

In retrospect, it can be seen that Agnon, when he insisted upon a return to Jewish sources and Jewish folk material, fulfilled a historic role. He sensed the alien and inhospitable spirit of Europe and early in his life he decided to turn his back on it. He freed himself from its influence and returned to his ancestral home and its values.

With his return he began, in good time, to build a monument to a world that was destined to be destroyed a generation later. Thus he showed the way, the *Jewish* way, to other Jewish authors.

To show this world at its best, to blend the Jewish and the universal in it, he broadened and enlarged it, ascribing to it all that was good and upright. As with the ancient rabbinic sages, the Torah was for him the blue-print of the world. "And the world operates according to the rules of the Torah, and every living thing derives its being from the Torah. And know, that the two hundred forty-eight members and the three hundred sixty-five veins that make up the human body are the servants of the two hundred forty-eight positive commandments and the three hundred sixty-five negative commandments of the Torah."

The material world is fused with the spiritual and man becomes a reflection of a higher being. The Torah of the Jews becomes a Torah for all the world and human life takes on cosmic dimensions. The early *hasidim* themselves, says Agnon through one of his characters, looked like the Hebrew letters of the alphabet. When they would lift their hands in prayer, they would look like the letter *shin,* the first letter of the word *shaddai* (the Almighty). Reb Yudel, the first and foremost of his characters, looks like an *alef,* the first letter of the alphabet.

"When Reb Yudel walks, with his cane in hand, bent over because of the bundle on his back, he is altogether like an *alef*. His foot is like the lower line of the *alef* and his bundle like its hump."

Even nature itself becomes almost piously Jewish. For example, when Agnon wishes to say that the days grow longer, he writes, "The time for yesterday's evening prayers has become the time for today's afternoon prayers." Time is measured by the schedule of religious services. And when he hears the sweet sad tunes of the shepherds' pipes in the meadows, he hears the melody of the *Yaaleh,* a prayer of Kol Nidrei night. The sun sets and the moon and stars rise in the skies not of their own power but "God brings forth the moon and stars and sets them to shine in the heavens." And in the story *In the Heart of the Seas,* as the ship sails over the waters at night on its way to the Land of Israel, there is heard not the ordinary beating of the waves, but the sound of the ocean's song of praise to God. The song reverberates from one end of the heavens to the other, reaching the gates of the sapphire spheres in the highest of heavens where all prayers are united. All through the night there ascends from the sea this song of love to the Holy One, blessed be He.

The simple character who spins the tale naively asks, "But how can water, that does not possess the power of speech, praise the Master of the universe?" Ah, but the explanation is—as those who know Jewish lore are aware—that it is really not the water, but the voices of the little Jewish children who, long ago, threw themselves into that very sea from the three thousand ships on which the wicked Titus was transporting them from Judea to Roman slavery. In other words, the waters of the sea really cannot sing, but the Jewish children who sacrificed themselves for the sanctification of God's name live to this very day in the heart of the sea and from its depths they sing their song of love to God.

In such fashion does Agnon clothe with Jewishness sea and dry land, field and forest, hill and dale. All the countryside is bathed in a gentle and *gemütlich* Jewish spirit. Thus, for example: "The smell of the field is like the scent of God's saintly ones." Or "the bare trees storm during the night like the dead deprived of their shrouds." And in the musical noises of the night he hears "the praying of Jews."

In addition to inanimate nature, Agnon makes animate nature Jewish as well. His wild animals, birds and domestic beasts are Jewish in character because they come not from forest, field or barn, but from the Psalms and Lamentations, Jeremiah and Job, from the Talmud and Maimonides. A rooster is named Reb Zarah. "And why Reb Zarah? Because it is written in the Book of Psalms, Chapter 113, 'Out of the darkness hath shone forth a *Zarah*—a light unto the righteous.' " Reb Note's two dutiful horses who carry Reb Yudel and Note on their journey are named *Mashkheni* (Draw me) and *Narutzah* (Let us Run); names based upon the curious verse in the *Song of Songs*. "Draw me after thee and let us run." There is no wayside inn whose owner does not recognize these pious beasts at a distance. They are not ordinary horses. They are two Talmudic scholars who use *Gemara* quotations like two rabbis.

When the travelers who have lost their way in the dark become frightened, it is of the fear of "the wolf and the lion, the bear, the leopard and the snake that are mentioned in *Baba Kama* and *Baba Metzia* of the Babylonian Talmud, and the lion, the tiger, the bear, the leopard and the snake that are mentioned in the tractate of *Sanhedrin*." Even *kadahat,* that fever which afflicts mankind, is the fever which starts in chills and ends in heat as mentioned in the tractate of *Shabbat*. And Agnon's characters imagine that the leaves of the trees in Zion have volumes of the *Gemara* inscribed upon them.

For such a complete Hebraization of the universe one must go back to Mendele Mokher Sefarim. Agnon, who is more sensitive and naive than Mendele, is also more pleasant and fascinating. The charm and tenderness of Agnon are almost unparalleled in Hebrew literature. One feels that in his stories evil impulses play no role at all and when they do appear in several of his characters, they are ultimately overcome. His heroes are humble folk imbued with the love and fear of God, with compassion and unstudied gentleness. The pious Reb Yudel, in *The Bridal Canopy,* wears the sort of halo which folk-lore and legend bestow upon saints. His trust in God, his faith, his meekness and his piety are genuine. The relationship between Yudel and Note, the coachman, is like that between

Don Quixote and Sancho Panza and yet as remote from Don Quixote and his servant as are Polish Jews from Spaniards. In Don Quixote there are knights-at-arms; here, *hasidim*. There, tilting against windmills—here, faith in the spirit; there, the rattle of swords and the flashing of spears—here, the quiet whisper of words of wisdom and of man's desire to fulfill the will of his Creator.

Reb Yudel asks himself a characteristic question, "Why was man given two eyes? He could very well have seen with one. Aren't there people in the world who have only one eye and manage to see all they have to see? Why should man have two eyes?" And even more characteristically he answers, "Man was created with two eyes in order that he might see with one eye the greatness of God and with the other his own lowliness." He illustrates his point. "Lord of the Universe, the world is full of people to whom I, Yudel, can hold no candle, and yet they have no food, no shelter, no couch on which to sleep, and I lie here in a soft featherbed, comfortable with pillows and blankets. Father in heaven, I know that I have no merits to make me worthy before Thee, but out of sheer compassion Thou lavishest Thy loving-kindness on me. Thus I see with one eye my own lowliness and with my second eye the greatness of God, our Father."

Such humility and love for mankind mark Agnon's characters. The saintly Rabbi Leib of Sassov "used to feel the sorrow of every man as though it were his own sorrow and from his meager earnings would feed little orphans as he would wash their heads and treat their scabs." He would say that he who has not kissed away with his own mouth the rash and the scar from the body of a little Jewish child has not yet attained half a degree of the virtue known as *ahavat Israel* (love of the Jewish people). Rabbi Elimelech, the scribe in *Two Couples,* would never write a divorce. Before Rabbi Elimelech had to prepare the documents he would fast all day, and at night would see the couple in question. He would plead before them, "I am a man weak in body. I cannot fast. Take pity on me and make peace." If they listened to him he would make a great feast that night. If not, he would fast again, praying that the couple would become reconciled. Thus he furthered domestic harmony among the children of Israel.

Reb Raphael, in *The Tale of the Scribe,* was a pious scribe who worked on holy scrolls, phylacteries and *mezuzot.* He was far from the cacophany of the world and was untouched by greed. His chaste, modest wife cooked and baked. They had no children. And why? Because the Lord on high who desires to hear the prayers of the pious, had closed her womb so that Reb Raphael would continue to pray for children, for God could not forego the pleasure of listening to the prayers of his pious Reb Raphael.

Out of material such as this, Agnon has created his characters. All of them trust in God, and if one is impatient with the sufferings and cannot endure the torments that come upon the pious and the virtuous, it is only because he lacks the quality of faith. Kindness and tenderness radiate from the author's pages. His restraint, his pathos and his unassuming gentleness tug at the heart. The light of confidence and faith gleams like a guiding star on the path which Agnon follows in his wanderings through the ghetto where the children of Israel find shelter. His love for his characters lifts them above their vale of tears.

In his many short stories and particularly in *The Bridal Canopy* he unfolds a panorama of bustling life full of many events. In the company of his heroes, we travel from town to town and from village to village meeting life in all its patterns and situations. We see Jewish business and Jewish poverty. We hear of communal affairs and of communal leaders who are far from being paragons of justice. We find money-changers and merchants, peddlers and smugglers, cheats and wags, gossips and synagogue loungers, hack authors, scholars and boors, *yeshiva*-students and free thinkers, arrogant rich men and fawning paupers, prejudice and superstition. In short, all the light and shadow of folk-life are described with unusual perspicacity and profound sympathy.

Agnon is a worthy successor to Mendele Mokher Sefarim. What Mendele did for Jewish life in Russia, Agnon accomplished for Jewish life in Galicia. But there is a striking difference between them. Mendele was a keen critic; Agnon is a sympathetic onlooker. Mendele indulged in satire, the other in gentle humor. Mendele made us shudder at the sight of poverty and decay. Agnon soothes us with a sense of love and pity.

Mendele was a scathing realist. He chose heroes, maimed not only in body, but tortured in spirit. His Fishke was lame, and those who were not cripples were abnormal in some other respect. Mendele delighted in revealing dirt and squalor, lice and disease. He mocked at human folly. But not Agnon. His heart is full of pity and love even when he portrays a cheerless and depressing life or when he writes of beggars. He takes no joy in exposing their wounds. His trust in the ultimate triumph of righteousness prevents him from falling into despair. His beggars are not, God forbid, mere ne'er-do-wells. Most of the time they beg for a holy cause and if they achieve their purpose, they leave off begging.

Agnon softens all bitterness with a kindly light of humor. Although he is youthful and gentle in tone he is mellowed by suffering. That is why his paupers and his beggars are satisfied with their lot. In *Ups and Downs,* the destitute rabbi says, "Were it not for the fact that I fast on Mondays and Thursdays, I would have starved, because there are more rabbis than there are towns."

Like innocent children, Agnon's characters know that they have a just Father. It may be that for the time being, He has become somewhat estranged and has withdrawn His loving-kindness, but it is not possible that His mercy will not reawaken and that His countenance will not shine over them again. Thus Menasseh Haim and his wife, Kreindel Charne in *The Crooked Shall Be Straight* simply await a more propitious hour. This family's vicissitudes are recounted delicately and gently and with a restrained pathos. Human dignity is not dragged through the mire, "and when a new garment was needed and was not had, one's Sabbath garment made its appearance on a weekday." Thus, "poverty donned clothes of beauty and wrapped itself in silk," but "a garment does not last forever, and a baker must use real money to pay for the flour which he buys from the wholesaler. And it happened that as the sun set and the eve of Sabbath descended, there was not even a piece of blackbread in the house, not to speak of the white Sabbath bread. Then Kreindel Charne went and took two small stones to look like two loaves and put them under the silk coverlet in order that no one learn of her suffering." What insight into Jewish self-respect and pride!

But when the last flicker of hope was extinguished and still God did not make his mercy known, the unfortunate family regarded it as a sign that it was the will of God that Menasseh Haim had to go from door to door to beg. Armed with his prayer-shawl, his phylacteries, a book of Psalms and a letter of recommendation from the local rabbi, he took to the road . . . "Oh, God of the Universe, Thou art just and Thy verdicts are just."

In the travels and adventures of Menasseh Haim as well as in the wanderings of Reb Yudel in *The Bridal Canopy,* we see the life of the people vividly depicted. It is marked by two dominant characteristics—poverty and the study of the Torah. In the despair and hope of the motley assortment of characters who cross Menasseh Haim's path, there is something sublime and majestic. One is moved by the sight of so much suffering and yet one cannot help admiring the people's simple faith. At times one gets the impression that these are not beggars and paupers but princes in disguise who at any moment may throw off their tattered rags and appear before us in shining splendor. Though they wear no splendid garments they are possessed of an inner spiritual beauty. Midas-like, the hand of a great artist has transmuted the grime of poverty into a golden dust. Agnon endows his characters with divine qualities without making an effort to emphasize the mystical. One senses this most strongly in his cycle of legends, *Poland,* in his short stories and in some parts of his *Stories of Love.*

A sizeable portion of Agnon's book, *Then and Now,* the third volume in his collected works, is devoted to Jewish life in Poland, but the fourteen sketches are all folk-legend in character. They are woven through with Biblical verses and miracles and are narrated in the pious style of the medieval *Maaseh Buch.* It will often occur to the reader that here is another Rabbi Nahman Bratislaver who poured such meaningful symbolism into his seemingly naive and simple stories and who created a lofty spiritual atmosphere, free from all external distractions, in his folk legends and children's stories. This spiritual world that Agnon built out of the material of diaspora life, he illuminated with the light of the Land of Israel. In his works, just as the boundaries disappear between reality and dream, this world and the next, so too do the boundaries between diaspora and the Land of Israel almost vanish. The Land of Israel, he says, is "a wedding certificate binding together the Jewish people and the Holy One, blessed be He, and our law states that a wedded pair may not live together without their marriage certificate."

In his love stories he displays his power of psychological portrayal with a delicacy of feeling and gentleness of expression. His love, even as his faith and mercy, is from beginning to end typically Jewish. It is marked by naiveté, demureness, purity. Love is a *mitzvah,* a divine command, and a God-fearing Jew who fulfills all the commandments must also observe the commandment of love.

Agnon delights in concluding marriage pacts and in describing weddings, because here the Jewish sense of love finds its rightful expression. It was in order to fulfill the commandment, "Be fruitful and multiply," that our author drags the quiet and simple hearted Reb Yudel out of his home and converts him into an itinerant beggar.

But his love is not only a mundane thing. Agnon is much more powerful when he tells of the higher love, the love that does not find its realization in the mating of sexes, but flares up into an irrepressible longing, a love that borders upon religious ecstasy, the love eternalized in *The Song of Songs.*

In the description of the holy ark which Uri, the Jewish master-builder, makes in *The Deserted Woman,* Agnon achieves the perfect blending of elements of love and religion. While Uri is polishing his sacred handiwork, he sings to himself. And Dinah, who secretly loves him, hears his voice and finds no rest. The souls of the lovers find their secret hiding-place in the holy ark; in every carving and fluting there is engraved a letter or symbol of devouring love. Yet, out of sheer jealousy Dinah shatters the holy ark which stands between them. She has committed an unpardonable sin and while lying in bed at night she is consumed by an infernal flame. And he? He lies among the trees in the garden and dreams of a harp whose strings had been broken and whose melodies are scattered to the four corners of the earth. And in that moment the ark appears to him "like a woman spreading her hands in prayer, and her two breasts are the two Tables of the Law that are borne out of her heart by the wings of prayer ascending to her Father in Heaven." Love and religion become one.

And then there is the other union—of love and death. For death is closely related to love. The poet of *The Song of Songs* had hinted at the relationship in his immortal verse: "Strong as death is love."

From *In Her Prime,* the realistic narrative with which he begins his short love tales, to *The Canopy of Love,* a true prose poem bathed in an ethereal beauty with which his book closes, love and death walk arm in arm. Man and nature merge in this mystery of mysteries. With epic calm Agnon unrolls for us a chapter of life in the environs of a graveyard. In the light of death all things take on a new aspect.

He has portrayed Jewish folk life in all its color and revealed its hidden beauty. Out of the bits of an already vanished civilization he has reconstructed a complete pageantry of life among Jews a century ago and has illumined it with his art. He has brought into view a whole gallery of types and personalities and an endless chain of typical events which are symbolic. In poverty and destitution he has found spiritual riches.

In bright, unerring dialogue, in pithy, sensuous description, in a language brimming over with life's vitality, he has revived Jewish folk-lore and brought it closer to all Jews. He has touched the very essence of the Jewish soul in its longing for redemption, and has groped in *galut* life for the mystic pearl called *Eretz Yisrael.*

A characteristic example is his touching legend, *Story of a Goat.* The goat belongs to an old man afflicted with a violent cough. For its cure he is advised to drink goat's milk. But the goat disappears. A few days later the goat reappears with its udders full of milk that "tasted of paradise." The same thing happens time and again. Once the old man says to his son, "My son, I should like to know where this goat goes to bring this milk that tastes so sweet and brings healing to my body." His son advises him to buy a rope and tie it to the goat's tail so that he can follow her when she goes off. The old man obeys. When the goat is about to wander off, the son catches hold of the dangling cord and is led to a cave.

"They walk for an hour or two, and perhaps for a day or two. The goat keeps wagging its tail and intoning its meaningless 'meh-meh' until they reach the end of the cave. When they emerge, they see high mountains and low hills where luscious fruit grows. Gushing streams tumble down from the mountains and a breeze wafts sweet perfumed scents through the air. The goat climbs a tree, managing to find support on the branches. And from the tree-top there begin to fall carobs filled with honey. The goat eats the carobs and drinks from a garden stream. Then the lad goes to the cross-roads and shouts to the passersby, 'Pray tell me, kindly people, where am I and what is the name of this place?'

"And the reply is 'You are in the sacred Land of Israel, and the place is near the holy city of Safad.'

"Then the lad lifts his eyes towards Heaven and says, 'Blessed art Thou, O Lord, that Thou hast brought me to the sacred Land of Israel.' He kisses the dust and sits down beneath the tree."

The lad remains in the Holy Land, but he sends the goat back to his father, placing a message next to its ears. "When the goat returns to father," he says to himself, "he will caress her and stroke her head. She will shake her ears and the note will fall out. Father will read the message. He will take hold of the end of the cord and will follow the goat to *Eretz Yisrael.*"

But the father does not find the missive from his son and in his despair over the loss of his son, he kills the goat. Only then does he find his son's note. For a long time he mourns the loss of his goat through whose assistance he might have reached *Eretz Yisrael.*

"Since then the entrance to the cave has been sealed and no longer is there a short route to the Holy Land."

This attachment to *Eretz Yisrael* which once could be miraculously reached within an hour or two, or within a day or two, with the help of a cord, finds an expression in more than one of Agnon's stories.

In *The Money-Collector From the Holy Land,* Agnon tells the story of a synagogue in a Polish town which detaches itself from its foundations and moves itself to a road en route to Palestine. The money-collector, one of a group of men sent from the Holy Land to wander from town to town to beg for the upkeep of houses of learning and for charity in Jerusalem and Safad, walks in front of the synagogue singing in a solemn voice, "God loveth the gates that excel in the Law," and adds, "All the synagogues and all the Houses of Prayer that are now in the *galut* are destined to move to the Land of Israel."

He walks slowly and the synagogue with its books, benches and tables miraculously follows him until he comes to a river. Then both the money-collector and the synagogue disappear. Thus not only human beings but buildings of stone and mortar can reach Palestine in miraculous fashion. And Agnon affirms, "And this, the attachment to Palestine, is the secret of the greatness and might and loftiness and love that throb in the heart of every Jewish person."

In his novel, *A Guest Tarried to Lodge the Night,* a sad story of disintegrating Jewish life in Poland, Agnon tells of his return from Palestine to his native land for a brief visit. Before he goes back to Palestine again he presents the key to the old little synagogue as a gift to the new-born son of his friend, Yeruham Hofshi. He reminds us of the Talmudic legend, that in the Messianic days to come the synagogues and Houses of Study will be uprooted from their foundations in the lands of the diaspora and will be transplanted in the Land of Israel. Let then the young generation have the key to the historic synagogue which will be erected anew in the Holy Land.

The Holy Land, in Agnon's works, is a land of mystical purity. It is for him more than just a geographical term, more than a politico-social entity. It is a place where the old become young again, the weak strong again. When an old man merits the privilege of going to Palestine, then all the years he has lived in the diaspora are erased from his allotted number and he begins the days of his life anew. It is *Bereshit* for him now. For living in Palestine is like getting a foretaste of the next world—and in that next world life begins again. That is why Agnon scarcely needs any young characters in his stories in order to portray youth. The old are his youth.

When these old people come to Jerusalem, they visit the Wailing Wall and with them, of course, is their guide and brother, Samuel Joseph Agnon. There stands a certain Reb Mosheh, for example, his head bowed against the Wall—the Wall that has never been deserted by the Divine Presence. With fiery enthusiasm he sings a verse from *The Song of Songs,* "The King hath brought me into his chambers" just as did his brother Gershom, before his death. With these words on his lips, Gershom's soul had left his body and the King had brought him into His chambers—of death. But when his brother Moshe, who has had the good fortune of coming to the Wailing Wall, sings these same words, he feels the joy of the Land of Israel and a new vitality coursing through his veins. The King has brought him into His chambers too—but for him, they are the chambers of life.

With this aforementioned novel, Agnon evidently brings to a close his diaspora-centered tales. For in his delicate and profound story, *In the Heart of the Seas,* he transfers his warm-hearted and enthusiastic Jews to Palestine, the land of his own adoption.

In Israel, he has in recent years begun a new chapter in his literary creativity. His first Palestinian-centered novel is *Yesterday and the Day Before,* a story of the Second Aliyah, that wave of immigration which settled, colonized and worked until its efforts were crowned with the birth of the Jewish State. Following the first such novel, there came *A Portion of the Field.*

But Agnon, prolific writer though he be, hews to his fixed and predestined line. His roots are deeply embedded in Jewish life and he is bound up with his characters by an unseverable bond. Many of his Jews—our Jews—perished in the Nazi holocaust. But some of them were rescued from the continent of destruction and had come to the Holy Land, a land that never grows old and knows not the meaning of total destruction.

Agnon always has marched along with his warm-hearted, enthusiastic Jews and always will. Circumstances may change, and perhaps the art of portraying personalities and events. For the rhythm of life in the Jewish State is different from that in the diaspora. The distant and the legendary have become the near and the real.

The first signs of this difference have already become discernible in Agnon's writings. True, the style is the same—epically quiet and midrashically wise. But more and more do present realities play a part, together with all of their difficulties and sufferings, their problems and contradictions.

Not long ago Agnon expressed the thought that his style and manner of writing had reached their climax and fulfillment. More cannot be done along the same lines. If one is to go farther, new ways must be sought, untrodden ways as yet not so clear. But one can rely upon an artist so deeply Jewish and so greatly sensitive as Agnon to find his new way amidst the new Jewish life, even as he found the old way in the old life. Just as he was able to bring the past with its riches into our present, so will he be able to bring the present into the future with its light as yet concealed.

THE STORY OF THE TWO BROD MERCHANTS, ONE WISE AND THE OTHER FRIENDLY, WHO JOURNEYED TO THE LEIPZIG FAIR TO BUY WARES, WITH ALL THAT BEFELL THEM ON THE WAY; THAT ALL MANKIND MAY LEARN THE FITTING TREATMENT OF GUESTS.

(Excerpt from *The Bridal Canopy*)

Two worthy merchants, Reuben and Simeon by name let us say, journeyed from Brod to Leipzig. Night fell along the road as they neared a village, so they descended from their wagon, entered the inn, washed their hands and stood to pray. But before ever they started, the innkeeper had put out his hand to greet Reuben who, instead of greeting him back, shouted at him, Go to the devil, fool that you are! So the innkeeper turned toward Simeon saying, Ho, ho, a testy Jew, a testy Jew upon my soul. Said Simeon to Reuben, You astonish me, Reuben; here's a fellow Jew greets you, and you have to shout at him. Do you call that politeness? Brother Simeon, replied the other, wait a bit and then utter your reproofs.

The innkeeper now offered his hand to greet Simeon. Simeon at once returned the greeting in polite style and friendly fashion, partly to appease him for Reuben's behavior and partly because Simeon was always good-natured and friendly. Blest be he who comes, said the innkeeper to Simeon. And blest be he who is here, Simeon responded. And whereabouts may you be from? the innkeeper asked Simeon. We're from Brod, he answered. From Brod itself? asked the other. Sure enough, he answered.

Then the innkeeper said, That there Brod's a real big city before God. Don't look down on me for being a villager, because all the same I'm as familiar with Brod as a Jew with the Afternoon Prayers. How many Jews, for instance, are there in Brod? And how many citrons, for instance, are sold in Brod? But before I begin asking your honor about the welfare of all Brod, 'twould be only fitting and proper for me to ask your honor your honor's name, as it says in Genesis, "For therefore are they come under the shadow of my roof-tree." For instance, what might be your honor's name?

I'm so-and-so, said Simeon. If that's the case, said the innkeeper, then your honor must belong to such and such a family. That's right, said he. Well, continued the innkeeper, and if your honor belongs to that family you must be related to this here family which is connected with that there family, and so it follows you're connected not only with this here family but also with that there family. Now I'm as knowledgeable about all of them families as I am, you might say by way of example, with my toenails and fingernails. And don't reckon I'm just an ordinary villager, because all the same I know how to mix with folks. And so we were just saying how your honor must also be connected with that there family.

Not exactly, said Simeon. That's a wonder, said the innkeeper, and how might that be? We were connected, answered Simeon, through such and such a woman who was married to so-and-so and was divorced by him, and so once she was divorced the connection came to an end. Now why did they have to get divorced, marveled the innkeeper, because couldn't they have lived together till a hundred-and-twenty years? And I'll ask you, if you don't mind, is there anything better, for instance, in the whole world than man and wife, like folks have the habit of saying, Man and wife is man and wife; and now why should they go and be divorced?

I don't know, said Simeon. Now that's just what I always say, said the innkeeper; townsfolk live a long way from one another, nobody knows what his neighbor's up to. But before ever I ask your honor about other folks' affairs I suppose I ought to be asking you about your own business, as it says in the Talmud, "A man's closest to himself." And so what might your honor be doing in these parts?

When we reached the village, answered the merchant, it grew dark and we came to the inn for a night's lodging. Well, and if that's the case, said the other, the question still needs to be asked, What was the point in your honor's coming to the village? We're on a journey, replied the merchant. And where might your honors be journeying, he asked. To Leipzig, he answered.

Thereupon the innkeeper clicked with his tongue, saying, To Leipzig; and what might you have to do with Leipzig? We have to buy goods, answered Simeon. And what goods, he persisted, might you be intending to buy? Fur skins, he answered. Then why must you go to Leipzig? continued the innkeeper. Because, replied the merchant, that's the proper place for such wares. And why, for instance, went on the innkeeper, shouldn't you go to Vienna, where you ought certainly to be able to find such wares?

There's not so much of it, explained the merchant, to be found in Vienna. Now that's a real wonder, exclaimed the innkeeper, that that class of goods isn't to be found where the Kaiser is. It can be found there, said Simeon, but it has to be brought there from Leipzig. And if, said the innkeeper, it's brought to Vienna, why shouldn't it be brought to Brod? Now that's what we're traveling for, agreed Simeon, in order to bring it to Brod.

Now why should you take so much trouble, went on the innkeeper? Your honor could just as well send an agent along, as it says in the Talmud, for instance, A man's agent is as good as he is. It isn't everybody, answered the merchant, that has an understanding of the quality of these goods. Now however can you say, exclaimed the innkeeper, that it isn't everybody, as understands the quality of these goods? After all, goods is goods, and what difference does it make where Judah buys it or Levi buys it?

Goods, said the merchant, need to be understood. What needs to be understood in them? he asked. Whether it's the pelt of an animal that died a natural death or whether it was killed; whether the hair falls out; whether its color comes from Heaven or is the handiwork of the dyer; whether the goods are in season and place, and whether they're worth the money paid for them. Now how can you know, he asked, whether the goods are worth the money paid or that they're in season and place, or whether the animal died itself or was killed, or whether the color is its own? Anybody knowing this class of goods, replied the merchant, will know for sure the moment he sees the stuff with his eyes and feels it with his hands.

Thereupon the innkeeper caught hold of his overcoat and began feeling it and said, You say that when a fellow sees it with his eyes and feels it with his hands he knows at once, but here am I feeling away with my hands and looking my eyes out, and yet I know neither the nature of the goods nor their value. Goods, said the merchant, have to be studied. And how's it studied? he asked. The fellow with eyes to see, answered Simeon, and a power of telling one thing from another and a life spent at this business—I can depend on him to know.

And if he caught a fox, pursued the other, and came to sell it—is one fox the same as another? There's one fox can be fat and in the pink of condition with a fine pelt and fine hair, and there's another which can be thin and wizened which is bad, with a bad pelt and bad hair. But as we're talking of goods I'll ask your honor something important. Do all the beasts o' the world come to Leipzig to be caught and skinned and sold there?

The trappers, explained the merchant, and those who buy them from the trappers, bring the furs there. If so, went on the other, why must they foregather only at Leipzig and nowhere else? The merchants, said Simeon, chose the place. If you'll permit me, said the innkeeper, I'll say something sensible to you. Let me hear it, said the other.

Then he said, I suppose the king of beasts dwells there in Leipzig and all the beasts gather to ask his weal and bring him gifts, and when the trappers see the beasts they betake themselves at once to their arms and kill all they can. But let's come back to what we were talking about. What might be the cost of a foxskin, for instance?

Do you know what your question is like? said the merchant. It is like the man who asked the shopkeeper, How much will a coat cost an orphan? I don't know rightly yet what sort of coat he wants, maybe jacket, maybe overcoat, maybe breeches and what kind of stuff does he want it made of, wool or flax? And how old is your orphan; is he little or big; and how much money has he to lay out on the clothes, and will he pay spot cash?

Said the innkeeper, What difference would it be whether he pays cash or not cash? If he pays cash, said the other, the price is reduced, while if he pays after some time the price must be raised. But the goods are goods, said the innkeeper. So what reason would the shopkeeper have to increase or diminish the price?

This is the general rule, replied Simeon. If the vendor receives cash he does not need to borrow money at the bank and he doesn't require to pay interest. And what's a bank? the innkeeper persisted. A treasury of money, said the other. If a man needs money he comes and takes it from there.

How fine Brod folk must be, said the other, if they make a bank for any man to come and take money. They don't give it, said the merchant, except to people who can be depended on to repay, and who they know will return it. So if you have to give it back, asked the innkeeper, why borrow?

Because, replied the merchant, meanwhile he can use the money for buying goods and selling them and making a profit; then he gives the money back.

And what happens, the innkeeper went on, if he doesn't give it back? They take him, said the merchant, and shove him into prison. Why, cried the innkeeper, this bank you're talking about is worse than Sodom, taking a Jew and shoving him into prison. It's done, explained the merchant, in order to keep the world in order and as a safeguard against swindlers. And does your honor, continued the innkeeper, also borrow from the bank?

But at this point Simeon grew furious to bursting and shouted at the innkeeper, What do you come worrying me for, you idiot? And before he had cooled down he took the wagoner's strap and lashed the innkeeper with it, crying out, Clear out of here and may all the devils take you! Have you ever seen the like of this fellow setting himself on me like a scab on the head, God forbid! And the innkeeper stared in astonishment at Simeon, the merchant, and said in wonder, At first I thought he was a friendly sort of fellow, but now I see he's as testy a Jew as the other.

And what had Reuben been doing while his companion was conversing with the innkeeper? He repeated the Evening Prayers, washed his hands, sat down and ate his supper, had a glass of something hot, stretched his bones to his satisfaction and smoked happily, smiling the while. Here's this nuisance been driving me out of my mind, complained Simeon to Reuben, and you go smiling! Didn't I tell you, replied Reuben, to wait a bit before you begin reproving me? If there's a chance that when I begin treating him in friendly fashion I'll have to finish by kicking him, it's better to kick him to begin with and then he won't trouble me any more at all. Brother Reuben, said Simeon, you're quite right. It's of you and suchlike folk that the Talmud says "Who is wise? He who foresees what must come about."

TEMPTATION ON THE ROAD

(Excerpt from *In The Heart of the Seas*)

The company traveled for several hours until they reached the Holy Congregation of Yagolnitzi, where they spent the night. In the morning they started out and came near Lashkovitz, that Lashkovitz where there is a great fair whose like is not to be found in the whole world; for more than a hundred thousand merchants come there year after year to do business with one another. At that particular time the fair was taking place, and they met small groups of merchants and wagons laden with all kinds of goods, so that the very earth groaned beneath them.

There it was that Satan came along and stood in their way and asked them, Where are you traveling?

To the Land of Israel, they answered him.

And how are you going to make your living over there? said he.

Some of us, said they, have sold houses, and others have other resources.

Don't you know, said Satan, that journeys eat up money?

We know it well, they answered. So each one of us has labored to lay up money for the expenses of travel, for inns and the ship's fare.

And how about stuffing the pockets of the frontier guards? he asked. And who is going to pay poll tax for you to the King of the Ishmaelites?

How much does he ask? said they to him.

May you have the good luck, he answered, to have him leave you food enough for a single meal. Well then, what you must do is go to Lashkovitz and earn money. Happy is the man who dwells in the Land of Israel and does not need to be supported by the Holy Cities. How people toil to reach Lashkovitz! And now that you have come this far, will you go away without doing business?

Busy as he was with the men, Satan certainly did not ignore the women. Kerchiefs and headcloths and dresses he showed them, until their hearts were near bursting after the fashion of women who see fine clothes and covet them.

When your mother Rebecca, said Satan to the womenfolk, reached the Land of Israel, what did she do, according to the Holy

Writ? Why, she took her veil and decked herself to show her loveliness in her fine things. And now you propose to go to the matriarchs and yet you don't behave as they did! Why, is Lashkovitz so far away? Why, it's in front of your noses. If a man sneezes here, people will say good health to him in Lashkovitz. Even the horses are turning towards it. The very beasts know where the road leads.

But Rabbi Shelomo took out his pouch and filled his pipe with cut tobacco leaf, and struck iron against a flint, and lit the pipe, and half closed his eyes, and began puffing out smoke fast, like a man who wants to get rid of a thought. He saw that the horses were gadding about in an unusual way, wanting to go on in one direction but actually going on in another. Whereupon he touched the wagoner with the long stem of his pipe and said, Take yourself towards Borsztszow. And he urged him to hurry, since folks who proceed to the Land of Israel are like they who go to synagogue, and are duty-bound to run.

The wagoner cracked his whip, and tugged the reins one way and the other, and whistled to the horses, and turned them towards Borsztszow. The horses tossed their heads and dashed on until the dust rose from under their feet. At once the wagons with the goods in them vanished, and the whole countryside filled up with the lame, the halt, the blind, and every other kind of cripple carrying waxen models of limbs, models of hands and legs. For it is their custom to take these to the graves of the holy, there to set them up as candles in order that the holy men might see their deformities and remedy them.

Thereupon the men of good heart understood that all those enticements had come their way only to delay them, so that while they engaged in business to make money with which to live comfortably in the Land of Israel, their souls would depart from them outside the Land.

Like the king who invited his friends to a feast. The wise ones came at once, saying, Does the king lack anything in his palace? But the foolish friends delayed until they had filled their bellies with their own food so as not to require the food of the king. The result was that the wise friends were seated with the king and ate and drank of his best food and wished him well, while the others stayed at home and became drunk on their own wine and besmirched their garments, so that they could not even show themselves in the presence of the king. The king rejoiced at his wise friends and held them dearer than all others, and was angry at the fools and introduced confusion in their midst.

In just the same way the King over all kings, the Holy One, blessed be he, invites those who love him to ascend to the Land of Israel. Is there anything lacking in the house of the King? say the wise ones, and proceed there at once and bless his great Name by the study of the Torah, with songs and praise; and the Holy One, blessed be he, rejoices to see them and does them honor. But the fools tarry at home until they fill their pockets with money, in order, as one might suppose, not to require anything of Him, blessed be he, in the Land of Israel. And at the last they grow drunk with their wine, that is, with money, and besmirch their garments, that is, the body, when buried in earth outside the Land.

Rabbi Alter the teacher spoke first and said, I hate the inclination to evil, which brings people to sin.

Rabbi Moshe responded in turn, The inclination to evil deserves to be hated, but I do not hate it; for all the merits I may have, come to me from the inclination to evil. But it is only just that the wicked should hate it, since it always leads them into evil; in spite of which, not only do they not hate it but they pursue it as though it were their own true love.

Well said, said Rabbi Shelomo.

But the wagoner said, Here are these people journeying to the Land of Israel and wanting to live on good terms with their evil inclinations. I should not wonder if they take it along with them up to the Land of Israel.

Don't worry about us, said Leibush the butcher to him. Instead, just touch up your horses with the whip a bit, so that Satan will not overtake you on the road.

The wagoner turned his face to him angrily and said, And could I touch them up more if I had two whips?

Rabbi Yehuda Mendel looked with friendly eyes at Leibush the butcher, whose words amused him, and put his hands into his sleeves; for the day was already declining and the heat of the sun had diminished.

The wagoner took the reins and urged his horses on. They dashed ahead till they reached the village near Borsztszow where all wayfarers make a halt. The horses betook themselves towards the inn and pulled up at the stable door. The wagoner got down and unharnessed them, gave them their oats and watered them, while Hananiah aided our men of good heart and took down the pillows and cushions and all their other goods.

Then the travelers stretched their limbs and entered the inn to give rest to their bodies and to say the Afternoon and Evening Prayers.

ON THE SEA

(Excerpt from *In the Heart of the Seas*)

At the midnight hour the comrades sat on their baggage and uttered songs and prayers in honor of the great Name of Him who dwells in Zion. The stars moved in the sky, while the moon was now covered, now uncovered. The ship went on, the waters moved as usual, and a still small voice rose from the ship. It was the sound of song and praise rising from one firmament to another, till they reached the Gateway of White Sapphire where the prayers of Israel gather and join together until such time as the dawn comes to the Land of Israel. Corresponding to the prayers of Israel, praises of the Holy One, blessed be he, rise up from the waters.

Is it possible for water which has neither utterance nor speech so to praise the Holy One, blessed be he? But these sounds are the voices of the boys and girls who once flung themselves into the sea. After the wicked Titus destroyed Jerusalem, he brought three thousand ships and filled them with boys and girls. When they were out to sea, they said to one another, Was it not enough for us to have angered the Holy One, blessed be he, in his house, and now are we to be required to anger him in the land of Edom? Thereupon they all leaped into the sea together. What did the Holy One, blessed be he, do? He took them in his right hand and brought them to a great island planted with all manner of fine trees, and surrounded them with all kinds of beautifully colored waves, blue and marble and alabaster, looking like the stones of the Temple; and the plants from which the Temple incense was made grow there. And all those who saw that plant would weep and laugh. They would weep because they remembered the glory of the House, and they would laugh because the Holy One, blessed be he, is destined to bring that glory back.

And the boys and girls still remain as innocent as ever, fenced about from all iniquity, their faces like rosebuds, just as we learn in the tale about the rose garden which was once to be found in Jerusalem. And the brightness of their faces gives light like the planet Venus, whose light comes from the shindig of the Beasts that are before God's throne.

And the children have no wrinkles either on their brows or their faces, apart from two wrinkles under the eyes from which their tears run down into the Great Sea and cool the Gehenna of those sinners of Israel who never lost faith in the Land of Israel. These children are not subject to any prince or ruler, neither to the king of Edom nor to the king of Ishmael, not to any flesh-and-blood monarch; but they stand in the shadow of the Holy One, blessed be he, and call him Father and he calls them my children. And all their lives long they speak of the glory of Jerusalem and the glory of the House, and the glory of the High Priests and the altar, and of those who offered the sacrifices and those who prepared the incense and those who made the shew-bread.

And whenever the Holy One, blessed be he, remembers his sons who have been exiled among the nations, who have neither Temple nor altar of atonement, nor High Priests nor Levites at their stations, nor kings and princes, he at once is filled with pity and takes those boys and girls in his arm and holds them to his heart and says to them, Sons and daughters mine, do you remember the glory of Jerusalem and the glory of Israel when the Temple still stood and Israel still possessed its splendor?

They at once begin telling Him what they saw in their childhood, and go on interpreting like Daniel, the beloved man, and Jonathan ben Uziel. The only difference is that Daniel and Jonathan wrote in Aramaic, while these children speak the Holy Tongue, which is the tongue the Holy One, blessed be he, uses. And at such times the Holy One, blessed be he, laughs with them; and you might say that at no other times does he laugh and smile as he does when he hears the praises of his House and the praises of those who came to his House. At such times he says, 'This is the people which I formed for Myself that they might tell of My praise.' And he also says, 'Comfort ye,' for in the future Jerusalem will be builded a thousand thousand times more great than she was, and the Temple will reach from one end of the world to the other and be as lofty as the stars of the heavens and the wheels of my divine Chariot; and the Divine Presence will rest upon each and every one of Israel; and each and every one of them will speak in the Holy Spirit.

Furthermore, all the years that those boys and girls have dwelt in the midst of the sea they have constantly awaited salvation, and there is no ship sailing to the Land of Israel which these boys and girls do not follow. For when they see a ship at sea, one says to the other, The time has come for the Gathering of the Exiles. Thereupon, each of them takes one of the great sea waves and mounts it as a rider mounts his horse and rides until he comes near the ship.

And as they ride they sing, 'I will bring them back from Bashan, I will bring them back from the depths of the sea.' And their voices are as golden bells in the skirts of a garment, and they are heard by those who go down to the sea. Indeed we have heard a tale from such as tell only the truth, of how they were sailing to the Land of Israel on the Great Sea and heard a voice so sweet they wished to leap into the sea and follow that voice; but the sailors tied them up with their belts until the ship had sailed a distance away from the voice.

The moon sank, the stars went in, and the planets went their way. The Holy One, blessed be he, brought forth the dawn and lit up the world. As the dawn grew bright the travelers saw the likeness of a man on the sea. They stared and saw that he had a full beard, earlocks on either cheek and a book in his hand; and a kerchief was spread out under him and on it he sat as a man who sits at his ease. No wave of the sea rose to drown him, nor did any sea beast swallow him.

And what did the Gentiles say when they saw a man sitting on his kerchief and floating in the sea? Some of them said, Such things are often seen by the seafarers and desertfarers. Others said, Whoever he is, he has a curse hanging over him so that nevermore can he rest. That is why he wanders from place to place, appearing yesterday on the dry land and today on the sea.

On that ship there were representatives of each of the seventy nations of the world, and each of them was overwhelmed and terrified at this apparition. So Israel stood on one side and the nations of the world on the other, fearful and staring, until their eyelashes became scorched by the sun. Then Rabbi Shmuel Yosef, the son of Rabbi Shalom Mordekhai ha-Levi, said, It is the Divine Presence, which is bringing back the people of Israel to their own place.

And Rabbi Moshe wept and said, 'The counsel of the Lord is with them that fear Him, and his covenant to make them know it.'

THE MINYAN

A Short Story

In Tiberias there lived a fine young man, the son of a widow, learned in the Torah and perfect in the fear of God, and all his days he was swift as a deer to do the will of his Father in Heaven. But, just as the skin of a deer can hardly contain its body, so the body of the youth could not hold in his soul, and one day he fell ill and was like to die. All kinds of remedies were used, and all kinds of doctors were called, but they were of no avail. If the Holy One, blessed be he, does not send healing from Heaven, what can men do?

In those days, Tiberias was full of *Hasidim* and men of good deeds, who knew how to pray before God. And when they heard that this young man was like to die, they were filled with pity for him, and they said to each other: "Let us pray for him, so that he may recover from his sickness."

So they all gathered together in a certain House of Study within whose walls the sound of learning and prayer was never silent, and they allotted a large sum to charity, which they divided into seven portions, so that the youth might be delivered from the seven punishments which are written in the Torah, and that there might be fulfilled for him the verse, "And charity delivers from death"; and they stood all day and all night in prayer and supplication. Then they went to the tomb of Rabbi Meir B'al Haness, and to the tombs of other Rabbis and sages and righteous and pious men, whose bodies were buried in the earth of Tiberias. And they prostrated themselves upon the graves with great weeping, and lit lamps, according to the number of years of the sick youth and according to the number of years of man in this world; till the holy city was lit up by these lamps. But the soul of the young man's life sank lower and lower, like a wick without oil.

When the *Hasidim* saw this, they said to each other: "Beloved brethren, what more can we do for this sick man that we have not yet done?" And they answered each other: "Beloved brethren, all that we are able to do, we have already done."

So they took their prayer-books and returned home in despair.

But the Holy One, blessed be he, still wished to enjoy the learning of the young man in this world, and he planted in the hearts of the relatives of the youth the idea of going up to Meron on Lag Ba'omer, to prostrate themselves upon the grave of Rabbi Shim'on Ben Yohai, that the merit of the divine sage might stand him in good stead and help him to recover from his sickness.

So they took him, in his bed, and carried him all the way until they reached Safad. And since Safad was full of many physicians, expert in books of healing and the ways of the human body, they brought the sick youth before them. When the physicians saw him, they lowered their heads, with a sigh and said: "We despair of him, we cannot lengthen his life for even an hour. But in the west of Safad there is an old burial ground with many caves; and in that place many righteous and holy men are buried, double the number of those who came out of Egypt. Take the sick man, and make the circuit of the burial ground with him; perhaps they will have pity on him and beg mercy for him." So they went and made the circuit of the burial ground with weeping and supplication, but they saw no sign of improvement in the sick man. Then they took him and went up to Meron with him, but when they reached Meron there was no life left in him. So they put down his bed, and laid him down in front of the cave, and wept loud and long, until all the companies of pilgrims who came to prostrate themselves upon the grave of Rabbi Shim'on Ben Yohai wept with them.

At that moment, all the sages of Safad arrived with scrolls of the Torah in their hands, dancing all the way in great joy, singing songs and praises and playing all kinds of instruments. And the Rabbi of the Safaradim walked before them, an old man and righteous, all the years of his life adorned with learning and prayer and good deeds. He saw all the people weeping and asked: "Why are you weeping?" They said to him: "A certain widow from Tiberias brought her only son here, so that he might find healing on the grave of Rabbi Shim'on Ben Yohai, and when he reached here he had passed away."

Then the Rabbi said: "God forbid that the Great Rejoicing of Rabbi Shim'on Ben Yohai should become a day of weeping and mourning." And he said to the attendants: "Send out all the men from the House of Study and from the cave, and let no man enter the cave until I call you." So they went out, and no man was left there.

The the Rabbi said to the bearers of the bed: "Bring the sick man into the cave." So they brought him in and laid him down on pillows and rugs. He said to them: "Go out"—and they went out. When they had gone out, the Rabbi sealed the cave and made the circuit of the cave, on the inside. And he continued in prayer until the time of the afternoon service.

When the time of the afternoon service came, he opened up the cave and brought in eight wise men, who had been careful all their lives to pray with the congregation, and stood with them by the grave of Rabbi Shim'on Ben Yohai, and said: "Ben Yohai, you know that ever since we reached the age of understanding we have never let pass the hour of prayer without saying our prayers with the congregation. And now we here are nine, and this young man makes ten; if you do not beg mercy for him that he may live, we shall lose the opportunity of praying with the congregation."

So they stood by the grave of Rabbi Shim'on Ben Yohai, looking at the dead lad, but they saw no sign of life in him. Then each of them put his hand in the girdle of his neighbor, and they said: "Ben Yohai, you know full well that ever since we reached the age of understanding we have not prayed in a congregation of fewer than ten, and today, on the day of your death, shall we stand here, ten men of Israel, and not say the afternoon prayer as a congregation?" Immediately, the old Rabbi began to say the *Ashrei* prayer, and he read each verse with fear and terror and awe and trembling and all his companions read each verse with him word by word. When they reached the verse, "The Lord is near to all that call upon him, to all that call upon him in truth," they heard a sound coming from the mouth of the sick youth. They listened carefully and heard his lips whispering: "He does the will of them that fear him," and they knew that their prayer had been accepted by God, and they knew that he lived.

This story is famous all over Safad, and I heard it from a certain man who heard it from a certain old woman who was there, but I do not remember whether the old woman came from Tiberias or Safad.

Gershon Shoffman, Portraitist and Realist

Gershon Shoffman, writer of novels and short stories, editor and translator, was born in Orsha, Russia, in 1880. He received the traditional *heder* and *yeshiva* education until, at the age of sixteen, he began studying the Russian language and literature.

His first stories appeared in 1899 and two years later he published a volume of short stories and sketches entitled *Sippurim Vetziyurim.* After three years of service in the Russian army he went to Austria in 1904 and lived in that country until 1938 when he settled in Palestine.

He has edited a number of literary miscellanies and, in addition to the above-mentioned volume, his works include the following: *Reshimot,* 1908; *Meidakh Gisa,* 1909; collected works, 3 volumes, 1914, 1927-35, 1946; *Beterem Argaa,* 1942; *Bemelkahaim,* 1944. He was awarded the Bialik Prize for literary distinction.

From the Russian he has translated Gorki and Chekhov and from the German selected works of the Austrian writer, Peter Altenberg. He is a contributor to the Israeli and foreign press.

I

Gershon Shoffman is a master of the brief compact short story. He is without peer for conciseness and for pointedness of expression. His phrases have a remarkable finesse and the glint of new minting. The reader from the very start is intrigued by an artist who is so rich in his gifts and yet so frugal in giving expression to them.

Some authors are expansive and their meandering may even have charm. But as a rule their work lacks precision. They like to verbalize and to weave a web of words around the reader. But Shoffman is ruthlessly laconic. His sentences are taut to the snapping point. This extreme condensation is not due to niggardliness of temper. On the contrary, it derives from Shoffman's very opulence so carefully controlled. Neither in style nor content does he mystify the reader. He cuts to the core of things and reveals their very essence. For he has no use for the outer shell in either language or content.

He does not suffer as an artist because of this strict selectivity. The theme that is promising and important finds ample room in his short story. With Shoffman one oblique glance, one adroit phrase, goes a long way.

Yet Shoffman not only knows how to tell a story and to portray a character; he can also entertain. That, too, he does with a subtlety all his own. From his carefully weighed and measured line, the initiated reader derives a refreshing satisfaction. This is due not only to his manner of composition and style, but primarily to his keen power of observation and his uncanny psychological insight. He can pique the reader's curiosity and arouse his dormant sensibilities. He can both magnify and minimize human weaknesses and he does not hesitate frankly to describe unpleasant incidents normally taboo among writers. For he knows that such incidents are common in real life. He is, therefore, not deterred from pursuing the truth wherever it may lead him.

Shoffman has a penetrating, all-seeing eye. Nothing is inaccessible to it, and whatever he discovers, he holds up as a mirror so that the reader may look into it and recognize himself.

He is convinced that it is the passions that hold sovereign sway over man. From them there is no escape. They deprive man of his independence while stirring him into feverish activity. After man has done their bidding, they play havoc with his life. They promise happiness and spread before his eyes beckoning vistas of beauty, but after he has heeded their call, the alluring horizons are invariably found to be mirages. What is man but the sport of these blind forces? He is not free. He is not "the captain of his soul," not "the master of his fate." His path in life is beset with insidious snares into which, sooner or later, he is sure to fall.

The whole world is but one large dark prison in which the prisoners are confronted by the blind walls of despair. That is why there are in Shoffman's stories so many emigrés, fugitives, prisoners and spies. One group, and by far the larger, is in jail or in hiding, while the other keeps watch over it or lies in wait, ready to pounce at any moment. The world is full of "eyes"—the vigilant eyes of police, visible and invisible, always prying, always pursuing their victims.

The convict's strongest desire, naturally, is to escape, to hide. And this is what most of Shoffman's heroes do. If one happens to be a rebel and member of an outlawed party, he lives his life stealthily, talks in whispers to his comrades, meets them at appointed places in the fastness of a forest until, seeking to escape under the cover of darkness, he succeeds in crossing the border, or else, falls into a trap laid by the police. If he is a soldier in the army of the Czar, he withdraws into his inner shell, feeding upon childhood reminiscences, abandoning his external self to the fitful discipline of corporals and lieutenants, and suffers blows and endless physical and spiritual mortifications until he deserts and steals across the border. Both the deserting soldier and the political fugitive hope that they will finally find freedom, but this too usually turns out to be an illusion.

A jail is a jail, whether it be in Austria or in Russia. Spies and detectives follow one wherever one goes, in time of peace or of war, into the cafes and on the street. The fugitive is constantly being tracked by ever watchful eyes. And thus his whole life is lived in the shadow of fear—fear of others and fear of himself.

What a dark and oppressive incubus weighs upon the lives of these uprooted characters who stalk through the pages of Shoffman's stories! Torn and far removed from home and hearth, love of home still haunts them. They roam about in strange towns to no purpose, aimlessly and hopelessly. They waste their lives in hostile surroundings. Their vacant and insipid existence is totally without meaning.

They fret away their days in cheap smoke-filled cafes, subject to suspicion and frightened by rumors. Ostracized by society, they kill time in these taverns frequented only by fellow-exiles, and cling to their cigarette butts as they do to their vanishing youth. Like the discarded cigarette butts, so too are the dreams of their youth trodden underfoot. Their gloomy fear-ridden days pass like swift-moving shadows upon the walls, and darkness frightens them with its nightmares (a word much used by Shoffman) as they sleep in their cheap lodgings two in a rickety bed, on dirty uncased pillows and straw mats.

Such is the fate of the disinherited. At home as children, when the innocence of childhood dreams enveloped them, there were father and mother and often a kindly and gentle sister—a lovely creature who appears to them still in a restless dream and draws them homeward. But now, in exile, they are alone—nobodies.

Strangers and suspects all, fugitives eluding pursuing eyes, eternal prisoners. Futile then was the escape from home. It brought no freedom. The fetters have grown even tighter. The prison at home has only extended its walls to swallow them up even here, far beyond their country's borders.

This imprisonment is both an outward and inner reality. Every man is in a cell. If he is really in jail, then certainly he is locked up. But even if he be at large, walking the streets, he is under the constant surveillance of the gendarmes. If he is sick, he is confined to his bed and subject to the orders of his physician. If he is insane, he is the prisoner of his hallucinations and kept under guard. If he is unmarried, he is the most enslaved—to the surging desire of youth and to the passion aroused by every passing girl. And if he is married, he is bound by marital ties and caught in the trap of matrimony. Nor is the male alone exposed to this doom. The female is no freer to control the destiny of her life. If she is pure and chaste, she is consumed by lust and passion until . . . she succumbs to temptation. And then—her demanding master, Love, flings her from one "admirer" to the other, from one lover to the next. And how many of the once innocent and sweet maidens fall into the trap at the edge of town—the house of prostitution. Their slavery is now complete, as the fat, dissolute "madames," having purchased their youthful freshness, sell them again and again to every passer-by. In that prison in the back alley, that blind imprisoning force, characteristic of life generally, pursues its hapless victims with a special vengeance, quashing the blossoms of youth, burying alive its innocence.

Little Ann too at the age of thirteen falls into this back-alley prison, wild and whimsical Ann, child of field and forest, a flower upon which the dew-drops were still fresh. The traffic to the disorderly house grew heavier, as the factory workers, themselves life's prisoners, after a hard day's labor, sought to free themselves momentarily from their slavery, to cast aside their anxieties and to sip the nectar from the fresh flower.

"In droves they would flock, life's disinherited ones, to that alley, singing and shouting their anticipated release—thither—thither—and from the threshold they would cry out impatiently, 'Where is Ann?'

"And the answer was always short and painful—'Busy!'

"The cruel hunger of those who were themselves victims of the big city and life's prisoners, the hunger that knows not satiety, fell upon this lovely creature, this flower of the field, quickly drained it of its nectar and then lustily demanded, 'More!' "

Ann did not last long. Life's hungry prisoners devoured her.

Hunger and yearning drive Shoffman's characters on and motivate their acts. They hunger for bread, they want a home, they are looking for a wife, they seek love. And just as they themselves are constantly longing to escape out of confinement into freedom, so do their passions seek an outlet, breaking out into the open, defying all barriers. The lust for life is irresistible; the quenchless thirst for happiness is irrepressible. Thus, all these lean and hungry characters make their way in a world, both alien and wonderful, hard and attractive, while within the fire burns unceasingly. Poverty and ennui hold them in thrall but boundless freedom and inexpressible beauty beckon to them. They become prey to hatred and despair, derangement and death. At the sight of them one is gripped by a deep sadness. What a procession—prisoners and fugitives, soldiers and immigrants, cripples and maniacs, wrestlers and thugs, servant girls and prostitutes, murderers and suicides, and, finally, figures swinging from gallows!

A sick and demented world! The only sure feature of it is torture and pain. It is always characterized by a passion for suffering and a love of madness. In thinking of Shoffman, one calls to mind the remark of the Russian critic, Michalovsky, about Dostoievsky: "What a cruel talent!"

This "cruel talent" gives him the courage and the ability to probe the innermost secrets of life's experiences as they are, to reveal the exact nature of reality with both its lights and its shadows. He is not a tender-hearted writer and he does not recoil from the gory sight of pain nor from the most exact description of it. For it is only after the correct word and phrase have been written that his creative spirit can find rest. This "cruel talent" preserves his integrity as an artist. For softness and gentility and the turning away from reality cannot serve a man in a world whose guardian angel is hunger and whose song is lust, a world ruled by sin and founded on physical strength. A singing sentimentality cannot help a man keep his footing amidst the raging of violent winds. One must gird himself with strength and fortify himself with cruelty so as to be able to rise again after each fall, to tread upon danger without succumbing, to behold horrors without being affrighted.

Yet Shoffman's sadism often frightens us. He paints human suffering with great faithfulness, almost with relish. "How pleasant is the shriek of pain, this human wailing that is swallowed up in the wide atmosphere. Let your hearts roll in pain a bit. It is good that way!" he exclaims in *Hanged*.

In *Ice Cream,* Socolin, the narrator of the story, says, "Out of this rapture I frequently used to awake from my sleep and I used to hear how Margolis (his room-mate and rival in love) would toss restlessly in his bed from side to side. Then I used to bury my head deep in my pillow and fall soundly asleep. How doubly sweet is sleep at the time when your friend, close to you, finds no peace in his slumber because of the pain of despair which you have caused him."

He shows animosity not only to the individual, but to the world at large. He is even moved by a desire for its destruction. In *Strain and Straits* he expresses himself thus: "The morning papers bring news of entire cities destroyed by cannons from both sides, from our side and from that of the enemy, laid in ruins not leaving one stone upon the other." And he rejoices: "It serves them right. Let them be destroyed, cut down, razed to the ground, these old cursed walls that have not a single unpolluted brick within them . . . Let them be brought to earth together with their owners, together with their wicked owners."

But in his sadism there is no blind hatred of man and life. On the contrary, there is a revengeful zeal to restore human dignity and to prevent life from being degraded. It is the cry of a man who sees evil and cannot remain silent. And he cries out, "Eye for eye, tooth for tooth!" so that human torture and humiliation may be expiated.

He describes a hospital where patients who have been operated upon suffer unceasing pain. The very door, swinging on its hinge, emits an almost human groan. For the hinge is only returning some of the endless human groaning it has absorbed here for so many days and nights. Here they lie, the mangled in body, the amputated of limb. Here is a Swabian whose ear was operated upon; there, a Pole whose legs were amputated; here a peasant boy who had broken his leg while skating and there a gypsy whose arm was broken by a kick from a horse.

"Not an easy operation," exclaims the surgeon as the patient, Alp by name, is brought out from under the knife. In their midst there flutters about a young nurse. The frozen grimace on her face masks her inner suffering. The pain all around her has put its stamp upon this fair and tender creature and she flits among the beds silently—the symbol of universal pain. As the last tongue of flame spurts forth from the embers of a dying fire, so too among these unfortunates bound to their beds there bursts forth in flame an intense passion for life. Love suddenly glows with a last blinding light and then expires. And the patient, whose name is Alp, has a hankering desire to tell the nurse that she is beautiful. Men thus become as children and awaken infinite pity and pathos. And so the end comes. The feeble sighs are drowned out by the shrieks. Here a man is breathing his last while there, outside, beyond this hospital wing, life moves on rich and quick and tumultuous. "And beneath the dull mental stupor there welled up a great anger at those miserable wretches outside carrying on their ordinary stupid business of life during these dark hours."

This sense of helplessness, in spite of the blind desire for life and in the presence of those who are shamelessly healthy, awakens in the heart of a sentient person, restlessness and resentment, envy and anger, hatred and cruelty. It is stronger than hunger and thirst in the discerning heart, the heart that sees all this cruel sport which is man's fate.

True, there are those naive enough to believe that one may pass by all this suffering and forget life's reality. But Shoffman would see life as it is. He loathes hypocrisy and prudery and scoffs at them. He knows smugness well and hates it thoroughly. His art is set in the framework of night, for darkness often reveals the truth. The grey eye of the cat flares in all its fearsomeness and ferocity only at night. The meanest passions, that lie hidden and buried during the day, awake into being with the coming of night; and the beast that lies lurking in man springs into the open when night grows darkest. All of life and love and lust are related to the night. They are wrapped in a mantle of darkness, unseen and fearing discovery. But he who has eye to see and ear to hear is aware not only of the visible secret police who lie in wait for us on all sides, but also of the inner "secret police," the hidden lusts constantly seeking to burst forth.

In one of his stories, Franchisek, the drunken sailor who is watchman of the insane asylum, waylays the proprietress of a house of prostitution after she had visited her son, a patient, with Stepka, one of her girls. She had lost her way and had wandered into the dark square, when suddenly out of the blackness of night there glinted at her the face of Franchisek "so pale and frightened as though he had just experienced a miraculous escape from the hands of murderers." And with the cry, "This is the end of you!" he jumped on the old woman and struck her dead. Then he made for Stepka.

"What are you doing, what are you doing?" Stepka called out to Franchisek who had formerly been her lover. A ferocious, bloodthirsty spirit took possession of him, no longer man but animal.

"Shut up, shut up!" he kept growling at her, and his firm, strong fingers gradually strangled her. "In the darkness he saw her dazed, entreating glance, that glance so well known to him and his old passion came to play, that passion to torture the helpless defenseless being, to crush, to kill."

This cruel desire "to torture and kill helpless defenseless beings," is common not only to the few. In one guise or another, in lesser or greater degree, it resides in all of us, and both in the individual and society. The murderer gives it simple and direct expression, powerful and certain. He springs out of the darkness and attacks his victims outright. Athletes and boxers disguise it under the guise of sport; and thousands of people who also secretly share the same desire for inflicting pain get a vicarious delight in witnessing various sporting events. Kings, statesmen, national heroes invest their savage lust for blood with moral purpose and hallow it with such names as "love of country" and "the sanctity of the law." And so they wage wars, instigate revolutions and crowd jails and prisons with unfortunate victims, with those who cannot defend themselves. No matter how much poets and moralists condone such conduct, its true identity is unmistakable. It is still savagery to inflict pain on others in order to enhance one's own joy, to destroy the other's world in order to build one's own.

Thus Shoffman divests man of all his garments and sets him down in all his nakedness, his sufferings and passions, his fate and his enslavement to the fierce ago-old struggle of life and death.

II

The contradictory forces in our life are secretly and continually at war with each other. The only faithful and reliable weapon in this struggle is physical force. This is the only instrument that can be successful against the hatred and compulsion working within us. This element of physical force occupies an important place in Shoffman's works. No one appreciates more than he the reality of physical force and the decisive importance of the body and its limbs. He takes great delight in athletes and shows intimate familiarity with sports. He enjoys looking at and describing the muscular figure of the wrestler. "The sinewy colossus," he tells us in his sketch, *Force*, "made a motion, took a light step, and in a swift movement jabbed without being touched himself." A company of soldiers who witness his performance go into raptures out of sheer admiration for this hero. "What strength!" exclaim both Chabotov, the cook, and the corporals. They admire the physical strength that enables him to throw great weights about like so many little marbles and to break an iron bar in half with his hands as though it were a hollow cake.

And in *Sergei Mamotov* he portrays the rugged wild strength of the athlete and the blind worship of force by the tender and weak sport-lovers. The hero of the story, Shakhna Green, is one of the Russian fugitives in Austria. He spends most of his days in the beer house, the "Port Arthur," a tavern frequented by his countrymen. He is greatly bored by the emptiness and weakness of his life, but when he reads an announcement of the arrival of a group of athletes, his heart jumps with joy. He will see wrestlers of various nationalities —a Frenchman, an Italian, a Pole, an American, a Jew and a Russian too. He is especially excited by the inclusion of a Russian name, Sergei Mamotov, among them. For in his heart of hearts he is still a Russian . . . "Do you know what Mamotov used to be in Russia?" he asks. "An executioner, yes, an executioner in Siberia. He himself boasted that he often used to hang as many as twenty-five people in one day. Enough to make you dizzy . . . and here he is, Sergei Mamotov himself."

At last, by some miracle, he is to see Sergei Mamotov, the executioner, in person! What an unusual treat! And what worship of vulgar physical force!

The match, to which the entire colony looks forward with impatience, and none more so than Shakhna Green, is described in great detail. On his way there Green encounters Shank, the anarchist, in the hands of a policeman.

"I was arrested and nobody knows it," says Shank to him. "Please go at once to the 'Port Arthur' and notify them."

But Green does not comply with his request. He says to himself, "It won't hurt him to be in jail a while," and he hastens to the sport arena. The hall is agog with joyous festivity. The first two wrestlers appear in the ring. There is Carfini, the Italian, and Tsiffs, the Negro from North America, who charms the crowd with his sparkling eyes and teeth. And here are the Tsignovitzes, two brothers from Austria. Polish blood mounts at once to the boiling point and the hall shakes with thundering applause. And the announcer continues, "The Jewish athlete, Hayyim Wildman." Sporadic, scattered applause is heard, together with jeering shouts. And the author adds parenthetically, were every young Jew an athlete like him, there would be little to fear from pogroms.

At last, Sergei Mamotov appears, "the real *goy*." The athletes wrestle, the big and the little. The little fellow flounders and wriggles, eluding the hand of his opponent quite nimbly. He is full of action, panting, perspiring and the heavy man works slowly, lazily, takes his time, and before a few minutes pass, throws the little man flat on his back. *Where strength is lacking, all the skill and maneuvering are in vain!* (Italics are mine—M. R.)

When Hayyim Wildman's turn comes to meet Mamotov in the ring, the Poles find themselves divided in their sympathies. But their hatred for the Russian soldier overcomes their contempt for the Jew and voices here and there call out, "Don't give in, Hayyim, don't let him beat you!"

But Shakhna Green, once a revolutionary and now a fugitive, is captivated by "the real *goy.*" He is swept away by the strength of the Russian. He watches the battle, and once during intermission when the wrestlers leave the ring wrapped in their towels, Green jumps out of his place, pushes himself into the aisle until he reaches the place where Mamotov is standing in order to see him better. But strangely enough, despite the fact that he is standing close to him, he fails to see him. He stares at him but somehow does not see him. Mamotov, panting and sweating, keeps wiping his naked flesh all aglow.

When his fellow Russians follow Mamotov to the wine cellar, Green goes along. He cannot free himself from the spell cast upon him by this Russian brute. He wants to sit near him, to see him at close range, to have a good look at him. His own companions, or those who had been his companions in the past, were undoubtedly looking for a chance to attack this wretch of an executioner and wreak their revenge on him for all the blood that he had shed in their mutual homeland, but he, Green, drinks a toast to his health. He quickly downs glass after glass. But, as in days of old in his native town, when he could not drink away his despicable fear of the secret police who might break in at any moment, so now. He keeps casting glances towards the door just as he used to do. Who is peering there through that black window-pane? And as though looking for protection and shelter under the massive strength of the athlete, at present sharing his own danger, he brings his chair closer to that of Sergei Mamotov.

The fear that shadows the weak and the persecuted makes of them slaves to brute force, confusing their thoughts, harassing their lives. Strong persons use their strength to their own advantage and to others' disadvantage. But the weak and the oppressed, afraid of their own shadows, spend what little strength they have to no avail. They fritter it away in satisfying morbid and loathesome passions. Whatever potential cruelty they possess is expended upon themselves. Instead of testy wrestling in the open, as do the healthy and the strong who thus sublimate their passions through physical action, these, the weak and the frightened, wrestle secretly with their passions and mortify themselves with their pains until the fire within them utterly consumes them.

Daniel Kuran in *The Fugitive,* had also been a revolutionary in Russia who had fled to Austria, but even here his constant fear of the detective continued. He lived surreptitiously. His energy found no outlet and he deteriorated mentally as well as physically. From afar, beauty was calling and happiness beckoning, but here the days were grey and drab. Only in his heart lust's fires flickered.

He would find solace and forgetfulness in the brothel, but it was only momentary. Upon his sobering up, the "I" within him would proclaim itself and he would bemoan his wasted youth. But ever since he had been torn from his native soil and cast far from the moorings of his childhood, he was unable to take root anywhere. And so he would go from one wench to another, as though others and not he, directed his destiny. He, too, was a wrestler, but his wrestling was with degeneracy and death.

"At night he would steal into the kitchen where the young servant girl, a modest, rustic maid was sleeping. She repulsed him violently, threatening, 'I will yell, I will call the mistress.'

"He became especially restless when they took in a Czech servant girl, Nunya, a pretty, blue-eyed creature, and the very first evening when the old lady of the house went away, he assailed Nunya in the kitchen with fresh importunities. He became indecently excited and sullied himself. In the meantime the door opened and the letter-carrier handed him a postcard. Kuran at once recognized his sister's handwriting and took it in in one glance. 'Last night Asher (his brother) was hanged. At least, suffer a bit, you too, if you can . . .' The bolt whizzed past his temple and missed! And without continuing his reading, he folded the postcard in two, put it in his bosom pocket and continued his siege of the servant."

Is it only carnal passion that burns within him now? No, it is no ordinary lust, but a destructive passion seeking revenge. The old flaming hatred in all its strength flares up against the women of the "others," the "others" who rule and oppress. He must avenge the blood of his long-suffering brother, Asher the quiet and sad, who had just been hung in his native Russia. He must take revenge for his own futile life wasted away under alien skies.

Indeed, this picture of Kuran, continuing to grapple with Nunya after receiving the news about his brother's death, is revolting. But such are the effects of despair nurtured for years by a hunger for life unfulfilled, a hunger that destroys the spirit. It is clear, all too clear, what Kuran's end will be. He had to free himself of the albatross of suffering that was slowly choking him. There was no other way out but to commit suicide in the prison where he was later confined.

"He knew what was good for him," said the warden when he came to inspect his dangling body at the call of the guard. "He must have been a murderer or a spy. Let him stew!"

Indeed, he knew what was good for him. He had no other way out. For there is no renascence for the weak.

The same fate overtakes Dora in *The Scorching Heat.* After a quarrel with her husband she runs away to the city of Kiev. Why there? Because in that town there lived a man who had been in love with her long ago and because there was a river there. (She will only go to bathe there."). And indeed, there, in the city of her dreams, in that very river, she drowns herself.

Similarly, in the story *Brother,* Lorka, whose "skin is so white and her face so very round," who has just begun to live, is crushed under the weight of her love. She had always sensed that Mundick would cease to love her and that she would not have the strength to carry on. "One morning between winter and springtime, Lorka threw herself out of the third floor window. She left a letter addressed to Mundick. 'I forgive you everything, everything. I loved your sad eyes and if I did not succeed in uniting with them in life, I may succeed better in death'."

It would appear that all of these victims are an indispensable part of the scheme of things. It is as though they help sweeten the taste for life. For the destruction of one person helps in the building up of another. And death makes one appreciate all the more the sweet mystery of life.

"This tragic event," the author adds, "casts a new beauty into the subsequent spring evenings, into the movements of the young girls strolling in their new hats, into the first rumblings of thunder, into the heavy drops of rain splattering on the clean sidewalk by the light of the street lamps. Clandestine love affairs take on a new edge now. Lorka's life blood seemed to nurture them all."

The blood of the weak and helpless, drips into the fountain of life. It makes the blood course more strongly in the veins of the man who lives and desires, who lives and suffers. For in all existence, out of every being there arises the call of blood.

III

Shoffman's sensitive ear hears the call of the blood both of the individual and of the people as a whole. His work is rooted in a strong nationalism, even racialism. He strains after those fine distinctions that differentiate nation from nation, race from race. When the Great War broke out with its destructive fury it revealed the world in all its nakedness. But the discerning ear could have heard even earlier the bubbling of unclean blood eager to erupt. From what he saw at the time, in the army, in prisons, in the gloom of Russia, in the lands of exile, he witnessed the hatred of the Gentiles towards the hounded, persecuted Jews. When Jews were being massacred, army contingents were sent to restore peace and order, but how could those soldiers restore peace when they themselves thirsted for blood and took delight in pogroms? Hence their captain kept detouring them so as to be sure they would not stumble against the rioters and interfere with their work. And the Jewish soldier relates, "Even the best of them, those who in the barracks are of a rather kindly and genial disposition, were seized by an ungodly fire and, exclaiming obscenities, greatly enjoyed all the violence they saw about them."

"Oh, how the Jewish daughters scream!" Our tortured daughters rent the air with their cries. And in that very hour when on one of the street corners the rioters were dismantling and plundering a Jewish grocery store, the Gentile women swooped down upon the booty, scooping handfuls of candy from the jars, laughing gloatingly as they watched an aged Jew being trampled down. "Lest the daughters of the Philistines rejoice,"—an old atavistic quiver shook me and my eyes grew moist from an inner tenderness towards David. "And he measured them with a rope, making them lie down on the ground, and he measured two lines of them to put to death."

And Shoffman ends with the exclamation, "David, our David! . . . " What do we have here but the call of the blood, of blood spilled without the possibility of revenge? And if the call be deliberately silenced in the world of consciousness, it breaks out again in dreams. If at times national boundaries seem to fade and different peoples reveal a semblance of kinship, and all mothers, sisters, brothers, seem to be alike, the happy vision does not last long. The call of the blood will not be silenced.

In *The Call of the Blood,* the differences between the Jewish fugitive, the principal character, and his Christian bride, Gretel, the Viennese, seem to disappear. She has a brother and a sister. So has he. Her mother's home reminds him of his own home in spite of the fact that worlds lie between the two. "This home even like his own, stands on the outskirts of the town, and the small frail woman with a shawl on her head coughs like his own mother and like her puts on her spectacles when she has to sew a patch on a garment. Everything as in his own home!" And her brother David, like his own brother Solomon, is shy, silent and self-sacrificing. And Bertha, her sister, like his sister Batya "comes from school in her black apron, and because of the poverty in the home, she makes light of her hunger and at once takes to her books . . . " The same integrity, the same understanding, the same patience. And even the midwife who hastened to his wife Gretel on a cold winter night is exactly like the *Baba* Mereh at home, and he thinks, "The agonies of war have wiped away all incidentals and externals which differentiate nations and races and have left only what is essentially human."

But this imagined similarity suddenly prevailing between distant and alien worlds is of short duration. It is sheer illusion that only the essentially human remains. At a decisive moment when his Gentile wife, Gretel, is gripped by pains of labor and he is waiting in the adjoining room, the call of the blood bursts forth unrestrainedly.

He dozes off and at once his ears are assailed by a remote, thin outcry. His native village is overcast by an eerie light, like that during an eclipse of the sun, and he is running down the street alongside the low frame houses, their shutters closed. A girl is running in front of him and he sees her curls flying in the wind for want of a pin. She is evidently much too frightened to have taken care of it. And there is the little garden of his childhood days. Three big Gentiles suddenly pop out from among the rows of flaming poppies, one of them wearing a soldier's hat, and giving him a spade, they order, "Take this and dig your own grave right here!"

And the distant cry grows louder and louder . . . his heart is split in twain. When his mother-in-law comes in with the news, "A boy!" he does not wake up.

For at the moment when the boy, his own little Gentile, comes into the world, he, the Jewish father, has dug his own grave. The peace was no peace. The tranquillity was no tranquillity. There had been only momentary self-forgetfulness and self-deception. And what had been consciously repressed and silenced had burst forth in the dream. The blood exacts its toll.

The most powerful, the deepest, of all passions is the sexual, the hunger for love. This is the most basic and the most mysterious. Like the rainbow's colors against a cloud, love shines through the works of Shoffman in all its hues and nuances. It is the driving force in his stories. In every utterance, in every motion, in every deed—there it is. For its decisive force is ever there to create and consume. It is man's good fortune and his evil star. It is his Song of Songs on earth in all generations. With it one is born and lives; with it he lives and dies.

In the fierce and cruel struggle of life, in the vying within man of complex forces, there is one force that both attracts and enslaves, redeems and sets free—love! By its light does man walk—suffering, struggling man.

The bearer of love is woman, but the bearer of its burden is man. And the heavier his burden of love, the greater her sway. Woman is the source of happiness, the giver of life, and to her is drawn parched dry-lipped man in order to drink and sate his thirst. Shoffman has elevated woman to the heights of a lofty power that rules and enslaves. She directs man's steps and he proceeds according to her will. If she wills it, he mounts the heights of bliss; or if she so desires, he descends to the depths of misfortune. A unique power was conferred upon her from her early childhood. Woman, weak and tender, frail and delicate, forever rules over man, strong and valiant, warring and conquering.

She herself may be naive, demure and innocent, but shrewd nature has made her the repository of limitless powers so that men, competing, quarreling, hating, envying, might be drawn to her and fight each other for her sake—all for the mirage of love and happiness that beckons from all her being. That is why she, the queen and goddess, often becomes the first casualty. For, in reality, it is not she who is strong. She is only the instrument of beauty's power that attracts men. And before this hypnotic flame within her can destroy those who are drawn to it, she herself is consumed by it.

For love is not like "the waters of Shiloah that go softly." It is not born in tranquillity and is not to be had for the asking. The same grim struggle waged in every arena of life rages with even greater fury upon the tumultuous battlefield of love. And in most cases in Shoffman's stories it is not a struggle between two, man and woman, but among three, the triangle of two men and a woman. Love and jealousy are intertwined. The woman is the altar upon which two priests strive to offer each his sacrifice.

Shoffman describes the ways of love and jealousy in a pithy, almost symbolic, style in his stories, *Love* and *The Revenge of the Music Box.*

In *Love* we are told of Joseph Smith and Moses Obsurov who had been friends from childhood. Their friendship was made the stronger because they both dreamed of love. The somber Obsurov with his wise wrinkles in his strong, firm brow entertained a paternal affection for the tender, weak and defenseless Smith, and the latter was attracted to his friend by his very sombreness, by the dark strain in his personality. Years passed and the boys grew to manhood. Each lived his own life in his separate town. One morning, Smith received a jubilant letter from Obsurov in which he wrote, "It often happens that fortune chooses to smile on one only in his latter years." He concluded the letter, "Before the summer is over, we expect to settle in your town. We shall come, both of us—I and my Julia; yes, I with Julia."

They came, but after their coming the old boyhood love began to wane, and in its place there was kindled in Smith a new love, love for his friend's wife. Instead of the old friendship there was now jealousy.

Smith, the weakling, rejoiced that his vigorous friend has sought and found this source of beauty now imparting its happiness to him as well. Yet when he would take leave of the happy couple and hear the door lock behind him, "he realized more than ever that he had no one to share with him the ennui and heavy emptiness of life. It appeared as though his former friend had cast off this burden from his own broad shoulders and thrust it entirely upon him, Smith. And instead of Obsurov's former friendship for him there was now only his sympathy."

Smith, envious of Obsurov's happiness, gradually fell more deeply in love with Julia. The sadness in his eyes deepened. Hungrily, he would follow her every movement. He thought constantly of "the tiny, beauty spot near her nose, the dimples in her cheeks, her chin." He desired her. His love was so great that it pained him. His passion was acute, almost morbid. He even hoped inwardly that Julia would die. "If I cannot have her, I do not want him to have her either." And once he told her, "You will not live long, Julia. You know, I would very much like to attend your funeral!"

One evening when she was lying on the lounge and Obsurov was out of the house, Smith went over to her, "took hold of her tapering chin, so dear to him and usually so very far from him . . ." She offered no resistance. When he kissed the dimple in her cheek, "he noticed in the semi-darkness how her eyes grew intense and dewy with love. And with that momentary illicit sense of happiness that lit up and warmed his entire being, he was seized by self-pity because of the empty kisses with which he frittered away the best years of his youth. It was then that he understood what Obsurov had meant in his letter. "It often happens that fortune chooses to smile on one only in his latter years."

But Obsurov, fearing the loss of Julia's affection, takes her to another city. He flees from his friend in his desire to save his own happiness. It is only after the catastrophe of Julia's sudden death in child-birth, that his old love for his friend returns and he wires him, "Come!"

Smith comes to Julia's funeral and he recalls how he once told her that he would like to go to her funeral. "And here it is, here it is," he says to himself. What is pain for some is joy to others. "With a sense of deep gratitude Smith looked at the gaping, sandy grave that voraciously devoured the new wooden coffin with all the beauty that it contained, the like of which was not left among the living." When Obsurov broke out in a hysterical cry, "Julia is no more!" Smith bowed his head towards him and all of a sudden, together with the old, youthful love for his friend that welled up within him, he now also understood him for the first time. He grasped the full depth of his wild cry and he too wept.

And upon the tomb of this buried beauty, loved and mourned by both friends, their old affection for each other comes to life again.

In *The Revenge of the Music Box* the sadness is somewhat softened, the plaintive note subdued. But the inner conflict and the rivalry are still there. In this story there are elements of a deeper understanding and a greater forgiveness, even a wistful smile. For one of the characters is blind and the reader cannot generalize and apply the suffering to himself.

Moses Rein, a blind music teacher, has a young, beautiful wife, Regina. Lank, an able pupil of his, has great admiration for the great talent of his blind teacher, but even more for the beauty of his young wife. His illicit wooing is carried on with an almost musical artistry. But not every husband is blind, nor can every talented disciple steal another's love betwixt the violin's chord and the music-box's melody.

Thus the author portrays his love-smitten characters. Like wolves hungry for prey, do the members of the artists colony seek love. And when Esther, the sister of the painter, Mando, arrives, all his friends are set afire with passion.

"And when he brought her one evening for the first time to the cafe in her black hat and in her clinging, revealing dress, all the men fell in love with her at first sight. 'There still are such, still are!' . . . They were thrilled, for they had thought that they had canvassed the entire field of beauty, and that no face in the world could hold any more surprise for them . . . 'God! If there still are maidens like these, then not all is lost'."

When Esther's brother lost his mind and was taken to an asylum, there was a quiet satisfaction in the colony. Now Esther was left alone without a protector against them.

Life took on a new interest for the artists. Each sought to outdo the other in showing kindness to Esther, rendering her little services, helping her to find a lodging, advancing her money. They would visit her brother at Steinhof where the asylum was located and in their hearts they rejoiced. There, to be sure, was a deranged friend, but here—a beauty! A beauty for the asking, flashing like the lightning, a beauty which can make a man mad. Around this young girl rallied all those famished for love, set aflame with passion. It was as though all the girls who had ever been loved were concentrated in this one. All of them, all of them were embodied in her, in Esther.

When one of the artists visited her brother in the asylum, he asked him, "Well, Mando, have you already painted your sister?"

And the deranged painter replied, "I have tried numerous times but without success. The image dissolved between my fingers!"

But that which the artists could not attain, nor the writers, poets and dreamers accomplish, was achieved by an external vulgar force. Austria fell at the end of the First World War. And with her fell her daughters. The Italian, British, Serbian conquerors came, "their hearts drunk with victory and their pockets bursting with money gained from the favorable exchange. The city on the Danube attracts them and their eyes go roving among her young daughters, those poor, orphaned girls who wander about, hungry, tattered and homeless. It is an easy hunt. Having first slain their fathers and brothers in battle, the chase is made very easy. Like dumb sheep the girls walk after them, and if one offers the slightest resistance, it is only because she is ashamed to be seen in her raggedness."

Thus the conquerors lavish their favors upon the daughters of the vanquished. They are intoxicated with all this available beauty, which not even the suffering of poverty could repress. They take them first to the clothing store, then to sumptuous restaurants and from there . . . "Well, let us go," he says. And she pleads, "Please, let us sit a while longer!"

Thus the girls fell one by one; the young and the not so young, the blondes and the brunettes, the pretty and the homely.

Esther too was among the victims. Another flower trodden underfoot, another bit of beauty consumed—and the hunger for love keeps on growing ever more.

Sad beginnings and gloomy endings. Wars and revolutions, fierce and painful. A yearning for life but strength is lacking. A craving for the light, but instead thick darkness. Is the darkness of life indeed so impenetrable? Is there no way out? Shoffman would not have it so.

The seemingly somber and pessimistic Shoffman is in reality not so. The zest for life and love that grips his characters lends a special enchantment to his stories. The passion for life underlies all his writing. And it is for it and because of it that there is so much suffering. It is this mighty will to live that casts into one's path all the stumbling blocks and pitfalls.

Shoffman is a stimulating writer and he can arouse all the emotions of the reader, keeping him on edge as though it were his own great personal danger or great passion. This is so because of the author's unique craving for life, which is his special strength.

While on the surface his stories appear to be devoted to sin and suffering, darkness and despair, helplessness and enmity, jealousy and hate, yet they are all suffused with the light of love and forgiveness, the desire for life and creativity. After all the arduous experiences and hazardous vicissitudes through which he leads the reader, the latter finds that the desire for life has somehow been enhanced and he is ready to turn even the works of the devil into seeds of blessing and of new growth. Shoffman has here blazed a new path. Instead of ephemeral saccharine sentimentality, he dares choose a bitter toughness as his vehicle for the transmission of a deep yearning for life, that zestful relish and sweet taste that life acquires after heroic struggles and defeats and after the final conquering.

He strings together from the gravel-stones of man's weaknesses and lusts a necklace that is both tough and gentle, frightening and comforting at the same time. That necklace he hangs upon the reader's neck so that he may gaze upon it and draw from it all that is precious and vital. He can tell the tale of man's struggle and suffering with restraint, in an almost epic mood. Lifting the veil of sin and filth, with an artist's deft hand he reveals the purity and beauty that dwell in the heart. Indeed, he may be cruel but this very cruelty is a method of revealing love and the stifled sob at the shame that can come upon it. How much sweet sadness there is in his tender stories—*Love, The Revenge of the Music Box* and *A Man Upon Earth!*

With his psychological insight Shoffman sees the world as it is, but he is not abashed by reality. For out of ugliness beauty beckons and out of hatred there rises an illuminating love.

And in *A Man Upon Earth,* a new sun rises, the sun that shines after the storm, casting its rays upon both writer and reader. A rain-storm had torn off half the roof of a dilapidated hut and it had collapsed together with all the cruelty that had lodged within it, all the rottenness and the two female witches who had been its inhabitants.

"What are we to do now? What must we do?" one tremblingly asks the other.

"First of all, we must save the child, the child."

They run away and save themselves from the destruction. But the child too is saved. "Everything about them cleared up and took on an air of tranquillity. The child opened its eyes and smiled, gazing at the rainbow, the perfect arch of glory stretching from horizon to horizon. That smile must have expressed the ultimate purpose of all the blind forces that had continued creating and experimenting to this end. And this sweet little creature is dreaming, dreaming of the beauty of nature about it, nature that has become cleansed and beautified through the storm."

And Shoffman, himself purified and strengthened, concludes: the blind forces, which apparently are not quite so blind, have finally achieved their goal—a man of beauty upon a beautiful earth.

GRANDPA AND HIS BOY

Asher was a lad of about eight or nine, pale, bashful, and given to laughter. Whenever a stranger looked at him he would laugh and dimple and hurry to hide behind his grandpa, Reb Yosef the teacher, the *Melamed*. The boy was extremely proud of this grandfather of his, and often wondered how other boys his age found any joy in life when they had gross, common grandfathers like Henich the lumber merchant, or Leibe the doddering ancient, or especially Zalmen-Idl the tailor. It seemed to him that his comrades, the pupils of the *heder* in his house, were jealous of him when he addressed their teacher not as "Rebbi" as they did but as "Grandpa."

There was reason to envy him! Reb Yosef was a head taller than anyone in town, his features were regular and clean-cut, his black ear-locks were curled beautifully and in his grey eyes—how much gentleness and modesty there was, how much reason and beauty! Compared to his speckled cane, so fine and elegant, the other thick, red sticks with their bent, common handles seemed dwarfed and of no account in the corner of the synagogue. His bone snuff box, too, was especially beautiful, not like the simple boxes made of bark owned by the other householders.

It was the likeness of this fine "Rebbi" that the little students used to see when they imagined Rashi, Our Teacher Moses, and even, if one may say so, the Almighty Lord Himself. When at times one of the students left the *heder* of Rebbi Yosef, for some reason of his father's, and entered the *heder* of Itzi the Melamed, his studies immediately lost value in his eyes, because all these imaginary figures instantly assumed the appearance of the new "Rebbi": his small stature, thin beard and ugly visage.

When Grandpa would stand up there would be only a little space between his head and the whitewashed ceiling. Asher used to envy him then because he could reach all those high places which were so far above the boy's reach and at which he always used to look up from below so respectfully. In those heights on top of the rafters rested the print for Hanukkah tops, the bow for Lag Ba'omer, all made by Grandpa's hands, and many, many things besides.

The house of Reb Yosef the *Melamed,* stood at the end of town in the alley of the *Goyim* and the peasant's houses with their peephole-windows under the rims of their straw roofs set off the lone Jewish house in sharp relief, with its large windows, its shingled roof, and the moss growing around its tall, red clever-looking, and, as it were, bookish chimney. The old beams were cracked at the corners of the house and the cornices were rotten and crumbling. When Reb Yosef took his walk on a Friday afternoon during the summer after class was dismissed, he used to stop to feel them with his fingers as though he were estimating how much longer this house of his would last.

In such leisure hours the boy used to watch his grandfather from afar, attentive to his every movement, and trying to guess his purpose and intention. There went Grandpa into the vegetable garden and from there into their neighbor Anton's fruit orchard, tilted his head upwards and looked at the cherries, still white but beginning to redden. And strangely, Grandpa, who was so tall, was then so small standing near the tree . . . At last he plucked a soft branch from one of the limbs of the tree and brought it home. There he drew his glasses from their blue case, mounted them on his nose, took the sharp knife, the one with the black bone handle with the brass dots strewn over it, and began to cut the twig with extraordinary skill so that it became a whistle. Grandpa himself blew the first note upon it, and then without a word he turned the whistle over to his grandson's hands.

Reb Yosef did not indulge in much conversation with his grandson, but sometimes he used to exchange glances with him that said much more than words. He used to look at him in this way when they said the proper blessings at the first thunder together, or at the end of a storm, or on seeing a rainbow; on Yom Kippur in the synagogue, also, when he underscored for him with gestures of his hands the sweetness of that wonderful melody which the cantor Kulye used for singing the verses of the *Piyyut:* "From carnal clods, from earth dwellers, from weak in works, from evil-doers."

Grandpa was an excellent craftsman with the hatchet as well as with the knife. Grandma, who was blind in one eye and sour-tempered, used to boast that in the past, "When Grandpa was still healthy, there was nothing so splendid as our Sukkah in the whole town, and people simply used to climb up on the roofs to look at it." Sometimes in the summer evenings Reb Yosef took his hatchet to the smithy of Beinush the blacksmith to sharpen it up a bit. With one of his hands he used to lead Asher along with him too. The boy ran barefoot on the grass which was wet with dew, and insects buzzed in the air and sawed away vigorously for a moment on the peak of his cap or on his forehead.

The bluish flame of the forge lit up the charcoal-blackened faces of Beinush and his two tall, strong sons through the darkness. The three of them were busy forging an iron horseshoe. As soon as they were aware of Reb Yosef's entrance, they welcomed him pleasantly.

"For the 'Rebbi' we'll do it at once."

"They still remember the beatings they got from the 'Rebbi,' " said Beinush smiling at Reb Yosef. He took the axe and placed its edge on the grindstone, and his two sons on both sides began immediately to turn the wheel with special diligence.

Everybody showed a mixture of awe and affection towards him. Even Meir, Zlate-Golde's son, who had just been released from jail and who used to cause scandalous rows in the synagogue, pulling the long beards of the respected men of the community, slapping the Gabbai, and nobody dared to oppose him, even this very Meir when he chanced to have some speech with Reb Yosef, at once became tamed and sweetened, and his thin dry scowling countenance softened into many little wrinkles by way of an ingratiating smile.

People used to come to Reb Yosef to confide secrets of all sorts, and to ask his advice in any trouble which befell them. Wrinkled women with aches, their noses blue and dripping from the cold of winter, used to hold whispered conferences with Reb Yosef for hours on end, and took their leave finally with faces glowing with a bit of hope. Old Haye Sarah availed herself of Grandpa's counsels more than all the others, she who was lately left a widow by her wealthy husband. At times Reb Yosef would visit her in her home, and Asher, who went there along with him wandered about in the chilly anteroom, with its ancient clock which had stopped ticking, and its dusty, sad black furniture. In the bedroom where the soul of the wealthy householder had taken flight floated some subtle, half-sensed odor which overcast one's spirit with an unbearable melancholy. Haye Sarah, her eyeglasses perched upon her rounded pudgy nose, whispered at length to Reb Yosef, and from the pleading tear-swept glance that she fixed upon her counsellor at intervals, one could see that her hidden sorrows were deeper than the sea. But Reb Yosef said nothing in return and instead of a soothing reply he climbed up on his chair and began to examine the bleak and motionless clock, feeling about among the inner works with one hand while with the other he moved the indicators upon its face. With a vicious whirring the clock began to sound out the hours and filled the emptiness of the anteroom, which resounded with queer, gloomy tones. The widow's face lit up slightly, as though together with the wheels of the clock something had moved in her jammed troubles also—and there was hope . . .

While Reb Yosef stood by others in their hour of trouble with advice and comfort, he was yet unable to help himself in his own straits, and he suffered his everlasting poverty in silence. The air of poverty broke in through the cracks in the walls, the nests of beetles and roaches, from the dark corners and the bookshelves. Grandma sometimes ate a husk of dry bread with an onion of so sharp a tang that it made Asher's eyes tear at a distance, but the single open eye of the sour-tempered old lady remained dry. At such times Grandpa would pace aimlessly here and there, look at the windows, take down from among the books his *Tanya,* the book he loved the best, look through it a while; but suddenly he would think briefly, return the *Tanya* to its place and take down his account book from the "tram" and make notes in it in his careful and attractive script: "To the woman Rachel I owe ten silver pennies for a loaf of bread." He would turn the page and write further: "To the woman Zippe I owe five silver pennies for a quart of oil."

Most difficult of all was the autumn season, when the cold outside grew fiercer and the firewood in the hall grew less. Grandma would light up the broken brick oven only on the very coldest evenings and she always hastened to shut the draft off too soon for fear that some of the heat might be wasted. Little Asher, who lay stretched out on the stove, was suffocated with the smoke and, getting down from there, he would fall to the ground fainting. Then Grandpa used to kneel over him and tap his nose with his fingers until he restored him to life.

Each morning the pupils of the *heder* used to come together bringing cabbage roots from home. Outside the first snow lay in drifts over the road-stakes and on the icy pools; the pretty maiden Beila, draped in a shawl whose ends were tied behind her, led her flock of fattened, squawking geese to the great round swamp near Timoch's house, where the water was now beginning to freeze over at the edges, and to look particularly black in the midst of the pallor of ths snow all around. And inside the enclosed *heder* they wrestled with the mysteries of Creation: "And the earth was without form and void, and darkness was upon the face of the deep, and the Spirit of God moved over the face of the waters . . . "

By mid-winter the geese were slaughtered, and the boys of the *heder* now owned their windpipes which they used as whistles. At intervals they would blow them and listen admiringly to the cut-off screams of a goose. . . . Each morning the tracks of wolves were seen on the surface of the snow which covered the vegetable gardens behind Reb Yosef's house, sometimes the scattered remnants of a torn goat, the jawbones of a horse. The nights were long, and Asher lay in his place, afraid to look at the windows for fear of seeing a wolf, a thief, or a drunken *Goy* wandering away from his path and seeking a place to rest. But soon he would hear Grandpa turn over in his bed and begin to groan and cough, as was his way, and fear dissolved in an instant.

Sometimes Reb Yosef's coughing would last till the break of dawn. The boy did not realize his Grandpa's torments because as long as he could remember it had always been so, but it was not long before Asher understood what this coughing meant.

Late one night Reb Yosef returned from a "Night Watch" (before the day of circumcision) at the house of one of his pupils' fathers, and tapped on the hall door which was always cross-barred. Grandma opened it to him and Grandpa came in and went straight to his bedroom, mumbling some unclear phrases to his wife, from which Asher caught the word "blood!"

His sickly mother, Reb Yosef's daughter, got up and hastened in terror to her father's room. She divined the truth and began to cry.

"Don't cry, now!" said Grandpa, scolding and pleading at the same time.

On the morrow the shadow of a horse and carriage passed over the frosted windows. A pale tinkling, a wintry tinkle was heard—and stopped.

"The doctor!"

Wartman, the tall old Christian doctor, came in, wrapped in his dark coat. He raised up the patient and examined him standing. Asher watched and measured them with his eye meanwhile to see which one was the taller.

"How old are you?"

"Fifty-eight."

After that began a treatment with slivers of ice to be chopped up for swallowing and for filling ice bags and bandages. But the spurts of blood did not stop and pot after pot full of congealed blood was removed from the sickroom to be poured over the hedge back of the vegetable garden and stain the snow there. They summoned Zarchi to Grandpa also, the short Jewish doctor with blue-colored glasses, and in a few days the room was filled with a mess of prescriptions, medicines, bottles filled with red drops (ordered by Wartman) and bottles filled with white drops (ordered by Zarchi). Asher thought of the words he had once heard Henich the lumber merchant say in the synagogue, "What Zarchi knows, Wartman has already forgotten."

Reb Yosef's neck became extremely distended, and he swallowed the pieces of ice with difficulty, like a sick fowl. His room was suddenly full of that subtle, half-sensed odor which overcasts one's spirit with an unbearable melancholy, and which can never leave the bedroom of the widow Haye Sarah and her anteroom with its dusty black furniture and its ancient, bleak and mournfully sounding clock. Late at night many of the respected men of the community would congregate here "to visit the sick" as was their pious duty and sit in a row for a long time on Grandma's bed. At last they took their leave one by one and only Leibe, the doddering ancient, the nonagenarian, was left, leaning his forehead on the head of his cane as though he were napping, until Reb Yosef took pity on him and awakened him.

"Reb Leib, why do you weary yourself? Go home and rest."

After the room was cleared of all the strangers, Grandpa's eyes caught those of his grandson. He looked at the boy as he looked at him only when they said the proper blessings at the first thunder together, or on Yom Kippur in the synagogue when he underscored for him with gestures of his hands the sweetness of that wonderful strange melody which the cantor Kulye used for singing the verses of the *Piyyut:* "From carnal clods, from earth dwellers, from weak in works, from evil-doers."

One morning, when Asher's sickly mother went to the apothecary to buy the medicinal powders that Dr. Zarchi had prescribed and Grandma was standing in the sickroom praying *Shmone Esreh* with her back to Grandpa, Reb Yosef raised himself from his bed and asked for something. Grandma, because she hesitated to stop in the middle of her prayer or perhaps because she was slightly deaf, did not answer immediately, and Grandpa roared at her in anger, a thing which he never did to his wife.

"Asher!" Grandma called out at once to the boy in fear and haste.

Asher came in and found his grandfather sprawling at length, his head and neck fallen crosswise over the pillow, his eyes open, strange, twisted.

Grandma screamed, "Go call people—he is dead!"

The bitter frost outside froze Asher's tears as he ran in bewilderment down the streets. Hither and thither paced men in felt boots. Andrei the water-carrier who spoke Yiddish sat on his icy empty barrel, whipped his horse and rode to the river. Asher opened strange doors heavy with frost; out of the dimness flickered contented, calm faces, and he cried and stammered, "Grandpa . . . Grandpa . . . "

He ran from house to house and deep in his heart a faint hope still stirred: were not Grandpa's eyes still open? (He had always imagined death in association with closed eyes.) But when he returned to the house and found the dead man stretched out on the ground in the middle of the house, covered with his winter overcoat, with two lit candles at his head, the dreadful certainty overwhelmed him, even though he still continued to believe that there must be some "mistake."

The confines of the narrow room, dark and damp, with the heap of "American" potatoes in the corner, were filled with men and women. His sickly mother burst into the room with a wild wailing, tore up the prescriptions, threw away the medicines and powders which she had just bought from the apothecary, and her weak voice seemed to split the Heavens: "I knew it, I knew it—my heart told me so! I have no father now!"

Strange faces flickered, healthy, glowing with the outer cold. A fresh white cloth was passed from hand to hand, rustled and was torn, cold verses from the Psalms floated in the air: The children of Adam and the children of men, the rich and the poor together. Andrei came in and asked as he always did for somebody to help him empty the water which he had brought.

Asher saw his grandfather for the last time in the twilight dimness when they "cleansed" him standing upon the bench, his tall naked body projecting above the heads of all those assembled.

With the removal of the corpse the house was empty, only a black pool on the ground remaining. The stove was lit by strange women, dripping whispered solace, and into Asher's eyes peered the eyes of his mother—shining and cleansed from weeping. Cracks of easement showed light in the wall of oppression. All night Reb Yosef lived in the dreams of his grandson; but the awakening at the break of dawn was terrible, the awakening into the emptiness of "Grandpa is dead!"

Yet, on the other hand, a certain new freedom was felt, a loosening of the reins: now he could climb up to all those unattainable "high places" as he pleased, he could touch and handle everything, everything, he could do whatever occurred to him to do . . .

But suddenly the infinite pity seized him, pity for his grandfather lying in his grave under the snowdrifts of the graveyards, and he sought to take hold of everything that remained of him: his books, his clothes, and those things which he had made with his hands. Asher placed one chair on top of another and took down from the rafters the print for Hanukkah tops, the Lag Ba'omer bow. He took the *Tanya* from the book shelf, opened it to the dog-eared place where Grandpa read the last time. Then he took also the account book and hungrily read the attractive, careful script in which Grandpa was so fully mirrored. "To the woman Rachel I owe ten silver pennies for a load of bread." He turned the page and read further: "To the woman Zippe I owe five silver pennies for a quart of oil."

DEBORAH

The people of the Valley either out of habit or because of "impatience of spirit and hard labour" are insensitive to the Biblical setting in which they dwell, and tread unheeding upon historic sites. But I, a visitor, am deeply moved and find it hard to grasp that here, indeed, this spring at the foot of Gilboa is the same where Gideon tried his men and chose them according to the manner in which they drank, "as a dog lappeth" or putting their hand to their mouth. Almost inaudibly the water splashes, pure as it was then, three thousand years ago.

And Gilboa! As if clad in some military fabric, some soldier's blanket, dun, dry, coarse. "Neither dew nor rain."

I can scarcely shift my glance from this chain of ridges and I hazard a guess where, on which crest, on what slope, Saul and Jonathan fell. An evil spirit has passed between them of late because of David. A bitter rebuke, "Thou son of perverse rebellion!" the father had hurled at his son, even casting his javelin at him. But now, in this hour of destiny, the son was at his father's side, together with him in his straits and together they fell, "Even in their death they were not divided." That tender youth sick with love, the object of whose love could understand neither him nor his love: "Wonderful was thy love to me . . . !"

For a long time I stared at Gilboa my eye unwearied, unable to conceive that here indeed it stood, while they, the men of the Valley, for days on end pass by with not even a casual glance in its direction.

But today more than all else my fancy is filled with–Deborah. The immediate cause has been a walk with a companion in the fields of Jezreel, all the while staring up at Mount Tabor with the foreign buildings on its summit. Here, here in these fields she hurried back and forth with the son of Avinoam and his host in the face of Sisera's threat. Here, here that great woman strode. Hence, she looked up, as I do now, to Givat Hamoreh. How fresh are the verses of her song, how real! "When the people offer themselves willingly" . . . "And the travellers walked through byways" . . . "The rulers ceased in Israel" . . . and then finally: "They fought from heaven" . . . Other prophets foresaw a distant era; but she, Deborah, prophesied for today!

I pondered on that "mother in Israel," and her love and anxiety for us, even us, until we entered the small, pretty *kvutzah,* luxuriating in its orchards and trees. A dark girl in khaki trousers passed by with a smile, the sort of beauty I have not seen for many a day; and yet, at the same time, suffused with something of orphanhood, that touched a chord of pity.

"Who is that girl?" I asked my companion, a member of the *kvutzah.*

"She belongs to the Youth Aliyah, from Czechoslovakia."

"Perhaps you will introduce her to me?" I asked.

He responded gladly and called after her, "Deborah!"

NOT TO SLEEP

"Not to sleep, not to sleep!" the little boy cries and seems to beg for his life as he is being carried in his mother's arms from his parents' shack, where he has been visiting toward evening, back to the children's home. He is eager to remain here with daddy and mother, to stay awake, awake.

Shadowlike, members of the Kibbutz wander about in the falling dusk, among the shacks, among the large packing cases brought over by German refugees, among canvas tents. Singly and in couples, they tramp aimlessly in the deep sand. "I knew her in Warsaw . . ." one of them relates. The large aluminum tea kettles sparkle in the lit-up kitchen. For a moment, the door of the shower-house opens and a stripped young fellow is seen inside, shuddering a little.

The guards are at their posts, and the large revolving searchlight guides its belt of brightness across the fields beyond, illuminating a kind of peculiarly reddish aftergrowth which is saturated, as it were, with the blood of battles of long ago. Farther, farther, way beyond, to the ends of the world, throw your searching brightness! For the whole world—is one camp of the enemy. On all sides, all around, they lie in ambush for us. They cannot endure it that we have found something of a foothold; they cannot endure it that we still breathe a little. It is not booty and spoils that they seek, nor to inherit our possessions. It is just that our life itself, our mere being alive hurts them.

We must draw closer together, our boys and girls, ever closer together. We must stand guard, be on the lookout, all eyes, to pierce the treacherous darkness. We must intensify our alertness a hundredfold—not to sleep, not to sleep! One's heart so trembles for the children, for the girl one loves, and there is a desire stirring to protect them with one's own body, right now . . . For the savage will not spare the most tender, the most gentle among us. He will not spare any!

Out of the thick darkness the sandbags glimmer at the bottom of the fence—those eternal sandbags, heavily piled one on top of the other, that do not permit us to forget the situation. Remote and cold and indifferent, the stars are radiant in their courses—those stars of Deborah's. Remote and cold and indifferent, and no longer reliable, as they were in the days of Sisera, when the battle now blazes. . . .

Singly, and in couples, the members of the Kibbutz tramp in the deep sand. "I knew her in Warsaw . . ." one relates. A girl's head bending over a book is seen by the light of the lamp through a shack transom. Stripped, all bare, a lonely young fellow shudders under the shower. The revolving searchlight illumines the reddish plain smeared with the blood of battles of long ago; it strains to extend its belt of light farther, over the whole hostile area, all around, farther, farther, to the ends of the world; and the little boy, being carried to the children's home, screams, begs for his life: "Not to sleep, not to sleep!"

Mattathias Shoham, Playwright and Poet of Ancient Themes

Mattathias Shoham (the nom-de-plume of Mattathias Moses Poliakewicz), poet, dramatist and essayist, was born in Warsaw in 1893 and died in that city in 1937. For a short period he was resident in Palestine.

In his early childhood he lost both his father and mother. Kindly relatives saw to it that he received a Jewish education according to the traditional pattern and the Bible became the dominant literary influence upon him. He received no formal secular education but, a voracious reader, he acquired a knowledge of European literature.

He married in 1915 and earned his livelihood first as a bank clerk, then as an instructor of Hebrew literature at the Institute of Judaic Studies in his native city.

His creative period lasted for only eighteen years, from 1919 when he published his poem, *Shulamit,* in the *Hatekufah,* until 1937, the year of his death. But during this comparatively brief span, in addition to his shorter poems and a series of essays entitled *Lizrot Ulehaver (To Sow and to Winnow),* he wrote his poems of stature: *Kedem* (Antiquity), *Ahavah* (Love), *Eretz Yisrael* (Land of Israel), *Ur Kasdim* (Ur of the Chaldees), *Hayehudi* (The Jew) and *Gadish* (The Stack of Sheaves), together with his poetic dramas on Biblical themes, *Jericho, Balaam, Tyre and Jerusalem* and *Elohei Barzel Lo Taaseh Lakh* (Thou Shalt Not Make Thee Gods of Iron).

His last poetical drama, entitled *Jesus and Mary,* was completed only a few days before his death. Unfortunately, the manuscript was lost in the havoc of the Second World War or during the massacre of Warsaw's Jewry.

I

Mattathias Shoham is a poet *sui generis* in Hebrew letters. The light phrase, polished style and lyric strain were foreign to him. Writing poetry was for him not just a pleasant pastime but a holy task. He was a meditative and profound poet for whom beauty *per se* was not sufficient.

He lived in Poland during the stormy periods between the two World Wars. Like all sensitive spirits who carry life's burdens silently, he inwardly bore the anguish of the era and with his mind's eye he recognized the portents of the coming catastrophe. But with all this he had the special gift of being able to rise above the world of reality, to enfold himself in the mantle of ancient days and to weave his tapestry upon the warp of poetry and the woof of history.

Shoham once said to Malkiel Lusternik, a young Hebrew poet who perished in the Hitler blood-bath, "Do you know that I wrote my drama, *Tyre and Jerusalem* with my blood? You may wonder at that, but I did write it with my blood. I was shaken, excited. Vision had turned into reality. I was transported to a far-away ancient world in a state of inspiration, of hallucination. I could not go among people. They disturbed me, they irritated me with their smugness, their self-satisfaction. Yes, with my blood did I write. I pierced my hand and with the red hot fluid I raised up my heroes from the abyss of oblivion."

Of course, Shoham was not the only poet who inscribed his visions with his heart's blood and who, when inspiration welled up within him, could not mingle with other human beings. All creativity worthy of the name comes to the true creator with agony of spirit and torment of soul. For so it is with him who dares to go beyond the limits of his own being and perception and to cast chaos primeval into a new creation. He who plumbs the wellsprings of the soul, both his own and that of the universe, in order to find form and purpose for man's life upon earth, he who thirsts to tear aside the veil from the secrets of eternity by the medium of words and phrases, lines and verses or by the means of paints, light and shadows, does thereby place himself upon the sacrificial block and yields himself to the tongues of flame that lick at and finally consume the soul.

A double share of this agony falls to the lot of the poet who sees visions of the days of antiquity. He treads upon vast stretches of time as he seeks to grasp the echoes of an ancient tongue, the shadows of worlds that are no more, the traces of personalities long perished. On the sands of the desert he searches for the footsteps of tribes and of peoples of thousands of years ago. Amidst the ruins of palaces and temples he looks for the living spirit of distant ancestors, whose being he feels, but whose image he cannot see. He examines old manuscripts and books of ancient history for hints that may throw light upon the song of warriors and prophets who fought against God and man, who conquered old territories and explored new worlds, then vanished into eternity.

And the poet, living within the boundaries fixed by a society differing completely from that of ancient man, held down by the chains of reality, wrestles all his life with the causes of his suffering, the pains of creation, the anguish of expression. He struggles to transcend the limits set by his life, to plunge into the vast distances of the past and to bring them near, to make them understood as a part of the present.

The poetry of the East, the poetry based on ancient history, whose echoes are now heard in the world of Hebrew literature is the poetry of the Return of the Jew, awakened from Europe's dream. The first builders of modern Hebrew literature brought with them the prevailing winds of the "New Era," the style then current in Europe. With the new springtime in modern Hebrew literature at the end of the nineteenth and the beginning of the twentieth centuries, the Jew mistakenly believed that salvation would spring forth from Europe. Hebrew literature, which had received the good tidings of the "New Era," began to sing the song of mankind, the song of the wide world. The Hebrew story and novel were a logical continuation of the European. Hebrew poetry became the poetry of the European individual writing in Hebrew.

But with the First World War, that shook the foundations of Europe and revealed its foulness and with the pogroms against Jews in the Ukraine and Poland following in its wake, the eyes of Jews were opened to see aright, to perceive that this culture that they aped and by whose light they did go was but "the staff of a bruised reed." With the progressive redemption of Palestine the way of the Return of Hebrew Literature was clearly marked—back to the source, whose origin lay in the days of antiquity. Poets who had displayed much talent in humanistic poetry, both lyric and epic, and in poetry descriptive of many lands, began to seek the road back to their own national being, to those qualities within themselves peculiarly Hebrew and to Biblical-historical symbols.

In this turn-about of values, Shoham's poetry plays a unique role. For while others wrote about historical themes also, he wrote poetic dramas with only ancient settings. With others their work based on historic subjects was simply an addition to their principal work; with Shoham it was the only work.

There is still another fundamental difference between the historical poetry of most of the Hebrew poets and that of Shoham. For the former the past was to be used as an illustration of the present. They probed ancient history for suggested solutions to contemporary problems. The past became an explanation of the present, its commentary. The heroes of the distant past uttered words and thoughts appropriate to the speech and spirit of modern man. But not so with Shoham. With all his might he sought to uproot himself from his own environment so that he might become completely swallowed up by the distant past. It was as though he himself had become one with the extraordinary figures whom he had rescued from the abyss of oblivion, as though he had become a man of the ancient world, both in time and in space.

To be sure, there is in his writings too a real connection between past and present and the one sheds light upon the other, as in all creative works based on historical themes. But for him the end-matter is not the present, but the past. He goes not from the then to the now, but from the now to the then. Antiquity is not a means to an end, but an end in itself for in it can be found the allusions to man's future destiny. The life-giving seed of human culture was sown in it. In it is hidden too the core of that miraculous ball whose threads, unravelling, have enmeshed all of the human race as it has made its long way from Genesis to the present.

Therefore, the principal characters in his dramas speak their own language—ancient, heavy and profound. Their speech, like that of Shoham's himself, is one of sublimity, of Biblical figures, of symbols, imagery and vision. It is the language of *Haazinu* (Deuteronomy,

Chapter 32), of the difficult chapters of Isaiah and Ezekiel. Shoham makes the language fit the characters who spoke it in ancient days. He removes it far from the present, the times of the blending of various styles, and brings the language back to its pristine days.

He does not like the *kal* mood of the verb. He prefers the stronger moods, the *piel* and the *pual.* Even among nouns he seeks those which give an impression of heaviness, of tension, of weight. His words and sentences seem to be power-charged.

II

His poem, *Kedem,* may serve as an introduction to his works. The poet introduces his reader into the mysteries of the distant past by means of broad, heavy lines carefully weighed and measured—passages laden with the wisdom of the ancient East and infused with keen historical feeling.

Throughout dark and silent nights he listens to the echo of forgotten generations and he hears the glorious song of the past calling to him from out of the barren deserts of the East. After imaginary wandering over seas and deserts, countries and empires, his soul is set aflame with a longing to return to the rock whence he was hewn—from which all mankind was hewn.

He sings of Egypt and Ethiopia, Ophir and Arabia, Tyre and Sidon, Assyria and Babylonia, Persia and Greece, China and Tibet; and the Nile sings its ancient, mysterious song, the song of a mummified civilization, *The Book of the Dead,* and the Song of Osiris and Isis. The land of the sphinxes and pyramids, which have stood guard in majestic loneliness over the riddle of their existence for thousands of years, this land spins its riddle now too for the Hebrew poet, lineal descendant of those who had participated in the Exodus from Egypt. The Nile's questions are his even as the sphinxes' secrets are his also.

The roots of his soul are there, in the lands of the East. From Egypt he goes to Babylonia to sing of her glory and decline. True, Babylonia was once the land of exile of his forefathers, where they had sat and wept on its riverbanks, upon whose willows they had hung their harps. But he does not look for the bitterness of the Jewish exile in that country. He sees only the antiquity and the grandeur of the land, its lust for life and its mysteries of love. Babylonia was satiated with pleasure and drank the cup of happiness to its dregs. It rejoiced over youth, scorned old age and delighted in every passion. It gathered treasures from all parts of the world, gold, mother of pearl and black marble "to pave the floors of pagan temples, to build rainbow-shaped bridges and to decorate resplendent towers." She wallowed in lust and sin, and she could laugh at fate. Yet when the Lord of Hosts arose to destroy the nest of kings, Babylonia was the dragnet with which he ensnared the most powerful of nations.

The poet knows that Babylonia is unworthy of a Hebrew's affection for she had been the queen and the harlot upon the cross-roads of the East, the destroyer of Israel. Nevertheless, the poet pleads with the prophet, "Forgive me, prophet of exile and affliction, mourner for the captive daughter of Zion, that on this dark and threatening night in the cold and bleak north, I recall proud Babylonia and I feel my heart palpitate at her memory." Something of her pagan lust still burns in his blood. After thousands of years, her unbridled coquetry disturbs his peace—the peace of a Hebrew poet in Slavic exile. His fingers yearn for the quivering breasts of the temple priestesses. The beauty of Babylonia, the pride of Chaldea—she who was the glory of Kingdoms—she who enticed every king and conqueror of antiquity, still lives in the contemporary world.

This conflict between the golden East and the dreary West still continues. It is renewed in every generation and in every age. At dawning, the East is supreme; at sunset, the West is victorious. Ormuzd struggles with Ahriman; light, with darkness; desert, with habitation; nature, with civilization; brute strength, with spirit; paganism, with Judaism.

From Babylonia he goes to Persia, the first of those who dreamed of world conquest. She opened up her copper gates to Babylonia and ensnared Lebanon, Canaan, Sidon and Philistia. She passed through every desert and wasteland, ploughed her way to the shores of Egypt, then descended to Ethiopia to conquer her. Yet all this was insufficient, so she sent her daring legions to far-away islands in the channels of the deep Western Sea, to lands of song and beauty, to plains of snow and mountains of ice on the other side of the mountains of Ararat. That brought her dream of conquest to an abrupt end. The ice froze the heat. The snow cooled the ardor of the eastern blood. The eastern star began to descend.

Thousands of years passed; the East climbed its own funeral pyre and was consumed together with its gods and its mysteries.

But the dream of the East did not die. In the heart of the Hebrew poet, it awakens and is kindled anew.

A broad, eye-filling panorama is unrolled in this poem. The iambic cadence and the majestic rhythm, which resemble the structure and the rhythm of Bialik's *Meitei Midbar (The Dead of the Desert)*, open great vistas stretching back to the beginning of human history, parading before the reader's eyes the evolutionary stages of our race from the dawn of mankind to the present. The seers of humanity from Zoroaster, the law-giver, who differentiated between purity and impurity and between light and darkness, to Buddha, the holy monk, "who yearned for eternal peace" and who strove to unite the torn elements of the universe and "to redeem them from the agony of eternal annihilation," to "the suntanned seers of Israel, who carry within their flaming hearts a wealth of rebellion, love, justice and great compassion for man"—all of them appear upon this dramatic stage to tell the story of man's travail and anguish as he searches for the answer to the riddle of his existence. For great is the wisdom of man, says the poet, and mighty is his lust for power. But superior to both is his dream, the echo of primeval man hidden in his soul. "In the silent rock and in the growing grass, in the gurgling stream and in the beast wandering in the forest, in the cloud lit by the sun, in the rainbow suspended in the blue sky, in the wind blowing on the fields, in the prayers of youth on a spring night"—in all of these he sees only part of his own soul, "and his soul, as a part separated from them." And his heart pours out a prayer to the source of all glory and eternity, to the living and creative God.

The living God whom man seeks is the only eternal remainder of the vast heritage of the East. For among the dead of Egypt, the ruins of Assyria, the wastelands of Babylonia, the slumber of Persia, there is nothing of substance; neither can they lift man's spirit that strives for the heights. They can neither light his way nor ease his burden. But the greatest of the prophets who fled to the wilderness to see his God face to face in the burning bush; and he who ascended to the heavens on the wings of a tempest; and the strong-spirited seers of Judah who saw the vision of the end of days at an hour when the world was still young and when the Divine Presence was just beginning to reveal itself—all these prophets did not die. Their image still radiates light and their word is still aflame. Their seed is scattered over all the fields of the universe and the fruit of their prophecy still blooms, as fresh as the day it was given. "And many a spring will pass before their day of reaping and harvesting shall come—the harvest day of the great East." The bearer of the great burden of the East is the Jew in the diaspora; the seer of its vision, the Hebrew poet. When the children of Israel went into exile, they knew that they were destined for a struggle of thousands of years, "like a rock standing amidst a tempest of ages." It was a struggle with peoples and cultures, faiths and beliefs. But they went forth to battle with the intent to return after their victory. "And the East listened intently knowing that its exiled sons swore fealty as they left for the lands of their conquerors, those distant western lands . . . The East remembers their oath to this day and believes in their return, even if they tarry for years and centuries."

III

Many long years had passed and the time had come for the return. After the poem, *Kedem,* which is the introduction to the songs of the return, there followed the poem, *Ur Kasdim* (Ur of the Chaldees). The history of the early ancestors of the Hebrews begins in Chaldea and from that country it is fitting to begin the return. At the dawn of history, God said to Abram, "Go from the land of your birth . . . and Abram went according to the bidding of the Lord." Many generations went with him to Philistia, Tyre, Rome, to the far ends of the earth. They set forth on a great historic mission, but now the circle describes a full turn and a descendant of Abram, the Hebrew, returns to his native soil on the banks of the Tigris and Euphrates.

This poem tells of the return of the Hebrew to the land of his fathers and his God. The earlier poem, *Kedem,* is primarily a descriptive poem of the ancient East, while in this poem the returned exile pours out his soul about the lands he has traversed, the wars he has fought, the remnant of the refugees he has saved from the fires of exile and the new joy of reunion with his land and his God.

By the stamp of his sufferings he reveals himself to his God and he asks, "For whom have you destined this yoke and this burden? See for Yourself, for whom is this everlasting sign stamped in blood on my sinewed limbs?"

This descendant of mighty and sacred seers, of simple herdsmen and rebels for the Lord, now kneels at their fountain, thirsty for purification, and writes a poetic letter to his "brothers in the East and to those who live by its ways." He asks them to plead his cause, "the exiled son of the East," who has been ensnared by "ornate western culture" and whose once fervent prayer, born in Eastern exaltation, has been corrupted by the cacophony of steam and electricity.

For thousands of years he had wandered along crooked paths. He had strayed into the encampments of strange peoples. He had led the flocks of his sheep into the pastures of the wide world. He had mixed his blood with the dung of cattle to fertilize the fields of others. He had subordinated his own will, the will of the East, to that of the West. He had absorbed its knowledge, penetrated into its wisdom and dwelt in its temple. He had torn off the veil from the holy of holies of the goddess of the West, removed the folds of her wrappings revealing her in her primeval nakedness—but he could find no answer to life's riddle.

It was all a false vision. For hatred was his portion. From the ambushes of the West enemies arose to destroy him, for they could not tolerate his strangeness, his uniqueness, his genius.

The mission did not turn out well. He beseeches his God to help him return to his pristine glory, to transplant him to the top of his mountains in the East as in the beginning and to grant him redemption and pardon.

And if someone should ask him, "What sacrifice of atonement have you brought? What remnant have you saved?" He would answer, From the jaws of stutterers I saved the clear exuberant language of the East, my ancient tongue. He had watched over Hebrew, the language of delight, to rescue her from oblivion and profanation; and above all, to guard her purity so that she should not wither. Like a faithful knight he had led her from Persia to Spain and to the lands of Magog and Meshekh, and she, in turn, had watched over his genius and his sanctity, over his Sabbath and holy day. In cold, strange lands he had sung songs of love and loyalty to her; he had whispered prayers and supplications and his heart had been warmed. In the language of his ancestors the returning son declared himself to his land and his God.

With *Ur Kasdim* the song of return began and in a later poem, *Eretz Yisrael* (Land of Israel), it is continued. The opening chapter of the latter is called, *Get Thee*—the same two pithy words which God spoke to Abraham and which were handed down to his descendants, down to Mattathias Shoham. But this *Get Thee* does not now mean *from* your native land, but *to* your native land. For, asks the poet, "Is it conceivable that a man should wander all his life from one strange land to another and die without seeing his native land? Can it be that a man should cherish the comforts of strange mothers and pass away without ever having suckled at the breast of his own mother?"

Therefore, the *Get Thee* of our day has come to mean ascent *to* the native land.

On his way home he writes a song of his journey, depicting the scenes through which he passes—the mountains, seas and islands. There are beautiful descriptions of nature, but they are used as a means for expressing his deep longing for his motherland.

In chapters like *In the Mountains, The Sea, On the Highways of My Native Land, The Plains of the Jordan* he reveals a deep-rooted appreciation of nature as well as a talent for the apt phrase and the poetic image. Yet there is no intrinsic pleasure in the reading of these descriptions. The melancholic reverie of the serious poet entirely absorbed in a far-away world is felt in each line. This is not physical return only; it is a return of the spirit as well, symbolizing repentance for the sin of exile. And it is the way of the repentant to pray and not to sing, to be downcast and not to rejoice, to bend under the yoke of life and not to ease the burden of pain.

The mighty Alps are overwhelming in their beauty; the poet sees not their beauty, but the "grandeur of their awe-inspiring presence." They stand "shoulder to shoulder with interlocking crags and they overawe him with the scrawl of their scars hewn on their cliffs." The mountain chains appear like "one anger chained to another." They command every storm and their backs are toward the sun. They depress one unbearably with their mood of calm and proud bereavement; and they have no regard for the creatures that walk in darkness and who desperately need a little hope, warmth and affection. These qualities they lack. Only when the poet bethinks himself of the mountains in his native land does the atmosphere become less oppressive and the breathing easier. "For there," says the poet, "in my native land I have mountains that have been measured by the yardstick of God . . . I have not as yet seen them, but from the days of my childhood have I known them, revealed as they were to me from the words of my prophets."

When he passes the Grecian islands, stations amidst the ancient seas, he is not moved by the sights he sees or by the deafening sounds of the waves, but by the visions of old that arise before his eyes. The external landscape is subordinated to the inner one, for the present is nothing but a reflection of the past. There is not so much significance to the scene for its own beauteous sake, as for the sake of what had happened when the ancients had lived there in the flesh, imprinting it with the seal of their image and the glory of their accomplishments.

The figure of father Abraham, prince of Mesopotamia, who was to become the hero of the drama, *Elohei Barzel Lo Taaseh Lakh,* appears before the eyes of the poet on the shores of the Grecian islands. The tumult of Abraham's revolt against the idols; the thunder of Mount Sinai; the power of the prophets who stormed against idol worship; and the battle of Tyre and Jerusalem and all the other wars of Judaism against paganism—the combined reverberation of all these exceeded the roar of the waves of the Mediterranean which carried the Hebrew back from the diaspora to his motherland.

Even this sea, so blue, deep and filled with ancient memories, casts aside its own fascinating recollections of ancient myths and is itself transfixed by the magic spell cast by the ancient Hebrew images. The sea hears the living songs of the pioneers "that ring out like the ancient lusty strain of the sailors of Tyre and Jerusalem" and this alien Mediterranean shifts its waves to the rhythm of the dance of the Hebrew *halutzim* returning to Palestine.

Here Shoham sings not only the song of his own soul, but also the song of the pioneer generation. The thousands of young people, the pride of their nation, know what it means to give up the pleasures of the world, the temptations of beauty beckoning to them from all sides, in order to offer themselves as a sacrifice to the motherland yearning for them. They too are poets who pay no attention to the sweet caresses of soft winds or to the beauty of Japheth. They go to seek their life's goal in their ancient homeland. For their blood, like the poet's, has remained pure; their vision is not blurred, their spirit not defiled, their holiness not profaned. They carry with them the scent of early days, the fragrance of their land, the sanctity of their tradition. They flee from the conflagration of the First World War, rescuing not only themselves and succeeding generations, but also the glory of ancient days and the grandeur of their heritage. Together with them returns the poet, and his motherland is to him both youthful mother and beloved bride who has conceived by the fragrances of her new springtime, concealing her pregnancy in the whiteness of the almond blossoms. He returns to renew the ancient covenant and to find redemption.

IV

The poet came back to the land of his origin. But both this return as well as that of the generation of pioneers of which he sang in his poem, *Eretz Yisrael,* is only a physical return in the immediate present. However, to a poet like Shoham the essential thing is a spiritual return to the past, for there is nothing in the present except that which has existed in the past. The past carries the imprint of the people's image and thus it indicates the path for the future.

Therefore he returns to ancient times, to hew from its depths mighty figures of prophets and path-finders, warriors and conquerors, and in the light of their lives and achievements he focuses attention on the long and arduous path of Jewish history. For this purpose he turns to verse drama.

For drama has more breadth and scope. There is more room for antagonists and their contentions and for the presentation of contrasting personalities. The battleground for individuals and peoples, for beliefs and faiths, can be more easily depicted.

His first drama, laid in Biblical times, is *Jericho,* the story of play as well as in his others, it is not brute force which commands the first conquerors of Canaan and their entry into Palestine. In this the attention of Shoham, but the spiritual power which defeats idolatry.

The Hebrews who come up from the wilderness to conquer a land and its people are not the best-armed in the world and the secret of their strength does not lie in the sword alone. They carry another power within themselves, neither visible nor comprehensive, an exalted power which casts awe upon peoples accustomed to the sword—the might of the spirit of the burning bush and Mount Sinai.

The pagan priests, the priests of Astarte and those of Egypt, Midian and Moab, who are in Jericho together with the king, are confounded and do not know the meaning of this new phenomenon threatening to destroy their countries and their gods. Even before the advent of the foe from out of the desert, they had already been subdued in spirit. They had ceased fearing their gods and had begun to quake before the God of Israel. The Moabite priest knows that Peor cannot stand up against the Lord of Lords and the Midianite priest knows that "Astarte, like Peor, is powerless against Him; He will raze Moab with His sword even as He did Philistia." For "these were not conquered by the power of arms."

The quaking Moabite priest covertly asks, "Is not their blood red? Are not the armies of the Hebrews made of flesh and blood?"

The Midianite priest answers, "You do not yet know them. For it is easy to slay thousands of them or tens of thousands. It is easy to conquer a people after destroying its land. But how can you kill the spirit of the God who commands them and lay waste a wilderness by capturing its limitless stretches of sand?"

These pagan priests know many gods: Dagon, Kemosh, Nirgal, Marodakh, Baal and Molokh. Each one has his own image and his own role. One is the god of fertility; another, the creator of light and the ruler of the heavenly bodies. Another is the god of wars; still another, the god of spirits. One is the god of light, dew and fruit; another, the god of the wilderness and the darkness. "But how can you depict Him, the God of the Hebrews? He is a Ruler without corporeal image." He commands the light and the darkness. He harrows the depths of the sea and He ordains the law for prince and slave alike. What else is left for any other god beside Him? And if He has not form, how can you break through to Him?

Rahab, too, the high priestess of Astarte, who foresees things hidden from the eyes of the priests, intuitively senses the new power now approaching her domain and she despises her own pagan goddess. Astarte seems to have lost her glamour as she is revealed in her nakedness. The priestess, knows that Astarte depends upon her for her very existence, because she, Rahab, has given her everything she possesses.

The social structure of the pagan world crumbles. The scorn of the priests and priestesses for their own gods and goddesses is the first significant omen heralding the victory of the Hebrew God and of Moses, His law-giver. A funeral procession for the dead gods is in order and the priests mourn their deceased deities and the destruction of their world. In contrast to the weakness and decadence of the pagan priests and their adherents, Rahab, the central figure of the play, loses neither her confidence nor courage. She dominates the scene through her arrogance, her beauty and her voluptuousness. The simple, concise story of the second chapter of the book of Joshua is elaborated, clarified and raised to the heights of a captivating drama. Rahab is magnified into a great dramatic figure. She mocks the pagan gods for she does not fear them any more, but neither does she stand in awe of the strength of the great God of the desert. She does not fear Him—she desires to see Him, to know Him. When she learns from the Midianite priest that Moses, the man of God, has married the daughter of a Kushite woman who had served Baal Peor, she envies the woman who could exchange Baal Peor for the Conqueror of peoples. In the nights of pagan holidays, while sitting in the temple of Astarte, surrounded by the sprawling forms of sleeping priests satiated with passion, she is weary of these orgies. She hears an inner voice calling to the Hebrew God—and she remembers the Midianite woman who has won Moses.

The dramatist in Shoham emphasizes the sexual urge as a driving power and the struggle between man and woman in the battle of ideas. In *Tyre and Jerusalem* he kindles a flaming passion for Elijah in the heart of Jezebel—a wild, consuming passion—and she binds up the fate of her war of Tyre against Jerusalem with her private war against Elijah. Hers is a battle of love. She wants to capture this primitive Elijah who robs her of her peace, in order that through him she may capture the God of Judah. The poet follows the same procedure with Rahab. He makes her the focal point of pagan lust. Even if she does not dream of Moses, who has by now passed away, just as Jezebel dreams of Elijah, her desire for him turns into a violent jealousy of Zipporah, the wife of Moses.

Rahab, the priestess of Astarte, having bared the helplessness and sterility of the pagan goddess, is now consumed by a driving youthful passion for the man who will master her. She seeks a Nazirite who will break his vows to his God and drink from her cup.

At this point two of Joshua's scouts come to spy out the land, Athniel and Akhan. Athniel is an old experienced soldier; Akhan an enthusiastic, exuberant youth. Like all young men he is filled with the passions of youth and the lust for life.

Rahab fills her cup for him at the feast she prepares and she urges him to drink. But heathen wine is forbidden to Akhan, the Hebrew, and he refuses to drink, for he had taken vows to the Lord and "My God may hold me to account," he says. After Rahab ultimately prevails upon him and he drinks from her cup, the ruler of Jericho asks her, "Were you so zealous for your goddess, Astarte, that you plied the Nazirite with wine?"

And Rahab answers, "For Astarte?–No. I was zealous for myself, the woman, to master both him and his God."

Thus Akhan, the young Hebrew, smitten by her beauty, is caught in her net. He who has come as a secret messenger of the conquerors is himself conquered. Similarly, she, the conquering woman, is held captive by the man who has betrayed his people and his God for love of her. Thus Shoham weaves a play within a play, joining together the struggle between individuals with that between peoples, so infusing fresh blood into the veins of dramatic action.

The enemy spy is changed into a lover bound by the chains of *amour*. When he hears the sound of the *shofar* trumpeted by the armies of the conquering Hebrews, he does not move a muscle, so infatuated is he by the charms of this daughter of the enemy. For one moment the door is open for him to return to his brothers and his God, to atone for his downfall with the blood of the sons of Jericho. But Rahab, determined and power-mad, daughter of warriors and noblemen, satiated with urban civilization, is now engaged in a life and death struggle with him who is both her enemy and lover, her captor and her prisoner, representative of the wild desert and the new culture now rising with a blinding light. She fights for her own soul and the soul of her people; she struggles for her fate and that of her country. She employs all her charms, all the wiles of the temple priestess to hold Akhan in her tent, so that he remain with her and become entirely subservient. With bold cunning she asks him,

> "Is it so easy to betray your God,
> And then to return to Him when you are in dire straits,
> To appease Him with loot and with the blood of the enemy? . . .
> What does it matter to Him that you return confused and weak with fear?
> If He is a real God, your bold rebellion is more pleasing to Him
> Than a pusillanimous atonement. . . ."

But if he wants to return, let him, because she does not desire so weak a man. She wants a brave man, a hero, who would wage war for her sake against his God, against his brother, against the entire world. She wants a heroic lover, whose image would be reflected in his shining sword, and who would capture her as the spoils of his victory.

Rahab wins and Akhan gets his booty, even though he obtains it by treachery. If she be sentenced to death, he tells her he will die with her; if she be sold as a slave, he will bend his back under the mill-rack and bear the burden of his love and his treachery. She has ensnared him with her love and with her forbidden wine, and subjected him to the possibility of excommunication by presenting him with an embroidered cloak of Shinar, inherited from her father, as a keepsake until such time as she would ask for its return.

Because of her, Akhan has thus befouled himself, for his soul is the price of her love. Rahab is to be paid with valor, sin and rebellion.

Thus one of the young Hebrew conquerors falls even before the fall of Jericho. He falls a victim of love, but even more, a victim of the spirit. This is one of the tragic concomitants of the battle of ideas. This love set aflame while the gods of Canaan are sinking low and the walls of Jericho are falling is a symbol of the confused soul of humanity struggling in bewildered agony.

The captor becomes the captive; the conquered, the conqueror. Rahab yearns for the vigor of the new faith arising from the desert. Akhan falls into the trap of the decadent beauty of the city. The symbol of this conflict and this sin is the woman. "On my way to God I always found thee, O Woman," says the Egyptian priest to himself, "Who can tell whether you will pave or block the way to Him?"

But even in the midst of sin God reveals Himself to man, for there is no medium for self-purging and for renewed devotion to Him as effective as pain and agony. Akhan has sinned and his sentence is death by stoning. However, in the last moments of his life this young man assumes heroic stature and becomes purified in soul. In his sin God is nearer to him than ever before. He says of God, "He answered me for the first time in the pain of my sin." He has heard God's voice not in the rebuke of the priest nor in the word of the prophet; it has come to him out of his own secret depths, and "the sinful soul entered into the shadow of mercy."

Akhan now becomes full of understanding and compassion because of his love, his self-sacrifice and his great agony. Though it was treachery in the beginning, it becomes sanctity and purity at the end.

Eldad and Medad, the servants and disciples of Moses, appear in the play in the roles of judges (unlike the Biblical story and in accordance with Shoham's practice of changing the roles and locales of Biblical personalities). These two pity Akhan and try to save him from death. But he does not want compassion, for his soul has become proud and elevated. He defends Rahab with all his might and he blames himself for everything. Eldad asks him, "Why do you incriminate yourself without benefit to Rahab?" Akhan answers, "Why do you want to acquit me and blame her for everything. She is innocent. If she is guilty then God himself is guilty for molding her ivory arms and fashioning her lovely image. . . . "

In the last moments of his life he sings with love's sweetness, "When the first stone hits me, I shall remember Rahab's embrace and the softness of her arms. When the second comes, a fountain of love for her will burst forth. When the third will split my head open, my lips will silently utter the name of Rahab and the name of my God . . . "

There are three acts in the play and three central points. Each act has a special function. In the first we find portrayed a struggle between two alien worlds: the world of the desert and that of civilization; the world of the ascendant monotheistic idea and that of decadent idolatry. The second act depicts the conflict of lust and love between Rahab and Akhan, wherein the man is defeated by the woman. In the third act comes the hour of denouement and reckoning. Judgment is passed upon the individual who has betrayed his people, who has sinned with his love for the daughter of the enemy and who pays the final penalty.

Thus the presentation begins with the problem of conflicting worlds, then pivots around the emotions of passion and love and ends with the dying echo of a lover perishing in the agony of his love.

Shoham did not write many love poems. He was impatient to take up his role as the poet of Jewish history. But his poesy of love was not wasted. It colored the structure of his dramas, filling them with an inner fire. Not only Akhan, but his creator was young when he wrote *Jericho* and that which he had only touched upon in his earlier poem, *Love,* came to fruition in *Jericho,* in the description of the love between Akhan and Rahab. Here there is ecstatic love poetry, great in its own right.

V

Shoham's first historical drama, *Jericho,* was his point of departure for travelling across vast stretches of time. He began with the conquest of the land in the days of Joshua. But the riddle of Hebrew existence did not start there. Historical eras had preceded it and the poet yearns for the very beginning.

In *Jericho* the characters are of the second generation after the exodus from Egypt, those who were closer to action and farther from prophetic vision. Moses is dead; Joshua ushers in a new era. A man of the sword has replaced the man of the spirit. Not only young Akhan is guilty of a strong passion for an alien woman who charms him with her wiles and brings him to treachery. Even Pinhas, the priest, who judges Akhan, is not guiltless of this strange desire. According to the poet, he is entirely "possessed by a tortuous desire" for Rahab and the fire of her eyes makes his blood feverish. In his severe sentence of Akhan there is more of jealousy of his young rival than of zealousness for the Lord of Hosts. He wants Akhan dead so that he may possess the living Rahab. The play ends under a cloud of vagueness, for the disciples and followers of Joshua, the man of the sword, have lost the power of vision.

Eldad and Medad, the disciples and servants of Moses, walk through the camp like shadows to whom no one pays attention. Their souls yearn for their teacher and prophet, in whose eyes shone the graciousness of God, which is no more. They preach of love for the stranger and compassion for man. They plead for the freedom of a captive woman, for the Law proscribes harsh treatment of a prisoner. But nobody listens. It is an era of material realization and none cares for the idle talk of these disciples of the prophet, the left-overs of former days.

So the poet, who would penetrate into the depths of ancient vision, goes back further to the early days of the desert generation, to the time of Moses and Balaam. He writes the drama, *Balaam*.

The main character of the play, as is evident from its title, is Balaam. But through this great tragic figure we see a reflection of the shining image of Moses and at the end of the play the greatest of the prophets appears and declares his message to the generations to come.

The Biblical figure of Balaam is one of the most bizarre and amazing characterizations created by the human spirit. It is for this reason that Bible exegetes and theologians are drawn to it. From the stories of the Scriptures as well as from the legends of the Midrash there emerges a strong, fascinating personality full of contrast and contradictions.

Balaam is a sorcerer and a magician, but he also "seeth visions of the Almighty God." He worships idols and is an intermediary between them and their worshippers; yet he also "heareth the words of God and knoweth the knowledge of the Most High." He is the greatest and the last of the prophets of the gentile nations and his strength and stature among them is equal to that of Moses in Israel. He is needed to complete humanity's wholeness and he serves the mysterious purposes of the Holy One, although by his very nature and inner compunction he aims to rebel against God and set His word to naught. He intends to curse Israel, but in the end he blesses them, for thus did the Lord command him.

Shoham delves into this complex and intriguing personality. He creates a brooding, suffering seer, who carries a heavy burden, fighting against his destiny without hope of victory.

Moses and Balaam were childhood friends in Egypt, but as they grow up their ways part. One is chosen for Sinai's heights, to give the Torah to Israel, to teach the blessing of God's unity and to reveal the lofty vision of "the end of days." The other becomes a "magician on the shores of the Euphrates," casting magic spells for kings and princes for silver and gold and pandering to the evil spirit of sinful man.

Balaam is the other half of the human-divine coin. He is the contrast to and the opposite of Moses. Moses is admitted to the mysteries of God; Balaam is not. Moses enters into the Holy of Holies and is there granted revelation; while to Balaam God appears from without. Moses is a prophet of God; Balaam, a soothsayer and conjurer. Moses is the prince of blessing; Balaam, the prince of imprecation. Therefore the face of Moses is radiant and the countenance of Balaam forbidding.

Shoham is sparing in his use of the rich mythological material dealing with the Balaam story. He prefers its symbolism. He even refrains from introducing the talking ass, or the angel with his drawn sword, for he does not wish to become entangled by miracle tales. He desires only to reveal the light within this tragic figure of Balaam. He seeks to grasp the mainspring of his being—the epitome of all that Moses opposes—the Curse.

The concept of blessing occupies a unique place in the Scriptures. The blessings of Abraham, Isaac, Jacob and Moses were given as farewell testaments and in all of them is hidden the deep meaning of the historic destiny of Israel. (Thomas Mann in his great trilogy, *Joseph and His Brothers,* grasps the significance of the Blessing and dwells at length upon it.) Shoham endeavors to reveal the nature of the opposite of the Blessing—the Curse—as exemplified by the personality of Balaam, the opposite of Moses.

In the struggle between these two powerful, contrasting personalities, the prophet and the soothsayer, the spirit of humanity is engaged in a struggle of light against darkness, of eternal life against life of the moment, of monotheistic Judaism against paganism.

The poet purifies the image of Balaam from the dross of mythology and discards all supernatural elements from his story so that the figure of Balaam attains spirituality. He creates about his hero an atmosphere of search for God and longing for redemption. The image of Balaam does not hang by a thread. It is set within the framework of an era, of a circle of wise men and visionaries who seek an explanation of the riddle of existence. It is a time of transition and "the desert generation" does not apply to the Hebrews alone, for all the men of the times form a confused and bewildered generation which now opens its eyes to the worthlessness of paganism and begins to seek a way to God. It is not only the children of Israel who leave the darkness of Egyptian bondage. It is as if the entire world has roused itself to go out of the darkness of its own spiritual Egypt and there are ferment and upheaval everywhere. At the head of this restless and turbulent generation march the seers and the wise men who seek the Lord.

In *Jericho* there appear the priests of various religions, the priest of Astarte and the priests of Egypt, Midian and Moab. In *Balaam,* however, there is only the one priest of Peor, but in addition there are two wise men from lands of antiquity, the Kittite, a wanderer from the West, and the Hindu, a wanderer from the East. (Wandering sages are great favorites with Shoham.) These wise men are superior to priests in their breadth of spirit, scope of knowledge and depth of understanding. The priests are concerned about their worldly wealth and their gods, their source of income; the wise men are naked and barefoot, wanderers over the face of the earth. They set their heart only upon the truth that is concealed and the beauty that is revealed, upon the pain of sentient man who can see the abyss. These are the seekers after God in all generations. Even in their apostasy there is faith.

Thus in this play, there appear these two strange wanderers, the Kittite and the Hindu. The first, the son of the West, seeks the secret of life and the truth of existence in the East; and the second, a son of the East, seeks the same things in the West. Each seeks his answer in the land of the other, for the soul of each is without solution for the eternal mystery. The seeking soul is thirsty for the living God; the heart of man, ancient as well as modern, fears chaos and emptiness. The wise men had abandoned the law of gloomy priests and had gone forth to find the blessing of life. In their search both the Kittite and the Hindu come to Balaam, the Master of the Curse and the genius of denunciation, who says of himself, "For none like him can curse so well."

The Hindu asks, "Where is peace?"

The Kittite asks, "Where lies the solution?" But Balaam is powerless to answer either for his is not the path of blessing and joy, of life and creativity. To him God had granted the curse alone.

Balaam is the poet of decadence and the philosopher of despair. When he beholds the eventide, he does not bless it with the joy of satisfaction; he only sees and feels the futility of it. When the sun rises he does not bless the miracle of light; he regrets the blight that will result from the heat. When youth rejoices before him he ponders about age and becomes melancholy. He is the prophet of doom.

There is something Job-like in Balaam and his agony. Deep and varied are the questions he asks. Why did God create the Curse? Why did God choose him to be the bearer of the Curse? He addresses himself to God,

> "Are you not the same God who created light and darkness?
> Then why did you set my path in the netherworld and the darkness,
> And why do you lead him (Moses) along the eternal heights of the sun?
> Are you not the source of all bitterness and sweetness?
> And yet you discriminated and gave one of your servants
> The heaviest burden of all mankind,
> And to the other, you gave light, goodness and happiness on earth."

Further—"why did you reveal yourself to me from the depths of Sheol and to him, the prophets of the Hebrews, you revealed yourself on Mount Sinai, so that the entire world and all the inhabitants thereof rejoiced at the message of the God of blessing?" He sees Moses as "travelling in the desert sated with his victory and commanding the hosts of his Lord. With a powerful hand he points out the path of redemption until the end of days." But he sees himself as cursed, decaying and forgotten by the sun. Like Job he summons the Lord to judgment.

If he is indeed the bearer of the Curse, does he then do it of his own free will? Did he choose his own path in life? Has he not worshipped God all his days in faith and honesty? He has only performed his duty and spoken that which was put into his mouth. Of course he has hardened his heart and withheld his compassion, while witness to suffering. But that has been his mission—the mission of a prophet of imprecation, who sees his visions at night and not by day, in the darkness and not in the light. If a tear of pity ever came to his eyes for a brother, weary of struggling, or for a harassed creature, God hastened with burning wrath to dry his tear. "And the curse was to me sister and servant, and death was my friend and slave."

If that is so, argues Balaam with the Lord, Why do you toy with me and mock me? Why did you create me to plague myself? Did I too not wish to be blessed and full of grace? Did I not wish to attain the light of God and the favor of His love? Like a live coal there has burned in my soul the desire to purify myself and all mankind, to taste happiness and share it with others. But you, O Lord, have planted your curse within me, so that I have preached its message and sought its honor.

Though God punishes him and humbles him before Moses, his rival, still Balaam is not resigned to his fate, for has the Lord only one blessing? So Balaam pleads for blessing, but it never comes. True, there is one blessing in his life, his only beloved daughter, Noa, but even she is taken from him and given to Moses.

Noa is a fascinating character in the play. In her moonstruck soul there is the play of light and shadow of two widely different worlds, that of Moses and that of Balaam. It is with her that the victory of Moses begins.

The women in Shoham's dramas are endowed with remarkable intuition. They see the march of coming events before the men do. In *Jericho* Rahab is the first to perceive the new turn of events. Even before the spies come to her she knows that the pagan gods have died, and the powerful, conquering God of the desert has appeared in their stead. In *Tyre and Jerusalem* too the most powerful force fighting for the paganism of Tyre is a woman, Jezebel, who senses with all her being that the war between the royal house of Ahab and the prophet Elijah is a war of destiny.

So too Noa, daughter of the conjurer, Balaam, is endowed with prescience, a somnambulist, who, half-awake, dreams as she climbs upon the mountains. Her figure floats and hovers like "a white-masted ship on the face of the deep." In her dream she sees her father pierced by a sword. After he is killed, the redeemer comes.

"Who is he?" Balaam asks, and his daughter answers, "He is the one whose name I have heard from your lips, the one you honor more than you hate"—Moses.

Thus Moses gradually overcomes Balaam through the medium of his own daughter, who perceives the blessing in the Man of God.

But Balaam is not easily subdued. He desperately fights the battle of his destiny and makes a last attempt to conquer Moses through the evil spirit dwelling in man from his youth.

The Scriptures tell, "And Israel abode in Shittim and the people began to commit harlotry with the daughters of Moab." The Midrash adds its colorful interpretation to this story. Shoham applies his poetic imagination to this material and unfolds the passionate love story of Zimri and Kozbi. Here too the priest, Pinhas, appears in the same negative role of a man who lusts after the daughters of Moab.

He longs for the priestesses of Peor who are not like the women of Israel. The latter were nurtured in the heat of the desert and their flesh is withered and their marrow dry. But the priestesses of Peor are soft and delicate and their desirable flesh is youthful and enchanting.

The tragic love of Zimri and Kozbi plays an important part in the drama. But the center of the stage is not given to them as was the case with the love story of Akhan and Rahab in *Jericho*. Here Balaam is the central figure, and the hub of the story is the struggle between him and Moses, both as individuals and as representatives of their respective civilizations.

Balaam knows man's soul and his weakness for the flesh, and by means of promiscuity he hopes to defeat "the redeemed people of Israel." He encourages himself by thinking, If the prince of the tribe of Simon, whom Moses sent into the camp of the enemy, could forget his mission on account of a woman, is that not an indication that it is yet possible to overcome all "this holy and pure people" whom Moses led out of Egypt to redeem it and make it an example for all other people? The flesh is the same among all mortal men. Therefore, he would kindle a flame of desire in the hearts of the Hebrews for the daughters of Peor and of the Emorites. He would defile their purity and set them against their God. Then the prophet would see that his effort to bring them out of Egypt and give them the Torah was in vain, and bursting with anger, he too would turn into a man of the Curse and would curse his people.

Thus the man of the Curse, would triumph over the man of the Blessing; the conjurer over the prophet. But the daughter, who sees far more than her father says to him,

> "By such means Moab will triumph over Israel,
> But not the conjurer, Balaam, over the prophet."

Noa, who drifts between a world of dreams and one of reality and between the world of Moses and that of Balaam, knows the way of the conquering spirit. The dramatist builds up the dialogue between her and her father step by step to the play's climax—the blessing of Balaam.

Balaam, who ascends the mountain with Balak to curse Israel, here attains the perihelion of his life. For this great moment he has hoped and prayed many long years. He reaches the heights of human prophecy and, thus, the apex of his own life's dream. He changes his black cloak for a white one and he is "clothed in white, in the light of the noonday sun" and "his voice henceforth is like that of a prophet at the moment of his vision." He is no more the man of the Curse, but the man of blessing. The divine spirit has transformed him from conjurer to prophet. The victory is both that of Moses and of Balaam, for Moses conquers his rival, but Balaam achieves his life's ambition—the bestowing of blessing! This climactic scene is an artistic chef-d'oeuvre, combining great poetic beauty and profound human wisdom.

Balak, the son of Zippor, and the princes in his entourage who have engaged Balaam to curse fall back in amazement. "The spirit of God has abandoned the seer!"—they cry out with fear. But Balaam who appears in all his greatness knows that this time the spirit of God rests upon him as never before. The clouds of his life scatter; his skies become resplendent. The blessing for which he has yearned is revealed to him. The light of Moses, which had first penetrated the soul of his daughter, now enters his own. He opens his mouth with blessing as he sees the Hebrews coming up from the desert to make their way toward the wilderness of humanity. The great parable of the end of days rises to his lips. He knows that whoever will curse the Hebrews will not himself be free from the curse of generations. "For they possess within themselves the blessing to the end of days." Balak and his cohorts await his curse, but Balaam has become elevated and transformed. The curse has gone from him like a far-away nightmare. God has poured new blood into him; he becomes "purified, clean and crying out the one word, 'Blessed!' " The redeemed people are revealed to him not as they are, but as they will become. The conjurer would see the present and discern nothing. The prophet sees the future and perceives everything.

He sees the Hebrews ascending from many deserts in the space of time to capture every land not yet visited by the spirit of God and he blesses this people distinguished from all others. Even if they be small among the great nations and their tent be humble, yet their spirit is a strong fortress. They will laugh at the tempests of future generations—"The hammers of the nations will be broken against Israel and the vastness of the exile will not dismay him."

Balaam penetrates the darkness of the coming eras and the circuitous way of God and he sees the path of Israel—he will pass through rivers of blood on his long journey "to the distant vast plains." Savage peoples will prey on his flesh, drink his blood, seize his best as booty, but he, the mighty in soul, the stiff-necked and great in spirit, will smite the immorality of peoples with the rod of righteousness and "with the torch of eternal redemption" he will light up their dark path. For beaten and confused peoples he will raise redeemers and messiahs, for in his own soul there lives the yearning for salvation and redemption. "Blessed is the people of redemption!" cries the sorcerer, now redeemed from the curse of his incantations and endowed with the blessing of prophecy.

This is the triumph of Moses as well as of Israel. For the greatest and the last among the pagan prophets sees for Israel a vision of the end of days, and the prayer, "How goodly are thy dwelling places," issues from his mouth.

After the Exodus, this was the first great clash of two great powers: the unity of God as revealed to Israel through Moses, prince of the prophets, and the polytheism of the desert people as represented by Balaam, the sorcerer and conjurer—and the blessing triumphs over the curse. The idea of the unity of God and of man, of love and justice, of morality and the spirit is victorious.

Thus ends the blessing of Balaam—thus too ends his life. Pinhas kills him. When Moses ascends the mountain to view the dead body of his rival, he commands unto the last generation that there be love and graciousness among men and that the spilling of blood be forbidden. "How long will you continue to think that you please God with your religious jealousies and hatreds!" Thus saying, his body stiffens, he stands erect and commands,

> "People of Israel, further, further,
> The road continues until the end of days . . ."

VI

In *Tyre and Jerusalem,* the drama written in Palestine in 1931, Shoham reached a new height. The structure of the drama is more complete and more compact. The language is more musical and has greater clarity. The characters, throbbing with life, express clearly the sharp conflict between external and internal forces, of living people and of pulsating ideas.

In *Jericho* and *Balaam* the scene is still the desert. The monotheistic idea is but in its infancy. The people have hardly found themselves, for they have not yet entered their land. On the stage appear stray individuals who represent new ideas, bearing the seeds of a world revolution. But the society of man which creates the background for the interplay of personalities and ideas is still wrapped in darkness. It is a desert generation and in the desert there is neither civilization nor culture. But in *Tyre and Jerusalem* the setting is Palestine many years after the conquest. The poet passes fleetingly over the period of the Judges and the early kings who had ruled over Israel. The people of Israel have already been united and have since separated into two kingdoms, Judah and Ephraim. The actual scene is laid in the period of Ahab and Jezebel, of Elijah and Elisha.

The dramatist looks for conflicts between opposing forces, not contenting himself with describing a period of peace and unity in the life of the Jewish people in its land. Therefore he chooses an era of storm and strife, of clash between two world outlooks, between two dramatic personalities engaged in a struggle for total victory or destruction.

These two world outlooks are the paganism of Tyre and the monotheism of Jerusalem; the spirit of Judaism and the flesh of idolatry. The two conflicting personalities are Jezebel, the sinful queen and the priestess of Astarte, and Elijah, the Tishbite, the prophet of the God of Israel. The two accompanying figures, heightening the dramatic effect, are Ahab and Elisha.

Jezebel is described with sharp, vivid colors as a very passionate woman. The poet makes her the living counterpart of Astarte and the symbol of the pagan world, which made of the priestess a sacred prostitute. In *Pantomime,* the introduction to the play, the poet uses his ability in prose to the utmost to describe the voluptuous surroundings and the promiscuity pervading the sacred precincts of Astarte. Jezebel, thirty-three years of age, "bares her magnificent body of its veils . . . strong passion pulses in her temples, breathes through her nostrils, beckons from every quiver of her muscle . . . One by one the princes of Elam and Egypt, the merchants of Lud and Crete, the potentates of Sheba and Tarsus pass by in the palace court . . . " Cobra-like, her body twists and turns seductively to every comer. Suddenly she stiffens and draws back without desire and her hand refuses the harlot's hire.

Like Rahab in *Jericho* and Kozbi in *Balaam* who pine for the new and who love a Hebrew, so Jezebel passionately yearns for the mysterious prophet, a thirty-year-old giant of a man who wears sandals of badger-skin. From under his hairy mantle one can see the bulging of his powerful shoulders and chest. On his forehead there is the stamp of nobility and his eyes are as sharp as spears. His entire bearing speaks of strength and echoes the thunder of power.

The pagan queen lusts after him. But the man of mystery, the powerful prophet and harbinger of the storm which will destroy the world of Tyre and the life of Jezebel, passes her by. He pays no attention to her seductive wiles and her enchanting beauty. The holy Nazirite despises the attraction of the flesh and rejects the blandishments of the sensuous high priestess who would defile his purity and conquer him with her unholy passion.

This is the first decisive triumph of Elijah over Jezebel.

Shoham makes their struggle both that of woman against man and of sacred prostitute against man of holiness. He indulges in daring descriptions of burning passion and fulfills the promise of his early love songs. The romantic fire, springing out of the recesses of his heart, then quiescent, now bursts into flame in the action of his dramas. Nevertheless, he uses this abundance of passionate expression with poetic wisdom. For where there is a clash of ideas and a struggle between faiths there is the danger of too much abstraction and the loss of realism. But here the sensuality rescues the situation and the characters become fully alive.

Jezebel is deeply chagrined because her beauty was rejected and her offer scorned. But with all her wiles and her enticements, she is more than just a woman—she is a daughter of Tyre and a priestess of Astarte. Her war against Elijah is more than that of woman against man—it is a struggle between Tyre and Jerusalem, between the impurity of paganism and the purity of Judaism.

In the person of this crafty beauty Baal girds his last strength to war against God. She, the queen, who rules over ten of Israel's tribes, suffers doubly—her beauty cannot captivate the man she desires and she cannot subjugate the strange people she governs so that they worship her idols.

Like a temple harlot she connives to inveigle the prophets one by one, but she cannot gain complete victory. True, the children of Israel stray after strange gods not infrequently, but they soon repent and mend their ways out of fear of sin and the moral rebuke of the prophets. The prophets cast their fear upon the queen, too. They have a peculiar power and their fiery words rob the listeners of their peace. From their mouths speaks the God of Israel. Therefore, her plan is to ensnare and capture by love and lust the most vehement and most dangerous prophet of them all—Elijah.

She is zealous for herself and her gods. She fights for her own life and for that of her culture and religion. She asks Micaiah, one of the prophets, "Does it not happen that a person will rise to war for his god but in reality he fights his own battle for his own personal vengeance?" She confesses her bitter hatred for the God of Israel.

> "I wanted to extinguish the fire on the altar of God
> And not to steal any brand for myself . . . "

For that reason she desires not Micaiah, who had been tempted by her, but his master, the greatest of the prophets, Elijah. She sends him to trap his master and Micaiah asks in fear, "He—for Baal?"

And Jezebel answers,

> "For myself! For is he not a man?
> Do they not say of him in Zorfat
> Which is in Sidonia, with a young widow he lived,
> If only for a day, for a brief moment,
> Endeavor to tempt him for me."

But Micaiah answers dejectedly, "I cannot do it. He is powerful. The two of us together cannot overcome him."

But Jezebel, who has captured lions and turned them into dogs, who has ensnared prophets and transformed them into lovers and slaves, will not desist. She says to Micaiah, "I shall mix into his cup all the wiles of a woman: mercy and enmity, anger and love, grace and guile. It will be a bitter-sweet potion."

Micaiah replies, "He will not drink from your cup. He will pour it out, for you are a daughter of Tyre, defiled by its idols."

Yet Jezebel continues and asks in the pain of her unrequited love and with the chagrin of a priestess and queen whose offering is deemed abominable,

> "Is the name of Baal engraved indelibly on my flesh?
> Or has he ever approached me,
> Rather than the king or the people?
> Has Elijah ever asked of Jezebel his desire?
> Has he ever asked me the price of my Baal?
> Perhaps Elijah would buy it from Jezebel?"

She wants to sell Elijah her gods. And what will the price be?

"He will pay for them with his God!"

That is the one and only price for the love of Jezebel, the priestess-queen. She knows this and the prophet knows it too. Hence the destiny-laden character of the inevitable struggle between them.

Such is the fate of those who fight for their faith, for their God and for their own way of life. For it is easy, says Jezebel, for a people to split into camps and to choose between a prophet and a queen or to waver between the two without much concern or anxiety. But that is not true of prophets or monarchs.

"For every Jezebel and Elijah, from time immemorial
There have been laid up their struggles.
To contend with the anger of eternal enemies, of uncompromising foes.
To deny and to believe one the other,
In the innermost depths of the heart, that is both repelled and attracted,
To fear, to hate and to love in secret
The man who is the enemy . . ."

This idea is a favorite one with Shoham and it runs like a scarlet thread throughout his works. In *Balaam,* the sorcerer says to Joshua, "Go, messenger, and tell your master, the prophet of the Hebrews, 'When the sun sets, victory will come.' "

"Whose victory?" asks Joshua.

Balaam replies, "He will understand . . . but if he continues to ask, tell him that it will be a victory for the two of us—for the prophet and for Balaam, son of Beor, the sorcerer."

Balak then asks, "How can it be the same victory for the two of you?"

Balaam answers, "It is one victory on the mountain tops of God. Only on a lower level, in the eyes of man, does it divide into two and it is then called defeat and victory or blessing and curse . . . Moses will understand this as I do. There is a realm in which only victory dwells. Those who come there will mock at the language of man."

So too in *Thou Shalt Not Make Unto Thee Gods of Iron,* Abraham says to his rival, Gog, "How you hate me, Gog! You did not know that on the day we were appointed to wander along the paths of the future—we, the eternal rivals—on that very day we were bound together by a secret covenant, in spite of our enmity, to stand up against every cunning foe."

Gog says to Abraham, "We shall yet meet again on the main highways and at appointed times."

Even if in the annals of mankind the two do not share a common ideal and a common purpose, they are alike in sharing "a continuous striving after great ends and a common antipathy to a mean task." Both swore eternal effort and unending aspiration for something extraordinary and boundless. Thus the Spirit and the Iron combine and become the two sides of the same coin—the coin of life, full of contradiction and struggle. Fear and desire, hate and love for his rival burn as one in the heart of man.

Thus the figure of Jezebel calls forth the figure of Elijah. This is the law of life. This is the way of man in the world. This is the eternal and incontrovertible truth.

The character of Elijah in *Tyre and Jerusalem* is powerful and stormy, like a lion of the wilderness. It is not the Elijah as he appears in folklore—that pious figure, that kindly old man who appears whenever Israel is in trouble, the beloved guest of the Passover *seder* table, who works miracles for the poor and marvels for orphans, the prophet who did not die, who suddenly reveals himself and quickly disappears, who watches over his people always. This folkloristic Elijah is not the hero of *Tyre and Jerusalem.* He is rather a prophet of wrath and flame, who causes kings to tremble on their thrones with his thunderous outcry—"Hast thou killed and also taken possession?" He walks about in the desert and appears on Mount Carmel to slay the false prophets, so that he alone remains as the prophet of the Lord. He lives amidst storm and rides up to heaven upon a storm cloud. In the hero of this play there are combined overwhelming grandeur and strength.

He is the one against the many, the seer among the blind. He is the divine revelation in the world which is full of man's pettiness and corruption. He bears the word of Jerusalem, but his is not the Jerusalem that is, but the Jerusalem that is to be; not the earthly Jerusalem, but the heavenly one. His is a vision of the end of days. Therefore, the life of the moment for which men struggle so much seems so trivial in his eyes.

He is the enemy of Jezebel because she symbolizes the lustful life of the flesh, the insignificant pleasures of mortal man and the worship of idols who are naught but false and empty delusions for lost man. He is the prince of the spirit, the Ariel of thought, the prophet of God, who sees a vision of greatness for man, created in the image of God. He is also the enemy of Ahab, because that Israelite king, although not so evil a man, is a mediocre person, concerned only with his small realm; one who watches over his limited domain and who wishes to make his people like all the rest. Ahab does not see the grandeur in the prophetic vision of the end of days when the entire world will be subject to the word of God.

The Israelite king knows that Elijah is his most powerful and most merciless enemy and there is no escape from him so long as he lives. He knows that Elijah could also have killed him when he slew the false prophets, but Elijah spared him until his appointed time. That his time would come, of that he was certain.

Whenever the hounded prophet appears at court, the king is in terror. The strength of the prophet lies not in the sword nor in physical prowess, but in the spirit, that mysterious and terrifying power granted to prophets and not to kings. The terror-stricken monarch asks the prophet in his palace, "Hast thou found me, O my enemy?"

And Elijah answers him, "Hast thou not sought me, O King of Israel?" Then follows the question that reverberates like thunder to this very day, "Hast thou killed and also taken possession?"

Elijah is the implacable foe of all who decoy men after false gods and false laws. The weak Ahab who pursues his wife's will and "the will of the people" claims that "the people love their idols," yet the prophet knows that in spite of the people and its kings the die is cast. "For not in vain is kindled God's flame in the hearts of seers nor will their prophecy come to naught."

At the entrance of the cave at the edge of the wilderness, Elijah encounters Ahikar, "a native of Tyre and a sage who wanders over the ancient pathways." Elijah reveals to him the tenets of his law and the truth by which he lives. The pagan sage perceiving life's emptiness and having no god in whom to believe—for cynically he would say, "Is there One to whom souls can be converted?"—took pity on the little people whose peace of mind was stolen by the stormy and revolutionary prophets. He asks Elijah, "Why do you disturb the peace of man? Why do you rob him of his calm and happiness? Why do you shorten his life in this world? Of what use are your fiery horses to him? Whither can he flee? Let the people alone in their darkness and in their filth. Then and only then will you do them good."

Elijah replies, "Cursed is he who lives in the darkness and is satisfied."

Ahikar asks, "What will you give to man in exchange for the peace you rob from him?"

Elijah answers, "A chariot of fire!"

Ahikar, the man of *nirvana,* the spiritual anarchist, reproves the prophets who speak in the name of God, and who try to plant in the small field that is puny man the seed of giants. Prophecy, he says, deceives the people and explodes their dreams. For there is no redemption; there is only suffering for man. "Where is your miracle, O prophet, and where your redemption?" Ahikar, the wandering, disbelieving sage, has pity for all creatures and because of his compassion for them, he wants to dispel the mirage of a prophecy of the final redemption of man, which commands him to cease from iniquity and injustice so that pain and suffering will vanish.

But such compassion does not please the prophet of Israel, for there is destruction in it. He will not run away from the battlefields of the generations nor surrender his vision. "By God and by man are we called upon to gain victory. We are sworn to redeem and cursed be all who seek to evade this responsibility or who deny the pristine purity of man and his final redemption."

The prophet too sees all the emptiness and the vanity, the wickedness and corruption, the pettiness and lewdness of the present, but within his heart he carries a world of the spirit and a vision of the future.

The vision of the prophet reaches its climax in the great debate between Elijah and Ahab after the battle in the Valley of Jezreel while the wounded king slowly bleeds to death. In both physical and spiritual agony Ahab graciously surrenders to the word of the prophet by whom he was defeated and he begs his forgiveness.

The prophet answers that were it not that God had goaded him, robbing him of his peace, and were it not that in his heart there burned the consuming passion for Israel's redemption, he would beg the king's forgiveness for having deprived him of peace, for having marred his every festival and victory celebration and for having embittered his love for his beloved Jezebel with the curse of God.

Ahab was a good king to his people, he says of himself in his dying statement. He had wanted to increase the boundaries of his land from Philistia to the Euphrates, but the prophet, always in his way, threatened him with the anger of God. He, the prophet, can be a lone individual, free and alone with his God; whereas the king must carry upon his shoulders all the burdens of Israel. The prophet is zealous for the God of Israel; the king for the people of Israel. The prophet reckons with a future era of a great kingdom of Israel; the king is concerned about the days of his own reign.

Ahab, like all other kings, does not worry about the future of other nations. For he asks, If we be concerned about others, who will fortify our own hills? Who will watch over the people of Israel in its own land?

To this Elijah answers,

"I am not like you, my king! . . .
For my people is holy to me.
Israel is the first fruit of God's vintage,
And His last ensign
On the day when the redeemed of all peoples shall be gathered. . . .
My victory is engraved with fiery letters
In my vision—though yet far distant."

Elijah is prophet for his people and for the peoples of the earth. He is universal, standing above his time and his era. His message rings forth—Not with the conquest of cities, the building of fortifications and the subjugation of peoples by mighty armies is it possible to secure human survival and man's happiness upon earth. That is not our way. Not by vast fleets nor by impregnable fortresses shall we preserve the word of redemption. Israel was the first of all peoples to be refined of dross, then going forward to seek solutions to the eternal problems. Having thrown off the impurities of the heathen nations, Israel had prepared itself for the great revelation—man's ability to see God.

On the top of God's mountain Israel unfurled its banner,

"To other people's joy, to the oppressor's dream
No more will it return; for a people will no longer be false,
Once having taught its young lions the roar of righteousness
and salvation."

The people of Israel had been defeated many times at the hands of more powerful enemies and on its long road ahead it would yet bear the burden of suffering and be defeated more than once. Down the far corridors of time the prophet hears the voice of the hosts of his people crying out from infernos of torture and degradation. He sees Israel's glory besmirched upon the dung-heaps of nations and its blood flowing into every pit dug by the ungodly. The agony of pogroms, the smoke of crematoria and the suffering of hell have been appointed for the chosen people and out of the darkness of its exile its entreaty will rise heavenward for the hastening of God's kingdom on earth.

Thus Elijah speaks his prophecy to Ahab, king of Israel. The dying king cries out in despair, Is this the reward? Where is the justice of God and where His righteousness? Where is His revenge?

Then Elijah delivers his prophecy of the end of days, the days of the Messiah.

First he utters it to the dying king, thirsting for his people's revenge, and then to his own disciple, Elisha, who according to the play was formerly a prince of Samaria and a lover of Jezebel.

Elisha who comes on behalf of Jezebel to ensnare Elijah is himself overwhelmed by the fire of the prophet's personality, by the might of his spirit and the grandeur of his vision. He attempts to flee and to return to the queen's palace but he cannot for "there is no escape from the word of the Lord."

The secret of prophecy is handed down from Elijah to Elisha. It is a heavy burden which no man chooses of his own free will, but for which he is chosen. Every prophet seeks a way out through some pretext—"I am a man of unclean lips." Impurity fears holiness; the flesh flees from the spiritual. Man's lust dreads his desire for self-discovery. But as great as is the temptation, so great is the victory; and as great the transgression, so the purification.

Elisha, bewitched by Jezebel and drawn by the allure of the queen's court, still struggles with his impurity. But Elijah purifies him with a holy flame and strikes off the chain of sin. He teaches him to carve out with a flaming sword of agony the vision of the future redemption. The prophet is but a symbol for his people and for humanity. Their tribulations are his; the passions of their lust and sin and the pains of their transformation and renewal he himself experiences. God chooses him, the elect, as a sign and symbol, to breathe the holy spirit into him, to purify his heart from the foulness of reality, from the lust of the flesh and from the passion for idolatry.

Therefore, he is zealous and avenging like his Creator. Therefore, he carries in his heart the flame of chastisement and in his mouth a barbed and wounding tongue. He smites and reproves himself and he teaches his fellow men to climb upward, to purify themselves so as to be worthy of the divine revelation and the miracle of redemption. The smitten and the rebuked accept their chastisement as a welcome gift and the curse, as a blessing.

This play reveals both the greatness of the prophet and all the force of the battle of Judaism against paganism. The two contending worlds are seen in their perpetual rivalry in the parables of Ahikar, in the heated conversations of Jezebel and Joram and the others who sit around her banquet table, in the minor characters of Salo, the son of Nabot the Jezreeli, Zedekiah the false prophet, Micaiah, Timnah, the queen's servant, and others.

Baal here wages his great battle against the Lord and he summons all his powers and his wiles to defeat his eternal foe. The sensuous Jezebel mocks at the high-sounding words—mission, justice, redemption. She asks, "Where is the freedom of man to live in joy, without worry for the future?" She cries out, Still another message have I for this people. Tyre and Jerusalem still face each other in all their glory and with contempt for each other.

Ahikar, the cynical sage, interpreting her intentions, seeks a union between the God of Israel and Astarte, a complete assimilation of Judaism by paganism.

But the end of this hope of Jezebel's and the end of the drama come when in the midst of the orgy, the licentiousness and the unbridled dancing of bodies consumed by wild passion, the awaited Elisha, the disciple and now heir of Elijah, appears and cries aloud,

"The word of the Lord has come to me!"

The vision of Tyre vanishes and the vision of Jerusalem appears again.

VII

Shoham, after dealing with the personalities of Moses and Balaam, Elijah and Jezebel in his earlier plays, in *Thou Shalt Not Make Unto Thee Gods of Iron,* retreats even further into ancient Jewish history to the days of Abraham. It would seem that in his great poetic design he was desirous of finding fresh strength by reaching back to the very beginning of Judaism, to the life of the first Jew. Thus it is significant that on the title page of this last play, which was written in 1934 and published in 1936, a year before Shoham's death, there appears the sub-title, *A Vision of Ancient Days.*

Although this play deals with the most ancient of historic eras, it is, nevertheless, more than any other of Shoham's works, a drama of present times. One feels the poet's desire to point a lesson for our own days.

The main characters in this book are Abraham, prince of Eber (Mesopotamia), and Gog, the son of and military commander for the king of the North. In their entourage are Sarah, Hagar, Lot and Melchizedek. There are also three men of mystery: one from the north, one from Crete and one from India. (In *Jericho* there were three priests: an Egyptian, a Midianite and a Moabite, as well as the local priests of Astarte. In *Balaam* there were two wayfarers: the Kittite from the West and the Hindu from the East. In *Tyre and Jerusalem* there was Ahikar, a native of Tyre, the sage who wanders over the paths of antiquity.)

Abraham and Gog are cousins. Their mothers were sisters whose brother was Melchizedek. Yet from the very beginning they pursue different paths. Abraham is a man of the spirit, Gog a man of iron. Abraham despises the ancient tradition of Gomer which taught corruption, separatism and the false strength that breathes hatred. He seeks the unity of God and the unity of mankind, equality and freedom. Gog seeks the opposite, for a life of freedom and happiness should be only for conquering heroes, for mighty nations, while the lot of the subjugated should be "slavery's frightfulness, terror's whip and the tyrant's rule." Abraham believes that all men are God's children, dear to their father and Creator. Gog considers himself and his northern people as a chosen and privileged race and the weak and the conquered are forbidden to rise to his level lest they defile him. Abraham is anxious to carve out new holy tablets which will proclaim peace for all nations and love of man. Gog scoffs at the dream of peace, which to him appears to be the fruit of cowardice and cowardice is an unforgivable sin. One sees in Gog the portrait of Hitler, who advocated the doctrine of race superiority with blood, fire and iron. Gog wants to soak the fields of victory in blood; Abraham desires to refine the spirit of man. As Abraham phrases it—Each opposes the other, each standing guard over a reciprocally hostile sector on a universal battlefront, Gog to subdue, Abraham to redeem.

Shoham puts words in the mouth of Gog and in the mouths of others concerning him, especially in the mouth of the mysterious man from the north who is a prince of Gog's people, which emphasize the insane theory of blood and race superiority. The entire philosophy of Nazism is thus incorporated in the words of the Prince of the North and Gog himself. The prince sums up the duty of the ordinary soldier in one word—discipline. That is man's greatest duty. It was only the teachers of the Orient who led the people astray by indoctrinating them with the idea that every individual has to watch over his own soul, to deal justly, to strive for self-improvement and to safeguard the dignity of man. But such is not the teaching of the North. In the North everyone is subordinate to the commander, to the leader. He is the chief and he can keep his word or breach it. If the commander tires of a treaty and breaks it at his whim, his is the right and his the law. "We follow our leader blindly . . . for we are not like the sons of the inferior races of the south. We are the descendants of a superior race."

When Gog goes to do battle against his enemies, he knows no mercy and he will not accept a peaceful conclusion of the fight, as Abraham does. He carries away all the booty he can lay hands upon and enslaves the vanquished forever. For once having the upper hand over his foes in battle, what need has he for law and justice? Force is his religion and iron his God!

Gog would not accept the yoke of the spirit advocated by Abraham and praised by Lot, who represents the average man, the man of peace. "This sin of weakness"—to yield to justice and to open the heart to love and mercy—cannot be found in Gog, who seeks with mailed fist to impose a rule of iron upon the nations of the earth.

Should Gog want peace, it will be only the peace that will come after all the other nations are vanquished by his might. Then, in the end of days, he says, "We will be a great people, a pure race, one and mighty."

Lot comments bitterly, "That will indeed be a wonderful day! No goat or lamb will remain among the flock of nations. Therefore the leopard and the savage will have no one left to devour."

Against this doctrine of Gog, there appears the first Hebrew, the idol-smasher, who enters into a new covenant with the God of heaven and earth, the God of the spirit and of morality, in order to create a new type of man in the world. This man will desire neither to spill blood nor to conquer. He will lift his soul to the heights of the mountain of the Lord and he will plant love and brotherhood among all men and all nations. Abraham preaches his doctrine everywhere he goes, to all who will listen. The emissaries of Amrophel and the princes of Pharoah, as well as the three princes, from the North, from Crete and from India, argue with him about his doctrine. They do not understand the essence of his being, his faith and his vision. They have never met a man his like anywhere nor have they ever encountered such purity of soul and such novel doctrines as are his. "How and whence," they ask, "shall we attain the knowledge to establish justice among small and large nations and to maintain order upon earth?"

Abraham, though he can fight fiercely when the need arises, goes among people with gentleness, imparting knowledge and pointing out the way for the confused and the perplexed. He is understanding and compassionate, knowing the weakness of man and the bitterness of his lot in this vast, mysterious and difficult world. He is the elect of God, entrusted with a divine keepsake—knowledge of the Lord and love of man. Even in his most dangerous hours, when Gog enjoys his greatest triumphs, Abraham does not lose his sense of balance nor does he know fear. His heart is firm and secure for deep within him is the knowledge of his Election—that is indestructible; so that when the entire world looks upon the victory of Gog, Abraham says calmly, "His victory is far off!"

Even Abraham at times has to make use of the sword against his enemies. However, he has undying hatred for war. He does not enslave the enemies he conquers; neither does he crave their wealth nor rob them of their property. He fights for a vision, seeking to win over the spirit of his enemies so as to have them enter into the covenant of God.

Why is it that he hates blood and loathes iron? It is not because of timidity but because the life of man is precious to him. Man's life must be preserved not only because "when life's thread is snapped, society lacks an individual or a generation of man and so too his production of bread, the deeds he would have done and the knowledge he would have contributed," but also because "the way toward his redemption is cut short and before he can achieve his goal, Iron cuts off his path to God."

Abraham always seeks the path to God and the solution to the riddle of existence. For it is petty for men to claim they belong to superior and privileged races "who slash the gardens of peace with the sword of warriors." It is not enough to build towers whose heights reach heavenward. It is insufficient for science to boast that it can cross-breed different species and combine differing elements into one. Beyond the knowledge and the understanding of man there dwells a mystery, a riddle, and the soul will know no peace, seeking the explanation and the solution. Blind and dumb Nature, which revenges itself upon man from time to time, as in the destruction of Sodom and Gomorrah, intimates that we cannot penetrate into the mystery of life nor delve into the secrets of the universe.

Abraham is the great seeker after the truth that may explain the riddle, the pursuer of the secret of God, Who at times in mercy reveals Himself to those who revere Him.

He is possessed by the tenderness of the poet-philosopher and of the father of a people destined to become the wanderer over the highways of the world, seeking a solution to the problem of its own existence and that of all creation. In the various characters surrounding Abraham, one sees the sons of many different nations, lost and confused, not knowing how to discover the truth, how to bring about the rule of justice, how to attain happiness. This is the era of the awakening of man and the dawn of the recognition of God's existence in the world. Abraham is the luminous figure who goes among men and peoples, bearing the message of renascence for the world and its inhabitants. Hence he leaves his native land to spread abroad the knowledge of God. His wife, Sarah, longs to return to her home and her native land, Shinar, but she will not return without Abraham who will not be false to himself nor fail his mission.

Sarah too is portrayed as a gracious character, understanding, patient and charming. In her love for Abraham and even in her jealousy of Hagar she shows the qualities of a great woman who secretly guides the steps of her husband, quietly and with dignity helping him bear his burden. Perhaps she does not understand all the intricacies of her husband's philosophy, for her way of thinking is different from his. But intuitively she senses its substance, the essence of the vision of the man who is her husband and her lord, her beloved and her guide. So she speaks his words and interprets the meditations of his heart to others.

Sarah personifies too the idea of endurance, of withstanding foreign influence and assimilation, an idea that occupies an important part in the play. She, the daughter of a Babylonian leader, the niece of Amraphel, king of Babylonia, cannot easily become rooted in Canaan. For such is the fate of the stranger, to purchase his tranquility by means of his talents, until he is again spewed forth upon the path of his wandering.

"Abraham," she says, "How I am wearied of knocking upon the gates of others! For every tiny parcel of land for sowing or for a small plot for our dead, no larger than the span of a shepherd's crook, we must pay the highest price to every farmer and to every owner of a well who niggardly measures out water for us—while there our land waits for us . . ."

To this plea of hers, Abraham replies, "The end of the appointed time has not yet come. For, lo, I have taken upon myself a command from on high to leave the shelter of my tribe, to uproot myself from my native land, the storehouse of science, injustice and the enchantment of idolatry, in order to become a foreigner among other peoples, until the day come when a new united race will appear to atone for the transgressions of the world. How, therefore, can I return to Shinar and stifle the voice of the future which sings aloud within me—a vision from generation to generation! A vision that shall never end!"

Sarah, who resigns herself to destiny and who gives way before her servant, Hagar, because of her love for Abraham, submits too to this call of the future and from the first days in Canaan, together with her husband, she bears the seed of the blessings destined for the Great Tomorrow.

The central theme in this play is the struggle of the spirit against the brute force of iron, as is indicated by the title, *Thou Shalt Not Make Unto Thee Gods of Iron.* In addition, there are many other ideas, major and minor, personified by individual characters. One of the principal themes is that of the existence of the ordinary man, the simple person who craves a life of peace and quiet, and who flees from the storm of conflict.

The clearest portrait of the simple, honest man is that of Lot, the owner of vineyards, who wants to protect his vine and fig tree as well as the peace of his household and of his country. He is also a judge and, therefore, he wuld preserve justice and equity so that society's equilibrium be not disturbed.

He opposes Gog, the prince of iron because of the cruelty of his doctrine and the sternness of his discipline; but the loftiness of Abraham's vision also upsets him. Because he senses life's tragic quality and is aware of the continuous struggle of mighty social forces and because of his even temperament and calm consistency, he too becomes a chief character like Abraham and Gog. As Shoham states, "He is a hero who speaks for the unheroic; the representative of silent multitudes who fights for the joy of small pleasures in the life of man, for morning's hope and evening's reward in day by day living, for the security of the ground under his feet and the roof over his head, his home, in whose shadow he can live in happiness or in sorrow." Lot is the hero and the symbol of the democratic idea.

He knows that amidst slavery a people can neither mature nor continue life. "If," as he says, "freedom be harnessed to the chariot of Gog, we shall neither plow the smallest of our furrows nor reap its harvest."

The Gogs of all generations rise up against the Lots of their times, casting upon them the bitterness of their iron rule and darkening their sun with the smoky clouds of their civilization. Mighty are the Gogs, who despise the weak Lots, suppressing them and finally chaining them to their chariots of iron.

As for Lot, he fights against Gog in his own way—with good common sense, with popular ridicule, and with the force of logic that stems from life's quest for certainty, order and calm. But the sublimity of Abraham's spirit also disturbs him, for the Great Vision of the end of days robs him of his peace of mind and deprives him of the actual enjoyment of the moment.

"You arrogant ones!" he addresses himself to Gog and to Abraham in the same breath. "How long will you yearn for the day of God, the day of great adventures and victories? If you want to contend with each other, to exhibit your valor before God, wherein lies our sin that we should be dragged into it? We are simple folk, modest in our ways. Unlike Gog, we have not defied God and unlike Abraham we do not pretend to walk before Him continuously. We have not broken His covenant as has the man of iron and we have not boasted of understanding the purpose of His ways, as has dared the man of spirit. In our humbleness we have not suffered our feet to tread upon His ways and only at the festivals did we seek His favor with sacrifice and prayer. So why should He be infuriated at us? Because of their sin and the evil pride of the two great antagonists, who fight the mighty battle of their destiny, we, the simple and modest folk shall perish."

Danah, the daughter of Lot, also asks the second man of mystery, "Tell me, is there not a god for the undemanding, a god of lesser qualities, who without anger or jealousy will apportion to his servants a measure of his grace according to their own righteousness, and of his punishment according to their own sin? Is there not a god unlike the God of Abraham or Gog?"

When the foundations of nature crumble and Sodom is destroyed, Lot feels all the more the futility of man. Of what use is the arrow or the battering ram? What does man's strength mean or his ability to construct? Nature is more powerful than he and at any moment it can wipe him out from under the heavens.

The vision of redemption is blocked for the common man, who sees only the battle of titanic forces and the upheavals of nature, and his own great helplessness.

The men of mystery, the princes of the nations, who have come to gather instruction from Abraham, also depart in sorrow and disappointment. They came to seek an answer to their questions, but they did not find it. No healing was found for the broken heart of the individual. No comfort was discovered for the pain of the woman in love for whom there had been no compassion. Nor was Sodom saved from the blind fate which razed her to the ground.

"Now," says the third man of mystery, "I shall return to the rivers of India, to my brothers who sent me thither, having heard of Abraham, the prince of Eber, who had rebelled against the ancestral gods, and thus shall I say to them, 'We have been misled by deceitful tidings. A faithful redeemer has not risen in Ur who will bring light to every eye, break the evil intent of the oppressors and taskmasters and make them understand that a unique and sharp pain, a pain of fateful grandeur cries out both from the blood of the murdered and from that of the murderer. For it is false judgment to show preference and mercy to the oppressed as against him who would slay him.' "

The judgment against the murderer and the murdered is the same. Fate is blind; its cruelty crushing.

When Sodom is destroyed, Gog sends his men to the village with a special order, "Pity no man. Save the iron!"

He has not yet learned his lesson. Like the prince of his own nation and the princes of the other northern peoples, his veiled mind does not understand. But it is Lot, the simple man, the common man, the homeowner and the judge, who knows what to do in such an hour of upheaval and devastation. He calls upon his guests to volunteer to go to the ruins of Sodom. "Perhaps we shall be able to rescue from the debris someone shrieking for help, a man, a woman, an orphaned child or an injured lamb."

The great Abraham feels put to shame that Lot should be the first to call for help and for divine compassion for unfortunate creatures on their day of calamity. Together with Sarah and Lot he goes to the ruined city bring flagons of milk and honey for the children, clothing and bedding for the injured and tents and cords for the homeless. "The common man" showed the way to the star-gazers. Thus the democratic idea becomes an augury of the longed-for redemption.

With this play, Shoham brought his creative work to a close. With his death in his fourty-fourth year there was lost a mighty poetic force which has had few parallels in Hebrew literature.

This last drama does not have altogether the completeness and the lucidity of *Tyre and Jerusalem*. The language is difficult, the dialogue abstract. A pressure weighs upon the poet, a portent presaging a doomed tomorrow. The play has a number of significant omens and many scattered threads of some great uncompleted tapestry. It was written at a time of twilight when both inner and outer boundaries were disappearing. Hitler was then setting forth from his thicket to subjugate peoples, plotting to conquer the world. The world was garbed in black. The thunder of the coming devastation was already reverberating across the skies of Europe and of its Jews. The poet had just returned from what was then Palestine to "The exile that is Poland," as he writes in his preface to *Thou Shalt Not Make Unto Thee Gods of Iron,* and from the pages of his last work he emerges weighed down with the meditation and the anxiety of a poet of antiquity who senses the approaching sunset, his own and his world's. The last rays of the dying sun light up the present, then gradually fade away—the darkness of death covers the earth.

EXCERPTS FROM THE VERSE PLAYS OF SHOHAM

From *Jericho*

(The courtesan mourns for the ruined dove-cote in the demolished temple of Astarte)

Cedar-ceiled, seraphic stood your cote
In the shrine of love where you were born.
First-fruits of corn and lentils Canaan's ladies,
Bereft of fruit of body, brought you hither
To placate the implacable Astarte.
Here incense-laden hands of courtesans
Patted tenderly your purple crop . . .
The goddess left, like you, this holy place.
We are her orphans in an abandoned nest,
Captured by a strange, avenging God.

From *Balaam*

(Pinhas praises the beauty of the pagan daughters of Peor)

The vestals of Peor are soft in temples
Their bodies mellowed; how unlike the women
Of Israel who knew the desert heat,
Whose breasts have shriveled from long wanderings,
Whose round and unanointed thighs have thinned
And lost their smoothness under hairy cloaks . . .

From *Tyre and Jerusalem*

(Jezebel swears vengeance against Elijah)

By my desecrated womb upon
The day of dedication to Astarte
I have sworn revenge upon the prophet
And his God till I erase my shame.

. . . And all the flames of my full summer
I will kindle for him, ecstasy
Of flesh which rises with the vintage, all
My paints and perfumes, pride and expectation
Of harvests of revenge I'll gather for him.

From *Thou Shalt Not Make Thee Gods of Iron*

(Lot, the common man, speaks)

I ceiled my house
With hardy cypress wood to give it strength in drought
And rain, I set my table in abundance and
I judged with reasonable wisdom. I secured
Grooms for my daughters.

(To Abraham and Gog)

Is this the fateful law of God
That we should pay with death for your exalted plans,
We—the humble and the innocent in life.

EXCERPTS FROM THE POEMS OF SHOHAM

From *Shulami*

Your sword is timid in the sight of my soft neck.
Its naked glimmer shuns the glamor of my flesh.
Between my breasts you sleep—a weakling and a coward.
My hero is a child . . .
You are strong and sturdy, I am weak,
A tender dove while you are the wild eagle.
My boy believes he is the stalwart king
Who treads in might and thunders his command.
I listen: he is but a boy who seeks
A dream, a legend, or a mother's wing.

From *Eretz Yisrael*

My land, my virgin-mother! When for a while you wrinkled
Your womb before me, wild and barren like your riven rocks
I thought the splendid buds of your breasts withered
In the sorrow of your virgin widowhood.
Suddenly you loved me and desired me
—your son—
Mirthfully and modestly, a bridal land,
Pregnant with the scented spring and hiding
Her pregnancy in her white almond sheen.

I will betroth thee unto me, my pioneer land,
In love and blood and eternal longing. . . .

Glossary

Aliyah—Literally "ascent," immigration. *Second Aliyah,* the second wave of immigration to Palestine from the first to the third decades of the present century.

Beilis Trial—The trial in 1911 of Mendel Beilis, falsely accused by the Russian government of the ritual murder of a Christian child. Diplomatic pressure compelled Beilis' eventual release.

Berditchevsky—Micah Joseph, Hebrew philosophical essayist and novelist, 1865-1921.

Bet Hamidrash—Literally, "the house of study," a small synagogue where daily study, as well as services, take place.

Bratislaver, Rabbi Nahman—Founder of a Hassidic sect, 1770-1811.

Cahan, Jacob—Israeli poet, editor, translator. 1881- .

Dolitzky, M. M.—Russian Hebrew poet, born 1856, moved to America 1892, where he wrote both Hebrew and Yiddish poems and articles. Died 1931.

Emek—The Valley of Jezreel in Israel.

Eretz Yisrael—The Land of Israel, Palestine.

Frischman, David—Polish, Hebrew and Yiddish writer of verse, fiction, feuilletons, criticism and translations, 1863-1922.

Gabirol, Solomon ibn—Outstanding Spanish Hebrew medieval poet and philosopher, c. 1021 - c. 1058.

Galut—Literally, "exile," the diaspora, lands outside of Israel.

Gaonic literature—Hebrew post-Talmudic literature, approximately sixth to eleventh centuries, Babylonia, Palestine and North Africa.

Gemara—That portion of the Talmud which is a commentary upon the Mishnah, c. 200 - c. 500.

Gordon, J. L.—Influential Russian Hebrew poet, essayist and novelist, 1831-1892.

Goy, Goyim (pl.)—Literally, "nation" or "people," usual reference is to non-Jew, although Bible uses it for Jewish people as well.

Halakha—Jewish traditional law.

Judah Halevi—Eminent Spanish Hebrew poet and philosopher, c. 1085 - c. 1140.

Halutz, halutzim (pl.), *halutzah* (f.)—A "pioneer," one who went to Palestine, usually to work in a collective colony.

Hassidism—Jewish religious revivalist movement founded by Rabbi Israel Baal Shem Tov in first half of eighteenth century, stressing close communion with God through prayer, cheerfulness and enthusiasm.

Hasid, literally "a pious man," adherent of this movement, *Hasidim* (pl.).

Hanukkah—The "Feast of Lights," literally "dedication," the Jewish festival marking the victory of the Maccabees over the Syrians and the rededication of the Temple, 165 B.C.E.

Haskalah—Literally "enlightenment," the Hebrew literary movement for enlightenment, second half of eighteenth and nineteenth centuries.

Heder—Literally "a room," referring to the traditional European Jewish elementary school.

Kabbalah—A medieval Jewish philosophy of mysticism, *Kabbalists,* those who engaged in this study.

Kaddish—A mourner's prayer recited in honor of the dead.

Ketubah—The Jewish wedding certificate.

Kiddush Hashem—The act of martyrdom, literally "the sanctification of the Name (of God)."

Kol Nidrei—The opening words, "All vows," of the prayer beginning the first service on the eve of the Day of Atonement and name given to the entire prayer itself or to entire service.

Kvutzah—A collective colony in Israel.

Lebenson—Micah Joseph, Russian Hebrew poet, 1828-1852.

Maimonides—Rabbi Moses ben Maimon, greatest medieval Jewish philosopher, born in Spain 1135, died in Egypt 1204.

Mapu, Abraham—Russian Hebrew author who introduced the novel into modern Hebrew literature, 1808-1867.

Mekhilta—Literally "compendium or rule of Scriptural interpretation," the oldest rabbinic commentary on Exodus.

Melamed—Literally "a teacher" who taught young children in a *heder* or at home.

Mendele Mokher Sefarim—Real name, Shalom Jacob Abramovitch, the father of modern Yiddish literature. Wrote novels of ghetto life. Born in Russia in 1836, died 1917.

Mezuzot, mezuzah (s.)—A rolled-up piece of parchment containing Biblical verses fixed on the door-post of the home.

Midrash—Scriptural exegesis, the ancient rabbinical literature of homilies.

Mishnah—The collection of the traditional oral law edited about 200 C.E. by Rabbi Judah Hanasi. It serves as the basic text for the discussion in the *Gemara,* both forming the Talmud.

Philo—Alexandrian Jewish philosopher, c. 20 B.C.E. - 45 C.E.

Piyyut—Liturgic poetry.

Saadya Gaon—Head of Academy of Sura in Babylonia, philosopher, grammarian, liturgist, 882-942.

Seder—The traditional family dinner, accompanied by the reading of the *Haggadah,* the story of the Exodus, held on the first two evenings of Passover.

Sheol—The nether world.

Shmone Esrei—The "Eighteen Benedictions," a part of the daily prayer service.

Shekhinah—God's presence.

Steinberg, Judah—Russian Hebrew writer of stories and notable interpreter of Hassidism, 1861-1908.

Sukkah—Booth or hut, built each year for use during *Sukkot,* the Feast of Tabernacles.

Tanya—Book of ritual laws and customs first printed in 1514 ascribed to various authors of an earlier period.

Torah—Originally the Five Books of Moses, literally "teaching," also applied to entire Hebrew Bible and to the complete body of Jewish traditional teaching.

Urim and Tumim—The oracles worn by the ancient High Priest on his breast-plate.

Yeshiva—A talmudic academy.

Zohar—The Book of Splendor, a classic of the *Kabbalah,* the occult medieval lore of the Jews.

Recommended Bibliography

For the reader interested in finding additional translations of the works of the authors treated in this book and related materials, the following books are recommended. The magazines listed are those which, from time to time, carry such translations or articles in their pages.

Agnon, S. J., The Bridal Canopy, translated by I. M. Lask, Doubleday, Doran and Co., New York, 1937.

Agnon, S. J., In the Heart of the Seas, translated by I. M. Lask, Schocken Books, New York, 1948.

Agnon, S. J., Days of Awe, Schocken Books, New York, 1948.

Ausubel, Nathan and Marynn, editors, A Treasury of Jewish Poetry, Crown, New York, 1957.

Beinkinstadt, Bertha, An Anthology of Poems From the Hebrew and Yiddish, Capetown, 1940.

Benshalom, Benzion, Hebrew Literature Between the Two World Wars, Youth and Hechalutz Department of the Zionist Organization, Jerusalem, 1953.

Bialik, H. N., Complete Poetic Works of, edited by Israel Efros, Histadruth Ivrith of America, New York, 1948.

Bialik, H. N., Aftergrowth and Other Stories, translated by I. M. Lask, Jewish Publication Society, Philadelphia, 1939.

Bialik, H. N., And It Came to Pass, translated by Herbert Danby, Hebrew Publication Co., New York, 1938.

Bialik, H. N., Far Over the Sea, poems and jingles for children, Cincinnati, 1939.

Bialik, H. N., Poems From the Hebrew, edited by L. V. Snowman, London, 1924.

Bialik, H. N., Selected Poems, translated by Maurice Samuel, New Palestine, New York, 1926.

Bialik, H. N., Halachah and Aggadah, translated by Leon Simon, Education Department of the Zionist Federation of Great Britain and Ireland, London, 1944.

Chomsky, William, Hebrew: The Eternal Language, Jewish Publication Society, Philadelphia, 1957.

Creekmore, Hubert, A Little Treasury of World Poetry, Charles Scribner's Sons, New York, 1952.

Eisenberg, Azriel, Modern Jewish Life in Literature, United Synagogue of America, New York, 1948.

Fein, Harry, A Harvest of Hebrew Verse, Bruce Humphries Inc., Boston, 1934.

Fein, Harry, Titans of Hebrew Verse, Bruce Humphries, Inc., Boston, 1936.

Fleg, Edmond, The Jewish Anthology, translated by Maurice Samuel, Behrman's Jewish Book House, New York, 1940.

Halevy-Levin, Isaac, editor, Israel Argosy, Numbers 1, 2, 3, Youth and Hechalutz Department of the Zionist Organization, Jerusalem.

Halevy-Levin, Isaac, editor, Israel Argosy, Numbers 4 and 5, Yoseloff, New York, 1956 and 1958.

Halkin, Simon, Modern Trends in Hebrew Literature, Schocken Books, New York, 1950.

Hameiri, Avigdor, The Great Madness, translated by Jacob Freedman, Vantage Press, New York, 1952.

Kahn, Sholom J., A Whole Loaf: Stories from Israel, Tel Aviv, 1957.

Raskin, Philip M., Anthology of Modern Jewish Poetry, Behrman's Jewish Book Shop, New York, 1927.

Schwarz, Leo W., The Jewish Caravan, Farrar and Rinehart, New York, 1935.

Schwarz, Leo W., A Golden Treasury of Jewish Literature, Farrar and Rinehart, New York, 1937.

Shenhar, Yitzhak, ed., Tehilla and Other Stories, Abelard-Schuman, New York, 1957.

Shimoni, David, Idylls of, translated by I. M. Lask, Jerusalem, 1957.

Spiegel, Shalom, Hebrew Reborn, The MacMillan Co., New York, 1930.

Tchernihovsky, Saul, Poems, edited by L. V. Snowman, London, 1929.

Wallenrod, Reuben, The Literature of Modern Israel, Abelard-Schuman, New York, 1957.

Waxman, Meyer, A History of Jewish Literature, Vol. IV, Bloch Publishing Co., New York, 1947.

Magazines and Pamphlets

Commentary, American Jewish Committee, New York.

Israel Life and Letters, American Fund for Israel Institutions (now America-Israel Cultural Foundation), New York.

Israel Youth Horizon, Youth and Hechalutz Department of the Zionist Organization, Jerusalem.

Jewish Frontier, Jewish Frontier Association, New York.

Judaism, A Quarterly Journal, American Jewish Congress, New York.

The Literary Review, Spring, 1958 issue, Fairleigh Dickinson University, Teaneck, N. J.

Palestine Miscellany, Pioneer Library, Youth Department of the Zionist Organization, Tel Aviv.

Pioneer, Youth and Hechalutz Department of the Zionist Organization, Jerusalem.

Poetry, July, 1958 issue, Chicago.

Reconstructionist, The, The Jewish Reconstructionist Foundation, New York.

Shalom, S., The Poet and His Work, edited by Preil and Kabakoff for the Histadruth Ivrith of America and the Jewish Education Committee, New York, 1950.

Acknowledgments

Special thanks are due to the following authors and translators for permission to use their materials in this volume: Samuel Joseph Agnon, Ben Aronin, Hilda Auerbach, Harry Fein, Reginald V. Feldman, Shoshana Grayer, Simon Halkin, Avigdor Hameiri, Sholom J. Kahn, Abraham M. Klein, I. M. Lask, Amelia Levy, Jessie Sampter, Maurice Samuel, Sh. Shalom, Zalman Shneur, Gershon Shoffman, Eisig Silberschlag, Morris Silverman, Jacob Sloan, L. F. Snowman, Yosef Wilfand, Esther Zweig.

Appreciation is also expressed to the Menachem Ribalow Publication Fund of Congregation Kehillath Israel, Brookline, Massachusetts.

Grateful acknowledgment is made to the following publishers and holders of copyright: America-Israel Cultural Foundation, New York: for "I Did Not Find the Light" by Hayyim Nahman Bialik, "In Praise of Jerusalem" by Jacob Fichman, translated by Hilda Auerbach, "In the Day's Radiance" by Avigdor Hameiri, "In the Woods of Hedera" by David Shimoni, translated by I. M. Lask, "Deborah" by Gershon Shoffman, "Command" by Sh. Shalom, "The Minyan" by Samuel Joseph Agnon, translated by I. M. Lask, all from *Israel Life and Letters;* American Jewish Committee, New York: for "The Hut" by Avigdor Hameiri, translated by Jacob Sloan, from *Commentary* magazine; American Jewish Congress, New York: for excerpts from the verse plays and the poems of Mattathias Shoham, from the article, "The Swan Song of Polish Jewry" by Eisig Silberschlag in *Judaism, A Quarterly Journal;* Behrman House, Inc., New York: for "The Kiss" and "Under the Hammer" by Zalman Shneur and "Credo," "Before the Statue of Apollo" and "Barukh of Mayence" by Saul Tchernihovsky from *The Jewish Anthology* by Edmond Fleg, translated by Maurice Samuel; Bruce Humphries, Inc., Boston: for "Yea, Even When My Course Is Run" by Zalman Shneur from *Harvest of Hebrew Verse* by Harry Fein, "Life," "Again the Dark Ages Draw Nigh" and "Exalted and Sanctified" by Zalman Shneur from *Titans of Hebrew Verse* by Harry Fein; Doubleday and Company, Inc., New York: for "The Story of the Two Brod Merchants" from *The Bridal*

Canopy by Samuel Joseph Agnon, translated by I. M. Lask; Histadruth Ivrith of America, New York: for "The Talmud-Student," translated by Maurice Samuel, "Morning Spirits" and "Go Flee, O Prophet," translated by Ben Aronin, "Upon the Slaughter," translated by Abraham M. Klein, "Surely This Too," translated by Jessie Sampter, "Out of the Depth," translated by Reginald V. Feldman, all from *Complete Poetic Works of H. N. Bialik,* edited by Israel Efros and "On the Watchtower," "Aboard Ship" and "On Guard," translated by Shoshana Grayer, "Man Is a Parable" and "When a Man Dies," translated by Eisig Silberschlag, "Five," translated by Yosef Wilfant, all from *S. Shalom, The Poet and His Work,* brochure edited by Gabriel Preil and Jacob Kabakoff for the Histadruth Ivrith and the Jewish Education Committee of New York; The Jewish Agency for Israel, New York: for "Samaria," "Samarian Nights," "Harvest" and "Hermon" by Jacob Fichman from *Palestine Miscellany I,* "In the Old City" by Jacob Fichman from *Israel Argosy,* "Jerusalem," "Go Forward Samson," "Kinneret" and "Epigram" by Avigdor Hameiri from *Horizon,* "Midnight" by Sh. Shalom from *Israel Youth Horizon,* "Redemption Has Come" by Sh. Shalom, translated by I. M. Lask, from *Pioneer,* "Samson," "This Is the Hoe" and "Lullaby" by Saul Tchernihovsky from *Palestine Miscellany I,* "Behold, O Earth" by Saul Tchernihovsky, translated by Shalom J. Kahn; The Jewish Frontier Association, New York: for "Grandpa and His Boy" by Gershon Shoffman from *Jewish Frontier* magazine; The Joint Prayerbook Commission of the United Synagogue of America and the Rabbinical Assembly of America, New York: for "Mourn Not" by David Shimoni, translated by Morris Silverman, from the *Sabbath and Festival Prayer Book;* The Reconstructionist Foundation, New York: for "There Are Times" by Zalman Shneur, translated by Amelia Levy, from *The Reconstructionist* magazine; Schocken Books, New York: for "Temptation on the Road" and "On the Sea," both from *In the Heart of the Seas* by Samuel Joseph Agnon, translated by I. M. Lask, "Ruth" and "Remember, My Heart" by Jacob Fichman, "Reb Mendel, The Brother of the Rabbi of Gur" by Sh. Shalom, "The Jubilee of Coachmen" by David Shimoni, "Not to Sleep" by Gershon Shoffman, "Martyrs of Dortmund" by Saul Tchernihovsky, all from *Trends in Modern Hebrew Literature* by Simon Halkin.